Real Country

Aaron A. Fox

Real Country

Music and Language in Working-Class Culture

Duke University Press Durham & London

2004

© 2004 Duke University Press

All rights reserved

Printed in the United States of America on acid-free paper ∞

Designed by C H Westmoreland

Typeset in Minion with Cooper Black display

by Tseng Information Systems, Inc.

Library of Congress Cataloging-in-Publication Data appear

on the last printed page of this book.

In memory of

Randall O. "**Randy**" Meyer (1940–2000),

and for all the kids.

Contents

Preface

In this book, I describe country music as working-class culture, approached ethnographically and with broad attention to the expressive practices of talk and verbal art as well as musical performance and interpretation. I aim to show here how complex, dense, and mediated the relationship is between country music and working-class social experience, and how rich and compellingly "cultural" class-based expressive and artistic practices can be. My central assertion — that country music is an authentic working-class art of enormous value to its blue-collar constituency — is straightforward and perhaps obvious, though it is an argument of a kind currently out of fashion in popular music scholarship. I hope this book is a convincing critique of such fashions.

Some parts of this book are relatively dense and technical, reflecting my approach to the subject through linguistics, anthropology, and ethnomusicology. The complexity of my analyses reflects the essence of my argument. Country music is, populist ideology notwithstanding, not simple stuff; nor is working-class experience uncomplicated. I treat country music and working-class oral discourse seriously as art forms here, and working-class practice and experience seriously as culture. To do so adequately entails deploying some complex theoretical frameworks. But most of this book consists of stories and transcriptions of recorded talk, and I hope most readers find most of this volume engaging and readable as a portrait of a community and its music and verbal art, whether or not they care about my academic agendas.

Because I am primarily concerned with the cultural life of *sound* here, the mute volume in your hands is an incomplete representation of the reality it describes. To remedy this limitation, many of the interviews, conversations, and musical performances described and transcribed in this book will be available as audio and video files on my website (http://www.aaronfox.com). And because I gloss rather quickly here over some technical matters of greater interest to my scholarly colleagues in linguistics and ethnomusicology than to readers in other walks of life, the website will also contain more extensive transcriptions, supplemental materials, photographs, and specialized discussions and materials (sonograms, detailed linguistic analyses, theoretical discussions, and bibliographies, etc.). I encourage readers to spend some time online, listening to the sound of this sound-centered community. The website is an important adjunct to the volume itself.

My descriptions, interpretations, and data in this volume are drawn from more than a dozen years of research, friendship, and music making, principally though not exclusively in a working-class community located around the town of Lockhart, Texas, and centered on a number of local taverns or "honky-tonk" bars. I entered this community as a researcher in 1990, early in my graduate school years, as I describe in chapter 1 of this book. I have never truly left it, and hope I never do. I claim not (or not only) the objectivity of social science but a subjective involvement with the life of this community, over a long stretch of time, as the source of whatever authority my descriptions and interpretations have. I am *not* a working-class person, but I believe I represent working-class experience here reflexively, without, I hope, descending into navel-gazing identity politics, the classic anthropological error of "going native," or a romantic minstrelsy of poverty and the laboring life.

Having explained the broad shape of this book, I will now, with great pleasure, thank the many people who helped it come into being over so many years. Ultimately, this book is most accountable to my friends, mentors, and interlocutors in Texas, and especially to their children and grandchildren, who might, I hope, someday discover in this book a fair, sensitive, and honest record of the cultural world of their parents. For this reason, I dedicate this book both to the late Randy Meyer, a truly great singer who stalks these pages, and to all the local kids I've watched grow up over the past dozen years, who are mostly—though not completely—absent from these pages, by my own ethical choice. I express my gratitude especially to Ann Roose, Audrey Meyer, Larry and Judy Hopkins, Becky (Rollings) and Smokey Ledbetter and the Rollings family, Justin and Sissy Treviño, and Ira Woolridge and his family. But I should also acknowledge so many others in Texas and Illinois that I cannot list them all here. I *do* list many of them in chapter 1, and although they do not always appear in these pages under their real names, most of them have been real friends.

I also owe thanks to dozens of musicians who talked with me, hired me for gigs and recording sessions, and patiently engaged with my endless questions over years of travel and performance. Again, I list most of these folks in chapter 1, so here I will just thank them collectively. Bartender, another round for the band, please.

The intellectual inspiration for this book came from my teachers. Steven Feld's work compelled me to pursue musical anthropology when I first read it as an undergraduate student, and his guidance and friendship have kept that inspiration alive for the almost twenty years that have passed since I sat in Harvard's Tozzer Library barely understanding *Sound and Sentiment* and yet somehow knowing that I had found my own calling in its pages. Kathleen Stewart, Greg Urban, Anthony Woodbury, and Joel Sherzer were the other members of my dissertation committee, and while each taught me a somewhat different style of thought and expression, I can no longer distinguish their separate influences on my work. I consider it my greatest good fortune to have been at the University of Texas in the early 1990s and to have had the chance to work with such a collegial and brilliant team of mentors. To list the names of all the other teachers from whom I have taken inspiration and knowledge would be to risk a thoughtless omission and would take several pages. For all of their examples and efforts, I am deeply grateful.

My fellow graduate students at the University of Texas, who also made those years of my life so memorable, as well as my colleagues during the years it took me to convert my doctoral dissertation into this book, have been unfailingly supportive and kind, not to mention endlessly patient. Since I do not name these friends and mentors elsewhere, I thank, in particular, Barbara Ching, Dieter Christensen, Erica David, Keila Diehl, Brad Garton, Melissa Hagstrum, Stevan Harrell, Kathleen Higgins, Marilyn Ivy, Calla Jacobsen, Mary Keefe, Julie Lindquist, the late Frank Magne, Louise Meintjes, Daniel Neuman, Ana Maria Ochoa, Robert O'Meally, John Pemberton, Tom Porcello, David Samuels, Elaine Sisman, Tom Solomon, Timothy Taylor, Christopher Washburne, Christopher Waterman, and Christine Yano. I owe a specific debt to Randal Tillery, who aided me immensely with my video documentary work in the field. I am also indebted to Charles Keil, whose reading of my dissertation influenced me deeply, and who remains an inspiration to all of us who think music makes an ethical difference in the world. I am similarly grateful to the second, still anonymous reader for Duke University Press, who made invaluable suggestions for improving this book in both its early and late stages. Peter Wolf and David Whisnant deserve special thanks not only for the profound knowledge of American vernacular music each commands but also for their willingness to read and comment on this book in manuscript form. Sherry Ortner likewise offered an invaluable reading of the final manuscript, years of dialogue and friendship, and, in her own work, an exceptional example of how to write anthropologically about class in the contemporary United States. And I deeply appreciate Ken Wissoker's editorial advice—rooted in his own love of both the subject of this book and his knowledge of my approach to it—as well as his patient confidence in this project.

The various chapters in this book have benefited substantially from responses and readings by many undergraduate and graduate students over the years, at the University of Washington and at Columbia University. I hope those students have learned as much from me as I have from working with them. There are too many to name, so again I thank them collectively. But I will single out Ryan Skinner, who created the index for this book with remarkable care and diligence, and Toby King, my hardworking student assistant at Columbia's Center for Ethnomusicology. Finally, I owe a special debt to my many working-class students (an invisible "minority" on America's campuses) who have read my writing over the years "from a native point of view" and helped me sharpen and refine and correct many of my ideas.

My father's rigorous scholarship, political commitment, and professional guidance, and my mother's ethics and selfless love of humanity have shaped every insight herein, and I thank them both for the music-steeped and socially progressive upbringing I enjoyed as well. I also thank my siblings, and especially my sister Mimi, whose knowledge of—and passion for—popular music has inspired me for three decades. I'm certain this project descends from the passions I was socialized into from the moment of my birth. Joan and Marty Lepselter have been unfailingly kind and supportive. And their daughter Susan, my wife and best critic and friend, gave more of herself to help this book finally exist than anyone else, indeed, far more than I deserved. Whatever I could say to thank her would not be enough. Finally, I thank my daughter Serena for letting her daddy go back to work every night for months when he should have been reading *Make Way for Ducklings* to his truest joy.

A Note on
Transcription Conventions

I use the following transcription conventions throughout this work:

Notation	Interpretation
Line breaks	prosodic junctures (usually pause-marked)
CAPS	syllables marked by strong prosodic stress
Italics	voice quality marked by heightened intonation
. . .	lengthy pauses (sometimes given in seconds)
=	rapid overlap; also indicated by line layout
"Quotation marks"	purportedly "direct" reported speech
Bold	words, phrases, or segments analyzed in text
[. . .]	transcript elides significant material on tape
[Brackets]	contextual glosses and paralinguistic descriptions
(xxxxx)	inaudible or questionable on tape

Where lines of transcribed discourse appear in parallel columns, this indicates simultaneous, overlapping speech. I have endeavored to match the visual appearance of these overlaps in the transcripts to the actual timing of the simultaneous utterances transcribed, but this often entailed significant approximation of the actual timing of the complex phenomena of interruption, overlap, simultaneous speech, and cross-talk. Although this transcription technique renders some of the transcripts in this book difficult to read, it captures an essential property of oral discourse in Texas working-class culture, which is characterized by what sociolinguists call "high-involvement style," and in which turn-taking rules are rarely rigidly sequential.

A further word on the transcription conventions used in this book is in order. I am principally concerned in this study with the musical, prosodic, grammatical, dialectological, and semantic features of oral discourse in a working-class Southern community. My disciplinary commitments to linguistic anthropology, sociolinguistics, and ethnomusicology made it imperative for me to represent the speech of my interlocutors (in most cases) with an accurate attention to the local dialectal features of grammar, pronunciation, and lexicon, as well as the prosodic structure of line breaks, emphasis, tone of voice, sentence intonation, etc. This creates, however, complex problems of representation, I am concerned here not to play into stereotypes of working-class speech as "lazy," "ungrammatical," or "substandard" in any respect. As any linguist knows, and as any educated person ought to know, there is no such thing as an "ungrammatical" dialect, and indeed one goal of this volume is to demonstrate the grammatical regularity and expressive power of certain features of working-class Texas speech, rooted in the persistent orality I describe as a central dimension of Texas blue-collar culture.

A second and more troublesome problem with my use of relatively exact transcriptions of naturally occurring discourse arises, however, out of the anxieties and objections of my interlocutors *themselves* not to be represented in ways that might play into such stereotypes, regardless of my intentions, and their equally understandable concerns over my representation of their discourse as "coarse" by the standards of more prestigious dialects of English. In particular, many of my interlocutors have expressed concern over my representation of their use of profanity, a rich and characteristic feature of their discursive practice, but one that they sometimes wish to disavow. This is an even more pressing concern for those who have become more religious and less inclined to participate in the tavern-centered culture described here as they have become older, which is biographically characteristic for working-class Southerners. Men, especially, often turn away from religion in their youth but return to it in their senior years. (Issues concerning the use of profanity and the stereotyping of working-class discourse and culture are discussed in more detail at several points over the course of this book.)

Although I was *never* surreptitious about my use of a tape recorder and always had the permission and approval of the principal actors in this ethnography to record their natural discourse (and was in fact occasionally asked to turn the recorder off, a request with which I always complied), it is in the nature of long-term ethnography that an ethnographer's tape recorder gradually becomes relatively invisible as personal relationships between an ethnographer and his or her interlocutors deepen, as well as over the course of particular recording sessions.

I have taken various approaches to addressing these issues. First, I hope this book stands as a testimony to the richness, grammaticality, and rhetorical brilliance of even "average" working-class Texas English discourse, and no attentive reader can fail to take from this book a case for respecting the beauty, skillfulness, and power of a dialect that is so often stereotyped as "illiterate" and "ignorant." Where I have felt that representing even artful and expressive uses of profanity (or other discourse features) was problematic for a speaker, I have either used pseudonyms (as I have in many cases for other reasons as well), "split" individual actors across several different names, some of which are pseudonyms, or made judicious elisions or modifications to the actual recorded speech I transcribed, although I exercised this last option very rarely (for example, substituting a locally attested euphemism, such as "God-DOG-it" for "God-DAMN-it"). Finally, I have endeavored over many years, I think with success, to explain the purposes of my project and my techniques for representing natural, oral discourse to my interlocutors, and most of the principal actors whose real names are used in this book accept the choices I have made, even if they are not always completely comfortable with those choices.

Real Country

Prelude

"Turns"

I pulled my truck through the gate of Hoppy's place in a cloud of dry dust thrown up from the unpaved, rutted surface of County Road 400, a nearly unmarked turn off U.S. 183, just a few miles north of Lockhart, Texas. Lockhart is a gritty little town of about 10,000 residents, a bit too far south from Austin to be a suburb. Its local economy largely depends on corn, cotton, and the South Texas oil patch, a few factories and service businesses, and a privately run prison facility.

These days, Lockhart is a stop on the highway for occasional tourists and weekend barbecue mavens and trucks carrying NAFTA cargo, although once the town had been a stop on the original Chisolm Trail, and the locals still celebrate Chisolm Trail Days every summer. And now Austin was building a new airport up at Bergstrom, as the booming city continued its inexorable expansion into its southern margins of fields, junkyards, small factories, and trailer parks. It was this very movement, in its earlier stages, which had pushed many of my friends around here out of Austin ("SOUTH Austin," they'd be sure to remind you) and south toward Lockhart to begin with. But now people said you could feel things pickin' up around Lockhart. And some people were beginning to think about how to move a bit further "out the country" again.

On the county road by Hoppy's place, it felt like I was "out the country," even though Lockhart's main street was only fifteen minutes away. And this was just how Hoppy liked it to be, the next best thing to living in a cabin in the mountains. I rarely went into the town for anything other than beer, batteries, and film. I spent most of my time in trailer-homes and beer joints on the outskirts of Lockhart and other small towns in this part of Texas. These places were planted in the middle of cotton fields and pastures stretching away from the highway. Or they huddled under the few remaining trees on this gently rolling silvery landscape, a land both beautiful and desolate, domesticated and fierce, that lay shimmering and parching in the blazing South Texas summer sun on this July day.

I hadn't been out for several weeks. Embarrassed by this, I'd called that afternoon to see if anyone would be making music over the holiday weekend. The question was rhetorical. There was always a "jam" somewhere, and if there wasn't you could always create one by showing up with beer and a guitar. But I hadn't expected the additional lure when Joanna answered the phone and casually mentioned that Johnny Mac was down from Fort Worth for a visit, and that I might want to get out to the "Five Acres," as Hoppy called his spread, right away.

I could have showed up without calling, since it was the Saturday of a holiday weekend. After nearly five years, I had achieved the status of someone who could just show up without having to be invited, certainly on a day devoted to musical leisure. But I hoped that securing the invitation would ease my return after my long absence. I remembered that the last time I had been away for three weeks, Hoppy had actually chewed me out, dramatically demanding: *"You forget who your friends are? I guess you're too busy to come and see US anymore . . ."*

Even after all the years and miles with Hoppy, it had startled me to hear the anger directed at me personally. I had never been so strongly upbraided, in the presence of others, by Hoppy before, but I was secretly somewhat proud of myself. Getting "chewed out" by Hoppy was a rite of passage, a sign of belonging and an acknowledgment of hard-won local status. Masculine interaction depended to a significant extent on this kind of verbal agonistics, and anger (real and theatrical) was a crucial dimension of friendship, often transforming rapidly into affection.

My immunity from Hoppy's criticism had actually become something of an issue. Once, someone had asked out loud, as Hoppy was upbraiding some other pickers on a job: "Why don't you ever chew out Aaron?" Hoppy shrugged off the question: "Because Aaron don't ever *piss me off!*" We all laughed, but I knew it had more to do with the obvious fact that I was, after years of hanging around, still something of an outsider. Although I was a good guitar player, and even a half-decent singer, I was, at that point, someone who might not understand that being chewed out and responding firmly was a deep idiom of male sociability, a crucial exchange in an economy of strong feelings. So the day I was finally chewed out was memorable, and I tried to do my part by pridefully arguing in turn that I had been too busy playing out of town, with my band. Performed with enough world-weary bluster, this was an appropriate, masculine excuse. My response preserved my honor, but it also offered compensatory honor to Hoppy. All those listening knew that I had learned much of what I now understood about the finer arts of country music performance from him, in this place and on so many beer joint nights, even if I was playing "that Top-40 crap" now, if only (as I insisted) to pay my bills.

I expected to get chewed out again this weekend. I had been making excuses for not coming out for weeks, as I was desperately trying to finish my dissertation in between weekend gigs with the band Modern Country, playing Top-40 country music at dance halls around the state. I pulled my truck up to the garage, where it joined a grimy brown '82 Ford Escort with its hood up, a white '84 Lincoln with its right front fender crunched in, and an assortment of other old cars, trucks, motorcycles, boats, lawnmowers, and less identifiable machines, lined up in front of the wooden two-story shack with the cheerful yellow sign up top: Hoppy's Auto and Cycle. I rarely arrived here during the day, and I thought of this building, which stood a hundred yards off from a trailer under shady trees, as "Hoppy's Bar," because upstairs in this building was where we drank beer and played music all night, surrounded by Hoppy's enormous collection of souvenirs of his musical life.

The place had other names too. When he was telling me what each object on the walls and shelves meant to him, Hoppy called this structure—quoting a Merle Haggard song—his "house of mem'ries":

HOPPY: The insulation on the ceiling,
right there
Ann gave me that
There's a Budweiser BEER
that's never been opened
That was my old BANjo player
that played with us, y'know
an' he passed away
He asked that we
put a beer up for him

An' that Budweiser can is his, y'know
we put that up for HIM
Got probably the ONLY gold record
I'll ever . . .
EVER have in my life . . .
You have to see this
It takes a LOT to get a gold record
but Sam GAVE me this gold record, y'know
An' I'm sure the PAINT didn't
cost him too much!
But y'know
it's a mem'ry and . . .
that's why I call it my house of mem'ries

And once in a while, in moments of very high feeling, as when a sick Randy Meyer had come to visit, Hoppy also called it *"this damn place . . ."*

HOPPY: Randy Meyer helped me BUILD this damn place
that's RIGHT!
an' I don't care what you say Randy Meyer,
because I LOVE you!

Today, however, under a blazing July sun, this building was simply what the sign said: a shade-tree repair shop, like the one in that silly Merle Haggard song that Randy sang if he was in a really good mood, "Harold's Super Service." Sometimes I wondered why the sign was needed. This dead-end dirt road runs off the main highway, just between the road to Lytton and the driveway for Peachtree Gas Supply. The road is, as well, not too far south of the beer joint that used to be Ann's Other Place, which people still call "Annie's," even though it has another name now and Miss Ann no longer runs it.

County Road 400 is easy to miss if you aren't paying attention, and that's just the way Hoppy likes it. In fact, the only people likely to come down it are the neighbors. And the neighbors all know Hoppy is a mechanic, and don't need no sign to tell 'em so. They wouldn't be very likely to take their car anywhere else for service when it broke down, unless they were fighting with Hoppy again, which was always possible with neighbors. Of course, Hoppy would probably do the work on barter, too, and that made a difference when you were retired from a factory job, or working at the Dairy Queen in town for the minimum wage. And he'd do it right, because he knew everything there was to know about the kinds of cars and trucks people out here drove.

Neighbors were a mixed blessing. When Hoppy had moved onto this lot in the late 1970s, the dirt road had stopped at his place, and the man who owned the property all around had assured him "I ain't gonna sell no more of it." Now Hoppy was dreaming of a place a little further from any highway, a place in the Rockies or the Ozarks, someplace with mountains where a man could build a little cabin and disappear with his family, the working-class promised land where the taxes are low and people leave you alone. Hoppy had been talking like this for a long time, and he made annual trips to the mountains to hunt and drink beer and look for such a place. But for the moment Hoppy's Auto and Cycle was still in operation. And for whatever reason, the yellow sign was there for the neighbors to see.

As my truck grumbled to a stop, I grabbed my tape recorder from the seat beside me, but changed my mind and set it down. I didn't know the other two men I saw working with Hoppy today, and I had developed a sense of the boundaries between my presence and my project that told me now was not the time to push my research agenda. I taped less and less as time went on, and as my relationships deepened and became more personal and complicated. But I remembered more.

Instead of the tape recorder, I grabbed a bag of M&M's and a twelve-pack of Lite beer I had picked up on my way over at the Tiger Tote up on the highway, where Cindy used to work after Doc got real sick. Today Harry had been working the counter, selling lottery tickets and beer. I'd heard he'd had to take the low-paying job because the bar he'd leased as a retirement project for the last two years had finally gone under. I'd played there regularly for almost a year with Becky's band, and we knew the place was doomed from the beginning. Sometimes we played to no one but Harry and his wife. So I knew Harry pretty well, and we talked while he was ringing up the beer.

He seemed out of place to me, his Navy tattoos on his bulging arms and his dignified presence dwarfing the apron with the smiling tiger. I told him I was moving to Seattle, and told me about his years in the service (he'd been based in the Puget Sound area before they shipped him off to Korea). The air was pungent with the irony of a man who had risked death for his country selling M&M's for minimum wage. We didn't mention his failed bar, of course. I paid, and he said "come back now, y'hear?" I said I would, and I meant it.

As I got out of the truck at Hoppy's place, I handed the M&M's to Amy,

Joanna's exuberant seven-year-old daughter. Amy was usually the first one to greet me, and she liked to tease me about being a "Yankee." She stayed up as late as the adults did, and she knew the words and the dance steps to an amazing number of Top-40 country songs, most of which her parents' friends professed to hate. I'd brought the candy for her, but I saw another little girl I didn't know, as heavyset and subdued as Amy was waiflike and exuberant, standing shyly a few feet away. With mock severity I admonished Amy to share the candy with her friend, and she smiled her vivid toothless grin and snatched her treasure and ran off to play with her friend and the dogs and the geese that rambled all over the lot, animals and kids blending into one chaotic tumbling maelstrom of nonstop movement on the periphery of adult work and sociability.

Twelve-pack in hand I walked across the compacted dirt driveway to the garage door, squinting through the sun, saying a quick hello to Joanna and a woman I didn't know, as they leaned back on the hood of a car talking quietly and smoking generic cigarettes the way women do out here, with crisp and angular movements of the hands, a hurried, needy inhalation, a stylized contemplation of the smoke swirl. I heard "girls' talk" as I passed, with its somehow greater and more practiced knowledge of the world of other classes in other places, its somehow greater sense of injustice and frustration:

JOANNA: An' I tol her
"Just because I work here
don't mean I don't know my RIGHTS"
She had no BUsiness lookin' at my records
and I told her
right to her face
"I may work for you
but I know my RIGHTS
and I'll get a lawyer if I HAVE to"
they ever try to fire me . . .
She had no business
that makes me so MAD
when they act like that!

"MySELF!" the other woman snapped, with a fierce punctuating drag on her cigarette. I smiled at Hoppy, who was standing near the garage door between two other men who were hard at work, one outside and one inside the garage. I stowed my twelve-pack in the Coleman cooler sitting on a tree stump, already full of cans of Lite and Milwaukee's Best. More beer was always welcome, although I think nobody understood why I always bought bottles, my slight concession to middle-class taste. At Ann's bar, she never had served bottles, believing rather dramatically that they were too dangerous as potential weapons. More practically, cans were cheaper and lighter, and you could fit more in a cooler. It was less often mentioned that the cops were more likely to notice a brown bottle than an insulated can in a driver's hand.

To my surprise, Hoppy didn't chew me out, even half-heartedly. He seemed genuinely happy to see me. But behind his usual broad showman's smile, infectious and photogenic, I sensed more troubles on his mind than usual. It might have been the bright sunlight drawing attention to the lines around his deep-set dark eyes and the gray in his black hair and beard. Or it might have been the bills. Something was *weighin' on him.*

"HE-HEY! AARON! ALLLLRIGHT!" he shouted from ten feet away, and he walked toward me, one hand extended to shake mine, the other reaching for my shoulder as he began the introductions: "This here's Timmy, an OLD friend of mine, like a son to me, like one of my own!"

A bearlike man emerged from under the hood of the Escort, his face and arms and bare shoulders and shaggy blond hair thickly coated in black grease, a torque wrench in his massive hand. He took a draw on a pint of Jim Beam, returned it to its resting place on the carburetor, and sized me up in a second. He extended his blackened arm, and sensing that this was an informal test, I grabbed it and shook it vigorously, feeling the engine grease soak into my own clean palms.

Grinning at some obscure satisfaction, he looked at my Mazda truck and asked me, "How do you like that little two-two?"

It took a second for me to process the question, to switch mental gears to a world where men talked of engine displacements as easily as the weather or the markets. He meant the two-point-two liter engine in my truck. Here it comes, I thought; that truck would always be an issue—too small, too Japanese, too urban. (Hoppy called it "Aaron's *Mercedes*," and when I was in Illinois it was a "rice burner.") Defensively I said, "That's the same engine that they put in those Ford Courier trucks, a two-point-two liter four banger."

"Naw, that one's PURE Mazda," he answered, "they put the two-OH on them

Couriers, piece of SHIT. But that two-two's a real GOOD engine, just got one myself."

I was trying to picture this huge man squeezed into a Mazda that made my average frame ache after a long drive. But with that utterly surprising approval of my vehicle, Timmy disappeared under the hood of the Escort again, reappearing a minute later having forcibly torn off the timing-belt housing, shredding the black plastic under the bolts. He waved the housing in the air like a flag before flinging it hard into the garage door behind him. With a grin at the other men, he said harshly, "That fucker ain't GOIN' back on. The BITCH don't need it anyway." To me, by way of explanation, he said, "It's a long story . . . This here's my ex's car. I paid two-hundred bucks for this piece of SHIT. And she cracked the FUCKIN' heads."

Hoppy interjected, telling the story the local way, dialogically: "And she's callin' here every day for a week, 'When's my CAR gonna be ready?' I told her, 'I don't know, I never said I would fix it." So she starts calling Timmy, and I told him 'Come on down this weekend,' because I happened to have an Escort head lying around . . . And she's DAMN lucky I did."

I asked Timmy "What'd she do, run it dry?"

Pleased that this guy with clean hands and bottled beer at least understood how one might go about cracking heads by running an engine with no water, Timmy spit out, in a savage, whining parody of a woman's voice, "*The light come on, but I didn't know what it MEANT.*"

And then he was gone, back under the hood. Hoppy laughed gleefully at this episode, and then, after a studied pause, pointed at Timmy and said, "Look at him work! I taught him, now look at him go . . . DAMN!" The torque wrench ratchet buzzed like a hornet and engine parts flew from the Escort, sailing over Timmy's head and sometimes crashing into the garage door as he methodically tore the engine down, working with a singular rage and at an incredible speed.

Hoppy motioned for me to follow him through the garage's side door to meet the other man: "Come in here, I want you to meet someone." John McArthur ("Johnny Mac") was the main reason I had come out that day, after Joanna told me on the phone he was down visiting from Fort Worth. Johnny was a revered guitar player, everybody's favorite "lead man" from the good old days, and he had played around Austin for many years with Randy Meyer and Hoppy at Miss Ann's old beer joint, The Little Bottle, on Manchaca Road (everybody called it "MAN-shack") in Austin. But Johnny had moved to Fort Worth in the early 1980s and only came down for an occasional visit anymore. I'd been hoping to meet him, and maybe even interview him, for years. Many people had told me that he knew a lot that I still needed to learn.

"He's kinda funny," Hoppy warned me quietly, seriously, as we entered the garage. The running commentary continued: "He got real depressed a few years back when his wife left, and he ain't been the same since. Got so tore UP he nearly killed hisself. You got to try to get him talkin', and then he'll talk all night. Johnny's like a brother to me. I wanted you to meet him. DAMN I'm glad you came out!"

"Try to get him talkin'." The phrase captured the essence of local ethnopsychiatry. Suicide and broken hearts were closely linked in country music and this trope veered into dangerous places. I thought of Maria. Everybody said she'd "died of a broken heart," "just walked out into traffic one day." I had been on a lengthy hiatus from the scene when it happened. That fall, Maria and I had talked a lot, quietly, mostly about music and loneliness, and especially about the intersection of music and loneliness in Alan Jackson's song "Here in the Real World," which Maria played obsessively on the jukebox. ("What is it about that song?" she would ask me nearly every night, and every night I would tell her "That's what I want to know too," and we'd laugh before the silence settled in again.) And then came the Gulf War and my own crisis of conscience. I couldn't bear to be in the beer joints anymore, surrounded by yellow ribbons and "Smoke a Camel" posters and "raghead" jokes. And the next time I came out, she was gone. The story hung around like a ghost, though, one of so many ghosts that danced through the beer joints.

Outside in the sunlight, Timmy had been all motion, volume, power, and drunken aggression, working furiously and yelling about his ex-wife. As we entered the dark and cool garage, a very different picture came into focus. Johnny was a small and delicate man, focused intently on the most delicate of tasks, alternately scraping the carbon off a tiny piece from a lawnmower engine's carburetor with a pin that he kept in his gimme cap, and blowing on the part with a compressed air hose to dislodge the gunk he had scraped loose. As he finally came to a break in this process, after we had stood silently next to him for at least a minute, he carefully set the part back down on his workbench, pulled his cap ("Fort Worth Power Supply") off, stuck the pin back into the material, and looked at me intently through his thick-lensed glasses.

Hoppy introduced us: "Hey John, I want you to meet somebody. Aaron's that guy I told you about, wrote that song about 'Rocky's Revenge,' and he's researchin' on country music."

John smiled at me. His teeth were a mess, and I remembered Joanna had told me he'd been suffering a lot of pain from an abcess.

John spoke first, and with surprising formality: "Glad to meet you. Y'know I've heard a lot about you. That's a *good* song you wrote."

I was full of desire for rapport and introduced myself stiffly. But when I offered my by-now greasy hand, John held his hands up in the air to show me that they were covered in grease and caustic carburetor cleaner. Unlike Timmy, John had no plans to anoint me with the sacred sign of the shade-tree brotherhood. "I'd shake your hand," he laughed, "but Hop ain't got no clean rags around here!" Turning to Hoppy he barked, "When are you gonna get some rags, Hop? And I gotta wash my clothes before I go into Austin tomorrow."

"What the HELL are you gonna DO in Austin tomorrow?" Hoppy asked, as I waited while the back-and-forth rhythm of ordinary talk was restored to this encounter. Johnny was unruffled: "Gotta get some parts." Hoppy barked: "It's the fourth of JULY! Ain't nobody gonna be open . . ." After a second, Johnny quietly but confidently declared, "Old James will, he's got some stuff out the house." Hoppy backed down: "Well, you're right about that . . . I guess you're right." Suddenly, Johnny winced in agony. "Do me a favor, Hop? Get the aspirin from my pocket. My hands are a mess."

Without another word, Hoppy reached into his friend's front pocket and pulled out a small tin Bayer box. Hoppy opened the box and Johnny opened his hurting mouth. Hoppy, laughing, tossed three pills, one at a time, down Johnny's throat.

Johnny swallowed the pills and washed them down with his beer. "Look at this," John said to Hoppy, and I leaned over too. He was turning the camshaft in the small engine, showing Hoppy how he had freed a stuck piston, which now gleamed with new grease covering impeccably clean metal. The engine looked like it had just come off the assembly line, although it was probably twenty years old.

"Is that a Briggs and Stratton?" I asked, summoning lawnmower knowledge from some deep suburban recesses of my memory.

"Nope, old Western Auto." To Hoppy again, he said, "She'll probably skip a little beat here and there, but I'll tell you what . . ."

"She'll run!" Hoppy finished Johnny's sentence with a wide grin, as if he had just heard Johnny Mac play an exquisite guitar solo.

"She'll run, that's for sure," Johnny rejoined. "Ain't like no Moline diesel, but she'll run." Back to me, he explained, "I was dreaming last night that I was fixing an old Moline diesel," and then, turning again to Hoppy, ". . . 'til YOU come in an' woke me UP!"

"You was makin' so much noise I didn't think you was SLEEPing!"

"A truck?" I asked, not following precisely what a "Moline diesel" was.

"Naaw, big ol' diesel tractor. I ain't no godamn LAWNmower mechanic."

"We gonna PICK tonight John?" Hoppy asked.

"I don't know. I need a shower, and I've got to get up to Austin."

"You can go to Austin tomorrow, and you can wash your clothes right here tonight. By GOD, John, I don't see you but every now and then, and we're gonna pick and drink beer."

To me again, Hoppy said, in mock exasperation, "You didn't bring your mandolin, I don't suppose?"

He always asked me the same question. That mandolin was a big deal. Hoppy had given me that old beat-up no-name mandolin (which had hung on Miss Dana's wall as a decoration for decades) for my birthday a few years back. Hoppy was always trying to subvert my preference for an electric guitar. "That damn electric guitar," he called it, which was always followed by the less equivocal sentiment "I wish you'd never picked that damn thing up." If I showed up without the mandolin, Hoppy would take it as an insult, so I always brought it, even though I played it very poorly compared to the guitar. And I'd have to admit that the old mandolin (even Hoppy called it a "piece of shit") meant more to me than any other instrument I owned. It was my own favorite speaking object, a cherished "mem'ry."

I assured Hoppy that I had brought the mandolin, and he pronounced: "He-HEY! Alright! Wait'll you hear this boy PICK, John!"

Johnny looked up from his carburetor, "Is this that guy who plays at red lights?" Hoppy laughed, and I smiled sheepishly.

This was how one became a full person "out the country," the same way I knew Johnny Mac long before I ever met him. You lived for people in stories of the crazy and idiosyncratic and artful things you did, which carried the reciprocal obligation to tell stories of the crazy and idiosyncratic and artful things that other people did. I was taken aback that the "red light" story had made it to Fort Worth, along with "Rocky's Revenge" (a song I had written to fulfill the latter obligation to tell a crazy story well, a song about a certain local character who had beaten a DWI rap by stealing the videotape of his field sobriety test from a police office, and barbecuing it at Ann's bar after a public viewing on the old VCR). It had delighted my friends to hear that, determined to be a better player, I had taken to keeping the mandolin on the front seat of my truck and practicing along with the radio at red lights, but that story had long since been submerged in local memory. And now it had made it to Fort Worth.

John turned back to his work, pulling the scraping-pin back out of his hat, signaling that he wanted to be left alone to finish his task, at which he now worked with monastic devotion: scrape and blow, scrape and blow. He'd been doing the same thing for two days, Hoppy later told me, getting that motor cleaner than a new one.

Hoppy motioned with his eyes, and I followed him out of the garage and up the wooden staircase that ran up the side between the garage and the little trailer where Steve's twin brother Phil was living. I hadn't seen Phil yet today, but his battered old Toyota with the "Vote Libertarian" sticker was parked alongside the trailer, so I knew he'd be around, and I remembered that the white Lincoln was his Lucy's car, which meant that they were back together again.

Hoppy and I ducked under the low wire that had been strung dangerously at neck level across the stairs for as long as I'd been coming out here. (Amy always warned the grown-ups "look out for the wire!" when we came down these steps drunk at three in the morning, but it still caught someone every once in a while, to peals of laughter.) We pushed through the screen door and into the bar at the top of the steps. It took a few seconds to adjust to the high-ceilinged ambience, the murky darkness and the delicious cold produced by the straining air conditioner.

The sensory effect was very much like entering a church, which, in fact, is about the perfect analogy. The room *was* a church, created in the image of the perfect beer joint, always open, devoted to the serious pursuit of a precisely sacred combination of music, memory, sociability, and an altered mental state.

Hoppy and I sat enjoying the quiet cold, smoking cigarettes and drinking beer, and talking in long, slow loops for several minutes, just catching up really. He reached for his old red EKO guitar, an Italian brand you never see anymore, an instrument one of his ex-wives bought for him with her tip money from waitressing in Austin back in the 1970s, a real "mem'ry." He preferred the EKO when he was in a reflective mood.

As he absently strummed a few chords, he spoke quietly, "I'll tell you what, you shoulda been out here. This place has been *craaazy* the last few days. Must've been fifty people around here at one point or another yesterday. Hasn't been a quiet moment." There'd been a lot of visiting going on over the last few days because Johnny was down.

Randy and Audrey Meyer had been out Thursday. Joanna had to go into town to the HEB supermarket to pick up Randy's trademark Pearl beer, since you couldn't get it at the Tiger Tote up the road. Randy had said "just get one six pack," but Joanna knew better and got two. No sense making a second seven-mile trip to town, not after drinking for a few hours, not with what a DWI would cost you these days.

Pearl beer was getting hard to find. But some of the bars around Austin still kept Pearl in stock just for Randy, just in case he stopped in on his way home, like the narrator in the incredible song he wrote years ago, "When I'm with Me." Hoppy still sang that song as a way to honor Randy, with a poignant cry break on "my greatest weakness": *"I'd like to change my life and live once more in your world, but then I stop for just one drink on my way home/ One drink has always been my greatest weakness, and the jukebox still plays my favorite song."*

And then came the lyric's denouement: *"What makes a man live in two different worlds?"* The song explores a particular image of an alienated self, its protagonist and narrator a man who is loving and upright when he's with his wife, but drunken and angry and depressed when he's alone with himself, "with me." And yet it expressed desire for this solitary despair, too. This kind of ambivalence reminded people of Merle Haggard, the greatest country songwriter that ever lived, and everybody said, "Randy Meyer IS Merle Haggard around here."

We were worried about Randy, because he was recovering from a second stroke, or rather, not recovering. This last one had almost killed him. It happened while he was behind the wheel of a huge dump truck. And now he'd had to quit working, and with his Social Security disability benefits hung up by bureaucrats, times were really hard. Still, he knew he couldn't get back in that truck, as he told me, using an image drawn from a dozen country trucker songs: "It's not myself I worry about, but what if there was a bus full of kids?" Of course the doctors had said no more beer and cigarettes, and this time he really meant it when he said he'd quit, and Miss Audrey had quit drinking coffee to participate. But, as Merle Haggard put it, the "reasons to quit" don't outnumber "all the reasons why." He'd held to his promise for a week after getting out of the hospital. Still, if anyone on earth could spite the devil, it was Randy Meyer.

I'd talked to Randy on the phone that morning, in fact. I'd wanted to come out and see him at his place in Spicewood on the same weekend, because I'd just transcribed an interview we'd done a few weeks back, and I hoped to follow up while it was fresh in my mind. But when I'd asked him how he was feeling, he had told me, indirectly, to leave him alone: "Aaaah, I'm not too good. Sick every day from the medicine they give me. Tell you the truth, I don't even want to see my own family right now, don't want to go fishin', don't want to do nothin'." I told Hoppy about this conversation, and the worried expression on his face deepened some more.

Randy and Hoppy and Ann and Johnny Mac went way back together. As the story (at least Hoppy's version) went, Randy was "the first guy that ever put me on a bandstand" in the mid-70s at Beverly's, a legendary dive on Congress Avenue. And there were all those adventures that lived in stories: the trips to Colorado, the late-night motorcycle run to the coast in pouring rain, building the "house of mem'ries" in which we now sat. Sometimes Randy felt like talking, and sometimes he wanted to be left alone. This shifting between depth and distance was the rhythm of so many of my relationships with country people, but I was coming to understand that it was a working-class way of managing "feeling" that was sublimely and adaptively rooted in a cultural dialectic of intensity and abandonment. It was the rhythm of relationships between fathers and sons, between lovers, between siblings, and even between close friends. And it was strong for Randy because serious illness brought out the unadorned truth of things in a man's mind, made every last ounce of life in a used-up body something to be conserved or else squandered on important things — cigarettes, beer, self-pity, and country songs, and later, as the end approached, Jesus, salvation, and eternity.

Our worried talk about Randy was interrupted by little Amy bounding up the stairs. She flew into the room in a pigtailed swirl, and I laughed at the chocolate stains on her mouth. She gave me a mock dirty look, and the words rushed out as she addressed her step-father: "Timmy wants to know how much torque to put on the head bolts."

Hoppy said, "Tell him probably fifty then sixty . . . There's a Ford book on the shelf in the garage." As I admired the ability of a seven-year-old girl to convey this sort of information, she was gone with a bang of the old screen door. We went on talking and strumming, drinking and smoking. The stories flowed as digression piled upon digression. Hoppy told me how Timmy had come to work for him years ago, knowing nothing of engines or the mechanic's craft, and how Hoppy had patiently trained him, struggled with Timmy's forceful- ness and aggression to teach him the finer arts of the torque wrench. And then one night somebody had broken into Hop's garage and stolen half the parts off of a prized possession, a hot-rod El Camino, and even siphoned off the gas. Hoppy knew it was one of the two guys who worked for him. But when Timmy came around to plead his innocence, he'd brought a motorcycle magazine with a picture of a bike just like Hoppy's beloved long-lost "Chopped Hog" Harley on the cover as an offering of fealty, and the verdict was in: Timmy became "like a son, like one of my own," from that dramatic moment on.

A few minutes and a few stories later, we heard an engine roar to life down- stairs, and even Hoppy was surprised: "THAT's the damn Escort!" Hoppy was proud, visibly proud, as his story of imparting his skills to Timmy was aurally manifested in the sound of roaring, popping cylinders outside. "I'd better check on that torque setting," he announced, showing a bit of the perfection- ism I knew he possessed as a mechanic because he possessed it as a singer, and I followed him downstairs. Walking behind Johnny Mac, who was still bent over his carburetor, Hoppy winked at me as he poured a dribble of icy beer down the back of John's pants. Instead of showing shock, however, John inverted the joke brilliantly, his face never registering surprise, his hands con- tinuing to work at their delicate task. After a moment's pause, in a measured and polite voice, he simply said "thank you." Hoppy burst into laughter at this as he made his way back to the corner of the garage to check his Ford book.

While Hoppy looked for his glasses and the book, I talked to John for a few minutes about how things weren't like they used to be anymore, how you used to be able to figure out how things worked and buy parts for them, but now they were all computerized and you couldn't fix anything, you just had to replace it now, and how the clerks at Radio Shacks and Wal-Marts didn't know anything about the stuff they sold, and about the time John had driven fifty miles to Wal-Mart for a sale on something and had arrived fifteen min- utes before closing time, and had been told that the sale didn't start until the next morning and he'd have to come back then if he wanted the sale price, *fifty* GOD-damn miles . . .

By now, I recognized this way of speaking as the most prosaic, the most "ordinary," register of rural working-class sociable talk, and I knew that a conversation like this would almost always work to open up a relationship. John and I both understood that our talk was more about talking than about Wal-Mart. The theme was ancient: a slightly sad, slightly bitter, slightly amazed reverie of nostalgia, the complaint of old men and slow-moving "ordinary" people everywhere: things aren't like they used to be, the good old days are gone, everything's so complicated now and it isn't any better. The trick, of course, is in the telling, the see-sawing motion of agreement and contradiction, the extension of the plaintive insight into sociability. It is absolutely necessary to move from the generalities to the stories and the images and the objects that embody those observations, setting up the lyric condensation of a diegetic narrative in a phrase which artfully sums it all up, a phrase like "doesn't last too long," or "wasn't too long ago . . ." A good phrase, like one of these, could be repeated and passed around like a "beautiful thing," marking the surprising recovery of meaning from talk of a lost world. And the art was to repeat it a few times until it became a poem, "Naaw, it doesn't last too long . . . doesn't last too long at all."

Johnny returned to his task, and I wandered back outside and talked to Joanna and the other woman for a while in the same vein: "They tell you you can't bring 'em back after you've worn 'em, but I swear he'd worn 'em one day, brand new pair of jeans, they don't make 'em like they used to, and they split right down the middle, not the SEAMS, y'know, but the MATERIAL, and they WILL take 'em back if you go down there and I WILL!"

In between complaints, we all watched Timmy work in between swigs of his whiskey, jacking up the car and crawling under it, standing up suddenly and cursing the fire ants that swarmed across his legs as he swatted at them. Again he leaned under the hood, impatiently. He had already tightened the new head down and was waiting for Hoppy to give him the exact torque specifications for the bolts.

From inside the garage, where he had his book open, Hoppy shouted at last "FORTY ALL THE WAY AROUND, THEN GO BACK AROUND ONE AND A HALF TURNS ON EACH, THEN BACK AROUND ONE TURN ON EACH!"

Timmy looked up from under the hood, seized by a sudden anger and frustration. This was too much precision and complication for an ex-wife's beater car. Timmy was a different kind of mechanic from Hoppy and John. To break the tension in the air, I said, "That sounds like one of those new line dances," referring to a current — and locally much derided — craze in national country music culture for tightly choreographed social dance styles, and the women laughed, and there was a pause in which the world suddenly seemed very still and a bit too quiet and I wished I had said something else.

Timmy stood bolt upright, not laughing. In a sudden burst of powerful, angry energy, he threw himself into the air, moving away from the car, spinning his body, greasy hair flying and torque wrench flailing, eyes closed, first revolving one way, then leaping and revolving the other way, all the while shouting repeatedly "FIRST ONE TURN, THEN ONE AND A HALF TURNS!" as his anger melted into delight in this literally centrifugal liberation of his body from its task. As Timmy became a giant dancing torque-wrench, we all stared transfixed and then exploded with laughter, as did Timmy when he finished and punctuated his performance with another shot from the pint of Jim Beam. And then, he was back to work, and John was back to his carburetor, and the women and I were back to our quiet conversation about the way things used to be.

A few minutes later, the baking air once again becalmed by late afternoon clouds and the return to quiet talk and hard work, Hoppy emerged, squinting, from the garage and I followed him back upstairs. We weren't done talking. He'd been thinking about Randy and the good old days, and there was something he'd meant for me to hear, something he had been listening to the last few days. Hoppy headed over to the pile of old stereo equipment stacked on the antique pump organ against the wall. "Listen to this," he told me, "if you want to hear some REAL country guitar playing!"

I recognized Hoppy's highest term of praise, that master trope for aligning the social and the aesthetic in a single evaluation: "REAL country." Nothing was more important to my friends, or more elusive to define, than "REAL country music." And yet, I was beginning to know it when I heard it, to understand that "REAL" country had to face both inward toward conventions of musical style and outward toward the deep social relationships that music constructed, and to face both ways in the same artful moment. And so I prepared to listen carefully to these "REAL" sounds and the relationships and memories they signified for my dear friend and mentor.

Hoppy sorted through a pile of hand-labeled cassettes, mostly off-brand tapes you could buy at Family Dollar for next to nothing and that were used again and again, layering memories on top of other memories, and he put on his reading glasses to confirm that he had found the right one. The speakers hissed, and then issued a glorious low-tech sound that moved us both to focused sentimental silence and a somber reflection on the passage of time: a young, explosive Randy Meyer, circa 1974, materialized in the room, singing Lefty Frizzell's melancholy and pensive classic account of the inevitability of loss, "That's the Way Love Goes."[2]

Behind Randy, a lead guitarist with an unusual instrument—a hollow-bodied Gretsch, I later learned—played slippery passing chords, and lovely delicate countermelodies that swelled up to fill each phrase break, with a slightly "popped" pick attack that brought out the high harmonics in each note. Johnny Mac's playing exactly balanced Randy's voice, which was hard-edged, Haggardesque, gruffly sweeping through the turns and twists in the melody with both rhythmic precision and a hint of anger and abandon that made the song's melancholy mood just a bit menacing, anchored by Randy's distinctive foursquare rhythm guitar playing and Nat Adelwine's solid bass line. Johnny's lead guitar countered with a precise and sweet tone, soaring into a decorated version of an already ornate melody for a few seconds during the ride but gently easing the singer back in at the end with a clean scalar "run-up" from the fifth, as Hoppy was always urging me to do when I played lead for him.

I had never heard Johnny Mac play the guitar before, but now I understood why he was so respected. I realized that I was listening to the musical translation of the kind of work I had witnessed downstairs. Randy's voice, even constrained by a soft, sad song, was all power, controlled anger, and centrifugal force. Hearing it, I recognized the younger version of the singer I knew in his fifties, a man who barely needed a PA system to work in a raucous beer joint, because his voice had so much power and presence; a man famous for his ornery, moody ways, his drinking, his fighting, and his passion. (He was a small-framed man, and speaking of his rough and rowdy days, he once told me, "I'd always whup the BIGgest man in the place, so that way everybody else'd know to leave me alone!") Randy was known for his hardness and edge, in both his music and his life. And this old, noisy taped vocal performance still had edge in spades.

Johnny Mac's guitar work was, like Hoppy's singing, full of grace and delicacy. It was limpid, plaintive, and constrained, sweet and precise. It was the centripetal balance to Randy's centrifugal edge. It made the song work—it gave the song "feeling," as Hoppy would say—by bringing out the underside of sadness in Randy's voice and in the song's resigned lyrics.

And then I understood Hoppy's point. These were two separate and complementary ways of being a good musician *or* a good mechanic, two ways of working on an engine or a song with "feeling," two ways of expressing a "tore up" self, and two ways of articulating sadness and skill in song. Randy's singing was obviously and proudly "redneck" in style and affect. Like Timmy's forceful way of performing the complex task of tearing down an engine, balanced precariously between control and abandon, imbuing work with anger. But Hoppy, who sang with Randy's authority *and* Johnny's lyricism, wanted me to understand another of his aesthetic reference points. He wanted to show me another connection I knew less about, a connection between the young hands caressing that Gretsch guitar twenty years ago and the old hands now painstakingly cleaning a tiny, worthless old carburetor to gleaming perfection with a pin and compressed air downstairs. Scrape and blow, scrape and blow. *She'll run!*

Voicing Working-Class Culture

[It is] . . . a contingent consciousness, burdened with matter which

here makes its appearance in the form of agitated layers of air, sounds,

in short, of language. Language is as old as consciousness, language is

practical consciousness that exists also for other men, and for that reason

alone it really exists for me personally as well; language, like conscious-

ness, only arises from the need, the necessity of intercourse with other

men . . . Consciousness is, therefore, from the very beginning a social

product, and remains so as long as men exist at all.

— Karl Marx, *Capital*

This is a study of country music as working-class culture, ethnographically observed in the small town of Lockhart, Texas. My basic argument is that, for working-class Texans, the voice is a privileged medium for the construction of meaning and identity, and thus for the production of a distinctive "class culture." Song and singing comprise the expressive apotheosis of this valued vocality, and song, in turn, is locally understood as a consciously elaborated discourse *about* (the) voice. Through song and its attendant forms of expressive, technical, critical, and playful talk (especially narrative and humor), working-class Texans construct and preserve a self-consciously rustic, "redneck," "ordinary," and "country" ethos in their everyday life.

I interpret this reflexive and deeply felt construction, in its contemporary form, as a class-specific cultural response to changes in the regional, national, and global economy in which American blue-collar manual workers have experienced a loss of both cultural identity and economic security. These recent changes are set against a longer history of tenuous gains and devastating losses of social power and prestige, and especially the era of the "postwar class compromise" (roughly 1950–75) during which many of the people who appear in these pages formed their social identities and their musical habits and tastes. In the face of hard and confusing times, and in an era in which mass-mediated culture has penetrated every corner of American life, speaking and singing artfully, improvisationally, and with minimal reference to exchange value have remained essential to the social construction of history, identity, and sociability for these Texans, and for a significant number of other working-class Americans who live in similar peri-urban and small-town communities.[1]

For the people who appear in these pages, country music is a vital cultural tradition, and a specific kind of intellectual property. Country music is, in Texas, an essential resource for the preservation of community and the expression of white (but not only white, as I explain below) working-class identity. It is also, of course, a canon of songs known through commercial recordings, a pantheon of mass-mediated "stars," and a suite of institutionalized forms of consumption. A reading of country music as working-class culture cannot be isolated from considerations of ideological hegemony working through figures of reified "authenticity" and the commodity form. (Such a perspective has become deeply naturalized in cultural studies, and more recently in country music scholarship, specifically.) But working-class country music is also the expressive, stylized, ritualized surface of a deep ocean of popular social experience. I view the significance of country music in Texas working-class culture as complexly shaped by — but ultimately theoretically distinct from — the logics of the music industry or histories of recorded musical style.

I approach this significance here through an exploration of the *cultural* processes, phenomenologies, and logics in which country music is embedded for a blue-collar community in Texas. Under the rubric of "culture," I emphasize themes of emplacement, embodiment, the organization of temporal experience and memory, and normative local understandings of emotion, subjectivity, and proper sociality. I examine the way these themes emerge within local expressive economies that conjoin referential language with poetics, music, movement, and visual art. My focus thus alternates between the discourses and practices of everyday Texas working-class life, and the rhetoric, poetics, and techniques of country music performance. Ultimately, I view performance as both a commentary on and a vital resource for ordinary social life.

More exactly, I examine how vocal expression (including verbal art, ordinary "talk," and song, as well as intersections and movements between these modalities) is used by working-class Texans to construct, interpret, and remake their own theories, models, understandings, and experiences of space and emplacement, of time and memory, of personhood and the self, of emotion and reason, and, especially, of sociability, social obligation, and class, gender, generational, and ethnic identity. I focus on the particular content of these cultural categories by, first, representing vocal expressions empirically (largely through transcriptions and descriptions of naturally occurring verbal and musical discourse), and then by analyzing the characteristic rhetorical, poetic, and grammatical tropes that recur in these sounding expressions. I describe—but also narratively evoke—the linguistic and musical practices that do the important work of symbolizing, interpreting, criticizing, reproducing, and synthesizing these tropes. I present metacultural arguments encountered in ordinary talk, in elicited discussions, and in dialogues about my own project and my own role in the community described here. And I trace the force of these arguments (as well as their limits and contradictions) through less theoretical, more practical forms of competence and consciousness—the "common sense" skills and orientations of working-class Texans.

Ritual and Sociability in the Honky-Tonk

While I document these voiced tropes and practices in a wide range of contexts characterized by voluntary social interaction between working-class people in Lockhart, my ethnography emphasizes the setting in which my interlocutors there cultivate live musical performance, dance, heightened sociability, and artful talk: the local tavern, "beer joint," or "honky-tonk" bar.[2] The defining feature of a working-class honky-tonk bar in Texas is the nearly constant aural presence of what working-class Texans call, with a very complex and elusive sense of irony, "real country music."[3] This phrase refers to live performance, usually by professional or semiprofessional musicians, of a defined canon of songs in a clearly delimited (though evolving) musical style. Such performance typically occurs in ritually framed events called "dances," and in more informal jam sessions or parties. The availability of the same musical canon in the form of recordings on a jukebox, performed by a set of venerated country music stars, is also essential for honky-tonk sociability. So, too, is the possibility of more informal live performance at any time by less gifted or polished local and amateur musicians, and the spontaneous emergence of artful, musical expression from the dense textures of "ordinary" social discourse.

Besides these musical characteristics, honky-tonks are defined by the presence of highly polished verbal artists of various kinds—storytellers, comedians, "liars," and "fools"—and by the expectation that most members of the tavern-based community are capable of verbally artistic participation in sociable talk to some degree. Ice-cold beer, a verbally authoritative bartender, dense cigarette smoke, loud, cold air conditioners, invisibility to passersby on the road outside, a visually riotous display of amusing and sentimental memorabilia, and a good balance of male and female patrons, each with the ability to "take a joke," are also key ingredients. Worn wood furnishings are always appreciated, and pool tables, game machines, beer posters of semi-nude women, and a back door are desirable optional elements. Honky-tonks are run by local owners from working-class backgrounds, and these owners must allow their institutions to be used for parties and for "benefits" to raise money for sick or unemployed patrons. In Texas, children of any age are permitted in most honky-tonks, especially during the day, at parties and benefits and at weekend dances. Honky-tonks thus overlap the more private spheres of domestic life. They are (at times) "family-centered" institutions. A successful honky-tonk must also be a comfortable place in which to conduct a wide range of deal-making activities in the domains of business, politics, kinship, and sexuality. The tavern plays a significant role in the economic life of the community, especially as an institution for the socialization of wealth and the maintenance of networks of reciprocity.

The local honky-tonks in which I spent much of my time during five years of fieldwork in and around Lockhart (and to a lesser extent throughout the state of Texas and elsewhere in the nation) all fit this description closely. Such places are historically central cultural institutions for working-class communities like the one described in this book (Halle 1984; LeMasters 1975; Lindquist 2002; Rosenzweig 1991). Honky-tonks are to some extent "public" institutions, and they function as nodes in a larger and more diffuse local working-class public sphere that also includes churches, workplaces, stores, and to some extent even homes and yards (which are far less private in this kind of community than they are in more urban and middle-class places). But honky-tonks are also less than fully public, in the sense that they are working-class–controlled spaces, hidden from outside scrutiny by windowless walls and a reputation for danger and debauchery.

As businesses, these taverns are, of course, open to the world and subject to the penetration of the commodity form and capitalist logics (in the consumption of alcohol, tobacco, and music especially). They are closely regulated in certain aspects of their functioning (such as hours of operation) by the state as well as by local customs, reflecting a venerable historical struggle over working-class alcohol consumption and the meaning, autonomy, and value of "leisure" practices (Thompson 1991). It is certainly true that these institutions both concentrate and help reproduce some social and individual pathologies, especially alcoholism, with occasionally devastating effects. But in essence honky-tonks are locally controlled spaces that share qualities of sacredness with churches (to which they are sharply opposed in other respects) and qualities of domesticity with homes, while they also embody their own specific qualities of poetic license, altered states of consciousness, and theatricality. They are deeply valued sites for the highly ritualized production of cultural identity and community solidarity, and they function as community centers in very practical ways.

Whiteness

Like the churches whose functions they overlap and complement and with which they compete to a certain extent for the loyalty of working-class people, Texas honky-tonks are relatively racially and ethnically segregated institutions, and are understood as such by locals. The majority of the blue-collar patrons in the places I worked were white or "Anglo" people. And the bars were universally referred to as "redneck" bars, by locals of all ethnicities and class levels, just as these same people referred to similarly marked "black" and "Mexican" bars along the state highway.

Many of the people who appear in this book would happily describe themselves as "rednecks," though they might resent being described that way by me. The prideful figure of "redneck" identity plays an important, though confined, role in contemporary commercial country music, and in ideologically charged situations this figure can elicit compelling identifications from working-class country fans. The term "redneck" has an obvious derogatory sense, when spoken by someone who does not claim the identity; and it has an equally well-known prideful sense. It names, in both senses, an identity that is canonically bound up with a defensive articulation of whiteness—a particular class-positioned way of being "white" (Fox 2004a). This is, however, *marked* whiteness, in the form of an accusation or in the form of an assertion, not an unmarked and hence unproblematically privileged whiteness. It is, specifically, working-class whiteness, an identity sometimes even polemically framed as "white trash" by its claimants and its critics. The embodiment of this identity entails a stereotypical range of class-marked attitudes and ideologies, including parochialism, nationalism, patriarchy, inscrutability, a penchant for violence, and an ingrained racism. (This final sense is so pervasive that the word "redneck" is sometimes used as a synonym for "racist.") And although the term has been adopted and used to refer to working-class people and ideologies everywhere in recent decades, "redneck" is still an identity rooted in the southern United States, and in the specific white supremacist, antimodern, and antiurban politics and culture of the Confederacy (inflecting the stereotypes of patriotism and nationalism with a rich irony). These roots, signifying a universally recognized conflict between tradition and modernity, have made "redneck" an appealingly rebellious yet conservative political identity for America's modern white working class.

"Redneck" identity is ambivalent and subject to complicated maneuvers and transformations. It is a relational identity, expressing dimensions of the social encounter between rural and urban sensibilities, and between "white" and "nonwhite" communities, in the historical context of the large-scale migration, proletarianization, and urbanization of America's rural and small-town working poor over the course of the twentieth century (Huber 1994). And "redneck" is emblematic of a much less clear contemporary historical moment too, in which American blue-collar workers and small-town communities feel a profound sense of political disempowerment and economic and cultural insecurity, and in which the dignity of embodied labor is in question as never before. In this moment, when historical ethnic and racial essentialisms have been reconfigured within emergent structures of hegemonic "identity politics," "redneck" has also acquired a specifically postmodern character that emphasizes "whiteness" as a cultural rather than economic or biological identity. And many white American workers see their own contemporary insecurity as a result of economic globalization, which has pulled them into a draconian competition with nonwhite workers around the globe (including new immigrants to the United States), setting back years of hard-won gains in working-class economic and political power. Drawing on older models, such competition is often and easily racialized. The "redneck" identity is overdetermined in American discourse by rhetorics of racialized nationalism, however ahistorical, stereotypical, inaccurate, or unfair these rhetorics might sometimes be. And they are not always so inaccurate.

Thus it is important to stress that this book is largely about "Anglo" or "white" working-class culture, identity, and musical practice. The majority of my interlocutors would and do self-identify as "white." However, like most public sphere institutions in Texas (and throughout the South) in the years since the civil rights movement, even "redneck" bars are not ethnically exclusive enclaves, and African American, Mexican American, and Cajun patrons were among the respected regulars at Ann's Other Place and the other honky-tonks in which I spent my time. (In fact, local bars that were marked as "black" and "Mexican" places were far *less* integrated than Ann's Other Place.)

Subtle forms of racialized hierarchy persisted, of course, structuring inter-ethnic sociability in "white" and "redneck" settings and in the local public sphere. These structures could be challenged and disputed by authoritative members of the community, including those from minority groups, usually but not always in an indirect and joking manner. In absence of minority patrons—but rarely in their presence—the derogatory terms "nigger," "wet-back," "coon-ass" (for Cajun), and "Messican" were used by some white bar patrons to refer to racialized social aggregates. But in five years of fieldwork, I never heard any of these terms used as a face-to-face insult (with the exception of white patrons jokingly insulting each other). And I heard them used in overtly political polemics against minority groups only on relatively rare occasions. (The term "minority" itself had some polemical force, however, and locals sometimes expressed anxiety about the emerging "minority" status of whiteness.) Nonetheless, racial ideology—in particular a defensive articulation of an increasingly denaturalized and deprivileged "whiteness" and a range of anxious and resistant responses to that articulation (such as racist jokes, particularly in the domains of sexuality and kinship)—played an important part in the construction of this community's culture as "country" and as working-class, and in the verbal art I analyze here.[4]

Even more important than the relatively "white" racial character of these institutions is the fact that these taverns are virtually class-exclusive institutions. Regardless of ethnicity, the principle requirement for participation in the social life of these bars was a working-class biography, most powerfully signified by the possession of an authentically working-class "voice" and by competence in (strongly gendered) working-class cultural domains. While race, gender, nationality, language, and rusticity were often the surface themes of public and private discourse in Lockhart, and in the honky-tonks, "class" was the deep-running current of shared experience on which these themes were carried, and it was widely understood that working-class experience did not conform to racialized boundaries.[5]

To the extent that I am familiar with African American and Chicano working-class culture in South Texas (the latter has been the subject of recent ethnographic attention [Foley 1990; Limon 1994], and I have increasingly applied my own ethnographic efforts to the former), I would maintain that many of the general features — the fundamental orientations to time, space, emotion, and other people — which I describe in this work as aspects of "working-class culture" are not simply aspects of *white* working-class culture.

On the other hand, culture *is* specifically inflected with whiteness in this ethnographic setting, as it is in other less stereotypically racialized sorts of American communities. In Texas (C. Davidson 1990; Foley 1990; Limon 1994), as in America more generally (DeMott 1990; Hartigan 1999; Vaneman and Cannon 1987; Wilson 1978), "racial" identity is a highly fetishized (albeit malleable) source of identity that divides social classes internally and also creates cultural and political alliances across class lines. In this context, whiteness provides symbolic capital which, for working-class people, has historically compensated for a lack of real capital — what Roediger calls "the wages of whiteness" (1991). And there is a deep history of real conflict, marked by periods of intolerable violence, which underlies the relatively calm surface of ethnic relations in Texas (King 2002; Montejano 1987; Paredes 1958).

But ethnic relations have changed since the 1960s in the South, in Texas, and nationally, and class relations in the United States have changed dramatically since the late 1970s, especially from the perspective of blue-collar workers (Dudley 1994; Harrison and Bluestone 1988; Vanneman and Cannon 1987). Alongside historically entrenched structures of racial domination, new practices, alliances, animosities, and attitudes are vigorously emergent. These shifts — and even apparently retrograde responses to them — must be considered in the broader context of working-class social history.

"Country" as Cultural Identity

The community on which I report here was just beginning to experience and respond to these large-scale shifts during the years of my concentrated field-work (1990–94). The emerging "postmodern" social order—in which traditional working-class family structures have become fragmented, women have become primary breadwinners and are often the heads of poor households, "welfare reform" has dried up public sources of capital, the overt racial segregation of public institutions has diminished, and working-class experience in general has become much more politically and economically marginal—was strongly resisted and resented by the middle-aged blue-collar workers I came to know well. Many of these people grew up in poverty but came of age in the relatively prosperous years between 1950 and 1975. Most considered themselves to be "middle class" or "working people," in the pervasive language of America's postwar class compromise with which they were strongly ideologically identified. When pressed, and in certain kinds of culturally and politically charged discussions, most of them would also identify as "poor folks," and as "working-class" (the term was rarely volunteered, but never denied when I advanced it in conversation). Often, too, I heard the term "redneck" (but never the less ambivalent "white trash") advanced as a self-ascriptive label, sometimes with pride and sometimes with shame and resentment (usually with a mixture of both sentiments). But despite its overwhelming salience for ordinary existence, "class" identity remained firmly embedded in the implicit phenomenological depths of *culture*, rather than rising to the explicit level of theorized "ideology" in this community, as invisible and enveloping as the air.

For most of these people, however, "country" was the clearest and most resonant term with which they summarized their political and cultural identity as hard-working and underpaid manual laborers, as prototypical independent and free Americans, and as members of a functional local community.[6] The phrase "we're just country people" recurs frequently on my tapes and in my notebooks, spoken by people of every locally represented ethnicity. "Country" simultaneously named the real and imagined place in which they lived *and* their most highly valued genre of artistic expression, a genre that celebrates both intense sociability and intense abject depression, often in a tense and mutually constitutive dialectic. "Country" mediates between the felt depths of culture and the explicit polemics of political ideology, and it foregrounds the centrality of "place" among the cultural categories I consider here. In Lockhart, if you want to be clear about what you mean by "country," then it is sometimes important to qualify it as *"real* country." "Country" is the local master trope, a concept that summarizes a dense constellation of ideas and embodied dispositions, experiences, and meanings. The qualifying term "real" advances a particular communal claim to the social and phenomenological authenticity of these ideas and dispositions.

"Real country" is a complex expression, a trope of social identity and cultural style, and it intertwines distinctive local understandings of place, sociality, character, temporality, style, feeling, and sensibility. But it also has an apparently simpler denotation as the most basic and widely deployed term of *musical* categorization and evaluation in places like Lockhart. My interest here is, precisely, in this fusion of aesthetic and social significance. In Lockhart, "country" as music is inseparable from "country" as an identity and a description of social experience, a linkage that is reflexively embedded in a matrix of verbal art, ordinary language, aesthetic, ideological and moral discourse, and distinctive forms of sociality, and that emerges explicitly in the rituals of country music performance. The medium in which this linkage is materialized— and literally embodied—is the medium of the sounding human voice.

In this book, I explore along the voiced paths that connect song and speech to identity and experience in a particular local, rural working-class world. These are the paths that lead to and across the cultural terrain referred to when Texans refer to themselves as "country people." "Country," as a trope of both cultural and musical essence, refers to the palpable historical ties of my interlocutors to rural values and ways of living now thrown sharply into relief by several generations of increasingly urban blue-collar experience and the steady encroachment of an urban regional (and now global) economy and culture into the peri-urban margin in which these people live.[7]

I will, in subsequent chapters, demonstrate in detail that music and language, song and speech, and singing and talking are configured in this particular cultural world through a network of interrelated tropes, or rhetorical, aesthetic, and expressive figures and conventions that invoke meanings running under the literal and referential surface of discourse. The explication and mapping of these tropes is what I call a "poetics" of this culture. I describe this poetics through close, detailed structural and grammatical analyses and readings of carefully transcribed conversations, interviews, songs, vocal techniques, music-focused discourses, and other (mostly oral) texts. These readings and analyses will be interspersed with a broader-brushed narrative phenomenology. This means, simply, that I will sometimes represent Texas working-class experience through stories and evocative descriptions rather than technical and theoretical analyses (a view of explanation that finds deep support among my interlocutors in Lockhart, who find a well-told—or well-sung—tale far more illuminating than pages full of "ten-dollar words"). But for the remainder of this chapter, I will frame the broad theoretical considerations that have motivated my approach to country music as working-class culture, which will require a few "ten-dollar words."

Country Music and Cultural Mediation

Intentionally, I de-emphasize here the view of country music as a commercial genre of popular music, explicable in terms of broad patterns and institutions of production and consumption, a recorded canon of songs and performances, or principal actors (especially musical "stars") on the mass-media stage. This distinction—between genres of popular music as fields of production and consumption, mediated principally by the relationships of economic exchange they structure, and genres of popular music as fields of popular practice, mediated primarily by ritualized forms of intimate social interaction—has been poorly theorized in popular music studies and ethnomusicology and requires some explanation here.

Most scholarly writing on country music has naturalized the former perspective, identifying "country music" principally as a category of commerce in sound, image, and ideology, coterminous with a rationalizing industrial enterprise of cultural production. On this account, country "is" a recorded, mass-mediated genre of popular music, although this genre may reflect, respond to, or resist particular forms of popular social experience. Several scholars have recently moved away from this bias and framed country as a space of cultural negotiation and interpretation in which the boundaries of the musical genre are contested and contingent consequences of particular claims to "authentically" embody its identity (Ching 2001; Ellison 1995; Fox 1992; Jensen 1998; Negus 1999; Peterson 1997; Tichi 1994). But even this work has largely continued to view country music as a field of popular consumption of a commercial product, in which the commercial product itself "speaks" for (or to) some segment of the field of the popular. In such a view, people who are not direct participants in the industrial production of country music have a limited structural identity, as "fans" or "consumers" of a particular kind of "product."

Here, I do something quite different, though this is not to diminish the understanding we have gained about country music from some of this recent work. Simply put, I describe the central place of country music in the *culture* of a class-based community—with "culture" understood as an active and hegemonic (or power-inflected) process of organizing communal experience and social relations. Within this cultural framework, I treat country music primarily as working-class *art*, some of the resources for which circulate as musical commodities. But my view of what "art" is entails embedding aesthetics in a nexus of social conduct, discourse, and ideology, rather than isolating canonical texts within a narrowly stylistic history or formalist analysis.[8]

I certainly do not intend, by de-emphasizing the idea of popular music as a commodity in favor of an emphasis on working-class musical practice, to discount the influence of the commodity form (or capitalist political economy more broadly) on the culture I describe. On the contrary, I argue (along with most contemporary scholars of working-class culture) that in Texas, working-class culture is in large part shaped in response to the commodification of human agency in industrialized capitalist society—that is to say, in response to "class" in all its sociological and lived complexity. The point of emphasizing that working-class interactions with musical commodities occur within an overarching context of alienation is to shift our understanding of what might be at stake in any particular claim on a musical style as a medium of class identity. Put more bluntly, my premise here is not that (some) country music is "working class." It is that (some) working-class culture is "country," entailing a claim on musical style that emanates from everyday experience in a blue-collar lifeworld, rather than from the commodified products of a rationalized music industry. In essence, I argue here that the working-class claim on "country music" is coherent, justified, and ethical—that is to say, "authentic"—in a way that a musical commodity simply cannot ever be.

To explain "country" culturally, in terms of forms of personal and communal local musical practices rather than industrially mediated processes, is not to "folklorize" country music, or to lose sight of political economy. "Working-class" experience is, after all, not merely a social scientific abstraction, as I argue in the following chapter. It is an enveloping material environment in which poverty and the risk of poverty are institutionalized at many levels, in which life is dominated by alienated, body-wrecking, and mind-numbing manual labor, and in which the state is both a hostile opponent and a source of compensatory, mystical identification. Logics of hypercorrection and covert prestige, ideologies of mobility and solidarity, discourses of ascription and achievement, emotions of shame and pride, embedded social hierarchies of race and gender, and epochal shifts in the quality and value of particular kinds of labor all connect the everyday "cultural" life I describe here to the material environment of capitalist modernity.

Tomorrow's exhausting shift at the plant—or the nursing home, or driving the school bus—is the looming horizon of "the real" toward which working-class Texans constantly look. Rarely does this gaze shift for long—though it does shift—toward the more distant horizon of individual or intergenerational social mobility, and when it does, the skies are generally cloudy. Almost never does this gaze scan the distant night skies for signs of a workers' paradise, a working-class revolution, or even a modestly more democratic state. But one can detect the faint outlines of an imagined paradise where the gaze does fall, usually during ritual experience, often with the aid of inebriants, and always accompanied by story and song. Significantly, this fantastic gaze often seems to be cast back over the community's historical shoulder, toward a "rural" past both distant and close, both mythical and clearly remembered, and largely stripped of its less appealing elements. This paradise is a fleeting image, viewed through a haze of sociable nostalgia in moments of inchoate, evanescent *communitas*. Its invocation—locally referred to as "feeling"—is a principal goal of country music performance in a Texas honky-tonk.

But even in the most nostalgic, sociable moments—the apotheosis of Saturday night, cold beer, good talk, and "real country" music sung "with feeling"—the logics of class domination can be discerned. In this sense, what I am describing ethnographically as "culture" might better be described in terms of "ideological hegemony," since "culture" has acquired a retrograde sense in much contemporary social thought as being conceptually inadequate for understanding the historical operations of power and difference. At best, as in the work of E. P. Thompson and Stuart Hall, "culture" is not only an ideological mystification of actual social relations. It is also a system of accommodation, resistance, catharsis, compensation, and (in Willis's famous phrase) "partial penetration" of dominant ideology (1981). At worst, culture is *only* a mystification of material relations of production, an "effect" of dominant ideology, the product of culture industries and colonial and state bureaucracies.

Certainly, many recent critiques of culture theory in anthropology (see Dirks 1998) have advanced this argument, seeing ethnography itself—and therefore, projects like mine—as a key site for the production of a mystifying "culture effect," and challenging culturalist tropes of coherence, objectivity, holism, ahistoricality, abstraction, localism, and psychologism.

Here, I nonetheless assert the continued utility of the "culture" concept for understanding the historical character of American working-class social experience. And I argue for a specifically musical and poetic perspective on culture as an object of inquiry. Working at the intersection of linguistic, cultural, and musical anthropology and critical cultural studies of popular music and working-class social life, I suggest that "cultural studies" needs to take "culture" much more seriously as an empirical, theoretical, and method-ological object. In particular, cultural studies needs to learn—especially from linguistic anthropology and ethnomusicology—a more fine-grained ethno-graphic practice, a more complex understanding of linguistic and musical structure, and a more phenomenological understanding of culture's materi-alities—especially the voice.

But this is "culture" imbricated with conflict. Ethnomusicology and anthro-pology have much to learn from critical cultural studies and the postcolo-nial critique of the "culture" concept about the nature of the popular and the hegemonic dynamics of ostensibly "cultural" processes as historical discourse formations. And from critical cultural studies of popular music, ethnomusi-cologists have much to learn about the social character of mediated musi-cal experience and market-oriented musical behavior (Negus 1999; Slobin 1993; Sterne 1997; Theberge 1997). Thus I also assert that anthropology and ethnomusicology have to take "popular culture" more seriously as a field of power relations and practices historically structured in dominance, especially by logics of social class and capitalist circulation (despite the strong empha-sis on racial identity in much popular music scholarship), and with a deeply nationalistic cast in many cases (despite the strong emphasis on "global" cul-ture in recent academic cultural studies).

An ethnographic description of music as "culture" need not close off such concerns, and may address them in important ways. Indeed, I would argue that we cannot understand history's epochal social conflicts without the idea of "culture." "Culture," as I use the term in this book, consists of both ideas and practices, and especially the process of calibrating ideas and practices in expressive discourses. Culture *is* structured in dominance, internally contradictory, and interwoven with the materialities it both shapes and responds to. As a grammar of human response to experience, "culture" is a flexible faculty of the mind, the hand, the body—and the voice. It enables and institutionalizes possible forms of both "resistance" and "accommodation" within particular hegemonic social orders—and it allows the imagining of alternative hegemonic social orders. Culture is an active structure of structured activity, not (or not only) a timeless template or a rarefied abstraction of a universal pattern. Culture has a principal dynamic logic of movement between the abstract and the concrete, the theoretical and the practical, the explicit and the taken-for-granted. And there is a specific mechanism for realizing this logic. This broadly "semiotic" mechanism is what I call (following the Peircian semiotic tradition) *mediation*.

"Mediation" is the discursive production of conceptual and intuitive links between domains of social experience. Mediation connects the practical and concrete domains of everyday life (work, play, sociability, worship, aggression, sexuality, performance, sound, smell, taste, kinesics) with more abstract domains of memory, historical consciousness, senses of emplacement and displacement, ideologies of class, race, and gender, models of self- and personhood, poetics, theories of emotion, and structures of feeling. This productive pivoting is both naturalized—taken for granted—*and* reflexively framed to some extent for the working-class people who appear in this work. Mediation works through diverse semiotic mechanisms (the iconic, the indexical, the symbolic) and expressive modalities (language, music, bodily disposition, economic exchange). But mediation is principally accomplished—both reflexively and without explicit comment—in discourse (including musical discourse).

At least in Texas working-class social life, the preeminent semiotic technology of discursive mediation is the sounding, talking, singing, crying, narrating voice—the actual medium of mediation, the principal tool of expression, and the material sign both of the essential self and of all the social relations into which the self enters through voicing. Vocal practice is my principal empirical object in this study, subdivided into the overlapping analytic genres of song, talk, and verbal art.

Vocal practice yields to three crucial frameworks of inquiry, which I will call the *theoretical/metadiscursive*; the *material/technical*; and the *poetic/performative*. I do not view these frameworks as rigorously exclusive—in fact, my argument is that they are not and cannot be. My goal here is, in part, to juxtapose them so as to evoke their joint and several embeddings in the cultural practices I describe. These frameworks are explanatory only in their inter-action. They "explain culture" both within the phenomenology of any par-ticular cultural formation and for a social science of culture, and, in distinc-tive ways, for both social actors and ethnographers of social action. But these frameworks explain to the extent that they represent and reinforce each other, and to the extent that their juxtaposition continually shifts figure/ground rela-tionships between the contingent, the normative, the taken-for-granted, and the simply known.

With the term "theoretical/metadiscursive" I call attention to the point that culture theory has no monopoly on abstraction, nor academic social science on intellectual argument. Ordinary life is shot through with both momentary and sustained critical reflexivity; indeed, reflexivity is institutionalized in cul-tural reproduction and in the figure Gramsci called the "organic intellectual" (1971:6). The ideas and ideologies that sediment in common sense, structures of feeling, the *habitus*, the "natural(ized)," and the given do not always stay so embedded; nor do they always arrive fully formed, in the night, and through the basement door.

In this sense, the analysis of cultural mediation entails a dialogic calibra-tion of the theoretical abstractions of social science (e.g., "class," "culture," "emotion," "art") and the theoretical abstractions emergent from particular domains of practice and discourse (e.g., "redneck," "country," "feeling"). In this study, this critical "local knowledge" consists of potent theoretical ideas, not necessarily about class identity per se, but about the essential qualities of place, history, personhood, agency, talent, character, aesthetics, and espe-cially feeling in the material context of a working-class lifeworld. These ab-stractions are the basis for the structure of this book, as I move from ideas of place and emplacement to models of temporal and historical consciousness, from understandings of self, person, and character, to beliefs about gender difference and the nature of emotional experience, and finally to working-class concepts of aesthetics and performance. I argue that these are issues framed in the "organic" intellectual life of the community, sometimes in simi-lar terms, but more often using local conceptual language.

With the term "material/technical," I mean to call attention to the richness of practical consciousness. I am concerned here with how working-class Tex-ans do things, and how they often know how to do these things without being able to articulate this knowledge abstractly. In particular, I am concerned here with working-class *style*, the deeply worn "grooves of experience" and intuitively mastered patterns of expression (Boas 1927; Feld 1988; Sapir 1925) that constitute the grammars of verbal interaction, musical performance and interpretation, narrative, and labor.

In this study, this practical consciousness is represented in descriptions and analyses of actual tokens of musical and verbal discourse and actual social interactions, both in terms of the social contexts of these expressions and interactions and in terms of the *forms* they embody. I consider "form" at several levels, ranging from narrative form and the grammar of reported speech to the normative formal properties of sound and sociability as aesthetic and cultural systems. In particular, I am interested in the elaborate skills working-class Texans have developed for deploying the voice in speech and song, and the enormous amount of cultural "work" that gets done through vocalization without necessarily being (fully) accessible to a local theoretical description.

Finally, with the term "poetic/performative" I mean to call attention to the always fraught emergence of reflexivity from practical knowledge, and the always fraught re-embedding of reflexive knowledge in intuitive practice. I am interested in a layer of cultural consciousness that lies "between" the technical and the theoretical, between "knowing how" and "knowing that." It is in moving through this "poetic" zone of culture that historically contingent structures of meaning, conduct, feeling, and value become objects of a denaturalizing technical manipulation, a critical gaze, and both playful and serious formal analysis. But it is also in moving through this domain of culture that contingent ideological narratives and theories become embedded and (re-) naturalized in the normative density of "the real"—in everyday experience and, again, in practical consciousness. Above all, I am interested in the dense texture of "reality"—in the phenomenology of what working-class Texans call "real life"—within social interactions occurring in, around, and through the arts of narrative and song.

In my view, art—including musical art—is not an *exceptional* domain of culture; it is the very *heart* of culture. Art is not merely reflective or anticipatory. It is not exhausted by explanations that foreground individual creativity, technical procedure, social "context," productive "art worlds," "corporate cultures," transcendent ideals of form, or innate natural faculties, though none of these perspectives is irrelevant to my concerns here. Entwined with ritual, the sacred, altered states of conscious, and especially with *feeling* (as a quality of experience and a topic of discourse), art—and perhaps especially music—is in many ways the very engine of culture as a dynamic, hegemonic process. Art is the terrain of focused cultural mediation. And in working-class Texas culture, the most important and ubiquitous medium of artistry is the voice.

Voicing Working-Class Culture

When I began the fieldwork for this project, I was already curious about the relationship between "real" working-class speech and the prominent representation of "ordinary" speech in country songs (Fox 1992). I wanted to understand why country music writers and performers seemed so focused on evoking the texture and style of the speaking voice and the familiar grammars of working-class verbal interaction. After hundreds of hours of listening to working-class Texans talk about music and sing about talk, I realized that for these people I was coming to know, speech and song were inseparable expressive modalities. Of course, music and musicians were ubiquitous everyday topics of conversation. But more than that, people also frequently sang when they talked, breaking into spoken and even sung quotations from songs in highly stylized and deeply personal ways. People referred to the singing juke-box as if it were an animated participant in their conversations. And people related to live musical performance and recordings too, by singing along with them and talking back to them. Singers (and even nonsingers) delighted in imitating the voices of their musical heroes, mentors, and models. Performers mixed speech into their songs, and song titles and bits of songs into their stage patter. Singers' stage patter itself mimicked features of sociable dialogue in a heightened vocal style. Songs seemed to establish fields of affect that substantially influenced the mood and topic of sociable talk occurring in their presence. And the moods and themes of everyday sociability in turn led to certain songs being played on the jukebox, requested from the band, and sung absent-mindedly into the silence of a quiet Thursday night. Speech and singing were sutured and tangled in this community, comprising a dense and irreducible field of discursive practice that was also immanent in every vocalization.

Only later, as I was engaged in transcribing the tape recordings made on these barroom nights (and in other situations), did I start to notice something else intriguing about the way working-class Texans gave voice to other speakers in their discourse—about the grammar of quotation in this community's normative speech style. The discovery was intuitive at first, and then I started counting. Among thousands of examples of oral quotation in naturally occurring discourse I had recorded, I found only a few uses of the grammatical construction that linguists call "full indirect discourse."

Full indirect discourse, which is arguably much more prevalent in middle-class and professional speech styles, and in normative plain-style written English, is a way of representing (or "quoting") the meaning or gist of another's utterance without claiming to represent the actual words s/he originally spoke. This detachment of meaning from form frequently entails a grammatical recontextualization of the quotation.

For example, imagine the need to report the fact that a male person who is not present had said the actual words "I'll be there tomorrow" on the previous day. Full indirect discourse in English requires the use of a subordinating conjunction ("He said *that* . . .") and a systematic shifting of the deictic features of putatively quoted speech to align the reported utterance with the reporting speaker's point of view. This can include changes in pronoun choice ("He said that *he* . . .), changes in lexical form and verb tense and aspect ("He said that he *would be coming* . . ."), and changes in spatial and temporal orientations to context, or "deixis" ("He said that he would be coming *here today*."). Grammatically, the reported utterance is modified so as to assimilate it to the reporting speaker's context. Little or even nothing may be left of the form of the original utterance.

The working-class speech I recorded in Texas was almost completely devoid of such constructions.[9] On the other hand, this Texas talk was saturated with floridly "direct" discourse.[10] Speakers in Lockhart have a strong preference for quotative forms that poeticize reported speech by representing the sensual form — especially the sound — of the speech being quoted. In their expressive speech, poetic and rhetorical form and especially the dynamic sounding voice are nearly inseparable from the "meaning" of utterances. To report *that* someone said something, you must report (or claim to report) *how* they said it, and to do so precisely and with vocal skill.

In the case of purportedly "direct" discourse, the form of the reported utterance is not modified or paraphrased, and hence its grammatical deixis cannot be altered to match the context of reporting. Any fitting of such an utterance to the reporting context must be conveyed outside the reported utterance, by explanatory framing, or within the reported utterance by prosodically and paralinguistically marking or "double-voicing" the utterance. In Texas oral grammar, often the only concession to this interpretive task is that some sort of prosodic or intonational quotative marker such as a pause, a change of voice quality, or a change of facial expression is required to mark the reported clause as an "exact" citation of an earlier utterance.[11]

In fact, the grammar governing these prosodic and proxemic markers of changes of voice and footing is elaborated and systematic, allowing the elimination even of verbs of speaking so that social discourse takes on the character of dramatic performance, with all new (i.e., introduced by the reporting speaker) contextualizing information conveyed by the speaker's voice and body. The texture of working-class Texas English (among speakers of all ethnicities) makes extensive rhetorical use of the possibilities for inflecting direct discourse with evaluation, as nearly any example taken from my transcripts immediately shows (though the effects in question are fundamentally oral and must be heard rather than read to be fully appreciated). In the following example, an African American truck driver tells the story of an encounter with a truck-stop manager after a racist incident:

IRA: Told the truck-stop manager
Said, [= "I said" — implies Ira's own voice]
"y'know that waitress in there
She won't serve my wife
cuz she's white
and she's with me
I just spent over three-hunded dollars gettin FUEL *from you"*
So he went
[imitates manager's voice]
"We'll take care of you,
eat on the HOUSE*"*
[returns to his own reported voice]
"Naaw, y'know
forget about it"
[imitates the voice of the manager]
"Naw eat on the house"
[returns to his own voice]
"I don't want to eat in here"

Such direct discourse canonically entails the oral representation of the original speaker's voice quality, prosody, pitch level, and distinctive accent, as if the reporting speaker's consciousness and body were suddenly taken over by the voice of another (or even of the self in a different context, as in Ira's last line). Often, too, these vividly embodied and enacted voices are saturated with the polemical intent of the speaker making the quotation, typically through caricature and exaggeration, emerging as parody, irony, sarcasm, reverence, or multiple other affective overlays. In Texas talk, purportedly direct discourse dramatizes the negotiation of meaning in social life. In such talk, "voice" is inseparable from the truth value of an utterance. A preference for direct discourse encodes an egalitarian respect for the irreducibility of the other's voiced utterance, though it need not encode respect for the other him- or herself, or for the other's intentions in speaking. It conjoins the idea of discourse as oral performance — as sound — with evidential and truth-conditional norms.

It was through a consideration of these two vocal phenomena — the intertwining of speech and song in everyday discourse, and vivid social dramatics of direct discourse — that I began to formulate the particular approach to culture through voice deployed in this work.[12] My data showed, incontrovertibly, the central importance of the sounding human voice for my consultants. As the most elaborated site of expressive practice, the voice appeared to mediate basic ideas about self and other, body and mind, individual and society, emotion and cognition, sound and meaning, subject and object, performance and competence, and the material and the ideational.

Realizing the massive importance of the voice and vocalization in Texas working-class social life led me gradually to see my project as an anthropology of the speaking/singing voice, with speech and music as equally salient objects. Such an anthropology advances a broad claim about human social life, seeing the voice as a key material and ideational site of culture as an active process. It differs from canonical approaches to music and language — including canonical social scientific approaches — in positing voiced sound as a coherent and important totality at the heart of human experience, distinct from the objects we blithely call "language" or "music," as if these existed apart from specific expressive social practices in which they might well be configured in an inseparable matrix. In Texas, this vocal totality is obviously emergent in musical performance, which is almost always framed and interlaced with evaluative, technical, and sociable speech, and in texted song, which explores complex relationships between sound and semantics. Texas working-class verbal art is likewise fundamentally organized around vocality, and oral narrative in Texas is riotously rich in complex uses of direct discourse (Bauman 1986). But it is crucial for this study to emphasize that the sounding voice is also, and perhaps principally, the medium of "ordinary" *talk*.

Assholes Talkin' Shit: The Nexus of Talk

Without voiced talk, which is massively present, intertwined with all other sorts of expressive practice, and essential to the reproduction of human social life at both minute and grand levels, from socialization (Schieffelin and Ochs 1986) to funerary ritual (Feld and Fox 1994), there is no culture and no ideology, and there is no "ordinary" reality. But talk is shot through with poesis, with both tiny and massive works of art that emerge in every conversation and across all the conversations that prosaically constitute ordinary life (Jakobson 1960). Talk constitutes everyday life. But as a privileged medium of ordinary experience, talk is subject to critical and poetic reflexivity. Talk, in the theoretical language introduced above, is a principle domain of mediation between reflexive consciousness and naturalized experience.

In working-class Texas communities, social life largely consists of a verbal stream of conversation, gossip, persuasion, reflection, and narration. Talk in this sense is, here as everywhere, the modality of the local, the personal, the interested, and the experienced. Talk looks at and into everything around it — relationships, objects, the natural world, art, and the world of feeling. Talk appropriates all of this, in a materialized form, to the social, the present, the flowing moment of experience, the "ordinary" — to what working-class Texans call "real life."

Talk is never guaranteed to bear this weight. It must be cultivated and practiced, and yet it must remain unmarked and ordinary. Talk is an art form in and of itself in this working-class social world, and skill in talking is an important axis of social identity. But talk is ironically figured as trash: "Aaaaaaaaah, we jus' ASsholes talkin' shit," old Rusty once told me, dismissing my attempt to value the intricacies of his verbal creativity, claiming to embody an abject "redneck" essence of the ordinary. To objectify talk, even to celebrate its beauty, Rusty implied, is to invoke the risk of mimetic displacement, of ironic nostalgia, of commodification, beyond a lived-in place and moment, beyond the "ordinary" and the "real."

Talk's alchemical authenticity survives on the margins of the geographic and metaphysical edifice of postmodernity, an evasive, invisible presence around which instrumental and technological debasements of talk swirl.

Fully copresent talk, the primordial foundation of shared human meaning and community, has in an increasingly displaced and instrumentalized social world ironically become a privilege of the powerful, a guilty pleasure for workers, a marketable commodity, and a simulated spectacle on talk radio, on the Internet, at conferences and board meetings, and in popular entertainments.

Frequently, talkativeness for its own sake is conjoined to the spectacle of social otherness predicated on race, class, and rusticity. The rural and periurban working poor, in particular, are practically signified in the American mass media by their talkative excessiveness as "rednecks" and "trailer trash." They appear as a dangerous, oversexed, inebriated rabble on the ubiquitous television talk shows and "reality" police shows, and as unselfconscious debased clowns devoid of style and sophistication in the plethora of interchangeable television situation comedies that foreground the American obsession with social distinction, an obsession shaped by the absence of a language of class.[13] In either guise, the diagnostic marker of cultural otherness is a proclivity to talk for talk's sake.

But talk (and talkativeness) is more than a stereotype, paradoxically inhabited and seen from afar by its subjects. For the Texans who appear in this book, talk is an expressive and experiential resource that must not be alienated from the living local world it constitutes. In order to challenge modernity's avalanche of desire and replacement, to resist the newest and latest and next best thing, talk throws itself into the space between loss and desire. Talk braces itself against the material world *as it is* in order to articulate a vision of the moral world *as it could be*, which in the local, working-class idiom means a world in the image of life *as it was*, before Wal-Marts, before CDs, before NAFTA, and before country music went to hell.

The medium of this primary form of social practice and experience is the socially and personally distinctive voice. And it is my contention that rural working-class culture is deeply oral and voice-centered because the historical project of this culture is to respond to and resist the alienation and objectification that is the heart of a class-based political economy. The voice stands for the embodied, socially embedded self; it stands also for a communal identity in which that self has a particular and irreducible dignity. The fragile but necessary living human voice, in all its individual embodied thought and felt particularity, and in all its iconic social symbolism and situational indexicality, is the object of a vigorous poetic entextualization in this class culture because it is also the heart of a cherished *critical* "ordinariness"—a way of occupying a defensively constructed "ordinary" identity on the margins of modernity.[14]

Theorizing Voice

I claim here and elsewhere (Fox 1992) that country music's aesthetic tension is rooted in a genre-specific opposition of a textual or "writerly" poetics of denaturalizing "ordinary" talk and practice, and a "performative" poetics of renaturalizing the meanings thus opened to scrutiny, a return of vocally achieved knowledge to the ordinary domain of talk. This distinction informs the highly conventional division of labor between writers and performers in country music production. Country's wordplay with everyday language use (clichés, puns, and literalized metaphors, for example) and its other speech-objectifying tropes (including the primary transformation of simply setting words to music) call attention to the arbitrariness and lack of a "natural" authenticity-to-experience of everyday spoken language. Country's performance conventions work to reinstantiate that writerly deconstruction of speech in the image of authentic talk, through framing song with speech, through talk about songs, through the uptake of song texts into speech, through stage patter that takes the form of dialogue with audiences, and through the constant objectification of talk's *sound* in song performance.

As a Western aesthetic practice, country music yields (perhaps unsurprisingly) to a deconstructionist account of textuality, fetishizing the "absent presence" (literally, in the case of directly reported speech) of the authoritative voice. But the double-voicings and dramatized engagements characteristic of working-class orality also confound the authority of the voice, both across time and synchronically in the characteristically dense, high-involvement, and agonistic sociable style of performative talk that working-class Texans call "talkin' shit." The other's voice represents the other's irreducible self, but it is also and always a text in process, open to interpretive revoicing, and subject to polemical revision (as in the example above, when Ira's direct reporting of the truck-stop manager's voice managed to impute insincerity to the manager's putatively ameliorative words).

As working-class discourse, country music stages a struggle between textuality and performativity that is both rooted in and responsible to the domain of talk. As a working-class art form embedded in a larger cultural and political economy, country music's identity as a class-specific expression is always at risk, and always traded on as a source of "authenticity" for projects of folklorization, cultural distinction, and nationalism (Fox 2004a). Working-class art constantly seeks to reclaim its own "authentically" working-class voice, often via a textual deconstruction of stereotypes of working-class expressive style (cf. Keil 1985). "Ordinary" working-class talk is always already layered with textuality.

Thus, in this study, talk constitutes a formal object of equal importance to song and verbal art, not merely as a context, background, or commentary on genres of expression normatively styled as "art." Talk is a crucial layer of sociality in Lockhart, where both song and verbal art find their materials and toward which both song and verbal art are performatively oriented. Deeply naturalized as practice, talk nonetheless frequently produces critical reflexivity into the textuality of social life.[15]

This book argues for the epistemological and empirical primacy of the living voice in social exchange, for the embedded, emergent textuality that is always intertwined with "ordinary" talk, and for the constant tension between impulses to order and to disorder in discourse emphasized in the work of Bakhtin (1981a, 1984, 1986) and Voloshinov (1973). Bakhtin and Voloshinov, whose work is central to my approach here, showed brilliantly how the social life of language is constituted "dialogically" at the level of inner speech and actual social communication. In particular, they argued for a focus on the way that conflicting, competing *voices* encounter each other in the dialogically constituted discursive sign, as a collision of accents, points of view, syntactic and perspectival unities, and embodied points of view.

They showed, in addition, that a key site for this "dialogism" was the phenomenon of represented or "reported" speech, the politics of quotation, the relations of power and difference that organize the presence of multiple voices in every single utterance in real social life, that is, in "talk" broadly conceived. In stressing quotation they emphasized the emergence of social conflict and change and struggle through the process of entextualization, through a making palpable of the *voice* of the speaking subject's other in a subtle and variegated typology of possible dialogic voicings. These voicings might range from the everyday use of typifications of others' words up to the high art forms of the polyphonic novel—or country music—and other "secondary speech genres" (Bakhtin 1986) that organize the less textual, more centripetal, more contained voicings of everyday talk.

The predominance of objectified, other-voiced direct discourse in Texas working-class talk is only part of a broader voice-centered cultural orality. The music of language and languages of and about music are equally salient in processes of poeticization, entextualization, de- and renaturalization, and in the modeling of social conflict and solidarity through talk's sociability. The musicality of language articulates another set of dialectical pivots centered on the voice: between the body and the mind, between disordering desire and ordering constraint, and between emotion's engagement and reason's estrangement, for example (Lutz 1988). The voice is the medium of these mediations. It is the principal domain of both practical *and* theoretical consciousness, and the pivotal site of their encounter.

In this book I stress, then, the centrality of the voice to link the politics of quotation, the music of language, the interactional density of "ordinary" talk, the individual creativity of speakers, and a local understanding of the embodied locus of feeling in social relations. And I stress voice, too, because I want to call attention to the textual interplay of voices that constitutes ethnography for me. This interplay is the talkative, poetic heart of the ethnographic critique of positivist epistemology and representation, as much as it is at the heart of a talkative, sociable community like the one described in these pages. The insistence on the irreducibility of the politics and poetics of the human voice constitutes, I believe, the "voice" of ethnography among the human sciences.

An important task for a critical and empirical and humanistic anthropology is to join a politics of (the) voice, in this latter ethnographic sense, to a formal poetics of voicing. Such an approach to the poetics of expressive culture—in particular of verbal and musical discourse—has emerged as a paradigm in the last decade in linguistic anthropology, ethnomusicology, folklore, and cultural anthropology. Viewing the voice as the medium of dialogic quotation in talk, verbal art, song, and their interlocking engagements in real discourse, I hope to make a linguistically and musically grounded contribution to the development of this paradigm, in the form of a voice-sensitive ethnographic poetics of Texas working-class culture. I propose that this model of and for an anthropology of the voice is a necessary dimension of humanistic anthropology.

Knowing Lockhart

Two Perspectives

They oughta make [Hank Williams's song] "Mind Your
Own Business" the national anthem of Lockhart, Texas!
—Candy Sue, *barmaid at Ann's Other Place*

In this chapter, I preface the polyphony of tropes and voices to come with a juxtaposition of two orienting perspectives on the community whose voice(s) I describe. The first perspective is subjective, and takes the form of a personal narrative. I will tell you when, where, and how I came to know something about working-class social and musical experience in Lockhart, Texas. The second perspective is, in conventional terms, more objective. I will describe the economy, demography, and geography of Lockhart and the surrounding region, in order to specify the material conditions that justify my extensive use of terms like "rural" and "working-class" in this book. Ultimately, I juxtapose these perspectives in order to underline this study's emphasis on the simultaneously material and meaningful character of working-class culture.

Arrivals: A Fieldwork Narrative

On a bright February afternoon in 1990, I walked through the door and into the cool darkness of Ann's Other Place for the first time. I had made the hour-long drive from my home in central Austin out to this roadside honky-tonk bar for a simple purpose: I was seeking a great country music jukebox. My search had taken me to a dozen bars in the Austin area over the previous few months, with mostly frustrating results. Ann's was further from the city than most of the other taverns I had visited, but a jukebox distributor named Birdie Barker had piqued my curiosity when she told me about a beer joint near Lockhart where the owner stocked the machine in her establishment with records from her own extensive personal collection. She added that despite its unusual paucity of current hit records (normally kept updated by the distributor), this jukebox was exceptionally profitable and the tavern in which it sat was a lively—and very "redneck"—place.

My interest in the jukebox as a site of social practice—as a principal and mythologized medium through which country music fans engage collectively and publicly in the consumption of songs—had been stimulated by work I had been doing on the ubiquitous image of the jukebox in the textual poetics of the genre, in songs such as George Kent's "Hello, I'm a Jukebox," Becky Hobbs's "Jones on the Jukebox," and Alabama's "Jukebox in My Mind." I had just finished a paper (published as Fox 1992) in which I argued that the image of the jukebox in such songs exemplified country's intense fascination with the poetic figure of an inanimate object that speaks with a human voice. This uncanny trope, I thought, involved a radical literalization of Marx's famous image of the commodity fetish, an image that conveys the hidden alienating logic of capitalist social life in which "a definite social relation between men . . . assumes . . . in their eyes, the fantastic form of a relation between things" (1978a: 321).

I was, at the time, a graduate student in anthropology, searching for a dissertation research project that would focus on working-class people and their musical experience, and that would enable me to explore the relationships between popular music and the cultural politics of class in the United States. In this context, I was struck by the potential significance of the "talking jukebox." This trope canonically represents the jukebox in dialogue with a "tore up" drinking subject. It blurs semantic boundaries between human and machine, use value and exchange value, and sociability and alienation. As a stylized, metaphoric description of a corresponding form of working-class social practice (drinking and socializing to jukebox music) conducted in a specific real setting (the tavern), it also suggested an opening for ethnographic inquiry, in a domain of practice seriously engaged with popular music as art.

I wanted to know if this textual trope of the "talking machine" translated, somehow, into real sociomusical practices among working-class country fans, the people whose social experience has typically grounded country music's claims to authenticity (and who have historically constituted a principal market for the country music industry). Did objects like jukeboxes really seem to "speak" in some way for these fans? Did "ordinary" talk resurface in song the way song seemed to suggest its own origins in speech? What "real life" traditions of verbal practice produced the voices of great singers, such as George Jones, Merle Haggard, Hank Williams, Johnny Cash, Patsy Cline, Dolly Parton, and Loretta Lynn, each the product of a small-town, working-class community? Why did those voices, distinctively "ordinary" and irreducibly unique at the same time, seem so central to and evocative of a broad history of American working-class experience? In what sense was country "working-class music," despite all the other claims made about, upon, and for it? How were working-class fandom, musical consumption, and local appropriation actually socially practiced? What creative possibilities for subjective identification and agency emerged from the mediated encounter between songs and social practice? What roles were played in this encounter by the voice, by conventions of musical and verbal and danced performance, and by musical metadiscourse — discourse *about* music? These questions compelled me to seek out an actual jukebox-centered musical scene, and eventually brought me to the front door of Ann's Other Place.

Poetically enough, this "place" was named through a trope of memorial displacement, its strangely resonant "Other" referring to a long-gone, more "real" place buried in the memories of the local people. That "real" place was the eponymous proprietor's previous tavern. Ann Roose had operated The Little Bottle in the 1970s, in the Manchaca neighborhood of South Austin. South Austin was, then, still the rough, rustic "redneck" side of a small city, almost as "country" then as Lockhart is now.[1] This is a reputation that persists, but it hardly describes the massive growth that has overtaken the southern section of the city since the 1980s. With its very name, Ann's Other Place suggested continuity, history, nostalgia, and a tangible link to a communal past that mattered very much to "Miss Ann" (as the bar's owner is known in deferential speech) and to her patrons. Indeed, many of the people I encountered at Ann's Other Place had themselves moved south over the past two decades. Ann had moved her tavern to accommodate this blue-collar diaspora. This community had maintained its distance from the expanding, modernizing city, continuing to occupy the peri-urban margin.

Ann's Other Place turned out to be an almost perfect example of the kind of situation I had hoped to find, a place where music in general, and country music in particular, mattered in a deeply local way. The jukebox was, in fact, at the center of ordinary sociability, and live music was even more essential to social rituals. At Ann's, country music and carefully cultivated forms of sociable talk and verbal art were highly valued by almost everyone who came through the double doors into this windowless, smoky, friendly tavern. And music and talk were combined with other expressive forms into an intense cultivation of the art of memory (or "MEM'ry," as it is locally pronounced). Graffiti, photographs, sentimental souvenirs, and funny, oddly labeled objects covered every available surface in a visual riot of text, color, and texture and layered, piled-up meanings. Ann's was never silent except in meaningful moments when speech and song both seemed inadequate. Even in the middle of the night, when no one was around, the jukebox was programmed to cycle through its playlist, pouring forth some random selection once an hour for the ghosts to dance to, as the police scanner chirped noisily with news of drunk-driving arrests, rowdy neighbors shooting off their guns, and another successful speed trap up the road in the infamous hamlet of Mustang Ridge.

Miss Ann herself, the proprietor of this former feed store and chinchilla ranch and flea market turned honky-tonk, is a vibrant, strong woman. She is the South Austin born-and-bred daughter of a master mechanic and a tough-minded mother, and she grew up deeply involved in the everyday political and cultural life of South Austin's white working-class community. As an "Air Force wife," she raised three children in a variety of places—Wichita, Abilene, Panama—before returning to Austin, divorcing, and taking up chinchilla ranching and saloonkeeping. She no longer raises chinchillas, but she is a legendary saloonkeeper, an occupation that had also attracted her sisters and that is a perfect match for her tough but gracious temperament, her skill at observing human behavior, and her deep love of country music.

Ann's life project, at least since her children have grown up, has been to create a musical and sociable home for the "real country" music and musicians she loves so much, and for their fans and students too. Her larger aim, though, is to contribute to the preservation of her community and the working-class values that define it. She was immediately welcoming to me, and she was extraordinarily articulate as well as generous with her time when we began to discuss my intentions in her tavern. I believe she took an interest in my project because it seemed to her that it was not so different from her own curatorial and emotional fascination with the meaning of country music in the life of her community. From the first evening I spent in her place, she helped me to develop relationships and overcome such obstacles as my need, as a linguist, to use a tape recorder. With Miss Ann's approval and participation — indeed, her patronage — my project, however strange it seemed to the locals at first, acquired an aura of validity it could not have otherwise had.

Ann's Place became my place. Weeks turned into months, and I spent three or four nights a week at Ann's for the rest of the spring and summer of 1990. I passed most of my time there listening to talk and jukebox songs and various bands and jam sessions. My interest in jukebox-centered sociability soon expanded to encompass the central roles played by live musical performance and knowledgeable musical discourse in barroom social life. In formal and informal interviews, and most often in formal interviews that evolved into free-form focus groups, I talked with Miss Ann, her patrons, and her employees about country music and jukeboxes and "feeling" (the key locally elaborated term of musical evaluation, discussed in chapter 5). My circle of interlocutors slowly evolved and expanded, as it became clear that Ann's bar was a key institution in a large and diverse musical community. Early papers and notes and tapes and an article from this period (published as Fox 1993), along with the stories that orally archive such memories for the community, now help me to reconstruct the way that this particular arrival took place over an expansive period of time and required numerous different attempts to forge a beginning. But my project had, in fact, barely begun.

Another Arrival — and a Departure

Ann kept several battered guitars leaning against the wall by the bar, and the house rule was that the jukebox and the TV were turned off whenever anyone picked up an instrument. The rule was frequently invoked. It was a rare evening when a locally celebrated musician did not stop by the bar, and impromptu performances and picking sessions in the front bar area were even more common than the weekly formal dances and organized jams held in the bar's larger back room.

I had downplayed my own identity as a musician, but on one quiet summer evening Miss Ann demanded that I pick up a guitar. On that night everything about my project changed, as if from black-and-white to color. Ann still tells the story of that day, which she remembers vividly. She jokingly accuses me of "lying" about my musicianship, of hiding my own musicality from my new friends and acquaintances for almost a year. "Nobody even KNEW you were a lead man," she still reminds me scoldingly, using the local term for a lead guitar player. Given the social importance of musical skill (especially as an index of masculinity) in this community, my reticence to display my own would have been constructed as rude if it couldn't be chalked up to my obvious otherness, signaled by the tape recorder and the notebook and an earnest way of speaking, by the way I nursed one beer for hours, and by my much-remarked-on quietness in the presence of so many fine talkers.

Once my skill as a musician was revealed, however, scarcely a night would go by in which I did not participate in the informal picking sessions at the bar. This change in role fundamentally altered my relationship to the local community. From jamming with the "old boys" at Ann's on Friday nights to playing with pickup bands at other small beer joints around Lockhart and Austin was an easy and natural transition. I had been a bass guitarist and singer in bands for most of my life, as well as a serious acoustic guitarist, and I had dabbled with country performance since college while working professionally as a rock and reggae musician. I could muddle, therefore, through the mixed sets of country and old rock tunes that comprised the basic canon of live music in Texas redneck bars, though I had a long way to go before I could claim the degree of mastery properly specified by the term "lead man" (the details of such mastery are discussed in chapter 8). Singers who fronted their own bands heard me at informal jam sessions and at more formal "gigs" (or "dances"), and called me to fill in when their scheduled guitar player didn't show up or showed up too drunk to pick. This steady stream of low-paid, often musically sloppy beer joint gigs allowed me to convert my rock, jazz, and folk skills gradually to the local "hard country" idiom, and even more gradually to start singing and writing acceptable country songs. Another sort of arrival was underway.

But even as I played more and more jobs as a working country musician, in the fall of 1990 I experienced a personal crisis of conscience that caused me to withdraw from socializing with my friends and acquaintances in Lockhart and to question my entire project. As the United States moved closer to an outright war with Iraq, following Iraq's invasion of Kuwait in August, I began to experience a sharp conflict between my loyalties to working-class culture and ideology and my opposition to jingoistic militarism and war. I became actively involved with the antiwar movement in Austin, attending protests and teach-ins on campus. As the nation moved into full-scale war preparations, I was increasingly distressed by the inflammation of long-standing conflicts in American society, and I found myself caught in the crossfire.

Out of personal interest, I had made efforts in my early period of field-work to identify and interview veterans of the war in Vietnam, who frequently turned out to be highly articulate critics of the ironies and hypocrisies of the social structures of class and race I saw as the focus of my work. It seemed to me that the Vietnam era had developed a near-mythological status among my middle-aged interlocutors. In their way of speaking, the war marked a moment when America had lost its bearings and blue-collar identity had begun to diverge sharply from a commitment to a nationalist ideology that had once lionized the (white) "working man" as the embodiment of American values. Much of the ensuing bitterness of the past few decades, for blue-collar Americans, can be and frequently is attributed to the cultural rupture of those years. And there is more than a grain of truth to this attribution.

The first Gulf War seemed to be opening up the poorly healed wounds of that era. Most of the older men in Lockhart were veterans, some from the Vietnam era, and others from the Korean conflict and World War II. Nearly every family knew someone who had died in Vietnam or come home damaged by the experience of fighting. The striking contrast between the veterans of the Vietnam era and the veterans of earlier conflicts, most of whom had returned to lead normal, locally successful lives, could not be denied and was a common topic of conversation. Vietnam vets were noticeably more likely to be alcoholic, depressive, physically disabled, and mentally injured. And they were implacably angry.

It was common to hear the blame for this difference in generational experience assigned to the unpopularity of the Vietnam conflict, and to the disproportionate load working-class soldiers had carried in that long and bloody war without appreciation from the broader society. Anger and resentment, stoked by ideological rhetoric, tended to conflate (again, sometimes fairly) leftist criticism of the Vietnam War and privileged exemption from its costs. And the militaristic patriotism swirling through America in late 1990 provided many working-class people a powerful, if (in my opinion) obfuscatory symbolic compensation for perceived injustices of the still vivid past. For my friends in Lockhart, the Gulf War provided a chance to redress these injustices by mustering an unwavering support for U.S. soldiers abroad, an unstinting criticism of any antiwar argument, and a class-conscious rejection of the antiwar movement as unpatriotic and bourgeois.

By the time the United States began bombing Iraq on January 16, 1991, an intense ideological climate had enveloped the beer joints where I hung out. Yellow ribbons, meant to symbolize active support of the war and the American troops in the Gulf, rapidly proliferated on trees, bumper stickers, hats, and t-shirts. I listened to racist jokes about Arabs and Muslims, from African Americans and Hispanics as well as from Anglos. These jokes were often told to goad liberal attitudes as much as to demonize newly discovered enemies. I heard sharp, bitter critiques of the antiwar protesters among whom I was spending much of my time. Whereas in the past I had been able to express disagreements with my working-class friends about difficult and controversial political subjects, and sometimes even to find common ground, now I found the door to debate tightly shut. My opposition to the war was, for these friends, tantamount to a betrayal. It was irreconcilable with my professed loyalty to working-class culture and to my country. It was only explicable in terms of my privileged habitus and historical ignorance of the working-class experience of the Vietnam era.

Many of my interlocutors had friends, spouses, sons, and daughters serving in the Gulf, or facing the imminent possibility of deployment, and for the first few weeks it was by no means clear that the United States would achieve the dramatic and relatively low-cost victory that ultimately ensued. With deep regret and sadness, uncomfortable anger, and a sense of intellectual and moral failure, I withdrew from fieldwork and social participation in the life of the bars in Lockhart and South Austin, although I continued to play regular jobs as a guitarist on many weekends, often spending breaks in my car listening to war news. I had run up against one of the major pitfalls of doing anthropological research in one's own society. My own identity as a liberal, urban, middle-class member of that society was symbolically significant for my interlocutors, just as their corporate identity was for me. I was accountable for that identity in ways that could not be transcended, ignored, or even dispassionately investigated. I had prepared to handle this problem directly, but the crisis atmosphere of the war gave me—and my interlocutors—no room to maneuver.

I avoided Ann's Other Place for several months and began to search for a new project. But after the war came to a quick and decisive end in March of 1991 I decided to return. The ideological conflicts exposed by the war persisted, fading with the yellow ribbons still tied to so many trees. But in Lockhart's working-class community there was a visceral sense that America had achieved a great victory and had thereby symbolically resolved many of the cultural conflicts that had festered since the Vietnam era. Gradually, the war receded as a topic of conversation and a barometer of class identity.

My return, however, was initially ambivalent both for me and for my friends, and ambivalence led me to wander down darker roads. The period of alienation had left me with a less heroic view of working-class life, and I felt compelled to learn more about the lives of the poorest and most marginal members of this poor and marginal social world, and to explore my new understanding. As I continued to play regularly with bands, I gained ethnographic access to a wider spectrum of scenes and a more diverse network of people. I spent increasing amounts of time in the rougher bars of South Austin and Central Texas, talking with criminals, prostitutes, drug addicts and dealers, drifters, depressed Vietnam veterans, and suicidal loners. At times I also crossed the line of local respectability by using drugs with some of my more marginal consultants and fellow musicians. The darker sides of country music and working-class culture came into sharper focus for me as I began to appreciate what was at stake in maintaining the sociable solidarity of "ordinary" life for my friends at Ann's Other Place.

At the same time, I decided to expand my project into another (less fraught) domain, and I began to study small-scale independent country music record labels run by entrepreneurs with a less polemical identification with (indeed, sometimes an outright cultural disdain for) the "redneck" community. I worked closely with the married proprietors of a tiny Lockhart-based record company (whom I met at Ann's place, which was the musical crossroads for the area). Don Jones and Sandy Samples (a fine gospel and blues singer herself) helped me broaden my project by introducing me to the busy world of small-time commercial country music recording and promotion at a level beyond the immediate local sphere. This is a world often driven by fantasy and greed and inhabited by a surprising number of people with a burning ambition to be famous but no talent whatsoever. But Don and Sandy were deeply passionate about country music and the musical life. Sometimes I thought that, with all their hardscrabble years making a living in the music business, they were more blinded by fantasies of musical grandeur than the naïve young singers and washed-up former minor stars whom they promoted. The next single or artist was always going to be the one that finally broke out. It never was.

In order to meet and interview the musicians who recorded for the label and who toured through the circuit of clubs, bars, and hotels at which Don booked jobs for his acts, I offered to write short promotional biographies of these artists. Such biographies are a standard part of the press kit (containing pictures, recordings, a biography, and contact information) these artists use to secure jobs and to market their recordings to radio stations. (The more local artists with whom I worked thought it an absurd pretension to use such materials to get jobs in honky-tonk bars, where one's biography was typically known in more detail than a press kit could ever convey.)

Through this process, I talked at length with Stoney Edwards, a once-famous African American country singer with a voice like sweet brandy, and with Dub Robinson, a longtime Gary Stewart sideman now fronting his own band and working the South Texas bar circuit. I talked as well with numerous other small-time singers, some raw and some hardened, and most with far less skill or charisma than Edwards or Robinson. All were dreaming of and struggling for that nearly impossible "big break" and trying as hard as possible to act the part of the "country music star," as if this could convert fantasy to the glossy, professionalized reality they glimpsed on CMTV and in the pages of *Country Song Roundup*. This dream reflects a key myth about country music stars as very "ordinary" people with "extra-ordinary" voices that catapult them, unerringly and unstoppably, to wealth and fame. Working-class country fans I met invoked this narrative all the time. Over and over I heard things like, "If those folks in Nashville could only just HEAR this boy sing, he'd be a big star by now!" or "She's BOUND to make it big!" Stardom was as palpable as heavenly salvation, and yet nearly as impossible to predict or engineer.

One of the artists on the label was a young singer named Becky Rollings, who lived in a small town I will call Parkville, in Central Illinois, where she had grown up on a wind-blasted prairie as the daughter of an insulation installer. Don and Sandy had, as the business jargon has it, "put out two singles on Becky," which were doing pretty well in the tiny markets in which Don worked. In November 1991 I was in Chicago for the anthropology meetings, so I rented a car, called Don to get Becky's phone number, and drove 220 miles through a snowstorm to conduct an interview, ostensibly so I could write a bio for Don to use in Becky's press kit, but with an unformed idea that my project might find new inspiration in the industrial Midwest, away from the self-mythologizing fantasies of Texas honky-tonk culture.

I met Becky at the (now defunct) tavern and diner where she worked as a waitress and cook. After we had talked for a few hours, I stayed around until well after midnight interviewing patrons and listening to Becky sing to a taped accompaniment before an audience of friends and family. She was a fine singer and a gracious person who became a good friend (and my employer), and I was intrigued by the community I discovered in this bar, which was in many ways similar to the Texas honky-tonks I knew, but in many ways also quite different. Life seemed less joyful in Illinois than in Texas—somehow darker and more severe. I heard fierce criticisms of the antiwar movement there too, but my political and cultural identity was less well known and my attention was less intimate than in Lockhart. My affiliation with Becky's record company provided a basis for rapport, because she was a local hero for her modest musical success. To the residents of Parkville, it seemed obvious that "a writer from a university" would be interested enough in Becky's singing to drive down from Chicago and spend the night in town. After all, she was bound for stardom.

Parkville is, like Lockhart, a peri-urban or "shallow rural" (Halperin 1990) working-class community, principally important as a switching point on a major freight rail line. The surrounding region is peopled with many descendants of migrants from Appalachia who had followed the soft-coal industry into Central Illinois earlier in the century. In the early 1990s, with the coal mines closed and the railroad in decline, most workers in the town traveled to factory jobs around the region or worked in service or industrial jobs in the nearby urban center of Champaign-Urbana. I was struck by both the similarities and differences between this place and Lockhart. I left Parkville at 3 A.M. for the long drive back to Chicago with new questions on my mind, and with a box of videotapes taken by Becky's family at "Opry Shows" and county fairs, entrusted to me without the slightest concern about my reliability. That was the first of several trips to Parkville over the next few years, and some stories from those visits will appear in these pages, especially when I want to suggest cultural interpretations that apply beyond the Texas setting that is my focus here.

In the summer of 1992, Don and Sandy convinced Becky to move to Texas, where they could concentrate their energies on promoting her career in a better live music market than the economically bleak Midwest provided. At Don's urging, I signed on as the guitar player in her band, along with a couple of excellent Nashville-based journeyman musicians on bass and keyboards and a series of local drummers.

Becky's show never did make it out of the dues-paying circuit, although we worked constantly across Central and South Texas. The band was, by the end, and for all of us, an experience of real camaraderie layered with deep frustration and road fatigue from too many cheap motels, too many corrupt and venal club owners, a miasma of drugs and alcohol, and the conflicting emotions that accumulate under such circumstances. But it was a good band, at its best a fine, funky bar band, and in it I grew into a professional country musician with my own fantasies and ambitions that transcended the fieldwork project that had brought me to this point. I had a gig with a new band the weekend after Becky, in search of a still bigger break, set off with her boyfriend for Nashville. For the next two years, until I left Texas to take my first academic job in Seattle, I worked steadily as a guitarist, "jobbing out" with dozens of different bands when I wasn't working with my primary employer, a so-called Top-40 band. This band—Modern Country—played covers of songs currently popular on country radio, traveling regionally with a large sound system, and working for good pay and principally for youthful audiences, with a clearheaded, and frankly middle-class, rejection of larger ambitions.

Like most working musicians, I have a stock of road stories from the years with Becky, with Modern Country, and with so many other bands, and some of these will find their way into this book. Certainly, as a professional musician working across a wide geographic area and in many different contexts, I came to a much deeper and more complex and modulated understanding of the details of country music's poetics and performance styles, and of the diverse meanings country holds for different kinds of fans too. I have played for audiences ranging from three working-class people in a tiny beer joint to dance halls full of rowdy teenagers, from fraternity parties to convention auditoriums and parties at the homes of millionaires. By 1992, my income from music began to pay my own bills and thereby to fund my research. Somewhere in this process, my fieldwork and my everyday sense of who I was and what I was doing with my life began to get blended, and my knowledge of country music became as much lived and performed as studied. At whatever cost in scholarly focus and objectivity, yet another kind of arrival had been achieved. Within the working-class communities in which I moved, I was no longer (only) a researcher. I had obtained a more familiar local identity for a young man: musician.

Arriving Again: Obligation and Ambivalence

All through these years from 1992 to 1994, I continued to spend most of my free nights at Ann's and at many other bars and homes around South Austin and Lockhart. I played frequently at benefits and parties and jam sessions and worked regularly as a substitute guitarist and bassist in friends' bands. I was by this time known in many of the bars and dance halls more as a musician than as a researcher because of my work in bands (although I continued to carry a tape recorder and a notebook in my guitar case and to seize frequent opportunities to conduct impromptu interviews). My presence as a picker, a singer, and increasingly as a songwriter provided exceptional opportunities for rapport, access, and reciprocity, requiring me to exercise more care about what I could document, and how. I became more personally embroiled, sometimes disastrously, in social and musical obligations that conflicted with my obligations as a researcher.

Gradually during 1993 I watched Ann grow weary of the effort it took to manage her bar. "They're killin' the beer joints," so many musicians, bar owners, and music lovers kept repeating, referring to the DWI laws, to the police cars that would wait right beyond the driveways of bars, to the ASCAP royalty collectors, to the TVs and VCRs that kept people at home, to rising taxes and insurance rates, to the emergence of the state lottery as an alienating sponge to soak up spare working-class cash, and more generally to the sense that there wasn't as much of that spare cash around as there used to be for a night out in the bars listening to bands and talkin' shit. Texas was just coming out of a regional depression, returning to the ordinary hardscrabble existence that people in towns like Lockhart took for granted. In Illinois a very serious industrial depression was still going on, and during the long hard years of the late 1980s and early 1990s, many aspects of rural working-class society had changed dramatically, and forever (O. Davidson 1990).

Things seemed to be coming to an end at Ann's Other Place. I made an extra effort during 1993 to spend as much time as possible there, on my rounds through the beer joints and trailers and jam sessions between gigs and on weeknights. Ann wasn't hiring many bands anymore, except for major occasions and benefits, and the crowds had shrunk to a reliable small circle of regulars on most nights. But the "old boys" (and some "girls" too) still met to pick there on Wednesday or Thursday nights (when those of us who worked as musicians would be less likely to have other obligations). Usually, these jams were led by Larry "Hoppy" Hopkins, a local singer with an extraordinary voice ("better than George Jones," some said) and a commanding social presence.

With some urgency, I worked to document this scene and this place and these people before it all faded away, which everyone seemed to think was happening. In the summer of 1993, I devoted myself to a period of fairly formal documentary work. I videotaped, tape-recorded, and conducted interviews at numerous benefits and birthday parties that were held at Ann's.[2] I made an especially extensive effort to fully document the annual "jammers' reunion," a nonstop three-day jam session attended by dozens of musicians who have known and worked for Miss Ann over the years, which was held for the last time, or so it seemed, in August 1993.[3]

My growing competence and confidence as a performer and my sustained involvement with the local scene had moved me, over the years, closer to the center of various local musical and social circles, although my partisan affiliations also cost me some relationships. I grew especially close to the most gifted and esteemed local singers who were associated with the jam sessions at Ann's place, especially Larry Hopkins and a young Mexican American prodigy named Justin Treviño. I had known them both since the beginning of my fieldwork and had already played quite a few jobs over the preceding years with Justin's band.

I had also jammed at many parties and benefits with Hoppy's band, which already had a superb guitar player named Steve Minnich, a sweet-tempered electrician and mechanical genius from upstate New York. Hoppy's band (ironically enough, he called it Classic Country, or perhaps it's the name Modern Country that's ironic) also benefited from the vocals and solid bass playing of Hoppy's longtime musical sidekick "Big Judy" Laughlin, a six-foot tall blond truck driver with a gentle personality and a hauntingly beautiful voice, both sweet and ragged, that could move me and many others at Ann's to tears, and just as easily to delight, often in the same well-phrased line.

During 1993 and 1994, I attended most of the regular Wednesday night picking sessions at Ann's. But in early 1994, Ann formally retired and leased the bar out to an Austin couple who remodeled it and made it so "sterile" (as ex-patrons said) that many patrons abandoned it.[4] The Wednesday night picking parties moved from the bar to the room over Hoppy's ramshackle garage, off a dirt road about a mile south of Ann's.

This room, which was anything but sterile, was a culturally specific fantasy come to life. Hoppy and another singer named Randy Meyer had built and decorated the place to reflect their vision of the ultimate honky-tonk, somewhere up in the mythical mountains, where time seemed to stop as long as REAL country music was in the air. It was a miniature beer joint in every respect except that it was private and everybody brought their own beer and if you were too tired or drunk to drive you could stay all night. Many nights, I saw the dawn out the passenger-side window of my truck as I crawled home to Austin on the dark, empty farm roads that my friends had taught me to prefer over the well-policed main highways.

Up there, in Hoppy's "house of mem'ries," we often achieved a transcendent level of music making. At those all-night-long Wednesday "pickin' parties," anybody might show up, even an old master like Randy Meyer or Johnny Mac. By contrast with these evenings, I felt more detached and businesslike about my paid weekend gigs playing "that Top-40 crap," as Hoppy always called it with a theatrical flourish. Still, Top-40 work paid my bills and gave me stature and self-confidence that could be earned in no other way, and through it I improved steadily as a player and singer. Although I often thought of Wednesday nights as "fieldwork" and Saturday nights as simply "work," in retrospect the distinction is not so clear.

Justin Treviño and I became friends too during this time, and I worked more and more frequently with his band, primarily around San Antonio. We spent many long days and late nights after gigs at Justin's trailer near San Marcos, where he had a small recording studio. We recorded each other's latest songs, laying down tracks and challenging each other to reach new heights on our instruments and vocals. But mostly we talked, about singers and singing and pickers and picking and where the night had gone right or wrong. Justin is blind, but this seemed at worst a minor inconvenience (and sometimes even an advantage) as he punched in tracks and set levels and programmed drum tracks on his machine and played guitar, fiddle, mandolin, and bass. He would play cut after cut from his record collection of classic Ray Price and Lefty Frizzell and Willie Nelson and Faron Young and Marty Robbins and Johnny Bush, as I mostly listened and tried to learn a fraction of what he knew, a mature master of his craft at the same age at which I had once dropped out of college.

Through Hoppy and Ann, I also came to know another singer who was among the most lionized of all the local singers on this scene and had been for many years: Randall O. ("Randy") Meyer. Randy was Hoppy's musical mentor and best friend, and he had long been one of Ann's closest friends as well. I had heard Randy sing, of course, many times, and had often listened to my friends tell me that he was simply the finest country singer who had ever walked across a Texas stage. But Randy was notoriously reserved and private and frankly ornery. I had never been able to develop much rapport with him, even after I had established an identity as a decent musician. It took many jam sessions and parties and benefits, where I took every chance I could to play behind Randy, before we began to talk a little. And then came the frightening moment in the spring of 1994 when he had a stroke while driving his dump truck through Austin.

To my surprise, Ann (and others) called me that very day with the news, and she strongly suggested that I should visit Randy in the hospital "before it's too late." And this admonition marked another kind of arrival, achieved only after years of music, fieldwork, and friendship. I suddenly realized as I hung up the phone, and only at this late stage in the project, that I had a responsibility to my interlocutors not only as a musician and a friend but indeed also as an ethnographer. It was a sobering realization. This was a responsibility that my friends took very seriously. I was expected to make the effort to interview Randy Meyer and to write about him, even if it was difficult, and the clock was ticking away.

I spent most of that week sitting with Randy's wife Audrey by his hospital bed, slowly laying the foundation for a proper interview as I kept Randy company and supplied him with Merle Haggard tapes. When Randy rested, Audrey and I developed a friendship too. I made regular trips out to their home (in another small town west of Austin) in the following weeks, eventually cajoling a wonderful interview out of Randy (and Audrey). Of course, once that was out of the way, everything got much easier for all of us. Randy dramatically announced, soon after his hospitalization, that he had "quit the music business," now that he had been *saved*. This embodiment of country music's hardest masculine, hell-raisin' tendencies reemerged as a devout born-again Christian elder, disdainful of the beer-joint society in which he had spent most of his life. Even so, and even in rapidly failing health, he pulled off some stunning performances at jam sessions and benefits, where he could always be cajoled into taking the stage, that rank among the most memorable and intense musical experiences of my life. I remained close to Randy until his death in January 2000, and I visited him regularly and played gospel music with him at religious revival meetings several times in the last few years of his life. His widow remains my dear friend.

Since I left Texas in late 1994, I have remained in contact with many of the people featured in this book, though some have died or lost touch. I have returned regularly for visits, including Randy Meyer's funeral (followed by a musical wake that lasted for two days), two "jammers' reunion" weekends, and an extended visit in the summer of 1998. My ethnographic attention has increasingly focused on the African American community in Lockhart, on the town's working-class public sphere, and on the incorporation of Lockhart into the Austin metropolitan economy and the larger regional economic zone. But I have continued to play music with my mentors and friends in Texas, and to document musical life there.

As this narrative makes clear, at times, and increasingly over time, "fieldwork" and "real life" have become mixed up for me. And that makes for some problems applying a rhetorical filter called "ethnography." The ethnographic scripting of my engagement in the world I will describe is intertwined with my "real life" experience of the same engagement *and* with a history of writing and singing about that engagement too. Fieldwork, music making, friendship, conflict, and writing have grown together into a dense thicket of stories in which knowledge, memory, emotion, and practice are simply inseparable. Making an analytic, scholarly path through this thicket is a tricky, though pleasurable, business. But let me first tell you some facts about a place called Lockhart, Texas.

Lockhart, Texas, U.S.A.

Lockhart, Texas, is the seat of rural Caldwell County, which covers 544 square miles in a diamond-shaped area south of Austin. The county, with Lockhart near its center, was founded in 1847 and has a colorful history in the cattle trade, as it was one of the first major stations on the Chisolm cattle-drive trail in the late nineteenth century. Since the 1950s, the county has been bisected by U.S. Highway 183. U.S. 183 is in fact Lockhart's Main Street for several miles, interrupting the highway as it flows south out of Austin and threads through South Texas oil, cattle, and cotton country. At the southern tip of the county, just past the oil-patch town of Luling, U.S. 183 intersects Interstate 10, to the east of San Antonio.

Although it is clearly demarcated from Austin, Lockhart has increasingly been drawn into Austin's economic orbit, especially since the passage of the North American Free Trade Agreement (NAFTA) in 1994. The passage of NAFTA dramatically increased economic activity and development in South and Central Texas and combined with the high-tech boom of the 1990s to make the Austin area one of the fastest-growing metropolitan regions in the United States. Austin has recently opened a new airport on its southern margin (on the former Bergstrom air force base, the 1990 closure of which signaled the bottom of an economic bust that defined the region's character for most of the 1980s). The sprawl of commercial development that inevitably surrounds a major airport has now begun to creep south toward Lockhart, slowly erasing the remaining rural zone that separates the town from the city.

The state of Texas is currently planning to extend and widen U.S. 183, largely to accommodate the region's explosive growth, and especially the resultant truck traffic that has choked Interstate 35 and created urban gridlock in San Antonio, San Marcos, and Austin. This congestion has pushed more traffic along the alternate U.S. 183 corridor, creating both possibilities for and limitations on the region's development. The enormous so-called SR 130 project has raised speculative land values along the right-of-way required to expand U.S. 183 north of Lockhart. However, the new highway is likely to bypass Lockhart to the west (several alternate routes are under consideration), making it possible for drivers to avoid the town entirely but spawning new development along the bypass route. New commercial and housing developments have sprung up in the pastures and fields that at one time marked a clear thirty-mile-wide boundary between the southern edge of Austin and Lockhart's northern margin, anticipating the inexorable growth to come.

In short, Lockhart is gradually being drawn into the suburban sprawl of the Austin metropolitan area, the larger South-Central Texas regional economy, and indeed global economic processes. As population levels, occupancy rates, rents, and real estate values in Austin skyrocketed during the booming late 1990s, Lockhart began to show early signs of becoming a middle-class bedroom community for the city (it is already, effectively, a blue-collar bedroom community). Several large high-technology plants that have been built in Austin's southeastern quarter since the early 1990s remain within an easy thirty- to forty-minute commute from Lockhart, where large, sometimes elegant Victorian homes are far less expensive than in Austin's more developed northern and western suburbs.

However, in the years of fieldwork I report here, many of these now irreversible changes were barely underway or in some cases not yet imagined. I think they *were* widely anticipated among Lockhart's working-class residents, as the inevitable expression of a historical pattern that has become harshly familiar to many American workers who have occupied the peri-urban or "shallow rural" margin. After all, these contemporary developments can be located in a longer history of rural incorporation and working-class settlement. As the national economy has siphoned people out of the rural occupations of agriculture and resource extraction over the last century, it has simultaneously absorbed formerly rural communities into the sprawl of development that marks both the residential and industrial wake of many cities. For many people, that boundary zone between the city (and its suburbs) and the isolation of the "rural ghetto" (O. Davidson 1990) represents a necessary ideological, cultural, and economic compromise. Living on the semirural margin of the city allows manual workers to partake of the benefits of an urban economy (unions, job choices, health care, anonymity, education, entertainment, bargain shopping) while maintaining a distinctively rustic cultural identity and while keeping the cost of living to a minimum.

In the early 1990s, Lockhart was, indeed, more "shallow rural" than suburban. The town felt culturally aloof from Austin—except as the latter was a key source of employment. Vacant storefronts were numerous in the town's center, and U.S. 183 was noticeably quieter than it is today. The town and especially the rural areas of the county were cheap to live in, but correspondingly bereft of local economic opportunity. This is less true, though only incrementally so, today.

What I narrate here as working-class "culture" must be seen in the historical context of a broad and sweeping process of social, demographic, and economic change, both at the level of the South Central Texas region and at the broader level of American rural, working-class society. These levels, in turn, must be seen in the context of global economic and cultural development impinging on every aspect of working-class life. And yet, the rapidity and totality of such development is all too easy to exaggerate. (Such exaggeration, in fact, has become the greater risk in recent anthropology, as it has in the cultural politics of the United States.)

The longitudinal depth of my experience with Lockhart, now approaching fourteen years, provides a complicating but important perspective on this project. For much of what I report here as a vital if threatened domain of cultural practice has since lost some coherence, some vitality, and some centrality. At least among the major characters who populate the stories in this book, death, illness, marriage, divorce, and out-migration have combined to scatter what had been a tightly knit community with roots reaching back to the 1970s. Certainly, other social networks of similar character have risen to take the place of the one I describe, and many individuals who are more peripheral to this ethnographic setting are prominent in other, more vital scenes. And in fact the local social network represented here is still in place, and still largely centered on the same physical place (Ann's tavern, under a new name and operator), though it has seemed to me to be less musical when I have returned to Lockhart in recent years. But in retrospect, this study captures a period during which a wave broke on the shore of American working-class modernity, and in at least that sense, the pervasive nostalgia of my interlocutors in this study was remarkably prescient in its anxiety about the fate of local country music and their distinctive musical culture.

I worry in particular about conveying the impression of a vanished, folkloric working-class cultural practice; but I also worry about implying that the scene I describe here in some sense typifies American rural, working-class culture. It doesn't now, and it didn't in the early 1990s either. I am certain that the community described here was unusually richly endowed with musical and verbal performative genius, overdetermined by its proximity to Austin, where Texas honky-tonk music and culture has already been subjected to several cycles of metacultural mythologization since the 1970s. In fact, this community's heightened critical and cultural consciousness and its unusually expressive performance of working-class and rural identity are essential to the aim of this book to construct a dialogic description of rural, working-class cultural practice and experience during an era of social transformation. I report on an exceptional community, but it was exceptional principally in its level of political and cultural self-consciousness.

Lockhart by the Numbers

Throughout this book, I refer — as I just have — to a "rural, working-class" cultural lifeworld, and for most of the remainder of the book I will be describing subjective social experience within this lifeworld. Here, however, I want to describe some of the objective material conditions that make this community "rural" and "working-class." These terms are often used without sociological specificity in ethnomusicology and cultural studies, making systematic and comparative inquiry difficult. My intention is to show that although the community described here may have been in a now-fading period of exceptional artistic florescence, its social experience was (and remains) as common as dirt.[5]

In 1990, when I began the field research for this book, Caldwell County had 26,392 residents, up from 23,637 in 1980. (The population is now well over 32,000.) The density of this population, in a county of 544 square miles, thus rose from around 40 persons per square mile in 1980 to 50 in 1990, and around 60 today. This low average density is deceptive, since nearly 50 percent of the population of the county lives in the vicinity of one of the county's two major towns, Lockhart and Luling (the latter's population is approximately 5,000). Caldwell County follows a typical American rural pattern of clustered settlements, separated by miles of undeveloped agricultural land with little housing or industrial development.

In fact, roughly three-quarters of Caldwell County land is classified as farmland, and slightly more than a third of all arable cropland is harvested in any given year. The average farmstead is between 200 and 300 acres, and almost all of Caldwell County's farms were classified as "family farms" in 1992. A numerical majority of these farms reported gross sales of less than $20,000 in 1992. Much of the farming community in the county must also depend on waged labor to supplement farm income, while some workers supplement their income with small-scale agriculture, especially by raising hogs and chickens. Sorghum, hay, cotton, and feed corn comprise the principal crops grown in the county, but amount to only about 15 percent of the value of all farm products sold; most farm income came from the sale of livestock, principally poultry, hogs, and cattle, and a great deal of the farmland in the county is in relatively disused pasture.

Most of Lockhart's working-class citizens, including most of those who will appear in this work, are not farmers or employed directly in agriculture. A significant number travel to work in Austin, San Marcos, and San Antonio, where wages for both skilled and unskilled labor are higher and jobs more plentiful. For men, this means jobs as truck drivers, electricians, factory and construction workers, and state or federal employees (e.g., road maintenance workers, postmen). For women this means jobs as nurse's aides, cleaners, waitresses, school bus drivers, and clerical workers, and assembly jobs in the high-tech factories of South Austin. The local economy includes a number of small manufacturers typical of the kinds of industrial operations that have arisen to exploit nonunion, mostly female labor in rural America in the 1990s. More stable, if dirty and dangerous, jobs exist in the oil and agricultural service sectors (drilling equipment maintenance, feed lots, and trucking). Many men operate informal small businesses in trucking, auto repair, or the building trades. Indeed, for some, country music is just such a business. Many women supplement family income with transient work as barmaids, supermarket checkers, waitresses, and cleaners. In a pinch, as in the case of an illness in the family, a divorce or breakup, or the loss of a business, minimum-wage jobs at convenience stores and fast-food restaurants are a frequent resort.

In 1990, nearly 49 percent of all Caldwell County workers over sixteen worked outside the county. In the same year, 6 percent of Caldwell County's labor force was employed in agriculture, 13 percent in manufacturing, more than 20 percent in retail and wholesale trades, and 8.3 percent in health services. Official civilian labor force unemployment was at 5.7 percent in 1991, down from 7.1 percent in 1986 (it is currently around 4 percent), but these numbers clearly and severely underestimate the problem of underemployment, marginal employment, and the seasonal unemployment typical of the agricultural and resource extraction workforce in Texas. This distortion is evident from the significant increase in nearly every other index of community poverty in the same period.

To a significant extent, Lockhart and Caldwell County have been spared the effects Osha Davidson (1990) describes as a process of "rural ghettoization" precisely because of Lockhart's proximity to Austin and San Antonio and the economic benefits of NAFTA on the region's industrial and service sectors. Also, unlike the American Midwest, South Central Texas has not been through a regional cycle of deindustrialization (except, to a limited extent, in the oil sector). In fact, the region has industrialized in part at the expense of the Midwest, especially since the passage of NAFTA (and also due to the political weakness of organized labor in Texas). However, the county has few local large employers. No single employer or industry thus dominates the economy or politics of Caldwell County, though there are powerful contenders. The county's largest local employer, the 500-bed Wackenhut prison facility, was built and went into operation during my field research. It employs approximately 120 local workers, not including the prisoners (who are waged employees of the LTI contract manufacturing facility in the prison).

In 1989, nearly 40 percent of Caldwell County's 8,700 households earned less than $15,000 a year, and over 60 percent of households earned less than $25,000. Median household income was around $20,000. Twenty-two percent of all families (up from 18 percent in 1979, when unemployment was higher; the figure is now around 21 percent) — and nearly 30 percent of all persons and 38 percent of all children — lived below the federal poverty level. Most of the people who appear in this book have known times of such desperation, and several families who are represented here were in such dire straits during the years of my field research. This was especially true for young families, single mothers, and for women raising children while involved with alcoholic and drug-abusing partners.

In 1988, 15.5 percent of all Caldwell County births were to mothers under the age of 20. From 1980 to 1990, the total number of female-headed households with no spouse in Caldwell county increased from 8.8 percent to 13 percent of all households. In 1990, there were over 600 female-headed, single-parent households with children under 18 in the county, representing roughly 7 percent of all households. Such families were more than twice as likely to be living below the federal poverty standard (47 percent) compared to all other families (22 percent).

For 1985, police records show a crime rate of 2,542 "serious crimes" per 100,000 population. The rate rose to 4,534 serious crimes per 100,000 population by 1991, an increase of nearly 80 percent. It has since subsided in concert with national trends, but not to 1985 levels. In practical terms, this means there were approximately 1,200 serious crimes in 1991, and there were several murders during my years of fieldwork in the county. Drug-related arrests were common enough to merit little comment.

Lockhart schools are considered adequate, though not excellent, by most parents and students with whom I have discussed the matter.[6] There are debates about how to calculate high school dropout rates, but Lockhart's Independent School District, which serves most of the county, appears to be on the high side of the state average.[7] The state of Texas has recently become much more concerned with measuring school performance, and a plethora of statistics rating school quality are available for the last few years from both the state and from private groups working to influence education policy. Lockhart's schools have recently been ranked as "acceptable" across a range of state-mandated metrics. Anecdotally, this does not represent a major change from the years of my fieldwork. High-achieving students, generally from middle-class families, often go on to great educational success in the state's public universities. In the last few years, Lockhart High School students have achieved an average 921 combined SAT score. But low achievement is common and all too unremarkable. A generational split in the structure of the community is palpable, as teenagers in particular create a separate sphere of social interaction. A teenage boy killed his parents during the early phase of my fieldwork; this was the subject of much commentary among the adults, who were deeply shocked. But at the time, a sixteen-year-old girl who knew the young killer told me she wasn't surprised in the slightest and that many of the boy's classmates were aware of his murderous potential.

Currently, roughly 27 percent of Caldwell County's population lacks health insurance, and the county has few local resources for low-income and uninsured patients. A third of all children are enrolled in Medicaid and/or CHIP (a federally subsidized health insurance system for children of the working poor, established in 1997). The nearest major hospital is in San Marcos, twenty miles to the west of Lockhart. The nearest trauma center and children's hospital are in Austin, thirty-five congested miles north of Lockhart, and subsidized by the much wealthier taxpayers of Travis County. Caldwell County lacks chemical-dependence treatment facilities and suffers from exceptionally high rates of alcohol-related deaths and accidents. (Although the county is dry, with no stores selling hard liquor, I suspect that it has an exceptionally high rate of alcoholism and drug addiction, though I do not have figures to support this claim.) As is broadly true in rural Texas, the demand for publicly subsidized primary care — and even privately insured primary care — far outstrips the supply. The absence of prenatal care for uninsured women is especially severe. The county is designated as a Medically Underserved Area and as a Health Professional Shortage Area by the U.S. Department of Health and Human Services (Morningside Research and Consulting 2002).

Roughly 14 percent of the population of Caldwell County was over sixty-five years old in 1990. Of these senior citizens, 25 percent lived below the federal poverty level in 1989, a slightly smaller percentage than applies to the entire population (30 percent). Senior poverty was ameliorated by military pensions, social security benefits, and pension plans from long-term employers. In addition, elderly people were more likely to be in stable long-term marriages (which improves economic status) and to have health insurance coverage through Medicare and military benefits. In addition, many elderly people worked part-time as retail clerks or in off-the-books jobs that allowed them to preserve their social security benefits. And since travel to work outside the county constituted a major expense for many employed residents, the ability of retirees to forgo this daily expense was also significant.

In the 1990 census, 70 percent of Caldwell County residents identified as "white," with German, English, Scotch-Irish, Swedish, Czech (or "Bohemian"), and Polish as the principal claimed "Anglo" ethnic ancestries. Roughly 11 percent identified as "black." Many of these are descendants of a few pioneering African American families who settled in the hamlet of Saint John Colony, just east of Lockhart, soon after emancipation. Nearly 38 percent identified as "Hispanic origin, of any race," while 32 percent reported speaking Spanish at home. Almost all those who reported a "Hispanic" identity were of Mexican and Mexican American descent, including both Tejanos— persons of Mexican descent, but from families long settled in Texas, and often upwardly socially mobile—and more recent and often transient immigrants. Evidently, a significant number of these same residents also self-reported as "white," but not necessarily as "Anglo." Not all "Mexican Americans" (the choice of a term is quite complicated, and this one is inadequate) in Caldwell County speak Spanish in the home. Indeed, in some of these families, Spanish is dispreferred as an impediment to social mobility. Many Anglos and African Americans know some Spanish. Thus, it is clear that the categories of "white," "Hispanic," and "Spanish-speaking" overlap significantly in Caldwell County (as is typical for South and Central Texas).

The town of Lockhart is segregated into ethnic neighborhoods and within private institutions, though the segregation is permeable and is often transgressed. In the taverns where I spent my time, Mexican American and Anglo patrons mingled and talked freely, while immigrant Mexican and African American men (but almost never African American or immigrant Mexican women) were more occasional patrons, although Anglo patrons were clearly numerically and socially dominant. The community included a number of Anglo/Tejano couples, and at least one African American/Anglo couple, who appeared to be readily accepted with little comment. There were both real friendships and real tensions across these ethnic boundaries, of course, rooted in a long history of often violent racialized class conflict in Texas.[8] (In fact, during Reconstruction, Caldwell County had an especially violent racial climate, for South Texas. The county had to be occupied by federal troops in the

1870s. At that time, the black population approached 40 percent of the total. But this number declined steadily, in part because of black out-migration and in part because of Anglo in-migration, until it stabilized at present levels in the 1930s.)

Anglos had historically dominated the county's political structure, police department, public administrative institutions, and social elites, although both Chicanos and African Americans were represented in these settings during the 1990s. There were occasional minor incidents of racialized animosity in the community, though I am not aware of any overtly racist violence in Caldwell County in the past two decades.[9] African Americans and Chicanos complained of persistent low-level racism, such as a white storekeeper refusing to touch the hand of a black patron while making change, the circulation of racially charged jokes and derogatory slurs, or the county's reluctance to maintain roads leading to black hamlets in the countryside. Bars, churches, and neighborhoods were clearly segregated by race. And although poverty crossed all ethnic lines, African Americans clearly were the poorest and most politically disempowered ethnic community. Ethnic holidays (especially Cinco de Mayo and Juneteenth) and intraethnic weddings and funerals were occasions for segregated celebrations. But there was also a multiethnic working-class community centered on semipublic institutions like VFW halls and restaurants, and visible in the town's retail stores and public spaces and in such fully public events as Memorial Day parades and the town's annual outdoor summer festival, "Chisolm Trail Days," which commemorates the town's mythologized history as a center of the cattle industry.

The working-class residents of Lockhart live in various kinds of housing and neighborhoods. Many of the people represented here live in "trailers"— mobile, prefabricated homes trucked on to a site and mounted on concrete blocks. These low-cost homes allow for home ownership, a strongly preferred option even among relatively poor families. Used, badly worn-out trailers (which can present serious fire, tornado, and flood hazards and which typically have very poor heating and cooling systems) can be had for a few thousand dollars. Nicer ones, up to and including quite comfortable "double-wide" models, still rarely exceeded forty or fifty thousand dollars. Residents of these trailers prefer to sink what capital they can accumulate into the purchase of as much land as they can possibly secure, either on a contract, through trade, or more rarely via a conventional bank mortgage.

Other families, especially the very poorest, live in rented trailers in trailer parks closer to the center of town, or in rented wood-frame houses in the many small rural hamlets that dot the countryside for miles around the larger town. Some of these families have no telephone,[10] though most have heat, electricity, and water most of the time. Better-off and more stably employed two-parent families either buy or rent frame houses in the town itself, on one of the shady streets that extend off Main Street. Some of these are handsome Victorian structures that have in recent years become desirable homes for an emerging commuter middle-class sector, driving up home prices and property taxes. Some families with steady income and construction skills are slowly building new houses on land outside town while living in rented homes or modest trailers.

In 1990, nearly 70 percent of the housing units in Caldwell County were "owner-occupied." For the remaining 30 percent who rent, the median rental was $300 in 1990. Owner-occupied units had a median value of only $44,200 (just over twice the median annual family income), which suggests how many of them were "manufactured" homes or trailers. It is important to remember that because these trailers are often purchased under a contract arrangement rather than with a mortgage, and because they deteriorate more rapidly than traditional buildings, these homes are not the stores of equity value suggested by the politically resonant discourse of "home ownership."

Lockhart has a quiet feel, although the perceived loss of that quietness was a major topic of discourse among longtime residents during my field research. And Lockhart has a host of social problems familiar to the residents of hundreds of American small towns I have visited in the last few years. Older people lament what they see as the rising visibility of drugs (especially methamphetamines or "speed" and, among the young, inhalants), alcoholism (though this term is rarely used), divorce and domestic violence against women and children, and a general loss of respect for traditions and authority. More recently, Lockhart's increasingly busy Main Street, which is simply the portion of U.S. 183 that runs through the heart of the town, has been cause for deep ambivalence, as people recognize the economic benefits of Austin's southward growth (a new sewer system was recently installed, for example, and the town's main supermarket has been renovated and doubled in size) but decry the arrival of an urban pace and urban problems, especially a spate of recent murders and drug arrests and an ever-increasing number of serious car accidents for which the county is not medically equipped.

Despite Lockhart's increasing orientation toward the urbanizing regional economy, however, most public-sphere interactions, such as those one observes in bars, restaurants, stores, and at public events continue to reflect a highly valued, deeply personalistic sociality, especially among working-class people and longtime residents of all classes. "Everybody knows everybody," as the local saying goes, and gossip and a generous, slow-paced sociability are basic, fundamental aspects of everyday life and social identity, as I discuss in the following chapters. Lockhart is neither as romantically idyllic as some country songs and not a few politicians would have you believe about small-town life, nor as darkly alienated as many other popular cultural representations assert (and as one often finds in more desperate places). It is neither so small as to be oppressive (in part because the cities of Austin, San Marcos, and San Antonio are close by) nor so large as to be impersonal.

The most common complaints I heard about Lockhart, from residents of all ethnicities and classes, reflected this balance: I was frequently told that gossip and scrutiny made privacy impossible, or that the town was "boring" or provided "nothing to do." But people frequently compared their experience of small-town life favorably with urban life, emphasizing attitudes of mutuality and interdependence—among the phrases I heard most often was "I could never live in Austin." Lockhart's working-class residents, as far as I can tell, appreciated this balance even when they complained about it. Lockhart, in their opinion, was still "country."

"Out the Country"

Space, Time, and Stereotype

The country and the city are changing historical realities, both

in themselves and in their interrelations. Moreover, in our own world,

they represent only two kinds of settlement. Our real social experience

is not only of the country and the city, in their most singular forms,

but of many kinds of intermediate and new kinds of social and physical

organization. Yet the ideas and the images of the country and the city

retain their great force . . . clearly the contrast of country and city is

one of the major forms in which we become conscious of a central

part of our experience and of the crises of our society.

—Raymond Williams, *The Country and the City*

"Down the road a piece," as the locals say, between the trailing off of the expanding edge of the city, with its office parks and planned developments, and the gates of the state park, with its protected stands of timber and its rustic redwood signs, the liminal industrial-agricultural wasteland disturbs the eye with reminders of the incredible transformation of the site and nature of material production in postindustrial America, America in the age of the global economy. The traveler passes those long, low factory buildings surrounded by snarling barbed wire, the railroad sidings overgrown with weeds, the rusted-out cars in huge auto graveyards, the shut-down mines, the landfills that rise like manmade mountains in the place of the ones that have been leveled, now closed by order of the EPA.

This dystopic vision is softened and modulated by the still-standing lone dilapidated farmhouse, whose interior enshrines a venerable nostalgic trope of simple, sacred, feminized domesticity. Through this nostalgia, disturbance is modulated in the pages of the home-decorating magazines devoted to "country" living and kitsch. Disturbance is swallowed up too by an expanse of pastures full of stock and fields of cotton and soybeans, their chemical toxicities and depleted soils disguised by the pastoral tropes of ancient agricultural fertility, "the breadbasket of the world." These icons conspire with American ideology to freeze, temporarily, the scene in the windshield into a lyric moment of panoramic completion and moral virtue, in the idiom of landscape inhabited by the "folk" and evocative of "nature."

And then, there appears suddenly and insistently the visual and aesthetic disruption of so much trash sprawled across a devastated afterimage of once-rural "nature." Not beautifully dilapidated farmhouses, but small, decrepit trailers surrounded by junked-out cars. Not fields of plenty on family farms, but massive tractors spewing neurotoxin insecticides over the eroded topsoil of land on lease to one of the agribusiness consortia (no longer the humble breadbasket, but now "supermarket to the world"), as migrant workers pick and bundle. Or we drive through town and see not tidy main streets, but huge, carbon-copy Wal-Marts and overflowing prisons, and their institutional nemeses, fundamentalist churches and dingy, windowless beer joints.

Drive on, and the trash recedes from view. With a sickly but still relentless nature overtaking here and there, as the grass grows up between the junked-out cars, the windshield-level view of all that trash is retransformed by resurgent "nature" and resurgent ideology into a simulacrum of the unspoiled, the bucolic, the heartland, or, simply, "the country." Somehow, all these decayed and rebuilt signs of human occupation strain to signify, ironically, the absence of the distasteful and conflict-ridden social sphere, if only as a loss, as the object of a contested nostalgia (K. Stewart 1988; S. Stewart 1984). We are in a comfortably familiar American pastoral landscape again, and a "past"-oral landscape at that. And then, a pickup truck roars by, cigarettes fly from the window, country music blares on the radio, a man in a feed cap takes a drink from his beer. Perhaps we notice his bumper sticker: "Don't Shoot! I'm a LOCAL Hippie."

These "locals," too, call this "the country," and they mean by that to invoke an ironic, nostalgic, patriotic, sacred, polemical, frightening, and unstable image also. But the image is different when it is inhabited rather than passed through, when it is seen through the cracked windshield of a beater truck rather than through the tinted glass of a late-model sedan or out the window of an airplane. For those who live among this junk, it takes on a life of its own. For those who pursue their vision of the Good Life in these churches and beer joints and Wal-Marts, who grew up working, and watching their parents work, in these fields, factories, railyards, and mines, this landscape speaks — "don't shoot!" — with a local accent.

This is, no less than the traveler's panorama or the layout in the home-decorating magazine or the crowded-on-Saturday meccas of barbecue-hunting tourists, the "country" of "country music." But to live *in* this country is to live, as those locals sometimes say if you ask them where they are, *"out* the country," the inversion of the preposition "in" calling attention to the "out-ness" of the decaying built environment "out" past the city limit, "out" of fashion, "out" of step with these postmodern times.

This country is, of late, a bizarre and ironic landscape for the working-class American dreamer; it entails a confusion of the signs of the garden and the junkyard, the sociable and the dangerous, kitsch and disturbance, the folk-loric pastoral and the apocalyptic postindustrial. You can see this semiotic confusion in the piles of junk in the yards, in the crazy jumbled roll-away road-side signs that are never rolled away but are left standing, bent lopsided, long after their referent has disappeared in a flurry of unpaid bills and crushed fan-tasies of the entrepeneurial virtue of small business. The signs, in a riot of vari-ously sized plastic letters, are advertising beer joints with unlikely and inscru-table entertainments ("Karaoke THursDay 8 to 11," "Turkey sHoot sUn") and oddly specialized services inside vacant-looking houses ("DOORs for sale," "facials and mAke-overs," "Navajo jewelry"), or more conventional services too, straining to conform to a rationalized national culture ("All Mechanics ASE Certified").

The uniform of this country is the black Harley-Davidson t-shirt, announc-ing "American Pride" while hiding a label that reads "made in China." The taste of this country, "the breadbasket of the world," is boxed and canned and washed down with cheap beer. This country smells of generic cigarettes, refineries, sweat and hog farms, marijuana stands and methamphetamine labs, and always of agricultural chemicals. The mascot of this country is a mangy dog chained in the yard. He might be better off dead or as a ward of the state, but just try to convince *him* of that.

The Sound of Voices

The people who live in these houses and trailers and drink in these beer joints here beside the state highway may work in the city, delivering propane and tortillas, driving a bulldozer or a dump truck, installing aluminum siding, and washing sheets on the night shift. Or they may scrape by somehow in the local economy, working for rock-bottom wages and no benefits at the bullet-proof vest factory or at the Dairy Queen, frying burgers. Others may not work much at all these days, some just given up and biding their days, some shackled to the bottle, some the victims of less censured disabling injuries — "ain't worked since I broke my back." And many have their time deeply invested in a sublime combination of both the bottle and a work-broken body. And if it's not the bottle, it's likely to be the Lord (these two sources of comfort are in an ancient contest among these people, and the fight gets serious on weekends). Finally, some are always passing through, drifters with an old dog and a few new songs and stories, or convicts or drug addicts or prostitutes or musicians or just people with an urge to see the world before, as one of those drifters once told me, it's too late and it all looks the same and "there's no 'there' there."

The injured and the subdued and stable may, if they get lucky, draw a workman's compensation check, and take to buying lottery tickets and name-brand whiskey for a while. More often, the job that did them in had no such benefits. So they're scraping by with the proceeds from odd jobs, and sometimes with food stamps and the proceeds from the local "benefits," advertised on the posters in the convenience stores and bars, that try to make up for the benefits jobs don't usually offer. Meanwhile, the ones still "working steady" (which is still most, though people seem to think it's less than it used to be) are getting by, marking time, until they can get that place somewhere *really* out the country, maybe even, someday, somehow, a little cabin up in the mountains, where the government leaves you alone and you can still hunt off your back porch and drink a beer in your truck and play music with your friends every night.

Most of these people *have* lived in the city, if usually on the outskirts, their families pushing out — or back to where they came from — as the city expanded inexorably into the countryside like a wave breaking on the shore, and tossing their lives in the foam. Many of them grew up "out the country," in Iowa, Kansas, Louisiana, upstate New York, Ohio, North Carolina, Oklahoma, and of course Texas, and remember upbringings filled with the effects of either religion or alcohol and always labor, and more hard times than good times. But not many want to live in the city anymore. They came back "out the country," if they ever left, and now they're of a mind to stay put, even if that means moving.

Climbing out of the car, and walking into Ann's Place, we can suddenly *hear* this "country" too. One day I was talking to Joey in front of the bar's door,[1] our boots digging into the gravel as we watched the kids pulling each other across the parking lot in Ann's "Little Red Wagon" (the newish Radio-Flyer was a birthday present from her friends a few years back, named after an old song that Ann had loved since childhood). Hoppy's band played the old Eddie Miller standard "Release Me" just inside the door, for a crowd of shuffling dancers. I asked Joey, a young man who'd wrecked his knees doing construction work, about his employment prospects. He hadn't worked in a while, but he wasn't about to start looking locally. There wasn't any point, he thought:

JOEY: I have to go to AUSTIN
to find GOOD paying work
I mean I could work out here
but there ain't any money . . .
I just drive into town
AF: That's the price you pay for living out in the country I guess
JOEY: I'd rather live in the country and just drive into town
and make a good dollar
than work out here
AF: Or live in the city?
JOEY: Well I CAN'T live in the city!

People choose to live here, "out the country," limping their beater trucks and used-car-lot specials thirty-five miles each way into Austin, Urbana, Savannah, Sacramento, Meridian, and so many other cities around America. If you stood beside the state highway, you'd see them slipping back out to the margins at sunset, back out for another night of beer drinking, cigarette smoking, music playing, slow dancing, talk-heavy sociability in those windowless beer joints that line the road, shielding their patrons from the gaze of cops and passersby.

In the first and most basic of many ironies I wish to explore here, this country is densely, irrepressibly social, despite its apparent visual sparseness. This is an ideological and sensory contradiction, and it rises to the surface of everyday talk among the locals. People say things like "I just couldn't stand to live in the city, what with my neighbors starin' in my windows and all." But they complain, also, about the lack of privacy in the gossip-saturated everyday life of a small town. And they speak fondly of the spare visual landscape of their peri-urban home, even as they are fascinated by its social density and riotously texted human surfaces.

To the stranger, this is a place to pass through quickly and quietly, those fences and dogs and windowless beer joint walls telling the outsider to keep on moving, following the signs to the famous barbecue joint in town. But "out here," your friends can walk into your house to say hello most anytime. In fact, it'd be rude *not* to drop by if you were coming through, even if you wanted to avoid them. "Y'all come back now, y'hear!" That's what people say as you leave, and they mean it. "When you live in the country," as Arleigh Duff's beloved song "Y'All Come" ironically goes, "everybody is your neighbor."[2] This is a moral lesson one learns early and often, as Randy Meyer once explained:

RANDY: Yeah I remember one time
I borrowed ten dollars from a guy that had a place of business down the street[3]
and I didn't have the money to pay him back
when it was due
and I'd drive waaaaaay around his place of business to go home
every day
and he caught me one day
and he told me, he said
"I don't care if you owe me money for the rest of your life
Don't avoid me"
y'know
"You stop by and say hello

or 'I can't pay you, but hello anyway' "
y'know
"Or at least acknowledge me
wave at me when you go by
but
I understand that times are hard
but you don't avoid your friends just cuz you owe 'em money"
From that time on
I never did avoid nobody

   The local rural, working-class public sphere, its sites and nodes and "places" separated by so much apparently empty space, is in fact hyperactive with gossip and sociability and schemes and deals and affection and conflict. A trip "up the road" — say to the Tiger Tote for beer and cigarettes — invariably takes longer than you might plan (if you were the sort to plan) because you're sure to have to stop a while, sure to mix business with the pleasure of talk. The bars and the benefits and the holiday festivals are crowded, densely packed with people (although some say they're less packed than they used to be). Unmistakably, these are working-class people, too painfully thin or overweight or muscled or bent or broken to be any other kind, perfumed with cigarettes and beer, still sweaty from the day's labor or dressed-up in Chinese-made Western-style clothes from the Wal-Mart. And where there's people there's gonna be talk.

   "Out the country," people are nearly always engaged in talk, which often seems to be the very stuff of their consciousness, unless a dangerous silence has suddenly taken hold like that cold front pushing down across the Hill Country from Oklahoma. "Doesn't last too long," people say of weather fronts and virtually everything else. And just as rain seeps immediately into the limestone aquifers underneath these parched fields, the effects of silences percolate through the conversations all around, a sadness running just below the surface of everyday life.

   This talk is always spiced with touch, a leaning together, a playful mockfight and a pretend punch, a warm hug. Or it veers, especially when lubricated with alcohol, into an angry advance, or even a real fight. But talk is salvaged by more touch and closeness as the women and the older men move in to pull the combatants apart, all the while keeping up a steady stream of talk, a phatic reestablishment of the essential bond of the social, a careful pruning back of vines grown suddenly tangled in the dark, intimate space of the tavern or a cramped and freezing trailer.

The affecting irony of "the local" — of emplaced identity — in rural, working-class life is my object in this chapter and the next. I will describe the way that rural, working-class social experience is sensuously modeled in the production of self and sociability in place and time "out the country." I am after a deep evocation of a local idea of "(the) country," in order to understand why "country music" matters so much to people who live within its compelling lure.

"Country" as a Logic of Space and Time

*In the literary artistic chronotope, spatial and temporal indicators
are fused into one carefully thought-out, concrete whole. Time, as it
were, thickens, takes on flesh, becomes artistically visible; likewise,
space becomes charged and responsive to the movements of time, plot,
and history. This intersection of axes and fusion of indicators
characterizes the artistic chronotope.* — Mikhail Bakhtin,
"Forms of Time and Chronotope in the Novel"

To get to this "country" will take a certain kind of movement, a calculated deployment of a rather shopworn anthropological trope of discovered cultural difference that I still find useful, like an old motor you keep in the shed just in case. Of Evans-Pritchard's frequent recourse to this trope, Geertz has said, "like all good ethnographers, [he] seems never to learn" (1983:78). This trope involves a spiraling motion modeled as a descent from the heights of abstraction to the intimate, microscopic oral/aural world of the concrete, the particular, the storied, the dialogic. I have taken you, already, down that road a piece, and I have told you something of the way I came down this road myself several times in recent years. And now I will escort you into the more voiced and personal interior of a beer joint called Ann's Other Place.

In working-class talk and song, the trope of "country" structures several dimensions of experience at once, resembling the kind of figure Bakhtin (1981b) called a "chronotope," an alignment of space, time, and subjectivity in a genre-bound narrative universe. This chronotope is implicated in ideas about the mimetic *space* in which social life and human movement happens, and in the way that imagined *places* come to occupy and organize that space. Space and experience align along different physical and imaginary scales, but the problem space presents to culture is always the establishment — the emplace-ment — of a knowable, narratively real locality (K. Basso 1990a; 1990b).

The chronotope of "country" also orders a way of living in, on, and with *time*, on both the intimate scale of conversations and the grand scale of gen-erations. Time is the woven cloth of experience, and the figures that pattern that cloth are named, for rural working-class people, with words like "feel-ings" and "mem'ries," evocatively grammaticized (and grammatically evoked) in the constitutive temporal tropes of song and talk, resonant figures like "any-more," "these days," and "doesn't last too long." The webs of meaning that link space, place, time, and memory will be taken up at length in this chapter.

The chronotope of "country" also makes its effects felt in the emergence of stock narrative figures, or "characters," those stereotyped genre-bound exemplars of embedded class-cultural worlds, making their way across the pages and grooves and screens of mass-mediated popular culture. In a process Charles Keil has shown to be fundamental to working-class musical expres-sion (1985), those stereotypes become the contested prizes in struggles for the meaning of identities, senses of locality and time and social "ordinariness." And in those figures we often find the experiential pivot-point between the poetics of literatures and the texture of actual lives. I conclude this chapter with a consideration of one such stereotype (the "hillbilly" or "rube") of the truly "local," and of its salience for the world it thematizes and parodies, "out the country."

Finally, the chronotope of cultural "country" resides in an alignment of intuitive and explicit notions about the social nature and moral hierarchy of human actors ("persons"), and the way that psychologically interiorized individuals and the real, embodied, conscious people these individuals are ("selves") experience the world and control their actions as persons. This con-figuration of person and self will be my concern in the following chapter, though I need to say a few words about it now.

"Mem'ries": Place, Space, and the Flow of Time

"Out the country," existence as a fully social person entails a heightened uniqueness and a certain degree of interesting "imperfection," a notion dis-cussed in detail in the next chapter. "Personality" is cultivated in conflict with the intense scrutiny of the local public sphere operating through performative, back-channel gossip, perhaps about a woman who swears too much, a man who drinks too much, or parents who have failed to control their children's drug use. It is also cultivated through more explicit public denouncements, like the time someone with a grudge took out an ad in the local weekly newspaper formally announcing the (made-up) "marriage" of a couple whose adulterous relationship, though conducted in public, was officially a "secret" from the prominent man's estranged wife.

Under the scrutiny of such aggressive censure, people say things like "That's just small town shit! It's gonna happen when everybody knows what's goin' ON!" But this "shit" makes it hard to keep a secret, which in turn can make it hard for a person to accrue the authority that comes with a masterful eccentricity, a "personality," which depends on managing your public self, both compelling and controlling the flow of assessments in everyday talk. Along with eccentricity, then, comes the constant risk of excessive and damaging revelation in the face of too much interest, too much sociability, too much contact. This is the risk of becoming the storied "fool" of public discourse and country songs, a personality whose excesses have overlapped sociability. Such foolish excess can lead to too much talk, and to talk that spills over the boundaries of syntax and sense. More dangerously, foolishness can produce asocial *silence*, a loss of words. So people cultivate a certain necessary inscrutability, which simultaneously invites and resists the scrutiny of talk, of "small town shit," the way windowless walls resist the scrutiny of passers-by on the highway.

One rainy and unseasonably cold Thursday night in March, Dave was talking about his new girlfriend, as several others were listlessly picking guitars and talking around a table in the quiet and nearly empty bar. Ann had been stocking the beer coolers. (These were modified ice cream coolers, which kept the beer cans that extra few degrees colder, a few degrees that could make or break a bar in Texas.) Miss Ann, that evening's bartender, caught a piece of our talk and headed over to our table for a visit, demanding to be included:

ANN: Who y'all talkin' 'bout??
You're leaving me OUT of this conversation!
I don't have no gossip!
DAVE:[4] Ah . . . on PURPOSE!
[laughter]
ANN: NOW I knooooooow . . . !

DAVE: Oh MAN I didn't want YOU to know!

ANN: I know that!

I saw you!

DOC: I'm 'onna tell you WHAT!

ANN sits back there with her EARS open!

She HEARS it!

DAVE: Okay, FILL me in!

Is she worth a SHIT?   [i.e., the woman they have been gossiping about]

ANN: Well I don' know if she is

If I DID I wouldn't tell you!

From the effort of managing one's social face there emerges a framed genre of moral discourse, a kind of organic libertarianism, which is also a key interpretive resource for making sense of everyday life. In fact, in a polemical moment, Candy Sue once announced that Hank Williams's song "Mind Your Own Business" ought to be "the national anthem of Lockhart, Texas." The dialectical tension between sociability and the foolish eccentricity of personality is made explicit in metadiscourse about "minding your business." I asked Ann, once, what made people angry or upset with each other in this local world:

ANN: YOU have your reasons

for doin' what you're doin'

It's none of my business

So why judge people?

So it ain't for ME!?

AF: That's where most people screw up?

ANN: But I still believe that saying of . . .

your rights END where my nose begins?

Well my rights ends where YOUR nose begins!

And I think if we ALL really lived along those lines

We'd be a LOT better off!

AF: You need to live in the country?

ANN: No, don'[t] have to live out the country

We HAVE to live together . . .

We HAVE to!

YOU know that!

People live together!

"People live together," Ann insists, in a dense, sometimes even claustro-phobic social space, and this requires an expanse of physical space to contain so much concentrated personality and eccentricity and imperfection and so many distinctive voices. Working-class Texans talk frequently about the im-portance of having this expanse of space around them. This is a space fig-ured through the barrage of words and deictic gestures used to locate a con-versation in an expansive space, a space measured in miles and roads, not blocks and addresses. And yet this space is also miniaturized and domesti-cated by sociable talk, brought into the close physical confines of the beer joint, through expressions like "I'm headin' to the house," which is "just up the road a piece," and the accompanying toss of the chin, which might mean five miles or fifty. This space is expansive and enveloping, a zone in which one can be both lost and hidden.

This ideology of densely inhabited but still open space emerges explicitly in ordinary speech genres. I was returning to Parkville for a visit with Becky and her family. They lived in a hamlet a few miles from town, and I hadn't been around for a while. So after getting lost, which seemed almost impossible in this flat country with its roads on a grid where you could see for twenty miles in every direction across the fields of soybeans and corn and not much else, I headed back into town and asked directions at the Pub & Grub. Somebody in the bar told me how to get to Pleasanton:

"You go out of town here, past the Post Cafe, across the tracks, about five miles, and make a left when you see the old mine and the shut-down dump off on the left.[5] Used to be you'd have to wait forever for a train most any time, but they don't run as many trains through here as they used to, any-more. You'll pass, let's see, one, two, three grain elevators. Turn left at the big pile of rocks and you'll cross some more tracks. Turn right when you can't go no further, and a couple of dogs'll start to chase your car. When they stop chasing you, turn right, and you'll see an old green Ford up on blocks. Go up a ways and make a turn where you see the white Chevy. That's where you want to be."[6]

The dogs did, in fact, stop chasing me, as predicted, and I found my way to Pleasanton, where I did indeed want to be. This Illinois country seemed, at first glance, to be a vast space with tiny pockets of human occupation dot-ting its surface, a place in which human sociality was minuscule. And yet, al-though it was certainly rural, this was also just as certainly a manmade space, its ground saturated with ammonia from decades of high nitrogen fertilization, its water tasting suspiciously as if the chemicals leaching from the closed landfill had made their way into the backyard wells.

And this landscape was known, in careful and historically elaborate detail, as a social space that was traversed daily in beater cars and muddy trucks, windows down, country music blasting, cigarettes piling up in the ashtrays. It was known the way tribal peoples know their rainforests and deserts, and the way urbanites know their blocks and neighborhoods. And like those other kinds of specialized, spatialized social knowledge, this space was known experientially, unevenly, by its surprises and storied landmarks. It was known by and through its *places*. Although the Illinois roads (unlike those in Texas) were on a numerical grid system, cutting through the fields like some demonic game of tic-tac-toe, nobody used those numbers to give directions. Instead, they used their own indexical grid, a grid of trashed-out places and objects, marked by these deposits of human effort, ambition, and failure.

The safety of this kind of well-known, only apparently empty landscape allows for a margin of error, an occasional wild swing of the wheel. (Though of course, the police are out here too, watching and waiting.) It permits room for that crucial measure of imperfection that escapes observation or severe consequences. There are those nights, for example, back in Texas, when you're driving home drunk. One night, José was standing around outside, behind the bar, with Quiet Paul.[7] The two Mexican American men, both regular patrons at Ann's Place, were watching the roaring barbecue and talking in a mixture of Spanish and English when I passed by and asked José whether he still hung out at a bar in Austin where I had often seen him. Not any more, he said, and he explained it this way:

JOSÉ: Thing I used to hate about partyin' at Harry's Place . . .
y'see 'ats the oool' [old] neighborhood crowd
y'get in there partyin' and drinkin' til one o clock in the mornin'
then I
then I go drive here
Y'see I just live down the road
[points away, up the highway]
Y'know I grew up right here
[nods head in a circle]

[laughs]

Y'get drunk then drive all the way back up here

That DOG don't HUNT man

[laughs, shrugs]

y'know

[mimics driving a car drunk, eyes squinted, swerving the wheel]

YEAH!

What did I DO this for?

AF: So then you drive over to San Marcos?

JOSÉ: Buda, right here

[points to the west]

live 'bout ten, fifteen MILE

make a left on one-oh-two

But no

I come back . . .

from here to one-oh-two is about seven-tenths of a mile . . .

[points around in a circle]

AF: After that you're home FREE?

[i.e., not likely to be stopped for driving under the influence of alcohol]

JOSÉ: Yeah, once you get to that back road

it's about four or five miles

right there on one-oh-two

old county road . . .

[points west]

take it from here to one-oh-two . . .

but yeah

if you're comin' from Austin

that's a horse of a different COLOR!

For José, space "out here" is paradoxically figured through a barrage of gestural and verbal deixis as fulsome and safely bounded: "just down the road" refers to a distance of "ten or fifteen miles." To leave this space is dangerous, disconcerting, and unnatural, a move out of the humane space of the local. José's metaphors capture this unnaturalness: "a dog that don't hunt," "a horse of a different color." To go home along these roads is to go "to the house," as if the miles of travel were as trivial as a driveway. One moves through a space that is both enclosed by the sociability of the local and empty enough to accommodate the eccentricities of the drunken "fool," sneaking home safely across the terrain of the local, on the back roads.

Those Sad, Slow Country Songs

Space, so conceived, is also a dimension of everyday talk and its organization of the time-scale and pacing of sociability. In those most "ordinary" moments of "talkin' shit," where the poesis of verbal art is only grudgingly emergent, time too flows slowly across the fields and highways, as if it would last forever, like "mem'ries." Such talk models a slow, lazy, disarmingly banal and apparently somewhat disengaged way of filling the time, and of filling a silent space with the murmur of familiar voices saying familiar things.

Such relaxed exchanges are, however, also felt as pleasurable build-ups to more intense forms of sociability. They tend to happen in quiet, hazy, and interstitial moments, late in the afternoon before the noisy crowds show up, or late at night over the last beer after most of the night's crowd has left. This liminal mood has a distinct experiential quality, one which lingers in my memory as an essential dimension of beer-joint sociability. This quality is signified musically, and instantly evoked, by a lugubrious beat, a whining, reverb-saturated steel guitar, and a voice dripping with sadness in its cry breaks. These are the songs people call "the sad, slow songs," and they typically tell of troubled moments in life: heartbreak, despair, regret, aging, leaving, desire for forgiveness, shame, and sin. Such songs evoke an intensely felt sense of location and temporality.

Clint Black's elegiac "Nothing's News (to Me)" played constantly on Ann's jukebox in the early evenings of 1991. This song, with its iconic "crying steel" introduction, clarifies the linkage between the spatiotemporal liminality of this barroom mood and the "feeling" of lived abjection that is so potently allegorized in "lost love" songs. "There's nothin' like a steel guitar cryin' in the night," Black sings in his everyman tenor, as the steel guitar wails mimetically. Black then continues, singing the praises of sawdust-covered floors, "friendly fights," and long sessions "talkin' 'bout the good old times."[8]

"Nothing's News," like so many other "sad, slow songs," also invokes the kind of nostalgic sociable "talkin' shit" that is the raison d'etre for rural beer joints, as Black celebrates "talkin' bout the good old times, braggin' on how it used to be." This musical icon of a hazy, lugubrious early-evening mood was a favorite at Ann's, especially among the "slow talkin' country boys" (as the local saying goes) who cultivated the lazy sociability that occurs at the seams of long conversations. The genres of discourse practiced at sunset constitute a careful approach to the more noisy, dense, artful, and agonistic forms of talk that emerge as the evening proceeds, as the jukebox gets louder and faster or a band takes the stage, and the beer and stories start to flow. These same slow ways of speaking also model closure and fatigue as the night winds down to a few minutes and a few last beers.

Such "slow talkin'" genres are also, for the same aesthetic reasons, highly poeticized in greetings and leave-takings. The canonical topic for such openings is the weather, which is often a mystically poeticized subject (as well as an occasionally very important one) "out the country."[9] One summer day a late-afternoon rainstorm had quelled the heat and dust, for a change, and was still moving across Caldwell County as Jake arrived from a day of hard work as an electrician.[10] Old Rusty, a retiree, was already in position on his stool, his third can of Milwaukee's Best Light just opened. He had been observing the rain for an hour or so through the open back door behind the bar when Jake pulled up a stool next to him. They began a slow-paced conversation:

RUSTY: Just get OFF Jake?

[long pause]

JAKE: Yep

[Jake stretches, yawns, and takes a drink]

RUSTY: We had a little SHOWer here a while ago

[pause]

JAKE: That's what JERRy said . . . Hmmm

[Jake had talked to Jerry in the parking lot]

[Both men look through the open back door of the bar, where the sky over the fields is clear and rain-washed, and the fields are glistening with water]

JAKE: It LOOK like it must've come this way

looooook like . . .

[pause]

RUSTY: Yeah, hell

I didn't even know it was s'posed to RAIN

them GOD-damn . . .

clouds a started back in HERE

[points west behind the bar]

come ON over . . .
[gestures movement past the bar]
[about ten seconds of silence]
RUSTY: Didn't LAST long[11]
but it was a . . .
good little shower . . .

The bar where we sit is an orienting point, a point of intimate, local reference, in this highly stylized, slow-moving, and redundant conversation. But
the bar is situated, and situates its patrons in turn, in a much vaster meteo-
rological space, space on the grand scale of clouds and cold fronts, and time
on the grand scale of seasons and years passing by. Indeed, the weather can
focus time and place in miniature too, in the form of drops of rain on your
face after two months of cattle-killing drought (we ran outside the Liar's Inn,
once, dropping our guitars and conversations to play in the sudden thunder-
storm), and as the chills that run down one's spine when a tornado seems to
be forming against the horizon.

The poetry of "ordinary" life is continually emergent against this grand
yet miniature, fulsome and enveloping, slow-moving, slow-talkin' totality of
weathered physical and conversational space and time. Poetic intensification
comes in the form of a "place" and a "mem'ry" and a certain suddenly heightened way of talking about and with a "place" and its associated "mem'ries,"
a sudden swelling of an "ordinary" moment to grand proportions. "Places,"
like the place where two dogs take off after your car, or like Ann's Other Place,
emerge against the background of ordinary time and space, in all of their full-
ness and closeness and inscrutability. *Talk's* "places" come in flashes of sung
and spoken poesis that emerge against the background of ordinary conversations only to resediment in that talk. They are like the ordinary objects and
commodities that suddenly become voiced, animate speaking entities only
to turn once again back into jukeboxes and stuffed animals and flaws in the
paneling and neon beer signs. Such "places" return inexorably to the vast
realm of pre-textual space and time, requiring an almost archaeological effort
to recover their momentary depth. And, in fact, "places" like Ann's Other
Place are made of these very objects and commodities and flashes of verbal
and musical poesis, all of which pile up in sedimented layers, waiting for talk
to discover them.

Country music gives just this account of the objects and stories that pile up and become possible texts, piles of bones waiting to be dug up, revealing the embedded, layered history of a "place" in time. Country is, classically, full of speaking, feeling objects: jukeboxes, walls, answering machines, suitcases, old photographs, and whole houses full of "mem'ries" (Fox 1992). The nostalgic, sometimes obsessive working-class gaze is precisely archaeological. This particular affective archaeology entails a careful peeling away of layers of encrusted sentimental meanings, an interrogation of the trash piled high around the house, the beer joint, and the mind, and a careful social recontextualization of these objects. Randy Travis sings about this gaze in his beloved 1985 hit "Diggin' Up Bones," where the narrator sits alone in his house talking to old pictures and mem'ries, "exhuming" his pain and "diggin' up bones" of a past that's better left buried.[12]

George Jones, one of the three or four most important of all singers for the patrons of Texas beer joints, takes this deconstructive project even further, discovering the way that moments of verbal poesis become the virtual walls and ceilings of the collapsing structure of a "Two Story House." (He says, "I've got my story," and Tammy Wynette reminds him, "I've got mine too").[13] Or he invites the listener to "step right up, come on in" to that fallen house of stories for "The Grand Tour."[14] Jones proceeds, in this song, to walk the listener through this "lonely house" until recently filled with the presence of a nameless "she," past the chair where she sat down on his knee, the bed where they made love, her picture on the table, and the nursery where their baby used to sleep, before "she left me without mercy." Each object pulses and speaks in the narrator's mind, as mnemonic obsessions pile up.

Once, with the video camera rolling and the beer flowing, I asked Hoppy to give me the "Grand Tour" of his many-storied "house of mem'ries," the room above his garage where we played music every Wednesday night. This room is piled high with stories-in-waiting, objects, signs, instruments, and what Hoppy calls his "mem'ries":

HOPPY: Oh, there's more stories to this place!
Sam bein' a friend of mine for years and years and years
we used to go to the Clachan Inn
down one-eighty-three an'
Mike'd get a little tooted up[15]   [i.e., drunk]
An' he'd swing on the rafters
They got the ol BARS up there   [open-timbered rafters]

So when Randy and I BUILT this place
there' was TWO things Mike liked to do
he liked to swing on rafters
an' he liked to ring bells
an' him bein' a good friend
that's why these beams are crossed here
[points to ceiling]
that's why it's a vaulted ceiling
and that's why the BELL is hangin' in the bar
an' that's the TRUTH
[nods, smiles with satisfaction]
I guarantee you!
Randy Meyer gave me the table
over there
Gosh I don' know
there's so much MORE in here that I couldn't . . .
the WOOD that this building is BUILT out of
a guy in West Texas gave me
to tear the house down
so the actual wood an' everything
We DID buy the four-by-fours up there
but if you look at the one-bys
it's out of the old house
the ship-lap   [i.e., tongue-and-groove wood paneling]
the insulation
everythin' in these walls
was given to me
y'know
Walt, that played banjo for me
for about ten years
that's gone now
passed away
gave me those
[points to some horse tack hanging on the wall]
The rest of the stuff is given to me
right down to actually the WIRING in the place
and I have had some times up here myself

there's one little story
if you look behind the bar
I don' know if your camera can pick this up
but you might be able to see it
be a little interestin'
[laughter, Hoppy points to an uneven spot on the wall near the door]
We's up here one time
We were puttin this ship-lap up here
Joanna's fixin' us drinks[16]
and I was smearin' the
stain on the wall an' stuff
an there's one board back here
right here
you can see it
SHIP-lap goes together
it's got a LIP that goes together
an' she was mixin' [drinks] for me that night
REAAAL strong
and I got that board on upside down
I didn't KNOW it
til the next day
an' I seen that board
I had it on upside down
I told her I was gonna LEAVE that there
cuz there's a mem'ry
there's a MEM'ry behind the board
Cuz that board got put on upside down
an' she always blamed it on the stain
because not havin her glasses
she made the drinks so strong . . .
PROB'ly not true!
[laughter]

Hoppy, no less than George Jones, literally deconstructed his "house of mem'ries" for the camera, piece by piece. This was a "place" where "mem'ries" and stories and meanings resided in the very planks and beams and wiring, as well as in the more obvious mementos and touchstones. Rural, working-class "places" resonate with these piled-up meanings and ideas and plans and stories and sad, sweet feelings, waiting for a question or an object to stimulate just such an archaeology of memory, a discovery of deep mnemonic meaning in an imperfection in the wood, "diggin' up bones."

This poetic discourse of place, the textualizing deconstruction of an inhabited space, can organize sociability, too, emerging not only in the form of directions to Pleasanton or as a performance for a video camera, but as an organic structure of dialogic "talkin' shit."[17] Once, on one of those lazy, slow-talking afternoons, I asked Rusty and Jerry what the barnlike building in which we were sitting had been before it became Ann's Other Place:

RUSTY: [to Pat and Jerry][18] What was the name of this damn place?
JERRY: Used furniture
stuff like that
but it was . . .
RUSTY: Tradin' Post?
[Turning to address Pat]
What'd they use to call it?
JERRY: But it was a flea market type of deal
PAT: I don't know Rusty
you have to ask Ann
RUSTY: Huh?
PAT: [exasperated] I don't *know*
you have to ask Ann
RUSTY: But it was written on the roof of this old bitch
You can SEE it
PAT: I don't know Rusty
I never COME this way
RUSTY: TRAdin' Post
I b'lieve it was . . .
JERRY: But it was a flea market type of deal
RUSTY: Yeah
AF: This is after they had the chinchilla farm?
RUSTY: Yeah, yeah . . .
yeah
Then they went out, uh, . . .
JERRY: Yep, but the thing is

Ann's has always owned the
property =   [RUSTY: Oh yeah.]
JERRY: Ann has always owned the
property =   [RUSTY: No, later on . . .]
JERRY: No
Ann owned it when it was a feed store. =
RUSTY: Oh yeah
she had it when it was a feed store
and that chinchilla thing
JERRY: Yeah
I know a guy that used to work for her . . .
he was a *mean* son'bitch . . .
RUSTY: Yeah . . .
then they, then they
"TRAdin' Post"
that was the name of this son of a
bitch =   [JERRY: "TRAdin' Post . . ."]
RUSTY: [satisfied] Yeah . . .
They had all
you know
the . . .
[rapidly overlapping with Jerry]
it's kinda like a goddamn =
JERRY: = It was kind of a flea market, used furniture store =
RUSTY: = Flea market and used furniture, yeah
yeah [pause]
JERRY: Doesn't last too long . . .
RUSTY: *Naaaaaw*, it wasn't here too long . . .

"Doesn't last too long," Jerry tells us, and Rusty agrees: "Naw, it wasn't here too long." The two old speaking partners thus conclude this section of a long dialogue with a powerful and poetic cliché, a move outward into the meta-discursive trope that organizes their talk: a sense of decay, loss, slippage, and nostalgia.[19] No less than ten-minute thunderstorms, "places" and "mem'ries" slip away across the interpretive horizon, leaving signs of their presence seeping into the open spaces, the fields and silences. It is this sense that the world isn't like it used to be "anymore" (to use the local term that stands for this entire structure of feeling) that stimulates the poetic construction, in wood, wiring, and words, of a named, meaning-full "place." Such a place is loaded up with signs, objects, and mnemonic devices that invite hermeneutic scrutiny against the faded background of time's passing.

Through their poetic archaeology of Ann's Other "Place," Rusty, Jerry, and Pat strip away layers of paint and time and signs painted over signs, discovering the history of still "other places" that lie behind the facade. The bar's very name—with its medial "other"—is already a metasign standing for the displacement of an *original* place, somewhere else and lost to time. Rusty and Jerry and Pat produce a verbal icon of their object as their words layer echoed phrases over each other, each speaker laminating his or her words on the words of the others, as close as layers of paint on the old sign, repeating themselves and each other word for word, as they co-construct the text of this "place." The poetic intensity of this talk is modeled temporally by an ever more dense dialogic overlap, an accelerating imitative pattern, and a sudden relaxation into the final lyric image of time's passage: "doesn't last too long." With their layered construction in words, they construct a new and temporary "place" of sociable talk, an "other" place, out of the remains of so many long-lost places.

Rubes, Hillbillies, and Country Pickers

"Country" is a cultural logic that organizes personality, place, and pacing when you live "out the country." But is what I have described merely the filling in of a stereotype? Are these sly, slow-talkin', sad-song-loving people "for real"? This is, after all, the notion of "country" that "country music" projects as a commodified image for mass consumption. It is, as well, the "country" we encounter in both mass-cultural popular entertainments and in many scholarly works. It is the "country" featured in those ubiquitous jokes about the slow-talking rube in the city.

Living "out the country" means identifying rural values with social "outness." It polemically marks a lack of sophistication, but also a disarming forthrightness of character. Not surprisingly, such images of "country" suggest sociable eccentricity, and always imply a hint of the sly trickster, who knows more than he lets on. At its extreme, in the figure of the dangerous hell-raisin' "redneck," "country" implies danger and violence, ignorance and arrogance.

"Out the country," though, where they see those same movies and television shows a little differently, the figure of the "rube" is more sympathetically portrayed, more multidimensional, more self-consciously apprehended as a confusion of the textual and the real. It is interpreted as both an unfair stereotype and a funny exaggeration, as a trope of explanation for actual, known people and for highly performative assumptions of the "hillbilly" identity. It invites subtle and partial identifications. This figure is pervasively keyed to musical signifiers; it is one of the most basic referents of "country music" and has been throughout the history of the genre (Peterson 1997). Perhaps surprisingly, but without a doubt, the figure of the hillbilly rube lives a vital life "out the country," even now.

One night we were playing music, as so often, around tables in the bar, when I played the introductory guitar lick from George Jones's "White Lightning," a classic country song about moonshining hillbillies.[20] Hoppy heard the lick through the miasma of talk and smiled. He reared back his head and let out a rebel-yelled, bluegrass-inflected rendition of the first line of the song, sung with a stiff diaphragm, at a very high volume and with a break in the voice: "In NORTH CAroLIna/way BACK in the HILLS!"

A few seconds of delighted silence ensued across the bar, with smiles all around at this musical found object that so perfectly entextualized the shared sociable "feeling" of that moment. Hoppy seized the performative opening and continued with one of the most recognizable vocal acoustic icons in country music: the palatal click followed by a sustained unvoiced breathy alveolar fricative giving way to a voiced, high-pitched rounded, labialized vowel with a long descending intonation and a sudden punctuated amplitudinal rise at the end:

! ["popping" sound] . . . *ssshhhwooooooooooOOOOO!*

This is the sound that George Jones makes, in his performances of this song, to signify breaking the seal on a bottle, taking a swig, and reacting to the fiery burn of the moonshine whiskey as it sears the drinker's throat.[21] As we enjoyed the sudden emergence and elaboration of this classic "hillbilly" trope, I picked out another rendition of the guitar lick, assuming Hoppy now wanted to perform this song. But Hoppy took the occasion for reflection. His eyes narrowed, in imitation of George Jones, who himself imitates a thousand other imitations of a "hillbilly" moonshiner:

HOPPY: *OOOOOOLD* George can do that!
[and then he sings again, without the click]
ShwooooooooooooOOOOOOOOOOOOOOO!
Heh heh heh![22]
AF: Like he MEANT it!
[laughter]
And I'm SURE he DID!
HOPPY: Boy
that's another one that jus' . . .
amAZes me to watch 'im perform!

Hearing Hoppy embody George Jones's embodiment of a hillbilly, it becomes clear how this rustic image of the rube is precisely a heightened performance, a metaidentity. The "hillbilly" image is frequently entextualized in such fleeting moments of nostalgic identification, half identified with, half laughed at, and never dismissed as irrelevant. But the figure of the rube can also become a more elaborated species of personality, a specific explanatory and inhabited identity, a means of socializing a certain kind of expressive foolishness, and for performing an excessive version of one's everyday self.

R. P. Sconci embodied that excessive figure in the beer joints around Lockhart. R. P. was an elderly musician and retired farm laborer. A self-professed "old Dago farmer," R. P. represented an extreme case of rural "hillbilly" eccentricity for the locals, with his quavering, highly modulated voice, his way of squinting intently as he talked, his formless, free-wheeling dancing, his archaic repertoire of country songs from the 1920s and 1930s, his radical looseness with rhythmic patterns and song structures, his way of calling people "Mister" or "Miss" at the beginning of nearly every turn ("Weeeeell, Mister Aaron"), his narrational fluency with animated, voiced direct discourse, his barrage of rephrasings and repetitions and sly asides apologizing for his own failures of memory and lack of sophistication, and especially his ability to tell inordinately long and hilarious stories, typically of his own experience as a rube among sophisticates.

R. P.'s stories proceeded through an unbelievable excess of embedded digression. R. P. was already in the middle of a digression from a conversation about his early musical experiences, telling me about his days in the Navy during World War II, when he remembered this story from his period of basic training before being sent to the Pacific theater:

R.P.: We had a chief
that I shall never forget
I shall never forget
he was my (chief)[23]
and he said
"Son, what's wrong?"
And I said
"Mr. D————"
I can recall his . . .
his name to this day
I said
"Mr. D————
I never have shot from the right side in my LIFE!"
I was a farmer
they KNEW I could handle the GUN
rabbits, and snakes
And I said
"I'm just a natural . . ."
He said
in other words
"Can I say that you're left handed?"
I said
"On that point, YES
With a carbine
or a shotgun"
I said
"Yes I am . . ."
And he stopped everyBODY
He got everybody up
"'TENTION!"
Everybody t'attention
"Okay"
he said,
"Now, switch to your side
and do it the way you do it BEST!"
and ah
I came within

I came within . . .
Now UNDERstand
that I'm gonna confess to this DAY
if I DID
I'm sorry that I said it
I'll apologize to the commANder
BUT thirty-seven, eight, nine years ago . . .
Now on my RIGHT side
I did not ever hit the FRAME
or the foundation
that was HOLDING the bull's eye
I did NOT
even get too CLOSE
to the foundation
made out of two-by-fours
I did not
He put me to the left side
and seven or eight rounds
I can't recall to this date
But I lived with it [the gun] thirteen months and eight days
twenty-four hours a day
on the islands
I'll testify to that
But I can't recollect
The CLIP
has me baffled
Course I know that the chamber held ONE
The clip
held six, seven, or possibly eight
I could be wrong
and I KNOW
I don't recollect of hittin' the bullseye
I mighta hit one time the bulls eye
but I got
CLOSer to the bulls eye
with them rounds of ah
ammunition

I got CLOser to the bullseye
than I would get to
any other circles
aROUND the bulls eye
aMEN
that's the best of my r . . .
and LORD
forGIVE me
if I'm not sayin' this right
I pray that I'm NOT
if I am
my recollection
and I
I BEG God's mercy
for this . . .
Alright, now
if we wanna get back to the music BUSiness . . .

Such excessive, digressive narrativity poetically explodes the easy, dialogic sociability it appears to embody, overflowing the bounds of any locally permissible turn-length or informational structure. On another night, while R. P. was carrying on, as usual, in this digressive mode, Owen tried to interrupt numerous times to cajole a song, instead of more stories, out of R. P.[24] Finally, in a moment of real frustration, Owen declared: "He won't give you a straight answer for NOTHIN'! He ALWays has to go into a story!"

"Going into a story" with performative flair at the right time and for the right reason is a cornerstone of sociable eccentricity, of "country" personality and verbal competence. Sociability both depends on the ability to tell stories and moves and develops through compelling characterizations by means of stories. The figure of the "rube," the "country picker," is simply an extreme, performative elaboration of this idea, the idea of "going into a story" taken to humorous, eccentric excess. Hoppy's fleeting flirtation with this figure and R. P.'s lived immersion in it represent two ends of a continuum of possible identifications with this slow but sly textual figure.

Hoppy and R. P. are working with inchoate, relatively unreflexive versions of this trope of the "rube." But occasionally, and tellingly, the hillbilly identity is metadiscursively foregrounded and interrogated. This happens, for example, in the standard genre of jokes about the hillbilly naif in the city. In these episodes, the textuality and ironic complexity of the figure of the rube is foregrounded, as in the following example:

ANN: You heard the story 'bout this guy
this hillbilly guy that went
up North you know
and went in this HIGH CLASS restaurant . . .
and he was
boy he was puttin' on the DOG thing
he was really RICH
[confidentially]
— course he was really just a country picker
didn't know too much —
and he was TALKin' bout how good he was
and how honest he was
and what a good ol' boy he was
as he was walkin' out of the RESTaurant
he picked up the toothpick
picked his teeth
and put it back in there
and he says
"Y'know, I'll bet you there's a lot of people stealin' these things!"
AF: OLD country!
[laughter]
RICHARD: [sings] *"Now that's coun-try"*
[laughter and pause]
Now I do that myself ever[y] once in't'while!
[laughter]

Richard's "I do that myself ever[y] once in "t'while" is a metaidentification, ambiguously situated between compulsion and choice, with the deep and polemically local meaning of the trope "country." This balance of felt necessity and articulated choice is what people mean when they say/sing, as Richard does here, "Now THAT's country." They are quoting from Marty Stuart's polemical song of the same title (which was, of course, inspired by the same phrase, which is widespread in rural American discourse). Stuart's song blends precisely the images I have been closing in on here; images of dense musically mediated sociability and also of ornery drunken rural solitude in a spatial expanse, figures of foolish rusticity and sly cleverness, moral ideas about self-sufficiency and bucolic scenes of fields of clover interrupted with socially meaningful trashed-out junk and funny eccentricity. Stuart's protagonist sings from his front porch, where he sits with a gun, a guitar, a dog, a bottle, and his truck in sight: "Now, that's country . . ."[25]

What Is "REAL Country Music"?

So *that's* country. And this blend of space and closeness, "outness" and quickness, trash and beauty is what people living "out the country" mean by "country" when they talk, as they so very often do, about being "country people," and about the essence of "REAL country music." The phrase "REAL country music," used ubiquitously as an evaluative index for musical quality, is an argument for the political and aesthetic necessity of local style as "country." It is the polemical delineation of a class community, an "us," and a "we," the "people out here." Ann pursued this refined definition in one of our earliest conversations:

ANN: In my opinion . . .
what the people out here call country is NOT
what you or some of the people you might run into call country
What WE call country is
Hank Williams
Hank Thompson
Ray Price . . .
especially EARLY Ray Price
Very few country music artists that come along toDAY
are considered country
to US . . .
Ricky Skaggs . . .
He was considered kinda a young man coming along
that did REAL country music . . .
and we're hopin' [Vern] Gosdin . . .
will not turn around and turn . . .
go the other way on us

People dispute these boundaries, up to a point, although few would argue with Ann's carefully refined and qualified definition here. The specific musical references implied by "REAL country" music vary, but the sense of the idea is closely linked to the idea of life lived "here in the REAL world," as Alan Jackson's hit song puts it. The aesthetic negotiation of the term goes on within discernible political and affective boundaries: the boundaries of the local world, "out the country." To abdicate responsibility to the local, working-class community and its deep sociality of "feeling" is, as Ann bluntly puts it, to "go the other way on us."

Indeed, the content of this sign is almost infinitely variable; though its broad aesthetic correlates are stable, they have surprising extensions. I remember, one lazy, hot afternoon, sitting at Ann's bar, smoking, drinking beer, and slow-talking to Ann and a few other regulars as the evening approached with its different valence of high-intensity interaction. Unusually, the TV was on behind the bar, piled on top of a wheeled cart full of various broken and half-working VCRs, its sound running through a crumbly old guitar amplifier. (This typical "redneck low tech" bricolage deconstructively echoed the idea of a middle-class home's "entertainment center.")

Besides the regulars and Ann and myself, another couple, older, quiet, with that dignified repose of the settled, retired working class, sat soberly getting drunk at a table close to the bar. The TV was tuned to the Austin PBS station, with the sound down low, the TV just another changeable sign in the raucous symphony of vivid-sounding signs surrounding us: "Shirts and Shoes Required/Bra and Panties Optional"; "Thank you for smoking"; "No soy responsible para accidentes." Out of the corner of my eye, I recognized the face on the screen: Mstislav Rostropovich, the virtuoso émigré Russian cellist, critic of the Soviet state, and expressive conductor of the National Symphony.

Ann saw me looking at the screen and turned her head as the image changed to Rostropovich conducting. Answering her unspoken question, I explained who he was, and why I had been distracted. In the way that the details of one's biography become crucial to sociability and friendship in a small, oral community, Ann understood my distraction. She knew I was a cellist and a Slavophile. Sometimes my friends would ask me how to say things in Russian, just for something to talk about and play with verbally. (There was always this delight in language for its own sake, and foreign languages and accents were major subjects of playful talk.) And this was the function TV served as well, on those rare occasions when it was on in the bar. TV was a stimulus to conversation, sometimes even a participant in the piling up of voices and images that made sociability dense and interesting.

Well, this *was* getting interesting, so Ann turned the sound up on the old guitar amplifier under the TV. And we found ourselves watching, riveted for an hour by the documentary on the screen, which followed Rostropovich as he returned to his beloved homeland for the first time since his defection. He was shown conducting an orchestra in Moscow, playing a Shostakovich symphony; visiting his first apartment and remembering the hours of music he made there with friends now long dead; touring the monuments of the Great Patriotic War in Leningrad with his daughter, remembering friends he lost there. The subject of the documentary was the intense and stereotypically Russian emotional linkage between history, homeland, memory, family, friendship, conflict, and, of course, a life saturated with music and poetry. Although the film was subtitled, the titles did not capture the interactional intensity of some reunions, or the emotional depth of Rostropovich's daughter's words as places and pieces of music conjured up feelings of nostalgia and loss. Even with only a few years of Russian, I could recognize scenes where more was said, more was exchanged, than the subtitles showed, and I pointed them out to my friends, who watched, transfixed, urging deeper interpretations out of me when it was obvious that more was going on than the film was making explicit.

At the end of the documentary, Ann turned off the TV, and we sat quietly for a few moments. The old couple at the table stood up to leave, having finished most of a fifth of Crown Royal in a brown paper bag. The woman, now drunk in a dignified way, walked over to the bar, until she was standing between Ann and me. She had tears on her face. "I just wanted to say," she said, "that was *beauuuuutiful*. You *sure* don't expect to see that kind of thing in a bar."

Ann's missionary zeal for her life's project, her musical sanctuary, animated her face. "We're into ALL kinds of music here," she said, "It don't MATter what it is, just as long as it's REAL. In FACT, if y'all like good music, come on back tonight. We'll have some of the old boys from around here pickin' and grinnin' and carryin' on 'til all hours. And when I stop sellin' beer, I'll have the coffee on and we'll play until the boys want to STOP. *Y'all come back now, y'hear!*"[26]

Swaddled in this most symbolic of Texas rural working-class goodbyes, the couple left, promising to return, which in fact they did do a week later. And back at the bar, we talked again, about music and home and friends and memories and how the linkage between them was really the same everywhere you went, even in Russia, even with classical music. The figure of the "rube" seemed a long way off at that moment. Now, that's country, too.

"The Fool in the Mirror"

Self, Person, and Subjectivity

When I'm with me, I go out to all the barrooms

Chase all the women, I stay out 'til one or two

When I'm with you, I'm a different kind of person

I change so much, you won't know me when I'm through

—Randy Meyer, "When I'm with Me"[1]

The Elusive "Subject" of Social Class

In this chapter, I explore the representation and phenomenology of the "subject"—the individual seen both as an autonomous agent and as an effect of ideology—in Texas working-class culture. Using a classical distinction in cultural theory, I will describe the cultural construction of the individual in terms of discourses of "selfhood" and "personhood." These terms refer to the opposition between the individual as a "person" constituted "externally" by generalizable social roles, rights, and obligations, and the individual as an irreducible "self," constituted by the uniquely "interior" qualities of subjective experience.

But these are not merely social scientific abstractions. In working-class Texas, this dual character of the subject is richly elaborated in metadiscourse, poetics, and practical conduct. I approach this elaboration through explicit local discourses about the nature of the subject (a frequent topic of working-class talk and of country music), and through several pervasive textual images or tropes that saturate both country music and everyday conversation. Specifically, these are the tropes of the socially engaged person as an idiosyncratic "character," both larger than life and authentically flawed, and the image of the socially disengaged "fool" with a "tore up" inner self.

The person/self framework is a subject of intense interest for many anthropologists, and it is a notoriously elusive aspect of "culture."[2] But like anthropologists working in Bali, Japan, or Pakistan, I believe that local ideas about what rules constitute a person and about what it feels like to be a self are essential to figuring out why people act, think, and feel as they do in particular places and moments. But of course, Lockhart, Texas, is not Bali, not Pakistan, not Tokyo. Indeed, a place like Lockhart is in some ways *more* inscrutable then such conventionally mysterious places. I am evoking the self-defining ethos of a "class culture," something not wholly other, something that does not exist in relative independence, for Americans at least, in the same sense as "other" cultures do. In some ways this class culture's orientation to time, space, and subjectivity is more than familiar—it is "ours."[3] It is, after all, an "American" ethos.[4] And yet, the argument that the logics of time, space, and subjectivity really are different, sometimes subtly, sometimes radically, for rural, working-class Americans is the basis for my effort to describing class difference as a culturally mediated phenomenon.

Against a background of apparent familiarity, subtle differences have a way of appearing transparent, especially when those differences are structurally incorporated—via stereotypes and stigmatization, for example—into the ordinary experience of both ethnographers and their likely readers, all of us citizens of a class society. What is more, the social reality that working-class culture shapes into a coherent form of individual experience—and into a political identity—is defined by conflict. Working-class culture is concerned with the dignity and agency of the subject in direct proportion to the lack of dignity and agency entailed in working-class political and economic experience, and especially in alienated labor. And working-class culture is concerned with the integration of the self and the person in sociable practice precisely to the extent that the pressures of poverty and alienation put the self at serious and continuous risk of disintegration. Being poor can make people crazy, a risk working-class Texans understand all too well. I conclude this chapter by showing how dangerous this risk can become.

In the previous chapter, I argued that one irony of the "country" as a social landscape is that an expansive "natural" physical space is densely and intensely social. I argue here that the closeness of all this embodied and spoken sociality registers in a dialectical movement that defines the local idea of an "ordinary" person as *ideally imperfect.* This "common sense" about the person entails an idea of an individual subject who is both open to intense social scrutiny and yet idiosyncratic, eccentric, unique, and ineffable. This is the way "ordinary" individuals appear, for my interlocutors in Texas, when they are known in great detail, as "characters" — a locally preferred term — on the stage of social life.

"I'm Only Human": Personality, Eccentricity, and Imperfection

The ideal of imperfection is expressed as an intense plea to a lover for forgiveness in "I'm Only Human," an obscure old Barney Tall song closely associated with singer Larry Hopkins, who sings it in every performance. Hopkins performs this song with a voice that comes close to crying on each stressed word in the refrain, as an icon of its self-revelatory intensity. The song's lyrics narrate the emergence of self-obsessed subject under the spotlight of social scrutiny with a flurry of pronouns:[5]

> *I'm only human, oh why can't I be*
> *all of the good things*
> *that you see in me?*
> *Yes I love you so dearly*
> *and I try to be true*
> *but I'm only human*
> *I'm not an angel like you.*

This song resonates precisely with a conception of the person expressed in everyday talk. Personhood is a function of performative "personality," a narratively produced effect of great depth and vivid recognizability, figured in the trope of interesting imperfection. This "only human" imperfection is a trope of almost sacred meaning in rural, working-class life, and the contemplation of imperfection in discourse is a valued source of the all-important affective condition of sociable "feeling" discussed in the next chapter.[6]

It was a blazing-hot Saturday afternoon in July. The intense Texas sun melted cassette tapes left on a dashboard, shimmered on the road, and stilled the fields. But inside Ann's bar it was dark and blessedly cool. The banner over the bandstand, at the far end of the long dance hall behind the front bar, read "Happy 50th Birthday Hoppy!" There was laughter in the air, mixing with the cigarette smoke and the music from the jukebox and the talk and the beeps of video game and the crack of pool balls and the buzzing neon and humming air conditioners.

The dance hall was packed with celebrants, there for a long day and night of revelry. One by one, Hoppy's friends came forward to stand in front of the stage, take the band's microphone, and speak a few words in tribute. Jimmy, a genial retiree, took his turn, dressed in a short-sleeved white dress shirt and a cap emblazoned with "#1 Grampa," a cigar clamped in the corner of his mouth. Jimmy was not yet showing the effects of the lung cancer which would take hold in the following months.

Jimmy (who died in 1995) was a fine verbal artist, and the room turned unusually attentive as he sat on the stool set up in front of the bandstand. A religious, though not always church-going man, Jimmy drew on the Southern preacher's art for his speech (Titon 1988), producing an intensifying, parallelistic, represented dialogue between a sinner and his God to convey the sacredness of imperfection as a valued quality of an important person like his old friend Hoppy, and, more slyly, as a quality he himself possesses in abundance:[7]

JIMMY: And I said,
"LORD what makes Hoppy so BEAUtiful?"
And He says
"So you will LOVE him!"
And I said
"What makes Hoppy play so good MUsic?"
And He said
"So you'll LOVE him!"
And
"Why is Hoppy so GOD-damn STUpid?"
"So HE'LL love YOU!"
AND . . .
I've LOVED you ever since Hoppy!

The sacredness of imperfection was in the air that Saturday. Hoppy had to leave for a while in the middle of the party, which continued long into the night. On his way out of the bar, he passed Miss Bettie, and even though he expected to be back in an hour or so, he paused for a heartfelt goodbye, humor leavening the serious feeling that is always emergent in leave-taking. As Hoppy embraced Bettie, warm words flowed between them:

HOPPY: You're a precious thing
BETTIE: Oh!
[They hug again]
HOPPY: I love you Bettie
you're so GOOD . . .
you try, and you know what hon?
We can never be PERfect
BETTIE: Your words are so PRETTY for us . . .[8]
HOPPY: You don't change a THING about you, okay?
BETTIE: Well gee THANKS! [but]
I'd like to get rich!
HOPPY: Well
I'd let you do that
but ONLY if I get SOME of it
[Hoppy departs]

There was a history of affection and acknowledged, cultivated imperfection behind this embrace, a history of evaluations and sharp-tongued gossip and warm support. Ann's was a place where eccentricity and imperfection were not only tolerated but carefully nurtured and curated. When Hoppy and Bettie embraced and spoke of each other's qualities and imperfections, they referred to this history of talk obliquely. It is this history of sociable intimacy that gives this brief and temporary goodbye its depth of feeling for both participants.

Once, for example, Hoppy ruminated on why Ann's was his favorite place:

HOPPY: If you make a mistake   [i.e., at Ann's bar]
It's kinda like settin' at home in your living room . . .
you can still feel comfortable . . .
and I don't think there's very many places in this WORLD
where you can feel that comfortable . . .
They've got to be
Ann and her sister   [Bettie]
two of the most SPECIAL people

as far as bar owners
I've EVER met in my life
and I've been in bars for the last . . .
I guess thirty years . . .
and more special people I've never seen . . .
Now they're HARD y'know
Ann's jumped MY bones a few times
straightened me out
matter of fact
one time
I got s'irritated
I wouldn't go down there for almost a year
I played ALL the way around here
and I wouldn't . . .
go in there
and it wasn't Ann's FAULT
I found out later
it was one of her help's fault
but they're HUMAN
and they make a few mistakes but . . .
aside from everything else
Ann's prob'ly about the STRAIGHTest
most honest person
you'll ever run into
especially for a bar owner
and she lets the musicians get away with murder
and I love that
we're all spoiled!

This imperfect, "only human" characterization, of course, worked in the other direction too. On one of my early visits to Ann's, Ann told me about her imperfect friend Hoppy; how he could be temperamental and "hard to deal with," but also how he had the most "beautiful voice" she had ever heard, a voice that earned him forgiveness for his imperfections. I remarked that this sounded like a description of the famous country singer George Jones, a notoriously imperfect man (nicknamed "No-Show Jones" by fans) with a transcendentally beautiful voice. Ann told me quite seriously, "No, Hoppy's WORSE than George Jones . . . but he's a better singer."

These mutually humanizing judgments, which carefully construct intimately known others as imperfect, richly eccentric, and yet larger than life in some specific and valued and redeeming quality, are folded into less reflexive speech genres, like greetings and goodbyes. They are embedded too in the kinesic rhythm of ordinary talk, coded with a knowing nod, rolled eyes, a half-uttered condemnation, understood well enough not to be fully stated. Indeed, they are foundational for interpretation, too, for the ways that such talk is aesthetically appreciated as artful sociability.

This aesthetics of eccentricity became clear after Hoppy left that afternoon. Miss Bettie, aware that the I had observed (and videotaped) the warm goodbye that passed between Hoppy and herself, turned to me with a smile and, putting herself in my observer's shoes, pronounced to me her textualizing, poetic judgment on the meaning of that moment: "Now . . . HAVEN't we got a bunch of CHARacters?"

"A bunch of characters," as Miss Bettie asserted, is an aestheticized prerequisite for working-class sociability of the sort prized at Ann's Other Place, just as it is a prerequisite for a novel or a television show or a drama, or for an ethnography. One night at Ann's, for example, we were sitting around a table reflecting on just this point over the last beer of the evening:

RICHARD: Life inside a Texas honky-tonk! [laughs]
ANN: I'm TELLIN' YOU!
[long pause]
A sitcom a day!
I coulda written a sitcom a day about this place!
RICHARD: Well we had . . .
we had one in here every day!
ANN: Oh YES!
Oh yes, it's great
great   RICHARD: Sittin right here . . .
These three way RO-mances that we had . . .
JOE: I thought Aaron was writin' somethin up on that . . .
where's he at?
[Joe looks over to dance floor, although AF is sitting next to him]

RICHARD: [laughing] He's right there!

[Richard points to AF; there is general laughter]

JOE: [to AF] Aaron!

was you writin' sumpin on that thing?

AF: I'm still writing!

JOE: No I'm serious, were you . . . ?

AF: Yeah, I'm still doin' it . . .

ANN: Well he wasn't writin' a sitcom

but he's probl'y gonna switch!

RICHARD: Where there's more money . . .

ANN: Base . . .

base it on CHEERS . . .

[long pause as Ann lights a cigarette]

RICHARD: Kinda like *The Young and the Restless*

a SOAP opera, y'know

every day . . .

day TV, y'know

but Texas honky-tonk?

ANN: Absolutely

OH YEAH!

Absolutely

kinda like Matt Dillon

and so forth

and what's her name . . .

Miss Kitty . . .

and them people

RICHARD: And we'll have Ol' Joe Briggs in there[9]

"A bunch of characters," discussing their similarity to a bunch of characters: this seemed to all of us at the bar that night to be the perfect reflexive
entextualization of this "ordinary" place (and the best way for me to "write
sumpin on it"). Rich characterization, through an individualizing, interpretive focus on the social uniqueness of another, is a crucial task of sociable talk
and verbal art in working-class Texas culture.

"Foolishness" and Sociability

There are limits to tolerable imperfection. Eccentricity can become excess, and absent-mindedness can become abjection. The performance of a flawed self can become socially aggressive and destructive, breaking the ordinary social frame of artful performance. A fine line separates a valued "character" from the frightening but compelling figure of the "fool," whose excessive eccentricity has the power to destabilize and disrupt sociability. At times, excessive, dangerous "foolishness" can shade into highly transgressive behaviors. But structures of discourse exist to contain such excess and to make transgression meaningful against a familiar, texted background of compelling explanatory tropes.

Returning to Hoppy's birthday party at Ann's Place, we can see this containment of foolishness unfold. More testimonials were being given, and Rick,[10] the biggest, orneriest, "craziest" man in the place, was doing his best to get a turn at the microphone. He'd been drinking hard, and nobody wanted to let him spoil the "feeling" that most of the celebrants were carefully developing for Hoppy on the occasion of his birthday. Rick, as most in the room knew, had an ambivalent relationship with Hoppy, at best. But the egalitarian ideology of this community mandated that every member had a right to speak on such occasions. Miss Ann had been controlling the microphone and organizing the flow of testimonial presentations when Rick made his insistent move to be heard:[11]

RICK: [shouting] MY TURN, MY TURN!
ANN: [exasperated, to the crowd] Oh, do I have to let RICK talk?
RICK: Yeah you DO!
ANN: OK Rick, I gotta watch on ya!
RICK: [to the crowd] Now the FIRST time I met this man
right here
[points to Hoppy]
we went to the COORS light place   [a brand of beer]
and HE told my old lady   [i.e., girlfriend]
which (is) the one I got NOW
he said
[imitates Hoppy's voice][12]

"who is that sucker you got?"
She said
"That's goin' be my next old man"   [i.e., boyfriend]
And he said
"You know who in the hell he is?"
He says
"Sis, why don't you find ya a decent man!"
She said
"I found the man I want!"
He says
"Naaw, you ain't found no man yet . . ."
He said
"That, that sucker's crazy"
'Til he got to know me!
an' hell, that's been fourteen years ago!
but ask him who he thinks 's his little bro now!   [i.e., "little brother"]
[in a high, intonationally dynamic voice]
just ask him!
look at him, look at him!
He's the one who's craaaazy!

Rick's aggressive foolishness was greeted at first with a wall of sustained talking. Whereas people had listened attentively to every word of some of the other testimonials (such as Jimmy's, described above), laughing at subtle jokes and recognized stories, they talked continually through Rick's increasingly incoherent narrative, which was layered with reported direct-voiced speech and hidden, coded meanings that only a few in the room could decipher.

Rick was clearly aware that others were interpreting his performance as dangerous foolishness, and that he was being pointedly ignored as other patrons tried to ward off the potentially poisonous effect of his drunken words. In response to this censure, Rick salvaged his performance as he concluded with a coherent mood-transposing trope, one drawn from country music, and also common in the testimonial genre.[13] He suddenly and disconcertingly revealed that the vividly animated story he had been telling as if it had happened days before had in fact occurred "fourteen years ago." As in so many country songs, the unbearably present feelings his story reveals were thereby suddenly repositioned in an obsessively persistent, but impossibly distant past (Fox 1992; Stewart 1993). The fool lost in his own past is an intelligible figure, richly elaborated in country music.

This temporal black hole is a frequently expressed trope among my interlocutors, one expressed directly in country songs beloved by working-class Texans, like Conway Twitty's "Fifteen Years Ago," in which a potently affective past-obsessed refrain follows the nonchalant line that ends the first verse: "He thinks I forgot you fifteen years ago," punctuated with a dramatic stop, before the singer, having suddenly heard the name of his lost love, announces dramatically: *"Fifteen years ago, and I still feel the same/Why did he have to mention your name?"*[14]

Rick's use of this trope, as the peroration of his testimonial, is exemplary. With its sudden, last-minute commutation of his anger, Rick's story of intense antagonism became intelligibly sociable after all. Rick reconstructed his story in its conclusion as a source of a real, if conflict-ridden, friendship. In a final ironic twist, Rick invoked Hoppy's *own* eccentricity as a form of praise, when he pointed at Hoppy, who was conspicuously ignoring this problematic "tribute," and shouted, "Look at him! He's the one who's CRAZY!" This echoed many other testimonials given that day in which speakers had stressed Hoppy's masculine virtue of "craziness," or willingness to do and say outrageous things in the pursuit of intense feeling—all aspects of his valued "character."

There are other less dramatic and more ubiquitous local techniques for socializing strong, dangerous "fools" and "characters." At Ann's, for example, Jane was known as an eccentric woman, given to fighting with men, running through husbands and boyfriends, getting dramatically drunk, and using strong profanity as readily as any man.[15] This kept her continually at risk of being a "fool"—a person whose eccentricities cannot be socially accommodated. Sociability, then, could not be assured when Jane was feeling "fired up" or "tore up." She got on people's nerves, and she made tempers run hot.

Jane's transgressive excess was an issue that came out in quiet back-channel talk to be sure, and such gossip is one way that transgressive "fools" become eccentric sociable "characters," through a poetics of critical indirection (Brenneis 1987). One night, the subject of women using profanity (strongly disfavored in this community) arose, and although no names were mentioned, it was clear who was being talked about:

ANN: Whenever somebody adopts that EVERY OTHER WORD
there's a THIS and a THAT
and a THIS and a THAT
when you KNOW it's not necessary!
SAMMY: Yeah . . .
and I don't use it around the KIDS   [he had admitted to using profanity
                                             earlier]

ANN: It's a HABIT
CINDY: Yeah!
ANN: So, I start callin' 'em down on THAT
And I 'll tell you WHAT
women
nowadays
have worse mouths then MEN do
when they get goin!
[Sammy laughs]
CINDY: That's TRUE . . .
We have LIVING proof of that!   [This refers to Jane]
ANN: DON'T we!

Such indirect gossipy criticism can keep truly excessive "fools" in line through the politics of reputation, but Jane was an exceptional and powerful voice. As a woman, in particular, she enjoyed a privileged immunity from physical confrontation, although she also suffered under much tighter constraints on appropriate speech and behavior than men did. One night, Jane had been drinking and carrying on, and her conduct was making her fellow patrons tense. She acted aggressively "tore up," in an excessively performative way. Suddenly, and loudly, she produced an explosive verbal flourish, calling attention to the transience of friendships and life itself. Jane had been considering moving, and someone, trying to be sociable, asked if she had moved yet. Jane was indeed "moved," but not in the sense the questioner meant:

JANE: We're s'posed to move back next weekend
but I don think it's gonna be next weekend cuz . . .
[heavy pause, continues in a growled, emotionally overwhelmed tone]
All my friends are leavin' . . .
and all my friends are DYIN'

and Y'KNOW . . .
We ain't gonna have time to DO all this shit!

Jane's complaint expressed real pain and loss and veered wildly toward foolish overexposure of her "tore-up" interior self. But there are conversational ways to resocialize such a fool, and Jimmy was an old hand at this, as well as a good friend to Jane. Jimmy tried to convince Jane that she was not without friends who were *not* "moving or dying," and in the process he artfully revoiced her foolish eccentricity, inhabiting her voice through direct discourse and making it an object of a gentle, sociable critique. Jimmy thus drew Jane out of her painful, solipsistic epiphany and into the joking sphere of ordinary talk. She was obligated to affirm her own foolishness precisely as a performance:

JIMMY: Well if you MOVE
who the hell's gonna call me up on my GODDAMN answering machine
and CUSS at me?
JANE: I still got your number . . .
JIMMY: Oh OK . . .
[pause, as Jane composes herself]
JANE: And if I call you up
and you ain't there
I'll leave MY number
you can call me back
and cuss me out!
JIMMY: [to others at the bar, as explanation]
She [Jane] call up one mornin' . . .
I got that answerin' machine . . .
[imitates Jane's loud, high-pitched, edgy, staccato voice]
"JIMMY,
shut the FUCKIN' *answerin' machine off*
and answer the GODDAMN *telephone!"*
[laughter]
JANE: That's RIGHT!
[nods her head with satisfaction]

Through a mirroring flash of direct discourse in Jimmy's kindly polemic, Jane became a "character" in a suddenly funny drama of her own eccentricity.

The effect of Jimmy's imitation was thus simultaneously a social embrace—indeed, a kind of verbal lifeline—and a subtle gendered critique. Jane's wild transgression was returned, if only for that moment, to the matrix of everyday, ordinary sociability. Jimmy brought Jane back into the communal fold by objectifying her voice and mirroring it back to her.

Working-class sociable talk is, as I discussed in chapter 1, dense with direct and quasi-direct discourse, lush with reported speech purportedly in the voice of another but unmistakably inhabited by the polemical presence of the speaker himself or herself. This poetic evocation of the distinctiveness of voice and person is embedded in the grammar and style of everyday talk. But it extends as well into the *thematic* topicalization of eccentricity and "character" in narrative and dialogue. This topicalization of a person's character is frequently linked to efforts to predict or explain the effects of a strong personality on a particular situation. "Character," the idea of an individuating but ultimately sociable eccentricity, is an everyday mode of explanation. Such explanation often elicits strong affirmation if it is felt as evocative and correct.

Once, for example, Miss Ann was explaining to me, with help from Richard, why it was a mistake to cross Old Joe Briggs, a big man, as Joe Briggs himself nodded his approval from the stool next to Richard:

ANN: I guess one of the first times I ever met him [Joe's antagonist]
he was in here
and Joe came in
and been drinkin' some beer or somethin'
when Joe . . .
started to walk out the door
I thought for some REASON
You weren't leavin'
You were jus' goin' out
He run over t'the'door and caught Joe
And *chewed his ass out* for BEIN here . . . ?
at my bar and not at his!
[Joe affirms with a nod]
RICHARD: And **Joe Briggs** didn't knock his LIGHTS out?
ANN: And you don't TELL **Joe Briggs** where to drink y'know
JOE BRIGGS: He ain't bother me
I stayed here!

[laughter]

I'ain' go to his place no more!

ANN: That was DUMB!

Even though Joe was sitting next to us, and even though he had been "Joe" throughout the previous few minutes of conversation, both when we addressed him and when he was referred to in the third person, he became "Joe Briggs" when the issue of his prominent social personhood was in sharp narrative focus. As part of a larger set of distinctive naming practices, the addition of a person's surname to his or her given name in discourse, whether in address or reference, calls attention to the named individual as a character in the social drama, a *kind* of person whom, for example, "you don't tell where to drink."

The "characterizing" tropes of personhood I have been discussing (e.g., ideologies of sacred imperfection, direct imitative voicing and double-voicing in talk, and personality-based narrative explanation) come together in a performative synthesis in instances of skillful public rhetoric in Texas working-class discourse. And the apotheosis of this characterization of the eccentric person comes when even the experiencing "self" is drawn into the world of voiced eccentric characters and represented as a simply another "character" open to social scrutiny.

One night, for example, at a jam session above Hoppy's garage, Hoppy used all these tropes skillfully to make a didactic point, as his teenaged son asked why Hoppy's old friend, Sam, had decided, rather uncharacteristically, to leave the party early:[16]

KENNY: Why did SAM run off?

JOANNA: He had to work tomorrow . . .

HOPPY: [speaking into his microphone, very slowly]

Sam was a little inTOXicated . . .

PLUS the fact that he's fixin' to get married

[laughter]

DAVE: [Sam's son] I CANnot believe that!

JOANNA: Neither can we!

It ain't . . .

it ain't happened YET

HOPPY: [slowly, dramatically] Well, Dave

the only thing that I'm gonna wait to see

is the total OUTCOME of this thing . . .

'cuz YOUR dad 's been single a LOOOOONG time . . .

[Hoppy switches to a conspiratorial tone]

and Nora is a *very possessive* person . . .

Now LOVIN' both of 'em like I do

all you can do is wish'em the BEST . . .

[quietly, warning]

but you stand there with one eye open and WATCH this shit too

[laughter]

This is gonna be . . .   DAVE: SING one for 'em then!

This is gonna be interestin'

right?   DAVE: SING one for 'em then!

That's . . .

That's like when your dad moved old

DEBbie

or that was her name?

or whatever her name was?

Gave me his table, chairs, bed

EVerything, y'know . . .

cuz she had all this stuff

he moved her in there and   DAVE: That's when I wasn't there

And I told 'im, I says

"Sam, y'know, I jus'

b'LIEVE I oughta put that stuff up, y'know?"

[Hoppy imitates Sam's rough, drawling voice:]

"Naw, I don't ever need it ag'in!" . . .

Well . . .

GUESS what table he's eatin' on toDAY down there?

[laughter]

the SAME table that he gave away

[trailing off]

and I took back to him cuz he didn't HAVE one!

[laughter]

   Ultimately, Hoppy's entire rhetorical performance was an explanation, using the trope of characteristic eccentricity, for Sam's decision to leave the party early. Hoppy's "on-microphone" turn contrasted sharply (being explicitly marked as performance) with Joanna's more generic explanation, expressed as a quiet aside in response to Kenny's initial question. Simultaneously, Hoppy articulated a gendered critique of a potential threat to male sociability represented by Nora's (highly stereotypical and narratively motivated) feminine "possessiveness" of Sam. Hoppy's commanding skills as a speaker are evident here, in his use of poeticizing devices like verbal iconicity (i.e., "looooong"), shifts of tone, volume, and rate of delivery, artful suspense through narrative digression, direct address to particular listeners, a climactic lyric image, and, of course, extensive directly represented dialogue. It is this command that makes him such an authoritative, respected figure in this rhetoric-centered local world.[17]

And the way this artful turn ended was important too. Hoppy's conclusion points to a surprising but essential quality of sociable eccentricity: it is a predictable quality that adheres to genders, characters, moods, and situations. Such predictability is socially useful, because it enables speakers to cast discourse turns on the basis of well-known "character" types and canonical narrative plots.

Hoppy's conclusion powerfully emphasized this point. Drawing on a trope that is yet another of the myriad parallels between country music song texts and working-class verbal art, Hoppy completed his narrative with a sudden "freezing" of temporality in a lyric image of time as a cycle of perpetual, predictable return. Here, as always, Sam eventually finds himself "eating off the same table" after a woman has ditched him. Hoppy thus marks the historical stability, the textuality, of Sam's eccentric yet sociable personality.[18]

Such tropes of personality are frequently used in talk in combination with pictorial, imitative reported speech. These latter voicing effects are also layered in Hoppy's performance. Sam's textual personality and the represented voices of Hoppy and Sam are, finally, joined with other rhetorical tropes in this episode and cemented by vigorous dialogic affirmation from the others in the room.

Hoppy's artful deployment of the image of Sam's predictably eccentric personality exemplifies the poetics of characterization that constructs the basic idea of the social person in this community. In successful sociability, the tensions between uniqueness and typicality, and between idiosyncrasy and predictability, are foregrounded and resolved in favor of the latter term in each opposition. It is no coincidence, then, that Hoppy's rhetorical tropes simultaneously perform the same kind of socializing magic on his own personal feelings of abandonment by Sam, as well as on those of the others in the room who look to Hoppy for an explanation for Sam's unusual absence. Hoppy's performance demonstrates that self-characterization is also an effective way of claiming and maintaining discursive authority for oneself. He has demonstrated that he himself has an eccentric but sociable and predictable "character."

The Fool in the Mirror

The discursive construction of individuals as imperfect, voiced characters in a social drama is one aspect of working-class cultural subjectivity. The individual is also constructed, in classically Western terms, as the domain of the unknowably interior, experiencing "self." But this "self" is in fact not unknowable, at least in its ideological aspects, because recognition of the "self" is crucial to the interpretation of the "person" in discourse. Such interpretation centers on certain stylized "figures" of narrative and explanation, especially the figure of the "fool." In working-class Texan discourse, and in country music songs, this figure is seen as "split," caught in the grip of a contradiction between inner experience and outer obligation.

Selves and persons are rhetorically and experientially constructed. But they are also distinctively juxtaposed in the dialogic structure of talk, in talk's form (especially pronominal grammar), and in a suite of embodied ways of dancing, sitting, and engaging kinesically. All of these modalities of self-construction and self-reflection are combined in the abject figure of the "fool," and especially in a trope of self-reflexivity and self-alienation that is foundational to the poetics of country music: the "fool in the mirror."

The figure of the self as an effect or "mirror" of social relations has been widely deployed in interpretive anthropology and psychology, as well as in country music. In both academic and popular discourses, the concept of the reflective self implies a set of cultural and ideological accounts of the subject of social action in relation to actors' sense of the locus of bodily control, and to the interiority, coherence, depth, and inscrutability of psychological experience. The self is invoked, again in both discourses, as a trope of immediate experience that otherwise evades objective description (as "subjective knowledge") *and* as an ideological and cultural system for interpreting, socializing, and disciplining inscrutable individual psyches. Like most Western philosophers, working-class Texans are committed individualists.

But the social person and the psychological self are inseparably paired in discourse, for example in the pronominal system. They are copresent in other forms of social action too, for example in the use of culturally appropriate means for expressing emotion (in Texas, thought to emerge from the depths of the experiencing self in moments of high sociability, as discussed in the following chapter). Person and self are likewise inseparable in the *interpretation* of discourse and action, for example in both vernacular and scholarly theories of psychological motivation. Finally, self and person are paired in social experience, in the dialectic interplay between externalized self-presentation and internalized self-representation.

The self as a posited psychological entity with a real phenomenal existence is foundational to a historically Western ethical system enshrined in such diverse cultural forms as anthropological humanism, the Christian idea of the "soul," and working-class individualism. This ethical system logically posits the dignity and isolation of the individual social "person," based on assumptions about the presocial sacredness of the imperfect but perfectible private self.[19] This emphasis on the dignity of selves is a highly salient aspect of rural, working-class sociability and ethics (where it is frequently connected to a political defense of Western culture that has become increasingly explicit in the last decade or so, filtering into everyday discourse as a distrust of "multiculturalism" and "political correctness").

In anthropology, the self is usually, and appropriately, a more elusive category than the person, and the very word invokes (though in anthropology it also often relativizes) a powerful Western ideology of interiority, inscrutability, and individual autonomy (and/or alienation) from ordinary social life.[20] Like the "body" from which it is inseparable, the self is, for anthropologists and blue-collar Texans alike, a mysterious and private text, in search of a sophisticated phenomenology that will reveal its secrets without demystifying its essence.

In working-class Texas, the domain of individual experience and motivation is inscribed with these qualities of interiority, and with very real but permeable boundaries between the private self and the public person. The discourse of imperfection that characterizes the fully realized social person as a voiced, eccentric, textualized individual posits just such a boundary between self and other. This boundary requires an interpretive and sociable effort to cross, and in the process to construct the "feeling" (the subject of the chapter 5) that harmonizes selfhood and personhood in social relations.

This talkative effort to link selves and persons through "feeling" is constitutive of sociability in rural Texas. It takes the form of gossip, narrative, and performative self-presentation, and it is powerfully mediated through country music performance. The characterized person is, as I have shown, continually socially scrutinized. The properly sociable response to such scrutiny is to participate to some extent in one's own characterization, through conversational engagement (as when Jane agreed to Jimmy's revoicing of her profanity) and through the sociable amelioration of conflict (as when Rick, under social pressure, reoriented his angry "testimonial" to assert that his conflict with Hoppy was the basis for a long friendship).

The "ordinary" self is culturally constructed through participation in this sociable effort at characterization, interpretation, and textual inscription. The other's self is ascribed a certain autonomy and inscrutability, and the local ethical mandate is to invest a personified other with a certain degree of intrinsic dignity as an individual and interest as a self. This in turn entails an effort by individuals to resist scrutiny, to retain a degree of mystery and self-possession in the artful sociable presentation of one's self. But the sociable project of coconstructing and co-experiencing "feeling" depends on a continual flow of enticements to engage in interpretive dialogue and public revelations of inner states. And thus complete self-*enclosure* is as impossible a choice as complete self-*disclosure*. To pursue either is to invoke extraordinary and dangerous discursive power, which can either magnify the person or collapse sociability.

This describes the delicate and particular balance between self and other that is the essence of successful personhood in rural Texas. Social encounters are ranked as aesthetic experiences and practical actions on a scale of the intensity of the "feelings" that a successful sociable moment can engender by carefully and performatively revealing the richly complicated interiorities of the engaged "selves." As a system for the production of a class-cultural subjectivity, working-class sociability is particularly adapted to an oral/aural habitus. And, of course, that discursive oral economy is itself in turn a product of this agonistic, emotionally and rhetorically expansive subjectivity. Subjectivity and sociability are intertwined aspects of talk.

Talk is the sociable background against which the rural, working-class subject becomes distinct as an imperfect, reputational text for others, and for the speaking subject herself or himself. Talk is the "mirror" in which actors see themselves as social beings. But, for the "fool," this mirrored vision of the social self is eerily wrong, and this dissonant experience engenders forms of abjection and alienation that take the embodied and communicative forms of a still, ominous silence or a babbling, aggressive verbal excess. At the extreme, fools can pose a serious threat to sociability.

Most often, such lost souls are simply "drunks," a word that conveys a deep spiritual need for alcohol caused by the cataclysmic trauma of "a broken heart," and not so much a biology-based addiction syndrome (the word "alcoholism" is almost never used in local discourse, and biological explanations for pathological drinking are vigorously rejected by many locals). "Hard" drinking is a highly symbolic self-administered affliction. Angry, antisocial "tore-up drunks" are prototypical "fools," "crying in their beer," figures in the grip of an obsession with loss who have shed, with alcohol's sublime, terrible help, their inhibitions against self-disclosure. In the process, they have likely also shed their respect for the hierarchy of social persons and the value of warm sociability. A true "drunk," as Pat the barmaid put it, is "not sure they WANT it out of their system," and what ever "it" is, "it" includes whiskey and it inspires madness:

ROBBIE: John's[21] really
he really is,
he's a really nice guy   ANN: Oh I like him
He'll do anything FOR ya   I like him! Oh yeah!
He might be
just the sweetest guy you wanna KNOW
[uncomfortable pause]
But you get him on that WHISkey
and he's MAD!   ANN: Is that RIGHT?
                                       I've never seen him . . .

Aw, MAAAAAAANNN!
He drank that whole bottle?
Man, he was bitin' BULLets!
But other'n'that I've never seen him raise his voice!

Excessive drunks, fools who cannot hold their tongues or their liquor, are closely attended to in the effort to maintain ordinary sociability. Ray, an Illinois bartender, told me about his bar's "fool," who was also "the town drunk":

RAY: Just like poor old Dick[22]
You talked to Dick today
Dick's a nice guy
He's considered the town DRUNK
This is the only place he can DRINK
and everybody's kicked him out
Most of DICK's problem is other PEOPLE
and like I told the day guy
said
the only difference between Dick and the rest of the drunks is
he ain't got MONEY
and ah
I'VE thrown Dick out on four or FIVE occasions
but I always let him come back
I never let him get to the point where he's gonna cause problems

The marginal figure of the fool is a standard narrative character in bar-room sociability—and in country songs. S/he is either vertiginously excessive or ominously withdrawn (and the two states can alternate rapidly). In either case the fool presents a challenge to sociability. Both reserved and excessive kinds of foolishness bespeak isolation, pain, and reverie. But foolishness also takes the form of a powerful symbol that is ritually central to the maintenance of sociability. The alienated, entranced, "tore-up" fool, in other words, can "meta-affectively signal" (Urban 1988) the fool's desire for renewed sociability, for transformation back into a person. Acting "foolish," put plainly, is a culturally stylized cry for help. If this effort is successful—if the fool can be rescued from abjection by social engagement—sociability is preserved and strengthened.

The fool's expressed desire for rescue is, in turn, intended to affect the fool's audience, especially when "foolishness" is being explicitly performed. Such moments of expressive, even dramatized contradiction—the direct encounter between alienation and sociability—produce a poetic intensification of the self/person dichotomy, through an enactment of a conflict between the two sides of the subject. It is in such moments that the discursive and social figure of the fool comes into existence and is named as such in talk and song.

The fool is a textual device for thinking about self and person, and also a practical tool for cathecting pain and healing injuries to the social body, especially through attention to individual affective crises among members of the local community. In Texas honky-tonks, foolishness can be both an existential condition of a truly troubled mind and a figure of artful verbal sociability— one can "act the fool" as well as "be" a fool. The fool is, in other words, both a real person and a character that can be performed either well or poorly. The two aspects of foolishness ("bein' tore up" and "actin' the fool") may not completely coincide. Sometimes, fools are simply good to think with, and fun to watch.

Some of the most appreciated verbal artists in rural, working-class communities are the local "comedians," as these artful clowns are sometimes called. The best of these seamlessly affect a lighthearted, drunken, and ironic self-presentation, while suggesting evasively with every non sequitur and joke that they are feeling deeply and inconsolably hurt. In performances of artful foolishness, the comedic fool is the principal investigator in a social experiment, a lightning rod for strong feelings, but s/he is not necessarily revealing personal abjection.

Sam, Hoppy's close friend and sidekick through many adventures, is a masterful comedian in this foolish genre.[23] Among his many artful routines, he is particularly skillful at performing one of the most basic and necessary functions of the fool: the restarting of sociable talk when it has ground to a standstill. The essential device for this kind of performance is the clever non sequitur, a humorous or raunchy aphorism launched into an uncomfortable silence and meant to engender laughter and rebuttal. One night, things fell eerily silent; we were all tired, the music hadn't been going all that well, and several people had already left. The whiskey was almost gone, and too much of it in everyone meant that tempers were a little frayed and quick. Sociability was on the verge of failure. Sam stepped into the silent and dangerous breach with a "fool's" aphorism:

SAM: [performatively loud, but spoken as if to himself]
Aaaaaaaaaaaaaaw SHIT!
Are we in the land of plenty . . .
or the land o'SHIT?
[laughter]
[Sam increases volume]
I think we're in the land o'SHIT!
[much laughter]

Sam's comedic foolishness draws frequently on the most powerful discursive device of all in rural, working-class culture, the exploration of the boundaries between speech and song (see chapters 6 and 8). Sam reserves this performative trump card for virtuoso turns of artful clowning, which he usually directs toward shattering a stagnant sociable mood.

Hoppy had been leaning a little heavily on the sweet, sentimental story-songs of which he was the unchallenged local master. The atmosphere was a bit maudlin and reverent as Hoppy finished "The Prisoner's Song," a cloying old Vernon Dalhart tune about the lonely, desperate longing of a prisoner for his beloved, beyond the prison walls:

> *If I had the wings of an angel*
> *Over these prison walls I would fly*
> *I'd fly to the arms of my poor darling*
> *And there I'd be willing to die.*[24]

Sam looked annoyed as the rest of us applauded, and he suddenly punctured the reverent, sentimental mood that lay heavily on the room, refracting the song in a viciously intoned parody:

SAM: HEY!
That's not the version I heard!
[Sing-song, spoken loudly]
If I had the wings of a buzzard
and the balls of a hairy baboon
I'd fly over these prison walls
and I'd
[slightly and deliberately sung]
corn-hole the man in the moon!   ["cornhole" is a euphemism for anal sex]

The room exploded in gasps and laughter, as Sam's vulgar sexual image instantly and totally displaced the saccharine reverence of "The Prisoner's Song." At first, Hoppy was annoyed. He'd worked hard for that mood:

HOPPY: Sam while you're back there mouthin'
gimme a beer . . .
SAM: I'll do this
[half-singing as he gets the beer]

Ain't no use a-duckin'
cuz you're bound to get a fuckin'
in that good old fashioned way!
HOPPY: [to all] Leave it to Sam!
We do a reLIgious song
and he comes up with that!
You knew SHIT was gonna hit the fan and life was gonna be a BITCH
didn't you?
That guy right there
[points to Sam and smiles]
he is coRRUPT
I mean
he is a corrupt little sucker . . .
I LOVE you
you do so good!
MAN we have a GOOD time!

Sam had continued nonchalantly to push the envelope of transgressive vulgarity, singing a raunchy verse of a bawdy ditty ("Put on Them Ol' Gray Panties"), refusing to acknowledge his powerful friend's anger. But Hoppy suddenly saw the talk-leavening delightfulness of this foolishness after all, and his conversion of mood was so total that a powerful moment of dialogic "feeling" between Hoppy and Sam ensued, marked by an emblematic pronominal shift from third person description ("**he** is corrupt") into second person address ("I love **you**"). Sam's high-stakes transgressive foolishness had successfully transformed and intensified sociability.

"Statue of a Fool": Quietness, Stillness, and Foolishness

The didactic and entertaining figure of the comedic fool embodies the excessive energies and obsessions of an unbalanced self. Such a babbling, overflowing, excessive character is, however, only one of the ways of being foolish. Stylized, poetic foolishness creates distance between the performer and the fool s/he performs. The result can be a highly objectified fool, one who is the source of a potentially antisocial silence and stillness, occupying a liminal position on the edge of sociability, standing for so much about the fool's self that cannot be said to others.

This is the completely objectified, frozen fool lionized in Jack Greene's classic song "Statue of a Fool," rerecorded (and a hit) in the early 1990s by Ricky Van Shelton. Both versions were important to my interlocutors and were at one point on the jukebox at Ann's simultaneously. In this song, a slobbering fool declares in an operatic baritone that someone should build a statue of "the world's greatest fool," and "name it after me."[25]

Indeed, a statuesque stillness and silence, or a strange, stiff, and robotic way of dancing by oneself, with eyes closed, head down, and movements precise and contained, can signify foolishness just as much as an excessive, overflowing sociability can. For loud, excessive fools, the "foolish" performance overwhelms and absorbs the abject self. But for quiet, marginalized fools, the obsessively remembering silent and still self absorbs all the exteriorizing energies of personhood. The effect is far more ominous.

This kind of withdrawal from sociability is, in part, a privilege of old age and its amplification of acceptable and delightful eccentricity. As Rusty once told me, "I get a thousand miles away, but an old man's got a right to." And nobody begrudged Old Rusty his performative orneriness, which emerged if he was bothered when he was "a thousand miles away" and he didn't feel like "talkin' shit." There is a structural position in talkative working-class sociability for quiet, quasi-marginal figures who absorb some of the darker and more antisocial energies of "ordinary" talk. It is a necessary role in discourse, a position open to old men and strangers, and those who are marginal for other reasons too.

Quiet Paul fit both requirements, as the elder statesman of the minority of Mexican Americans who were patrons at Ann's.[26] Paul, like a few of Ann's other patrons, had been a regular since back in the "Little Bottle" days. An even-tempered, exceedingly soft-spoken man, Paul was regularly asked to break up and settle fights, to listen to private troubles, and to provide verification for the narrative claims of others.[27] Everybody knew that Paul was a keen observer of, if not a loud participant in, the bar's public sociability. Paul was spoken of in glowing terms when he was not around, and shown great respect when he was. His absence could put a strain on sociability, so necessary was his silent presence. Whenever rounds of beer were bought within smaller conversational circles, Paul would often be included in the round whether or not he was in the conversation, and by the end of the night he'd have so many drinks stored up "in the hole" (that is, held by Ann in the cooler) that he'd have a head start on the following day.

As a steadily employed man, Paul was a quiet but important donor in bar-centered charities and benefits, and he always volunteered his labor (and thereby volunteered the other Hispanic men who patronized the bar, all of whom looked to Paul as a leader) for the difficult, time-consuming task of running the barbecue and cooking enormous pieces of meat during benefits and other large-scale bar events. As the driver of a food truck, Paul occasionally showed up with huge boxes and bags of food that had passed its freshness date but which, if it survived a few hours of sitting in the bar, often went to feed one of Ann's quiet "charity cases."

But Paul's high level of social involvement was paired with an affect of deep introspection, a stillness, quietness, and precision of movement that announced through Paul's soulful eyes a carefully guarded and slightly but ominously loss-ridden self. His unique social identity was foregrounded in the casual expression often used to refer to him: "Paul, y'know, QUIet Paul?"

Paul's soft presence, with its dignity and guarded sadness, was an anchor for sociability. When even the most skillful talkers failed to have something to say, when a heavy pause descended on the place, people would turn to Paul for a stylized, friendly, sociable dialogue, itself practically a symbol for talk's form rather than a substantive exchange. Sometimes this was no more than a few words about the weather, or somebody asking Paul how to say something in Spanish. But what such exchanges modeled was a kind of emergency sociability, reduced to its barest dialogic skeleton. One afternoon, for example, a glum silence fell at Ann's, and although we'd all been sitting there for an hour, Doc looked to Paul as if he had just walked in and asked loudly, so that all could hear him:[28]

DOC: [loudly] "PAUL! HOW'S IT GOIN'?"

The atmosphere was charged with the air of an experiment in progress as Paul replied, slowly and quietly:

PAUL: Pretty goooood . . .
DOC: Is that Ford pickup still runnin'?
PAUL: Yup . . .
DOC: You got to be the LUCKiest guy I know
PAUL: Naw, not so lucky [laughs]
DOC: It's LUCKy that's still running
[to everyone at the bar]

God I got to BITCH at you guys
I went down to buy a CARburetor kit
for a TWO barrel Ford carburetor . . .
You know what list PRICE is on that thing?
Seven-ty-four dol-lars!
RICHARD: a KIT?
DOC: Yes sir . . .
RICHARD: I bought a alternator Tuesday
for her car   [her = his girlfriend]
DOC: *God-DAMN!*
RICHARD: Know how much a alternator for her car was?
Sixty-five dollars . . .
DOC: *Wow . . .*
RICHARD: Sixty-five dollars, man

Doc and Richard and the others kept on talking about the price of car parts for a long time after this, but the whole conversation would not have been restarted without Paul's artfully minimal sociable response to Doc's plea for engagement. Doc knew to turn to Paul for this function, and Paul obliged, reenergizing talk by reducing it to its bare minimum for a few moments.

However, despite the surface minimalism of his contributions to public discourse, Paul was an especially engaged private talker. He pursued serious topics in one-on-one, close-up conversations. Paul talked most often to the other Mexican American men who patronized the bar, and to Miss Ann and a succession of barmaids to whom Paul represented a sensitive listener who stood apart from the emotional (and sexual) politics of the rest of the talkers. Paul occupied a reserved seat at the end of the bar closest to the cash register, near where Miss Ann or the barmaid would sit. The bend in the L-shaped bar even set him off a little from the others spatially, creating a confidential space where the barmaid or someone standing and talking to Paul would be slightly removed from the more polyphonic and permeable sociability of the others at the bar—and where a few quiet words would not easily be overheard by others.

When I would sit next to Paul at the bar, I would sometimes be privy to these asides. Indeed, I also fit the bill as a good listener in the early days of my fieldwork—I was there, after all, to listen. I was still marginal to the emotional politics of the place, and not as yet enmeshed in conflicting loyalties and relationships. There was an afternoon, for example, when Pat needed to get something off her chest. But Paul, her usual confidant in such situations, had not yet arrived from work. José, as he walked into the bar, called attention to Paul's absence with a query:

JOSÉ: [to Pat] Paul been around?
PAT: [exasperated, loudly]
I wasn't here last night, José
I got mad last night and left
They SAID he was here last night
I went and bought me a twelve pack
and got drunk

The reminder that Paul wasn't in his usual position seemed to annoy Pat, who looked like she really wished Paul would show up. Her bearing and her tone suggested that she needed to talk about something serious, while the other men told fishing stories and dirty jokes, and as Lynn Anderson's mournful last-goodbye song "Then Go" was wailing on the jukebox. José took up a cautious, generic tone, sensing the foolish heat in Pat's tore-up declaration and edging away from becoming involved in her mood:

JOSÉ: Long as you get it out of your system . . .

Pat is a fine barroom speaker and verbal artist, which is unsurprising since the sharp comeback is a skill that is virtually required of barmaids. She had more in mind than José's generic dismissal of her complicated mood with a punned cliché about alcohol's pharmaceutical effect and its similarity to a bad emotional feeling that gets "in your system." She wanted to *talk*, and she announced this with a surreally poetic crystallization of the sublime trope of the "tore-up fool," muttered as a cryptic, introspective aside, but meant to be overheard:

PAT: I'm trying to decide whether I WANT it out of my system or not . . .

Pat had revealed a guarded side of her self, as a challenge to sociability meant to invite some healing attention. But the bar chatter continued all around us. José, who is a light-hearted man, retreated deftly to talk to someone else, and Paul wasn't there. Pat and I had already been talking rather formally for a few days, and now, aware that I had observed her intensity of feeling, she came over to me at the end of the bar and spoke quietly and seriously.

We talked for several minutes about relationships and why they went wrong, both of us speaking from our own experience and with care and concern for one another. For the moment, I took Quiet Paul's place for Pat.

This self-disclosing conversation happened on the shady, introspective edge of barroom sociability, in that enigmatic and detached zone where loss and grief doubled back on self-fascination with the almost pleasurable undertone of real pain. Pat shifted suddenly, through a flash of poetic brilliance, from her front-stage person (her public role as a feisty, back-talking, hard-partying barmaid) to her backstage self, so quietly intense and "tore up."

Pat thus took a masterful, subtle turn through the trope of the fool in order to restore her sociable balance. And she drew on an arsenal of sad country songs for her models. The fool of country songs might be the heartbroke, tore-up slob of Lefty Frizzell's much-loved "I Never Go Around Mirrors," a man poetically spinning through a vertiginous space of self-despisal, avoiding his own reflection at all costs. This fool "can't stand to see a good man go to waste," a man who "never combs his hair or shaves his face."[29] But like Pat, on the surface this fool is cooly and bemusedly narrating another's abjection.

Frizzell then delivers a devastating punchline in which this "other" becomes the narrator's reflected self, and the fool in the mirror comes vividly to life: "That's why I never go around mirrors/I can't stand to see me without you by my side." The same trope reappears as a drunken cowgirl poet sitting off by herself, angrily accusing her mirrored self of foolishness by stringing together the titles of George Jones songs as an interiorized voice, in Becky Hobbs's "Jones on the Jukebox." The song opens with the image of a "fool in the mirror, looking back across the bar." This fool discovers the polysemy of "reflection" which joins self-objectification and thoughtful interiority as she continues with the pun "reflections of a woman whose world just fell apart."[30]

"Bartender's Blues": Pronominal Rhetorics of the Split Subject

I was talking, early one evening, to Ray, the owner and bartender at the Pub & Grub. It was a bitter late fall day in Parkville. The Illinois town of 2,500 sat in a cluster of closed-down coal mines and landfills and factories, surrounded by dead flat corn and soybean fields stretching off into the horizon. Darkness seemed to have set in at about 3 P.M., making the cold somehow more intolerable, and the bar that much more inviting.

It wasn't long before Ray started telling me about the "hard times on the area." That's how everybody seemed to put it, as if the bottom dropping out of the local economy was just like the dark clouds that also "came up on ya" and tended to accompany these early, brittle evenings in late November. Ray had leased the bar with every penny of his contract buyout offer from his downsized job as an engineer on the Missouri and Pacific line, after taking early retirement in his fifties. Working with his sons, he had rebuilt the former Lion's Club lodge room at the end of Main Street near the switching yards. Ray was proud of the place. And now business was steady on weekends. But it wasn't so good the other nights, and the best-avoided truth was that it wasn't getting any better. Like so many others in town, Ray was worried:

RAY: Oh there's some HARD times, man
Yeah the area is real bad
Tonight's Friday night
We got a pretty good crowd
We had a big factory over in Tuscola shut down
The COAL mine's shut down
And it just hurt real bad here
Real bad
'Cause a lot of people WORKED there . . .
And then the RAILroad industry
which is . . .
y'know this is a railroad TOWN
THIS is a railroad TOWN
THEY'RE not doin' like they did
[suddenly urgent]
and people are kinda SCARED right now
And it SHOWS!
You can really TELL it in THIS business!

Ray's comments reflected the gloominess of the times and the season. But he also cultivated a necessary but earnest optimism for the circle of working-class friends and relations who were his customers and his community, and he struggled to preserve his business, which was this community's key public institution. He hoped, with his small dark barroom and the homey restaurant, to offer a compromise between the more libidinous, dangerous bars out on the county road, spaces for hardened, bitter young men, and the plush, staid bars like the place down the street, where older people and folks with a little money might go. These kinds of places split people up, Ray thought, and that wasn't a good thing:

RAY: Well, people tell me they come in here
and, especially the young guys
They come in here
They can
DRINK beer
PLAY pool
Don't have to worry bout anybody HASsling 'em, y'know
They like to be BY themselves
PLAYin' by themselves
and ah . . .
I ain't gonna mention no names
but one of 'em's had a lot of trouble
Gotta a lot of guys tryin' to PUSH him
They like to come here cuz they don't HAVE to
And the guys next door . . .
You got more of a MONEY crowd . . .

Ray's idea, as the father of several sons of an age to find trouble in bars, was that a place with a bar, a restaurant, live music, and a pool room would keep families closer together, if in separate spaces, on Saturday nights and would pay his bills in the process. He was proud that his place of business, right on this ghostly Main Street, drew the young men in Harley shirts and feed caps who came in to shoot pool with their girlfriends. But it also drew blue-collar families out for Saturday dinners and then maybe a dance or two on the little patch of linoleum in front of the tiny stage where local singers like Becky Rollings, who also worked as a cook at the restaurant, performed country songs to taped accompaniments.

It was a bit of a balancing act to keep the families and the drinkers peacefully together, but Ray had a knack for controlling the drunks and the fights and the desperation that welled up after a few too many at the end of the work week. Like most working-class bartenders, Ray was an expert on fools. He had to be. The danger of foolishness is its power to disrupt talk, its power to engender strong feelings of anger, and an intense subjective social detachment in which the loss-obsessed self overcomes the sociable person in a sudden heavy silence or a flurry of crazy transgressive words. Subtle harmonies connect specific affects that slink about in this liminal darkness: resentment, fear, outrage, mistrust, ennui, pain, heartbreak, rejection, loss, dread, frustration, regret, "orneriness," gloominess, annoyance, betrayal, shame, guilt, concession, dreaminess, obsession, or surrender. If you feel many of these things at one time, people say you're feeling "tore up." And if you're "tore up," you're in danger of "actin' the fool."

Ordinary sociable talk struggles constantly to contain these antisocial feelings. They are sought out and defused in jokes and carefully controlled in small talk. Such discursive strategies pay close attention to the repair of damaged personhood, and to the maintenance of reputation and dignity. But these strategies aim deeper thereby, when they seek to repair a damaged, fragmented, foolish self, imagined in all its dense, interiorized, and inscrutable Western glory. Such strategies seek to reconnect the person and the self, and to reveal the ways this hidden self motivates the social actions of persons.

Self and person are constantly being taken apart and realigned in discourse, through subtle uses of the pronoun system and poetic metaphors and the indirection of gossip and the affective gestalts of country songs. These tools enable talkers, confronting a fool, to pay close attention to producing the positive intersubjective "feelings" people come to expect from their friends in a rural beer joint. These tools are used to repair social ruptures with the strong feelings engendered by dialogic sociability.

Every good working-class bartender carries these tools. Bartenders practice a kind of semiotic tinkering with the balance of self and person. Mythically this power is said to destroy its bearer's own balance, like the "tore up" bartender in George Jones's song "Bartender's Blues," who has become the very kind of alienated fool he despises, hating his job even as he lights the cigarettes and laughs at the jokes of his customers while watching them "fall down on [their] knees."[31]

Ray cultivated these verbal arts himself when there was social work to be done. As he continued talking about those "hard times on us," one of the community's many unemployed young men came in with an icy blast from the front door. He shook the cold off and sat down at the bar next to me, in front of Ray. Ray's attention went to the new arrival as he pulled a draft for him:

RAY: [to patron] Your buddy was in here a while ago . . .
PATRON: Huh?
RAY: The [name omitted] kid?

PATRON: Oh YEAH

RAY: Yeah

PATRON: Well I hope he stays away from me

RAY: Well, like I told him . . .

PATRON: Well, you know what I mean

I'm not gonna start nothin'

I don't even want to talk to him

RAY: Well, he mentioned your name

PATRON: He did WHAT?

RAY: He mentioned your name

I said

"I'm'onna tell you WHAT"

I said

"If he happens to come IN here"

I said

"there's not gonna be any trouble EIther"

PATRON: I'm not gonna say nothin'

RAY: Yeah

PATRON: I tell you what

He DOES get under my skin

RAY: I can SEE . . .

He gets under mine.

In this conversation, the cost of fractured sociability is made clear. Anger means an absence of talk, the spread of misinformation and hot words, and with young men in particular, it means the threat of physical confrontation and serious, spreading disharmony. Such dissonance is inimical to the spirit of feelingful sociability that makes a working-class bar popular, pleasant, and profitable.

Ray's rhetorical project here is to get the patron to commit himself to the cessation of anger, to move beyond the patron's surface assurances that he is not bothered, when he clearly is. But the patron seems eager to drop the subject, and he attempts to keep a distance between Ray and himself. He tries to achieve a minimal, strictly formal level of dialogue necessary for closure with his first use of a second-person address in a question meant to affirm his sincere lack of serious "self" disturbance: "**You** know what I mean? I'm not gonna start nothin'."

Ray is not convinced that resolution is so simple. He wants the patron to show more of his injured self. Social repair depends on discovering and manipulating damaged selves and depends on the fool's self-revelation. Ray places his patron's person very much at stake when he reveals that the absent antagonist has "mentioned [the patron's] name." Names are, after all, the essential markers of social personhood. But selves are also in contest here. Ray's challenge to the patron's person reveals an interiorized and embodied zone of anger and bad feeling, which emerges into discourse through the patron's expression of anxious disbelief: "He did WHAT?"

It is this suddenly revealed anger that Ray must ameliorate by drawing it out in talk. Even though the patron has signaled that he would rather drop the subject, Ray goads him with the image of his social person in an opponent's hands. He repeats himself: "he mentioned your name." Ray has opened a discursive space for the patron to display his unguarded self, but he opens the door to that space slowly. He continues with a fragment of speech styled as direct discourse, in which Ray represents himself as using the full authority of his social person against the excessively tore-up self of the patron's antagonist:

RAY: He mentioned your name
I said
"*I'm'onna tell you* WHAT"
I said
"*If he happens to come* IN *here*"
I said
"*there's not gonna be any trouble* EIther!"

Through Ray's dramatic recreation of an agonistic engagement, in which dangerous negative feelings are acknowledged and aired at a poetically objectified distance, the patron is encouraged to reveal his self. But the patron resists, responding at first with a minimal, noncommittal promise to avoid a fight, this time by avoiding any talk where feelings might come out: "I'm not gonna say nothin'."

The patron assures Ray that he has no intentions of drawing out the conflict with his antagonist. But then, almost as an afterthought, he adds "I tell you what, he DOES get under MY skin." Ray instantly recognizes the patron's dialogic modulation of the tone of this conversation. The patron is offering a glimpse at his interiorized self to Ray as if to prove that his balance and equanimity has been restored. The patron uses a second-person pronoun with a verb of saying (as a performative metadiscursive truth-marker, i.e., "I tell you what") to prepare Ray for his pronouncement of a metaphorically embodied and interiorized private state. This is the hidden zone of experience the patron lays bare and invites Ray to occupy intersubjectively, with an everyday meta-phor that locates the deep, hidden self "under **my** skin."

The patron signals, through a self-revealing glimpse "under [his] skin," that he is offering to rise above the conflict. Ray cements this worked-for result by sharing a similarly interiorized feeling back with his patron. He uses a first-person pronoun to convey his own self, which normally remains guarded underneath his identity as a morally and pragmatically authoritative social person.[32] "I can SEE," Ray says, "He gets under MINE."

With this visual literalization of the patron's metaphor, suggesting he can "see" the patron's interior state, he activates the canonical image of the self as an interiorized entity, which can nevertheless be "seen" in social dialogue, and interpreted and healed in discourse. Such healing depends on a fluent ability to assess and control the pronouns and metaphors of self and person, and the feelings of anger and sociability.

Ray's use of a nonformulaic "I" in "I can see" differs from his previous uses of "I" in formulaic expressions with verbs of saying or in direct, voiced dis-course ("I tell you what . . ."). The nonformulaic "I" is Ray's "real" self speak-ing. Ray has exposed his self to contextualize his conduct as a person. Con-trolling this combination of semiotic identities is an important dimension of performance, creativity, and discursive authority in working-class communi-ties.[33]

This usage's self-revelatory sense contrasts with Roy's other uses of "I" in this example. His earlier uses of first-person pronominal forms are all attached formulaically to verbs of saying that are used to introduce and focus the illo-cutionary force of the segments of objectified, voiced reported speech they introduce ("Like I told him," "I said"). Indeed, in one case, the formulaic use of "I said" is used to introduce an embedded, voiced, and reported variant of this same formula:

RAY: And I said
"I'm 'onna tell you what . . ."

Here Ray embeds one forceful and even antagonistic variant of the reporting construction ("I + [verb of saying]") within another, less strongly assertive version of this same performative construction. "I'm [g]onna tell you what" gains insistence from its explicit use of the second-person indirect object — "you"—which is often prosodically stressed and/or kinesically marked, for example, by a finger to the chest or widened eyes. But this strong usage is introduced with the default neutral form for reporting without strong self-commitment or marked disagreement: "[And] I said . . ."

This speech-reporting formula (with its many variants) is a generic trope of working-class narrative performance. Its conventionality subtly indexes an objectified person rather than an interiorized self as a referent for the "I" which speaks it (Urban 1989). The conventionality of "I say [to you]" (and its variants, such as "I said," "I'm gonna tell you," "Like I said," etc.) backgrounds the self of the speaker as it dramatizes the speaker's person. This is, at least in part, because the use of first-person pronouns in constructions with verbs of saying is enmeshed in discourse functions that focus on the dialogic and performative structure, that is, the *intersubjective* structure, of sociable talk rather than starkly indexing or diffusely symbolizing the interiorized "self" of the speaker.[34]

Along with their poetic configuration with verbs of saying and expressions of self-revelation, the pronouns of self and person are elevated to constitutive tropes in country music's thematization of the experience of foolishness, in which the self and the person are thrown out of balance. In these depictions of self/person conflict, we encounter the classic country music image of the "tore up fool" as a *split* subject, the "fool in the mirror." The self's "I" gazes obsessively at the person's "me," trying to discern some pronominal logic that might bind the two together into a coherent whole. Such a split between an extroverted public figure and the privately "tore up fool" this masks is re-created in the pronominal rhetoric of sociable self-narration, as in Randy Meyer's "When I'm with Me":

> *When I'm with me I go out to all the barrooms*
> *Chase all the women, I stay out til one or two*
> *When I'm with you I'm a different kind of person*
> *I change so much, you won't know me when I'm through*

This song gains extra power among those who grasp its autobiographical quality. Hoppy had just sung "When I'm with Me" for Dennis, a musician visiting Texas from Tennessee, and Dennis showed his enthusiasm for the song, which he was hearing for the first time:

DENNIS: Hey! I've LIVEd that song!
HOPPY: We ALL have!
But RANdy's lived it TWICE!

The subtle pun may not have been intentional, but "When I'm with Me" *is* about living "twice," and twice as hard, as a subject *and* as an object of aesthetic contemplation. Drawing on the rhetorical device of juxtaposing subjective and objective pronouns — "I" and "me" — Meyer's song uses one of country music's most exemplary grammatical tropes, one that appears in songs like George Strait's "If I Know Me" and Lefty Frizzell's "I Never Go Around Mirrors," which links startling reflexive play with pronouns of self and person to the similar objectification of the subject in the figure of the "fool in the mirror." Frizzell's mirror-gazing "fool" (who is the song's the protagonist) declares, for example: "I can't stand to see me without you by my side."

Such obsessive self-objectification is in turn a dominant trope of sociability when talk concerns itself with the social meshing of self and person. The rhetoric of pronouns extends from songs into speech, for example, in the strongest expression of agreement that can be offered in Texas rural, working-class talk: the forcefully articulated, drawn-out pronouncement "myyy-SELF!" This one-word sentence is ubiquitously used as a rejoinder to expressions of "liking" to do something, either positive ("I like to jitterbug") or, more rarely, negative ("I wouldn't like to be the one to tell her"). "Myyy-SELF" is a mark of desire for closure with full agreement:[35]

SAMMY: But there is rock   [music]
They PLAY rock in country   [music performances]
But you keep it in perspective
with the country music
it'll work
CINDY: Yeah cuz I like to jitterbug
ANN: Myyy — SELF!

"Myyy-SELF" is a signifier of maximal agreement. It commits the objectified "self" of the speaker to the point being agreed with, achieving conversational closure with an image of the revelation of the — "my" — self. This mutual revelation is essential to the notion of "feeling" I discuss in the next chapter. What is more, this objectification of the self appears not only as a logic of pronominal usage but as a whole embodied and performative suite of self-objectifying tropes commanded by "tore up fools" and other such split subjects.

"The Bitch about Country Music": Split Subjectivity as Lived Experience

I was talking with Jim, a middle-aged man who often sat by himself at a table near the jukebox, repeatedly playing the same few Patsy Cline record-ings—"Crazy," "She's Got You," and "Sweet Dreams"—as he nursed his after-work beer:

JIM: If anybody told me that they were gonna stop country music
tomorrow
I'd possibly commit suicide
[laughs]
I really would
If there was not gonna be any other music on the radio
Shit . . .
I'd probably leave this world tomorrow
You can relate to this shit
At least I can anyway
Like if you're gettin' over a heartbreak or somethin' like that
it might tear you up, just listenin' to the songs . . .
AF: But that's the point, isn't it?
JIM: Yeah, but I mean, a lot of people don't want to get tore up
And that's a lot of the BITCH about country music
God do you want to cry in your beer?
No!
Hell, the cryin' in the beer part is not part of it

Country, despite its apparently monochromatic pathos-ridden "sad songs" and manic rave-ups, is emotionally complicated music to create, perform, and interpret. At one extreme, the discursive subject, who is both the subject of the country song narrative and a "real" person like Jim who "relates" to such narratives, is immersed in the experience of loss, pain, misery, and heart-break. Such feelings are represented as antisocial, dangerous, obsessive, and "crazy" in country music songs and by working-class listeners. They mark a disengagement with ordinary modes of sociability and a descent into abject self-immolation (Fox 2004a; K. Stewart 1993).

At the other extreme, the discursive subject in country music achieves a reflexive distance from these same feelings. This subject watches, narrating its obsessive, fixated doppelgänger with amusement, as if it were that fool's reflection in a distorting mirror. By means of this talkative, sociable mode of attention, the dangerous and antisocial "tore up" figure "crying in his (or her) beer" is resocialized. A potentially disruptive (indeed, as Tim remarks, even "suicidal") feeling of abjection (being "tore-up") is brought within the interpretive boundaries of "ordinary" talk, and a frightening withdrawal from sociability is converted into something good to talk about.

Maria often sat without talking to anybody at the bar for hours on end, nursing her beer, smoking dreamily, and intermittently singing along with the jukebox for a line or two.[36] Talking to Maria over the course of many nights, I learned that she was obsessed with memories of her once-happy marriage, which had ended several years before in a bitter divorce and left her in poverty with an adolescent son to raise on an income she earned by sewing garments at a local factory. Our talk centered on the lyrics to sad country songs and on phrases from those songs that she would repeat over and over as touchstones for reflection, expressing a loss of words, and the inadequacy of talk to her deeply "tore up" condition.

The song that most transfixed Maria was Alan Jackson's "Here in The Real World," a slow, sad, ironic song that dwells on the way "the boy don't always get the girl/here in the real world," via an obsessive reflection on the tropes of cinematic happy endings. The song deeply moved Maria, who played it repeatedly on the jukebox. Night after night she would stare into her cigarette's smoke-swirls as Jackson quietly and poignantly lamented that "here in the real world, it's not that easy at all," as he compared the "real tears that fall" to the world of movies where "cowboys don't cry."[37]

When I asked Maria why she was so moved by this song, she told me that the song expressed perfectly the way she had been feeling since her divorce. "That's how it is," she said with long sad pauses, "the dream just ended, I guess . . . the dream just fell apart . . . it just fell apart."

She told me the details in bits and pieces. She had grown up speaking only Spanish and had never left the central Texas area where she was raised in a conservative Tejano family until she was married. Her husband, a more assimilated Mexican American, had insisted that they move to Lockhart, to be near his family. When their son was born, he insisted as well that they speak only English at home, to ensure that the son would become a fluent English speaker. When her husband had left Maria and her son six years previously, she found herself unable to speak her native Spanish at home with her son, who didn't understand it, and she gradually withdrew from speaking it outside as well, except on trips back to her hometown.

Though we talked in English without difficulty, she claimed to be a poor English speaker and blamed her sense of isolation on this as well as on depression over her divorce and her lack of communication with her son. She had been immersed in this silent, abject domain of lost language and intense remembering for six years and had, she said, to "convince herself to come out" to beer joints, because she wasn't really "a party girl." Her withdrawn silence made this seem like a serious understatement to the others in the bar, who observed her isolation with worry and trepidation and treated Maria with gentle caution.

When she talked, it sometimes seemed as if she were watching herself in the fool's mirror. She was eerily amused and fascinated by her own experience of loss. Repeating the questions I posed to her back to me, she asked me several times why Alan Jackson's "Here in The Real World" had the effect on her that it did. I would throw the question back again, and she would repeat the phrase "the dream just fell apart" as if it were a verbal touchstone, deconstructing the cliché and getting distance from the feelings it signified, with its specification of a collapsed self.

Maria was in that zone Jim had ominously warned me about: she was "tore up." Like Maria, Jim was particularly fascinated by the power of songs to focus and intensify feelings of intense loss, and for Jim it had been Patsy Cline, the most esteemed of all female country singers, who carried this eerie ability in her velvety, controlled voice, which ironically sang so often of the loss of emotional control and of the raw, "crazy" depths of heartbreak:

JIM: It's the idea that I can pick . . .
out a certain song
like Patsy Cline's songs, for example
I could listen to her every day
It reminds me a lot of **her**
maybe

but there's nothin' to CRY about
and . . .
they'll never REPLACE her . . .
and she's on
DAMN near
every jukebox
that I've ever been in contact with
at least one or two of her songs
is always on there

Jim allows a potent pronominal ambiguity to reveal the tension between his earlier argument that "cryin in your beer" is "not part of it," and his implication of the depth of feeling country music mediates. The "her" of this fragment refers ambigously either to Patsy Cline or to Jim's ex-wife, whom he had been discussing in relation to the idea of being "tore up" and "crying in your beer" as aspects of the "ordinary" experience of "D-I-V-O-R-C-E," as he put it, quoting Tammy Wynette's performance of Bobby Braddock's classic song.

Jim's reference to Patsy Cline is exact. His careful consideration of being musically "tore up," and Maria's somber obsessive self-objectification, both converge on the image of the fool who narrates Cline's classic "I Fall to Pieces." The image (the narrator "fall[s] to pieces" each time she hears her lost lover's name) conveys the literalness of "split" subjectivity and the idea of being "tore up."[38]

Patsy Cline's poetic exploration of the image of the puppetlike, "broke-down" and "tore-up" fool makes her work a canonical textual account of deep loss for working-class country fans. Her voice, and these songs, have a shrinelike sanctity. Patsy Cline stands, "out the country," for the whole affective disposition occupied, in distinct ways, by "tore-up" fools. Cline's songs calmly narrate their protagonists' depths of anguish (e.g., "Crazy" and "I Fall to Pieces"); they lovingly fondle "mem'ries" of long-gone love (e.g., She's Got You"); they obsessively return to past moments (e.g., "Sweet Dreams (of You)"); and they project dreamlike future encounters (e.g., "Walking after Midnight"). Clines's voice accomplishes an extensive aestheticization of feeling "tore up" and inspires a careful attention to the unbearable loss she sang of.

Patsy Cline remains the preeminent female country singer for working-class (indeed, most) fans, decades after her tragic early death. Her work both mastered and also subtly feminized a male-dominated affective trope (K. Stewart 1993). This lonely figure of the abject, "heartbroke tore-up fool" walks through many of the most canonical country songs in Texas beer joints, "falling to pieces" while narrating his or her own misery in a detached, disengaged monotone, in a visually claustrophobic and aurally narrowed ambitus of feeling. George Jones cuts this figure, for example, in "She Thinks I Still Care," as he careens through the bars — and his entire, enormous vocal range — insisting that even though he still talks about his ex-lover, mentions her name, and calls her phone number by mistake, she's crazy to think that he "still cares."[39]

After moving through an ever more unlikely sequence of obsessive nostalgic actions, including haunting "the same old places/where the memory of her lingers everywhere," Jones is suddenly unable to keep up his facade of cool, poised disdain, and like the "fool" he sings of, he explodes in excessive display, as his voice suddenly goes wildly swooping over its full range while he reasons that she must think he "still cares" because he "saw her, and then went all to pieces."

Jones packs two identities into the "I" of this song. One is falling "all to pieces," like Patsy Cline's "crazy" and "tore up" sung self, and the other, again like Patsy's sweet-voiced narrator, coolly and compellingly reflecting on the whole scene, the "I" that can say "she thinks I still care," wavering between objectifying poetic mastery of the moment and the abject subjectivity of the fool, caught in the grip of a memory. (As Patsy Cline sings, "I've got your memory, or . . . has it got me?"). Once again, the split subject emerges in a juxtaposition of poetically resonant pronouns.

This split between narrating and narrated self is also vividly foregrounded in Merle Haggard's somber "Today, I Started Loving You Again." This song, like "She Thinks I Still Care," is a canonical barroom standard. But here, the rhetoric of pronouns is even more subtle, revealing the unstable structure of the "I" discussed above. Haggard begins by intoning: "Today I . . ." He then pauses before he sings the rest of the sentence: ". . . started loving you, again." He reports being "right back" where he'd "always been," even though he thought he was finally over his pain. On the last line of the refrain, he lightly summarizes the whole situation: "Today . . ." (and here he pauses again) ". . . I started loving you again."[40]

Haggard, too, masterfully deploys a subtle prosodic manipulation of the pronoun "I" in order to call attention to the split, "tore-up" subject, and to emphasize the depth and intensity of the word "today." Like "anymore," this use of "today" is a lexical trope of temporal displacement. Both figures emblematically posit a past that weighs heavily on the mind in the present.

It is one of the most subtle and important marks of a "REAL country singer" that he or she has mastered the subtle rhythmic articulation that makes "Today, I Started Loving You Again" work for many working-class listeners.[41] The *first* "I" is run together with "today" in a single upward-moving melodic phrase, followed by a significant pause before the clause is completed. The final "I," at the end of the refrain, comes after a pause following "today," and it is joined in one melodic phrase to "started." Haggard's phrasing iconically plays with two ways of positing the narrating "I" of this anguished song. When the pronoun is run together with "today," the construction emphasizes the backwards-looking, backsliding obsession ensconced in the temporal trope of "today," an explosion of memory in which the self's "I" is swallowed up in the past, and in which each future-oriented action loops back in an impossibly expansive "now." The entire phrase, the "Today-I," thus becomes the agent of the verb "started." When, at the end, the pronoun is articulated distinctly as part of a separate verb phrase following a long pause after "today," Haggard artfully models the compulsively narrating self's "I" as a detached agent of its own poetic misery: the fool in the mirror.

Where the Mem'ry of Her Lingers Everywhere

Maria occupied the far dangerous extreme of "foolishness," refusing to re-engage socially, lost in her own reverie of deep sadness and loss. She came to the bar most nights for several months, but talked very little unless Ann or Paul or I made an effort to draw her out. She gave people an uneasy feeling, and she was the subject of much anxious gossip. Such obsessive self-fixated abjection had led in dangerous directions for so many people, and it was frightening to watch in another, especially an attractive young mother.

I was away from Ann's for several months after the period in which I came to know Maria. While I was gone, she became romantically involved with one of the other Hispanic men who hung out at Ann's—lighthearted José—but still she remained darkly, quietly "tore up," people later said. And she kept playing that jukebox song, "Here in the Real World." I had been back for a few weeks before I thought to ask if Maria was still coming around. In all those weeks, nobody had mentioned her name or spoken of the day, during my absence, when she had walked out of the bar and onto the middle of the state highway out front, where she was run over and killed by a truck. It could have been an accident, but nobody believed that. Not long after that, Alan Jackson's "Here in the Real World" was gone from the jukebox. Some songs are just too dangerous.

"Feeling" and "Relating"

Speech, Song, Story, and Emotion

Sensations that are not in some way colored by feeling

have no existence in reality. — Victor Zuckerkandl,

Sound and Symbol

If You Have to Ask:
On the Cultural Construction of Aesthetic Categories

This chapter explores the social semantics of the words "feeling" and "relating," which are the most pervasive terms of sociomusical evaluation in Texas working-class culture. I describe the complex but categorical and comprehensive structure of meanings to which the term "feeling" refers in the context of local aesthetic ideology. I take as a premise here that lexical semantics — the formal analysis of the meaning of words — can reveal repositories of cultural knowledge and models for social action. In particular, I follow a long tradition in the anthropology of aesthetic systems and of religion, by focusing on a powerful cultural/verbal master trope for emotional depth, rightness, and intensity.[1]

Summarizing lexical tropes, such as "feeling," connects sensory experience, embodied attitudes, and rational thought to the domain of social relations. Above all, such tropes permeate affective dispositions that organize encounters between social actors, shaping what it "feels like" to be a particular person in relationship to others. "Feelingful" qualities shape the texture and tone of

interactions in ways that become generic and institutionalized, especially in
contexts — like a Texas honky-tonk — where the *form* of interactions is ritually
elaborated and texted. These dispositions constitute a context for elementary
social obligations and expectations. "Feeling" is thus essential to "sociability,"
a term I use to capture the qualities of improvisation, compelling necessity,
and mutuality that define an ideal for social relations in the rural, working-
class vision of "ordinariness." "Feeling" is both the goal of sociability and its
very basis.

Feeling and Relating

One quiet night, Ann, Sonny, Shirley, and I were talking at the bar, and our
talk drifted predictably toward country music, and music in general. Ann
observed that many of the musicians who hung around her bar singing and
playing guitars late into the night were not particularly masterful performers:

ANN: So that's why I really admire these guys that come in here and play
just cuz they like to sit around and play
AF: I think that . . .
One of the reasons I'm here,
One of the reasons I'm doing what I'm doing
I agree with you to a point that musicians are important
but I think they get too much credit . . .
They've gotten a whole lot of credit . . .
for making the music
But in my opinion it's the people that listen to them . . .
ANN: That's right
that make them money . . .
AF: Not only money but
through a whole system of understanding that tells them what to do
and gives them a way of expressing themselves
They didn't make that up
The people that listen to them
made up the words to those songs, really
In the sense that for those songs to work
people have to understand the feelings in them . . .
In that sense the songs are coming FROM the audience

ANN: [animatedly] The musician has to *feeeeel*
what other people feel
or he couldn't put those in words
He couldn't put those words down unless he felt things
that maybe we don't feel

AF: No, I don't think so   SONNY: Oh yeah, you have to
                                            feel it

I think we feel 'em
He just spends his life
learning how to put that into a form that you can . . .

ANN: But he can take what I FEEL
what he might see me do
and make a song out of it
I couldn't make a song out of it

AF: But if you didn't feel it
he couldn't make a song
or no one would listen to him
That's my only point
that musicians get a whole lot of credit
People go out and study musicians all the time
They go out and study some brilliant guitar player or singer or whatever
and people never study the people that are listening and dancing
and that creates the possibility for that musician to work

ANN: You see, I think the SMART
What I call the smart musician . . .
could be on that bandstand
and he sees ALL of these people up dancin'
and he stays with whatever that particular group of people are reLAting to
and has sense enough not to go off into some out . . .
left field
and they all sit down and hold their hands
and wish that they weren't there . . .
And there's so many people
that don't have sense to say
"Hey, THIS works
This is what THIS group relates to
This is what we're going to DO tonight!"

And without going
too far in the one direction
or too far in the other direction
but keep the people invoʟved with them
make them ꜰᴇᴇʟ good
if they're feelin' good
they're up ᴅᴀɴᴄin'

This expression "(a) feeling" and the linked expression "to relate (to)" evoke and specify a central social and musical—indeed, properly sociomusical—concept for working-class Texans. This concept is central to local styles of aesthetic and social evaluation, and especially musical evaluation. "Feeling" and "relating (to)" are diffuse, integrative, summarizing ideas. These terms, which fulfill a variety of grammatical functions, often appear to refer to essentialized, ineffable properties of social and aesthetic experience: if you have to ask what "feeling" means, in other words, you'll never know, and that's the point. "Feeling" is an inchoate quality of authenticity. But this phenomenological knot can be analytically untangled to reveal an orderly, dynamic, and elegantly binary semantic field. "Feeling" connects and naturalizes the distinction between two fundamental phenomenological and social subdomains. Each subdomain is highly valued on its own, but it is their fusion that constitutes musical and social "feeling."

These two subdomains of "feeling" are, first, *verbal* acuity, cleverness, structural complexity, or beauty, and, second, infectious, compelling *embodied* movement, especially rhythmic "feels" that produce dance and other impulses to bodily displays of emotional and physiological movement ranging from "tappin' your toe" to "cryin' in your beer." In other words, "feeling" is a concept (and an ideology, a symbol, and a heuristic) that mediates between cognitive and embodied domains of cultural experience. Ideally, "feeling" (especially via the social and psychological process of "relating") integrates these domains into a higher socio-aesthetic-psychological unity, a "felt" whole that is both poetically heightened and deeply naturalized.

"Feeling" links these subdomains of words and embodiment, comprising an overarching and conceptually distinct third dimension. This dimension draws together, as the immediate and usually implicit referents of "feeling," notions and principles of memory, emotion, sociability, narrativity, and especially the materiality of the speaking and singing voice, which is the very meeting point for words and embodiment. The relationships among these terms might be diagrammed as follows:

"FEELING" and "RELATING" (to)
connecting emotion, significance, and sociability
the essence of musical meaning and meaningful music
expressed in musical "feel"
inherent in "the OLD stuff"
requires "a song with a story to it"
"something that *reminds* you of something/somebody"
characterized by "repetitive singularity"
necessary for personalization of the performer/listener relationship
a quality inherent in "REAL country" as music and social identity

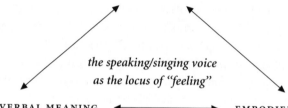

*the speaking/singing voice
as the locus of "feeling"*

VERBAL MEANING ←——————→ EMBODIED MEANING

song lyrics as discourse	dance, drive, "delivery"
singers as (agents for) songwriters	singers as musicians
"pretty words"	melody, timbre, groove
"you know every word"	affect as embodied, e.g.:
"talking" (about music, about "feeling")	"heart [and soul]"
narrativity, entextualized stories	"a feelin' [like . . .]"
reflective vs. direct expression	"sittin' and thinkin' " vs.
cleverness, sincerity, articulateness	"cryin' in your beer" vs.
	"tappin your toe" (etc.)

"Heart and Soul": Feeling and Embodiment

"Feeling" refers, along one semantic axis, to musically stimulated and coordinated movement and bodily experience, including but not limited to dance. The locus of "feeling" is conventionally located in the body, and especially in

the metaphoric and metonymic *heart*. The distinct embodiment of "feeling,"
for Illinois country singer Becky Rollings, involves an affective quality that
is bound up with inarticulate embodiment, something like the idea of being
"moved *by*" (as opposed to just "moving with/to") music:

BECKY: I think the interest in country music in this area
has gone EXTREMEly up in the last two years[2]
I don't know WHY
I think people are just startin' to listen and actually FEEL the songs
because a country song can get in your HEART
And rock songs . . .
There's a few that can
but mostly they're just to listen to
dance around
jump around
have a good time with
Country songs you FEEL . . .

As Becky told me then, using a coronary idiom that recurred frequently in
these sorts of conversations, "feeling" is concretely embodied in the way music
can "get into your heart." Conversely, the task of a musician who, as Ann says,
"relates back" to listeners who "relate to" the singer's music, finding a way to
express and create those "feelings" that nonmusicians "might not even feel,"
is to be able to "put his/her heart into it." Hoppy, for example, describes his
own commitment to country as a drama of this coronary investiture, using
the idiom that makes the link between "heart" and a sacred imperfect "self"
explicit, with the phrase "heart and soul":

HOPPY: It seemed to be something I always
felt close to
things like that
I mean
that was more reALity to me than
I seen a lot of
—pardon the expression—
CRAP in my life
And I just

never got into rock and roll because it wasn't
the way I *felt* about things
and I think JUSTIN kinda explained it one night
he told somebody on the BANDstand
he said, he said
"I never did want to do anything
that I didn't feel like I could do well"
And I don't have anything AGAINST other types of music at all
matter of fact I LISTen to a lot of types
y'know different things
But for ME to do it
and if **I can't put my heart and soul into it**
I'm not gonna do it

Miss Ann, too, argues vigorously that jukebox music in her beer joint must be both dance-inspiring and also affectively potent in embodied and imagined ways that go beyond inspiring dance. But embodiment is only part of what Ann means by deploying the primary local verb of active "feeling" when she says "you have to be able to *relate* to it." The structure of her argument suggests that "relating" moves us closer still to an idea of emotion as emergent in human relationships, and again, beyond the embodiment of dance, suggesting that embodiment itself is subject to some further theoretical elaboration and refinement:

ANN: It's a whole different ballgame for jukebox music
You have to dance to it
You have to be ABLE to dance to it
first of all
Especially if you're in a bar that has dances
Number two, you've got to be able to *relate* to it
And these people sittin' in the bar
They've all been hurt
They've cried in their beer
They've done all the things EMotional
So those songs have got to have some emotion to 'em
and yet they've got to have a good beat
But you put somethin' on there that won't

that you can't dance to
and you can't FEEL
they won't even play it!

Ann here succinctly locates embodied "feeling" both in the notion of dance
and the embodied experience of emotional loss, canonically expressed as "crying in your beer." In turn, this moves relatively raw and naturalized ideas
of embodiment, seen as an organic response to musical form, into the more
stylized forms of socially conventional embodiment and ways of signifying
"feeling" in song and social life.

Even the interiorized embodiment of the "heart" image can become a public sign of the person, conjoining nature and biography, for example. We
can see this in the following comment by Randy Meyer, where the aging
singer locates the feelingful difference—which he believes he has lost with
old age and infirmity—in the "heart" of his "feeling" body. It is this "heart"
that a great singer like Hoppy or Randy Meyer is thought to put into his or
her music.

One afternoon, sitting in Randy Meyer's home, I asked the singer why he
had decided to stop performing country music in the taverns where he had
spent his musical life:

RANDY: I decided **if I couldn't put my heart into it**
I wasn't gonna just try to do the WORDS to a song
and not have a *feeling* for it, y'know?
AF: Well, that's what I think is so remarkable about your style
It seems like you're living those songs to me
like they're really in you
RANDY: Yeah I did, y'know
but it got there toward the last that I just
I wasn't feeling the FEELING of the song, y'know?

Meyer argues, in close parallel to the way Ann and Becky discussed embodiment's inclusive transcendence of dance above, that the invocation of feeling
in musical performance must go deeper than the verbal surface of the song
text, or any danced response to a compelling rhythmic "feel." A singer has to
"have [indeed, 'feel'] a feeling" for a song, which means he must "put his heart
into" a song's verbal meaning, emotively embodying its text with his own life
force. Otherwise, he is "just [singing] the words." But the metaphor was glar-

ingly literal, as Meyer reclined on his couch, a once manic energy now stilled by advancing heart disease. Meyer literally had "put his heart into" his musical life in the bars, smoking, drinking, fighting, and loving with such intensity that he was widely understood to have "lived" the life he sang about (or as Dennis said, "lived it twice").

"A Song with a Story to It": "Feeling" and Narrative

Despite this emphasis on "feeling" as embodiment, the language of song is not only its surface, against which embodiment's authenticity is posed. Later in the same conversation, Randy Meyer again stressed the ubiquitous linkage between "pretty" words and "feeling." He located this intersection in what he called "the old songs," defined not by simple chronology but by their relevance to a particular, necessarily time-worn personal history of sociability. Meyer then ascribed the categorical difference between "old" and "new" songs to an objective difference in the quality, variety, and cleverness of song lyrics, a widely voiced critique of "the new stuff" among working-class country musicians, for whom contemporary country music displays a definite decline in artfulness. These Texans often cite a well-loved song, Marty Robbins's "Pretty Words," to name this dimension of "feeling." "Pretty words," Robbins sings, "make a fool out of me." "Pretty words," that is, words that are clever, complex, artful, and original within the constraints of the genre, are crucial for the production of "feeling." At the same time, Meyer introduced yet another idea that takes us even deeper into the idea of verbally affective "feeling":

RANDY: Those old songs that they'd come out with
had a lot of meanings to 'em . . .
feelings
They got so many of em now jus' . . .
they're repeTItious
they say the same things over and over again
You can write all the words down to a song in FIVE lines
that's about it!
I like a song with a sTOry to it
verses and a chorus
You used to do a verse
then you'd do a chorus

then you'd do another verse
then back to the chorus,
then put an ending on it
Now it's stuff like Eddie Rabbitt
[sings] *"I love a rainy night, I love a rainy night"*
It's over and over and over again!

Randy Meyer here adds yet another term to the multilayered definition of "feeling," and therefore to the expressive domain that mediates between words and embodiment, sense and affect. He is here exploring the *verbal* axis of "feeling," He speaks of "meanings" or "a song with a story to it." Verbal cleverness becomes something minimally affectively potent only when it suggests or explicitly tells a "story." This does not necessarily mean that a song "with feeling" must be in the "epic" mode (where the use of the third person and the past tense describe an objectively distanced past event). While the epic mode characterizes a true, and relatively more rare, "story song," as the local phrase has it, "a song with a story to it" has a broader and more complex meaning. Meyer insists that "a song with a story to it" creates a conceptual space for a locally meaningful narrativity to emerge in the process of interpretation or "relating to" the song. Such a song conforms to some moment or scene in a well-loved cultural metanarrative, such as obsessive lost love, or the guilty conscience of a "cheatin' heart."

In fact, most country songs that fit this definition of "meaning" (i.e., a "song with a story to it") move *between* epic narrativity (the "verses" Randy mentions) and the lyric crystallization of the repeated "choruses" or refrains, which tend to contain the dominant verbal trope of the song—the essence of its "feeling." This crystallization is typically enshrined in wordplay, puns, and deconstructive references to aphoristic fragments of "ordinary" working-class speech. Lyric refrains or "choruses," in other words, typically depart from the epic narrativity of verses, and yet they contain the crucial creative element that earns the evaluative characterization of "a song with a story to it." The repetition of the refrain must be motivated, so that each repetition of the lyric image is deepened and transformed by the intervening narrativity of the verses. (This is discussed in more detail in the next chapter.) It is this development of narrative resonance that the repeated one-line chorus of "I Love a Rainy Night" lacked, or appeared to lack, for Randy Meyer. Crucially, the song has little wordplay, and little overt evocation of working-class language.

But Meyer was not finished with this song. There is more to the idea of a "song with a story to it" than textual narrativity. Songs with "feeling," songs that you can "relate to," evoke a *lived* story. Such songs assist in the narration of lived social experience. A song with "feeling" has "a story" that specifies a local, personal history of use and interpretation. This story is actively told and retold in the repetitive contexts of sociable evaluations. This quality of narrativity, which is external to the song text itself, can even redeem a song that lacks the necessary verbal narrativity, complexity, or beauty to qualify as feelingful on its face.

Randy Meyer, in fact, was making just this point about "I Love a Rainy Night," Eddie Rabbitt's bouncy, radio-oriented hit song from 1980 (and a song that I have never heard played by a live band in Texas).[3] This light-rock song virtually lacks a textual narrative and expresses no emotional conflict or drama, only a vaguely nostalgic reverie. But even this kind of song can be subjected to a renarrativizing verbal recovery. This recovery foregrounds, ironically, the very same qualities that form the basis for Meyer's critique of the song: its lack of inherent poetic verbal quality, and its ceaseless repetition of its title phrase without developing any lyric intensity in relation to a dramatic narrative.

This playful recovery of feeling through a story emerged polemically on the heels of Meyer's critique of the song. Meyer, like Hoppy and other local singers of similar high stature in Texas, was also a practiced rhetorician. His speech typically exhibited an extremely clever, situationally sensitive attention to narrative form and topical organization, especially in his onstage patter, but also in everyday talk. Therefore, immediately after Randy had dismissed "I Love a Rainy Night" for its repetition of the title phrase "over and over and over again," his wife Audrey and I both laughed. We knew a redemptive story was coming next, or Randy wouldn't have bothered to specify the song by title and artist, let alone dismiss it so vehemently. As expected, Randy obliged us:

RANDY: Well that's another story there
Me an' my brother went fishing one night . . .
one weekend
It started raining when we got there
I set up a *brand new tent*
Had my radio out there

and everything
It kept raining
and kept raining
four days and nights!
AND the fourth night
I already SUNK the boat
lost a lot of stuff out . . .
and had to go down the river looking for everything
everything that'd float
Burnt the starter up
and then that TENT started leakin'!
A ninety-eight dollar tent!
Just bought it brand new!
And I went out
and I had a big fire going
and I just set out in the rain
and we kept the fire going
and I was listening to the radio
and that SONG came on
Eddie Rabbitt
"I love a rainy night, I love a rainy night"
And that made me so mad I picked the radio up and throwed it in the fire
My brother was dying laughing rolling around in the tent
and it's leakin'!
And I told him
"Come on let's GO!
We're goin' home!"
I loaded up the boat
Left the tent sittin' there
brand new
still set up . . .
AF: Let somebody else get wet!
RANDY: We came back to Austin . . .
He picked a hell of a time to sing that song
[sings]
"I love a rainy night"
Me sittin' out there in it!

Randy has added another dramatic layer, then, to the verbal dimension of "feeling." His conception of musical meaningfulness not only foregrounds the textual narrativity of songs but depends on "going into a story," "reminding [one] of a story," or "having a story." This extratextual narrativity can assimilate diverse kinds of musical materials to the local idea of "REAL country," or music that "you can relate to," because it has "feeling." Nearly any song can have a meaningful personal story attached to it, even if its verbal artfulness is inadequate in itself. Even a forgettable piece of fluff like "I Love a Rainy Night" can become a song with "feeling."

Feeling and Deep Narrativity

One afternoon in 1994, after we had been talking and playing music together for several years, I decided that I needed to arrange a long-delayed formal interview with Hoppy. My years of full-time fieldwork were winding to a close. I had a list of questions that needed to be approached directly and formally. The situation was slightly uncomfortable, until we had made our way through the first of several six-packs of beer. After all, I was strangely reverting to this most unsociable of discourse genres after years of playing music together, sharing songs and stories and adventures.

Eventually, and predictably, the interview evolved into relaxed conversation in the late afternoon calm, before a long night of music. And in this context, Hoppy's "answers" to my questions became more elaborate "stories." Hoppy's sociable point not only extends my argument about the deep narrativity of musical meaning but still moves me deeply when I reflect on it. In that movement, my own, there lies another layer of the idea of musical "feeling."

We were talking about how Hoppy conceives of "REAL country music," the kind of music he can "put his heart and soul into." But Hoppy managed to turn the "interview" around:

HOPPY: I don' know
it's just y'know
it's an opinion
everybody likes one thing
It's like some of the songs I do
you might get one guy that likes one thing
another . . .

I know this is supposed to be my interview
but I always enjoyed your acoustic work
much more than your electric work
on GUItar
I mean if I can put an acoustic in your hand
I'm just in HOG heaven
I LOVE it
cuz you do all the fingerpickin' an stuff
that I enjoy
On electric you seem to get away from that
AF: Yeah
I'm a schizophrenic musician
[we laugh]
I do my different things
But I actually I like the acoustic stuff much better too
It's where my heart is
HOPPY: I think there's a lot
I know some of the . . .
you done some of
kinda FOLKie type music
and I enjoyed that
Some of the HAPPY moments in my life, y'know
I had some FRIENDS that was in the military and stuff
That I used to play with out in Colorado, y'know
We'd sit in City Park
up in ah Denver
and go out on a mountainside
a rock or somethin', y'know
He'd play banjo
mandolin
I'd bang a little rhythm'n stuff
and we had a GOOD time doin' that . . .
Got throwed out of a bar one time
way back then
for doin' ah
[pauses as he thinks to himself]
"TALKin Vietnam Blues" I b'lieve it was

AF: Right, you told me this story
but tell me again!
HOPPY: Well . . .
We was in a little place
just outside of Denver
up by EVERGREEN
and this guy's name was Bill B ———
and he was stationed in Colorado Springs, y'know
gettin ready to go over to 'Nam   [i.e., the Vietnam War]
and we got to pickin' together
And he rode the little motorcycles and stuff, y'know?
We done a lot of things together
An' we went up there and we . . .
He done that "Talkin Vietnam Blues"
and it said somethin about smokin' POT!
Well they kicked us out!
[we laugh]
AF: Well that whole thing is about pot
that whole song!
Did you tell me Bill DIED in Vietnam?
HOPPY: [sadly] Yeah
yeah I found out
I called one time
he . . .
y'know as many
BAD jokes as I make about the North country
and the Yankees
and stuff
up there in New York
strangely enough
I've found a lot of good friends that
came from up there
I don't really remember
I think he came from ah
like New Jersey
I think's where it is
And I called up there cuz I figured

well it'd been
several YEARS y'know
And I called up and asked for Bill, y'know
at the number he'd gave me
And they said
"WHAT?"
Y'know?
"He got killed over there!"
And I went
"ooooooooh, shit!"
There's . . .
I still got pictures of him somewhere
I still got some tapes
Pickin' and singin'
He was a REAL good picker
He did a lot of fingerpickin'
that I just LOVED
Matter of fact, he was around when I wrote
my famous song . . .
you'd better shut that [tape recorder] off!

In this example, the relationship between a song, an extratextual story, and sociable feeling is even more complicated and densely layered than in Randy's story of fishing in the rain. Here, the song Hoppy reflects on is Tom Paxton's 1968 folk-style song "Talking Vietnam Potluck Blues,"[4] which has no canonical status among country fans whatsoever (although a similarly titled and styled Johnny Cash recording is well known).[5] But an extratextual story—one that makes this song "country"—occurred to Hoppy as he thought about the significance of "folkie type" acoustic guitar playing in his youth. Hoppy's digression suddenly fractured the "interview" frame, as he focused on *my* guitar-playing style (folk-style "finger-pickin'," which comes up as a summary image at the end of this example as well). Having projected the talk into the realm of our friendship, Hoppy, as so often, turns in a masterful rhetorical performance.[6]

Hoppy's discourse here is a reflection on the way that musical "feeling" mediates friendships, and it proffers an analogy between his long-dead friend Bill and me, both of us, ironically and pointedly, "Yankees" from the "North country." Hoppy uses the song-inspired memory of shared musical sociability with Bill to reflect on the different paths that *our* lives are sure to take in the coming years. This reflection is embedded in a tragic memory of the way that history and chance, and perhaps class-specific biography, can combine to separate friends in spite of deep musical bonds, leaving behind only some old tapes and pictures, some old "mem'ries." And the point of this story and the others we exchanged in this meeting is surely an exhortation we are making to each other, at this advanced stage of our friendship, not to lose touch.

We were both, Hoppy and I, aware that the pretext for this interview was my need to "wrap things up," to collect some final important details and "mem'ries," as I was preparing to move to Seattle the following month. This punctuation in our relationship is less dramatic than a draft notice in wartime. But it nonetheless inspires Hoppy's story, which invests our shared musical sociability, this anomalous friendship between the son of a Kansas salt miner and the son of a New York professor, with the depth of meaning that emerges from Hoppy's connection of this moment to a storied past, to another remembered moment playing in City Park in Denver with his old friend from, of all places, New Jersey. More precisely, this moment is connected to a memory of being kicked out of a bar for playing a particular song that has evoked, by its mere mention, the tragedy of war, death, and time's passage, framing this entire exchange of question, story, and remembrance. This telling, at this moment, gives new meaning and depth to the stories Hoppy may tell in the future about a guy from New York who used to hang around and play the guitar and tape-record everything that went on and write articles full of "ten dollar words" that, at least, had some good stories, stories worth remembering. And it gives, I hope, new meaning, new "feeling" to the stories I tell of Hoppy and the others here, and to all the "mem'ries" upon which these stories will hang: still more pictures and tapes, and perhaps a few more ten-dollar words.

Musical "Feel" as the Foundation of Musical "Feeling"

Country music is FEEL *music.* — Ron Stendquist, country musician.

I really like a song that you can get into and just FEEL *it, and get the crowd to feel it the way* YOU *do.* — Becky Rollings, country singer.

In country musicians' discourse, "feeling" is often interlocked with the idiom of musical "feel." "Feel" is an idea that aligns particular genres, rhythmic grooves, tempos, themes, individual performative idiosyncrasies, or, as musicians also say, "styles." Like "feeling," musical "feel" is modeled across the mind/body boundary. For example, Becky Rollings carefully contrasts, in her comparison of two of her own recordings, two different "feels" or "styles" (Becky uses both terms), which are characterized respectively by verbal directness (linked to physical animation) and reflective contemplation (linked to nostalgic solitude).[7] Both "feels," however, can implicate embodied, cognitive, and mnemonic "feeling": they "catch a listener's ear" with their different kinds of "meaning" and "make you think about something that's happened to YOU in the past." "Feel" is simultaneously a characterization of musical sound and musical meaning. This became clearer when Becky drew a distinction between the two songs:

BECKY: [The song] "Rusty Nail" 's got that . . .
you just gotta tap your toe to it
and [the song] "I Gave All I Had to Him" is kinda . . .
makes you sit back and think about life
and relationships
and just kinda makes you think about things
Where "Rusty Nail" just says "this is how it is,' 'this is how I feel!"
There're two different STYLES
but they come across with the same kind of energy
They catch a listener's EAR
Least they caught MINE!
And I critique music all the time
I can sit down with a new song
and I know what the song is saying and what it MEANS before I know any of
the words . . .
AF: From the delivery?
BECKY: Yeah, from the *delivery* . . .
And just by listening to it
You get the general feel of the song
[ca. five minutes elided from transcript during which we talk about lyrics and
rhythm]
BECKY: If you've got those two things [intensity of lyric and rhythmic feel]
and can convey that to the audience
then you got it!

[a song] makes you think about something that's happened to YOU
in the past . . .

Rollings's point resonates with my earlier claim that "feeling" articulates
embodied movement and cognized verbal meaning in relation to personal
memory. Echoing Randy Meyer and Miss Ann, Rollings argues that the textural quality of "feel" in some sense can be said to precede the referential
meaning of a song's text, although ideally the discourse of the song text will be
matched to the "feel" of the performance and the generic quality of the song's
rhythm and arrangement, as a lilting waltz, or a "cry-in-your-beer" slow song,
or an up-tempo swing tune, to name only three possibilities. Each "feel" produces its own specific embodied affect. Becky lists two: "tapping your toe,"
and "sitting back" and thinking.

Rollings compares two songs here, to clarify her concept of "feel." "Rusty
Nail," her first commercial single, is a fast, hard-driving song in a "straight"
(unsyncopated) 2/4 "feel." This song falls into a generic thematic category as
it announces that the long-suffering narrator (typically female) is not going to
put up with a "broken heart" any longer. (This trope is used in women's barroom talk about relationships too.) Vocally, this trope is signaled by the use of
a wide tessitura that emphasizes Becky's forceful low midrange and her tendency to "growl" aggressively when she sings in that range. The line's phrasing
produces an acoustic icon of the narrator's "long suffering" coming to an end.
This phrasing drew much commentary from fans and the other musicians in
Becky's band. It involved the clustering within a single breath group of a long
string of syllabically set, rapidly articulated words in the final phrase of the
song's refrain (*"So if anybody wants this poor old broken heart to hurt some
more/you'll find it hangin' on that rusty nail beside the door"*). "I Gave All I Had
to Him," on the other hand, is a wistful 4/4 syncopated swing ballad (about
half the tempo of "Rusty Nail"). This song articulates the conventional pretext
for songs like "Rusty Nail," as it tells of a woman who obsessively dwells on a
lost love. It uses a high, airy tone and tessitura, and a long slow crescendo from
a very quiet beginning, coming off the bridge (it is in 32-bar AABA form) at
full volume, to represent intensification. In form, melody, chord progression,
and theme, and in its use of performative dynamic intensification—that is, in
its musical "feel"—it strongly evokes Patsy Cline's "Crazy" and, to a lesser extent, "She's Got You," both of which are canonical examples, widely imitated,
of the same female-gendered trope.

In this sense, "feel" resonates with the performative and interpretive idea that Feld theorizes as "groove" (1988) and Keil formulates as "engendered feeling" and "embodied meaning" (1966). Not surprisingly, country musicians speak consistently about musical quality (for example, in evaluating the skill of another musician) in terms of an all-encompassing notion of the mastery of musical and emotional "feel." With this usage, they are glossing some of the same notions that jazz musicians intend by their use of the terms "groove" and "swing." "Feel" refers both to typical dance-based rhythmic gestalts and their associated moods ("swing feel," "shuffle feel," "waltz," "train beat," "two-step") and to a musician's grasp of the subtleties of expression that such gestalts demand in domains like timing, mood, and textural density. A musician who knows how to play tastefully within the constraints of the major rhythmic and emotional gestalts of country music (neither too many notes nor too few; neither too much drive nor too much drag) is said to play with "a good feel" for country music. And there is no higher praise for a country musician than to say s/he plays or sings "with a good feel." "Feel" in this usage is distinct from "technique": it is possible to say of a musician that s/he plays or sings "all the notes, but with no feel."[8] This is unacceptable, because musical "feel" is an essential aspect of "feeling," and thus of "REAL country music."

"You Can Relate to This Shit": Memory, Personalization, and Obsession

From the elements thus far discussed, we can begin to assemble the meaningful components of musical "feeling." Specifically, these various reflections and narratives suggest that "feeling" articulates (i.e., it both connects and gives voice to, which is also the double meaning of the verb "relate") verbal and embodied domains of experience. Feeling then *adds* something else, some "meaning." This meaning is often glossed with the idea of a "story," or with an actual story, a "mem'ry," or a fixation on something that "reminds you of something."

The active effort to interpret musical experience in terms of acts of "remembering" is one aspect of "feeling" that is even more closely focused and lexically refined by the verb "to relate (to)." Unlike "(to) feel," which has the nominalized form of "(a) feeling," "to relate to" is exclusively a verb, though one with diverse meanings. Consequently, talk of "relating" focuses more exclusively and powerfully on the *active* qualities of feeling. Furthermore, "to relate to" compels the specification of an object that is the medium of "feeling," (i.e., one must "relate *to*" a song, a singer, or a situation). "Relating" creates more distance from the content of verbal/embodied meaning, focusing instead on the process by which that meaning is encountered as "feeling."

"Relating," like "feeling," entails articulations of embodied and verbalized meaning (which is why I treat them as a paired concept here). Pat the barmaid suggests that song's mnemonic power is, for her, closer to the verbal axis of relating to music when she "relates" to a song, stressing the textual mediation of "feeling" that "relating" brings into focus as an object. To "relate" to a song is to remember something important with the song's assistance:

PAT: I like this song,   ["I'm Just a Man" on jukebox]
this is Hank Williams, Junior
If I like a song, the words to the SONG
it doesn't matter who it is
Like Lorrie Morgan
I like a lot of her songs
But I listen to the words of the SONG
If I can reLATE to it
I understAND it . . .
It remINDS me of something

Jim, whose comments on "relating to" Patsy Cline I quoted in the previous chapter, was, like Pam, not a musician. But he was extraordinarily articulate and reflective on these subjects in my conversations with him. Jim drew out a subtle linkage between memory and the apparently contradictory realms of repetition and uniqueness in his consideration of relating to the music of Patsy Cline. In so doing, he too made a connection between the interpretive concepts of "feeling" and "relating" and two important tropes of sad country songs: immersion in an unforgettable past, and fixation on a unique and long-gone object of desire (Fox 1992, 1993; K. Stewart 1993). Likewise, Jim linked the idea of "feeling" to the key local idea of being a "character" (see chapter 4), in which eccentricity and predictability, "foolishness" and sociability are held in a careful balance. Jim articulated what might be called a trope of "repetitive singularity," in which a unique voice and object of desire multiplies obsessively in the imagination of the "tore-up fool."

In both songs and "real life," this repetitive singularity can be figured as obsessively and repeatedly playing the same song on the jukebox in the bar (a widely recognized symptom of being "tore up" or "actin' the fool"). Indeed, the listener's mind is often itself figured as a jukebox in which a song plays repeatedly. The mnemonic articulation of obsessive repetition, uniqueness, a personalized relationship to the singer (who is so often a cipher for a lost love or some other "real" relationship), and the interiority of the "jukebox of the mind" is a characteristic trope in modern country music. "Jukebox in My Mind," a 1990 hit by the group Alabama, is only a particularly extravagant example of this figure, as the singer (Randy Owen) declares: *"In the corner of my mind stands a jukebox/ playing all my favorite memories."*[9] This recording is especially compelling for working-class country fans because it embeds a representation of a "real" jukebox as a sign of fixated repetition. After the song has ostensibly ended, the sound of a needle dropping on a scratchy record—the same sound that also begins the recording—restarts the final chorus, implying a ceaseless reenactment of the narrator's abject obsession.

Obsessive repetition is an important aspect of "feeling" in song, and of "relating to" musical experience for working-class Texans. Rodney, an electrician, suggested this linkage one night when he explained the power of "the old stuff" for him. Again, Rodney articulated the domains of embodiment and verbal meaning in the transcendent idiom of "feeling." The past speaks through the "feeling" body to the "knowing" mind via the singular, suddenly remembered verbal song text, repeating inexorably across the years. The physical "chill" he feels when the words resonate with his experience is the very essence of embodied/verbal memory, an apotheosis of "feeling":

RODNEY: It's like when there's songs
you don't even remember you know
They give you a **feeling like a chill**
when you hear 'em
and you **know every word!**

For Rodney, then, the words of songs come back as embodied sensation through a history of evocative and timely repetitions. The major elements of "feeling" and "relating" come together nicely in this brief quotation. Pairing this sort of embodied and cognitive modeling of the experience of "feeling" with Jim's attachment to Patsy Cline and his ex-wife, or with Pat's insistence that good songs "remind you of something," implicates another submerged meaning of "relating." Relating articulates a personal memory of a song with what is remembered in addition to the song, namely, a particular social relationship.[10]

In country music, the idea of "relationship" is remembered and amplified by emphasizing the figure of the singer as a metaphoric old friend or lover, an omnipresent other who is longed for and obsessed over. But this other is also subject to the rules and constraints of local sociability. The crucial idea behind the delineation of "real country music," often expressed as a preference for "the OLD stuff," is the linking of the identities of particular performers with particular places and times and known people. Heroic status is accorded to local country singers and national stars alike whose personalities have compelling force for what Rusty called the "common people." Even the biggest stars are imagined as participants in the deep locality of sociable discourse. This creates the possibility for "relating to" singers, and the obligation for singers to "relate back" to their fans.[11]

This intense personalization of the performer/audience relationship, and its construction in memory, emerges in a history of engaging with the particular performer in question through listening, through talk, or through stories in which country stars are imagined as "common people." This history is foundational for musical "feeling." "Relating" is a dialogical process, assimilating texts, songs, and singers to local ideologies of conversational style and sociability. Ann once explained to me why Randy Meyer was the most powerful singer she had ever known:

ANN: People JUST LOVE him
He's like MAgic
He's one of the FEW musicians
That I've ever run INto
that sits up
that gets up on that stage and it's MAgic
EVerybody in the place reLATES to him
and he relates BACK
And everybody LOVEs him
and he loves 'em back!
AF: Yeah?
ANN: And he can have . . .
he will put 'em ALL
in the PALM of his hand

whenever he . . .
opens his mouth
and they WON'T get OUT
til he QUITS!
[long pause]
[sharply rising intonations]
Temperamental?
Stubborn?
And do it MY way?
RANdy Meyer!
huh!
pure country . . .
And he'll turn around
and he'll tell a drummer
[imitating Randy's edgy voice]
"you wanna DROWN me out, you just PLAY this solo!"
He will chew a drummer out in a HEARTbeat . . .
And everybody loves Randy
Everybody you SEE knows him!

The importance of "relating to and relating back" can be transposed from the local level, where "everybody you see" really does know a performer, to the level of relating to the music of even major national stars. This is evident in widely told local stories of meeting country stars. Ann, for example, tells a story of meeting Jim Reeves as a customer when she was a waitress in a steakhouse, focusing on his kindness and "ordinariness." Almost all musicians and many nonmusicians have these stories at the ready, and they are widely repeated. Sometimes these meetings are more obviously located in the realm of the imaginary, as when the musicians who jammed on Friday nights at Ann's asserted confidently that Johnny Cash would waive the ASCAP royalties bars are supposed to pay, even for amateur performances, if they knew who was playing them and where the bar was. Betrayals of this personalized relationship can be the cause of real anger:

ANN: I HATE Reba McEntiiiiiiiiiiiiire!
NONE of her records are on my jukebox!
[confidentially]

First of all cuz she insulted Texas
She shouldn't have done that!
When she played the Aquafest [an Austin outdoor music festival]
she wouldn't let any other woman on the bandstand
Then she went over to do Austin City Limits
and wouldn't let us
have "Texas" behind us![12]
She made 'em take that off!
SO
I said
she doesn't NEED my money!

These mythic but intimate relationships are binding on stars and local musicians alike in their efforts to perform effectively (that is, with "feeling") and to promote their careers.[13] Even the biggest national stars continue to engage with working-class fans as if they were neighbors and old friends, as in this next example from a national radio call-in show, in which Reba McEntire (the same singer Ann disparaged) deploys a full range of working-class women's markers of dialogic engagement. McEntire's speech is characterized by an ensemble of prosodic and interactional features marked as "gossip," the female equivalent of male "talkin' shit": huge intonational movements, leading questions, back-channel encouragements, and shifts between forceful enthusiasm and gentle confidential rapport. And the caller expresses her attachment and satisfaction with the encounter by using the idiom of "feeling":[14]

FEMALE CALLER: Yeah, HI REBA!
MCENTIRE: Hello!
CALLER: Hi, I have been wantin' to talk to you for years!
I jus' wanted to tell you . . .
Hey, I'm from Nashville too!
MCENTIRE: Oh ARE you?
CALLER: Yeah . . .
when you came out with that song,
"You're the first time I ever thought about leavin' "   [i.e., "You're the First Time
                                                     I've Thought about Leaving"]?
MCENTIRE: uh HUH?
CALLER: That was a major turnin' point in my LIFE
And I jus' wanted to TELL *you*

that I lived that song
And I **felt like** you wrote that song jus' for me!
MCENTIRE: Well, that's great!
CALLER: And I'm happily married now . . .
MCENTIRE: GOOD DEAL!
CALLER: And, ah, I jus' wanted to tell you, ah . . .
I just . . .
I felt like you were a friend
that understood **what I was feelin'**
I jus' wanted to TELL you that . . .
MCENTIRE: Well, I appRεciate that honey . . .
CALLER: And I thank you so much for that song!

Above All, You've Gotta Have a Certain Amount of Heart

It was late on a hot August night, and we'd been playing music and drinking beer for hours together upstairs above Hoppy's garage. The usual pickers were there: Hoppy, of course, and Justin, Phil, Linda, Judy, myself, and a few others who always showed up to hang out and listen and drink and talk and maybe sing a song or two. But it was a special night, because Randy Meyer had managed to make it out for the first time in a long time, and only the second time since being released from the hospital. When Justin found out from Hoppy that Randy would be coming, he made sure to call me, and I broke other plans to be there. We all felt like we might be having our last chance to pick with Randy. And sometimes he'd show up and not even want to sing, which made everybody worry, because for Randy singing and living were simply the same thing.

This night too, Randy had been reluctant to sing at first, but just like in the old days, he relented after our clamor became irresistible. But this reluctance was studied and stylized. We had all seen it many times—Randy had a knack for declining to perform in impromptu situations until the clamor to hear him sing became emphatic, and attention became much more focused. Randy settled down on a stool with Justin's Ovation guitar in his hands, and ran through a couple of funny and raunchy songs, to lighten the mood in the room and get the pickers tuned in to his groove, keeping up the stream of talk and messing around with lyrics and dirty jokes. But a heavy moment of "feeling" was coming, and we all knew it. After about fifteen minutes, Randy grew silent. Justin and Phil and Hoppy and I waited reverently around him, our instruments poised and our minds focused to catch the first line he would sing so we could join him with precision.

Randy liked to test good musicians, to make them find the beat and the key in his voice as he sang the first line, although if he wasn't sure about the pickers he would call the song and the key firmly. Randy could work with any band, and with any pickers. After years of playing the beer joints with whatever musicians could be rounded up for low pay on short notice, Randy rarely counted on anyone else to kick off songs. He retained absolute control of the flow of musical time even when he was relaxed. To measure out the time between songs, he would reach for his trademark Pearl beer and take a drag on his cigarette. The almost mechanical precision of these gestures was widely recognized by his fans as an aspect of his commanding style. Working without a set list, Randy used a distinctive stage patter full of self-deprecations ("Drink up folks! The more you drink the better we sound!"), dedications, and sly sexual and scatological puns with which he engineered the seamless sequencing of requests, the songs he felt like singing, and the appropriate mix of tempos and dance steps. These were (and are) uncommon skills, acquired over a lifetime of practice. Randy was a master performer, someone you could "relate to" and someone who "related back" too. And so even up at Hoppy's, even informally, we strained to come up to his level and to learn something in the time we had.

Into the expectant, hushed silence of the cramped room, Randy sang his favorite song with all the world-weary weight and intensity of his fifty-nine years:

RANDY: *"Wish I were down
on some blue bayou . . ."*

We'd all played this song before. We'd been waiting for it, and we joined Randy seamlessly. My mandolin, Hoppy's and Phil's guitars, and Justin's bass punched out the oddly perfect though idiomatically unusual flat seventh chord moving to the subdominant chord (C to G, in the key of D — or "Dog," as country musicians call it). The progression arched across the syllable break on the word "ba-you," changing chords on successive beats and locking in to the lugubrious slow 4/4 meter of the song. We pulled the groove from Randy's strongly articulated opening line and (for all but sightless Justin, who relied only on his ears) the little jerk of his guitar neck that located the downbeat of the second bar while his exaggerated hand position on the neck announced the key.

The song was Merle Haggard's "The Way I Am," a darkly resigned, even mournful lament (written by Sonny Throckmorton) in the voice of an "ordinary," imperfect, weary working-class man trapped by life and labor and time in a confining "reality" but dreaming and singing of escaping to a life of fishing, a life in the country.[15] In recent years, Randy, a roofer, framer, father, husband, bar fighter, truck driver, fisherman, and legendary singer, had made it his own theme song, a song layered with "feeling" widely understood to express Randy's own sentiments about the working life and its disappointments and responsibilities. It never failed to have a powerful effect on his friends and fans.

Randy launched the song with a dramatic a cappella rendition of the first line, forgoing the instrumental "kick-off" found on the Haggard recording. A palpable shiver of emotion ran through the room, tears came to many eyes, and a rush of "feeling" caused someone to call out "Alright!" before falling silent again. (This was a rare tribute for a country beer-joint musician, who expects to compete, always, with a wall of talk.) Randy continued in a quiet, thoughtful voice: *"A bamboo cane stuck in the sand/ But the road I'm on don't seem to go there/ And I just dream to keep on bein' the way I am."* And then, altering Haggard's original double-verse slightly in favor of the more standardized verse/ refrain/ verse/ refrain pattern, Randy reared back for the powerful, cathartic refrain which soared up to the subdominant (IV) chord: *"The way I am, it don't fit my shackles/ The way I am, reality."*

After Phil and I split the lead ride, Randy continued again with another hushed verse, vowing to stay the course at a miserable job, before returning to the roared self-declaration of the refrain again. The last lines of the song wordlessly repeat the alternation between constrained, quiet reflection and wailed resistance, moving from a hummed wordless version of a verse line to a final eerie "high lonesome" yodel. As Randy's final yodel faded away, the dreamlike darkness of the song was brilliantly illuminated in a sociable wash of applause and delight amid the neon beer signs and Hoppy's many mem'ries covering the walls. For this night at least, Randy felt like singing, and he owned the evening, ranging over his huge repertoire of songs by Haggard, Ernest Tubb, and Hank Williams, and other strange and obscure and sentimental and funny songs. Randy's own songs too glowed like rare jewels hidden in the box of small-time obscurity. He sang them all the way he did on tapes from the 1970s, tapes that were jealously hoarded by his fans. His vocal signature was on every edgy, angular nuance of phrasing and feeling. He looked weary, but he was smiling, and his eyes were dancing. Still, in the following days, people who had been there that night looked sad and many said "you could *see it* in his eyes." Even in this sociable moment, the knowledge that time was always short lay heavily on the room.

As the night wore on, Randy tried several times to leave, saying he needed to "go to the house," his trailer home forty miles to the west. But Hoppy tricked Randy into staying for "one more song" several times. In a spectacular bit of rhetorical manipulation, he cajoled Randy into singing Joe South's "The Games People Play." This piece of country-pop trivia from 1968 would not merit attention from a singer like Randy under normal circumstances. But it was, as Hoppy knew, "a song with a story to it." Randy sang it only when he told the story of how he had learned the song by listening to it once on a beer-joint jukebox. He had done so on a dare from a fan who said he couldn't learn that sort of "new stuff," and in the process had turned a relentlessly repetitive and not particularly artful song (not unlike "I Love a Rainy Night") into "real country music."

Finally, however, Randy was making his way to the door at last to begin the long drive back to the hill country where he lived. Randy declared he "wasn't feelin' too well," and that he had better get back home. But Hoppy, Randy's longtime friend and student, working with Phil's assistance, pulled out one final, masterful rhetorical trick, bracing himself against the door of onrushing time. And Randy took the bait, recognizing the tribute that was layered into Hoppy's agonistic invitation to join just one more conversation about the old songs and the old days and REAL country music and "feeling":

HOPPY: I don't care WHO you are
whether you're Merle Haggard   RANDY: No!
or whatever
you can't ALWAYS **feel** great
PHIL: Don't you HATE to see it
when you
when you see a guy like Merle Haggard
and you KNOW he ain't **feelin** good?
RANDY: Right, right

PHIL: It's painful
because you can SEE it

PHIL: But you understand
y'know
SOME nights
that guy can do it
but somebody like you
would watch him
and you'd KNOW
you'd KNOW

PHIL: That's the only way!
A songwriter . . .

PHIL: Oh yeah

PHIL: Well he could do it
good point

HOPPY: It really is
RANDY: Playin the SAME old songs
over
and over
and over
and over
and over

RANDY: I'd have to be a
songwRIter
where I'd have to write me
a new song
EVERY night
that I played

That's where I could say
"comin up with a new one here
in a minute
workin' my way up to it!"
And I'm gonna see how it
(goes over)
But . . .
to do the SAME old crap
over and over
without leadin' up
to somethin NEW

RANDY: I used to LEARN a
a NEW song
once't'week . . .
Every week I played

[high-pitched]
fifty-two weeks
a god-damn . . .
YEAR
or whatever
y'know
I used to learn a
a NEW song
every week
so it'd GIVE me an incentive
to ah
get to do that SONG
Said "OKAY FOLKS
Here's a new song!
We just learned this one!"
and cut out and . . .
Knock 'em BACK!

HOPPY: The only problem I GOT with that
Randy
is you're absolutely RIGHT
but I . . .
I've got a problem
see I've gotten stale
I haven't played really in . . .
several years
I come nearer t'quittin than YOU did
tell you the truth . . .
And THIS bothers me too
what you're saying
the thing of it is
that
[staccato delivery, slightly pitched]
they aren't comin' up
with anything NEW
that's turnin' my crank lately
for me to WANT to learn it
see?

RANDY: They're not comin' up with
any SONGS
that I . . .
Merle HAGgard
is my IDOl
an' he hasn't come up with
NOTHin'
in the past ten YEARS
y'know
other than
[sings]
"Wish I were down
On some blue BAY-you"
I mean y'know
songs like that . . .
I can reLATE to
Y'know I
I can get INto it!
And I said
"Yeah !
I wanna LEARN this [one]"

PHIL: The last album was
a big disappointment

But songs that . . .
HOPPY: But how many new ones
have you HEARD lately
Randy
that you want to . . . ?

RANDY: Randy TRAvis
is a great song
singer
far as I'm concerned
But I haven't learned a
DAMN SONG he'd SING
It's because of
the NEW generation
that's comin' aLONG
[staccato, forceful]
is not
down

old
country
style
PICKin'!

PHIL: mm hmm!

JUSTIN: Absolutely
absolutely!

JUDY: That's right!

ANN: Yep, yep!

PHIL: Those guys are a lot . . .

RANDY: And you know WHAT?
I've found out
where you can GO to a crowd
of PEOple
that are from
say THIRty years
to EIGHTy years old

PHIL: mmhmm

And PLAY the SHIT
like WE'RE playin' right HERE
And they'll go CRAzy over it

JUDY: Yup!

PHIL: No SHIT!

And I mean
the OLDer it gets
the more they LIKE it

PHIL: mmhmm!

And you put that NEW shit on 'em?
Oh yeah
you'll catch the YOUNG generation
runnin' out there
lookin' around from

[assent from all]

playin' a game of POOL
or sumpin
But WHO's interested
in them fuckers anyway?
You want the guys DANCin
on that DANCE floor!

PHIL: S'right!

JUDY: Yeah!

HOPPY: Even if they're DANCin'

they're not hearin' what you SAY!

PHIL: That's true!

RANDY: I 've . . .
How many TIMES
have I slipped things in a SONG
just to see if people're LISTENIN'?
y'know

HOPPY: Justin does that a lot!

JUSTIN: I do that shit!
I do that a LOT
All kinds of NASty shit!

PHIL: Oh yeah
He DOES!

PHIL: I can tell you man
It's the same way . . .

RANDY: Oh YEAH
Yeah SHIT
[rhythmically, slightly pitched]
"How can I get over YOU?
[laughs]
When you're always . . .
[laughs]
under him?"

JUDY: The whole dance floor was FULL
and NOBODY even really
REALized what it was you did that
Justin!
at KELLy's that night
with (people dancin' to it)
And nobody KNEW
what you were SAYin'
except US!
Knew what was . . .

JUSTIN: I find . . .
(what) the hell was wrong

HOPPY: And NOBODY
Nobody but US

PHIL: I saw ONE table crack up!

HOPPY: You DID?

PHIL: And there's one other PERSON too
One other . . .

RANDY: But you don't
you know
people are DANcin'
They're generally TALkin'
or somethin'

JUDY: Nobody pays any attention!
Yeah yeah
[other assent]

JUDY: They don't pay you no mind
HOPPY: Well that's why I
think it's . . .

[assent, some side conversation]
HOPPY: AIN'T the same!

PHIL: No!
it DON'T matter!

PHIL: NO
you gotta have
a CERtain amount of ability

but

above all

**you gotta have a certain amount of
HEART**

JUDY: Yeah!
OTHERS: YEAH!
yeah!
yeah!
mmhmm!
JUDY: Naw . . .
It's just that . . .
That's what you chose . . .
PHIL: Well that's like ME
Because I've been around a bunch

y'know
They still don't HEAR you

RANDY: But it's the LIVE music
that BRINGS 'em there
and you gotta remember that!
A JUKEbox is NOT
the same
I don't give a damn
how BAD you are

If you're LIVE
You're up there TRYin'
THEY're gonna give you a HAND
if you're not just
plum-ass LOUSY, y'know?

JUSTIN: Ability, yeah!
RANDY: They're gonna give you
a good HAND
They're gonna give you TIPS
They're gonna buy you
DRINKS
They're gonna enJOY you
For just ONE PERSON
I KNOW
because I went
all over the U-nited STATES
by mySELF
pickin' and SINGin'
and it's not that I'm that GOOD!
It's just it's . . .
LIVE!
It's LIVE!

and I ain't
no SINGER at ALL
HOPPY: They don't do that NEAR as much
anymore as they used to, Randy
But your . . .
y'know
I'll bet they DO it though
They do it from MAINE
to California   RANDY: I'll bet you ten dollars
JUSTIN: Randy   you and I . . .
y'know
y'know I . . .   RANDY: I'll bet you ten dollars
                              you and I
PHIL: Right NOW?   could hit the road
You'd be great!
HOPPY: I'll bet we COULD!
                          RANDY: It's FRIday
                          By SATurday NIGHT . . .
                          we'll be PLAYin' somewhere
PHIL: You COULD   and makin' money!
There's no question ABOUT it!
                          HOPPY: We went out
                          And Justin . . .
                          I've got to tell you about this
                          Me and Randy went deer
                          huntin' . . .

For most of this chapter, I have been arguing from metadiscursive evidence for the ethnotheoretical and phenomenological reality of a specific rural, working-class conception of musical "feeling." I have drawn evidence from interviews and conversations about musical aesthetics between working-class musicians and listeners and myself. That is, I have reported what working-class country fans and musicians have to say about "feeling," "relating," and music's powerful meaningfulness.

With this example, however, I wish to emphasize the conversational density and ubiquity of the discourse of "feeling." The category operates pervasively in sociable activity, whether or not it is explicitly articulated. I have shown how "feeling" aligns verbal and embodied domains and is predicated on a deep intertextual narrativity. "Feeling" infuses sociable relationships between musicians and listeners, and among listeners themselves, refining intense affects of nostalgia and loss. "Feeling" is, ultimately, essential for the production and curating of social memory. In this sense, "feeling" is a quality that transcends lexicalization and abstract recognition. It is an essential, irreducible, only approximately specifiable quality of authenticity.

At the deepest level, this conversation's music-saturated "feeling" was about an ineffable sentiment of loss that pervaded the room as Randy Meyer prepared to go out the door and down the stairs alone into the hot darkness of the August night. The biographical and allegorical quality of his departure, as he was "not feelin' too good," after a long and intense night of music and sociability, was lost on nobody in the room. Hoppy's herculean effort to keep Randy with us for one more song, and one more, and one more, and finally for just one more conversation, represented the endless struggle between musical sociability and all those forces that pull people apart and take them away, leaving only "mem'ries."

The focused social emotion we shared in this moment for Randy Meyer was modeled through many of the markers of "feeling" and "relating" that I have already described. Hoppy began by making an analogy between Randy's "not feelin' too good" and Merle Haggard's hypothetical bad nights. This conflated the figures of Haggard and Meyer, a long-established and even canonical local comparison; as Ann once told me, "Randy *is* Merle Haggard around here." As Ann also said, "Everyone you *see* around here knows Randy Meyer." Here, then, Meyer and Haggard were conjoined in the image of a figure who is "not feelin' too good." Phil's rejoinder suggested that this real/imaginary relationship was a long and intimate one. And it was even more intimate for the object of this tribute, Randy Meyer: "somebody like you would watch him and you'd KNOW, you'd KNOW [that he wasn't feelin' good]."

But it was Randy, accepting this deferential identification and invitation, who stressed polemically that the source of a singer's malaise is boredom, the ceaseless repetition of "the SAME old songs over and over and over and over and over."[16] This was an unusual stance, but one Randy took often in the years I knew him. It was made logical in this context by being explicitly linked to the desire for verbal novelty within stylistic continuity. This in turn emphasized songwriting and the singer's role as the mediator between the songwriter's emergent vision and the audience's rigorous, conservative standards for music they can "relate to." Randy was both a poetically innovative songwriter and a conservative performer: everything he sang automatically turned, for his friends and fans, into "REAL country music." For such a master, a demand for verbal novelty was perfectly compatible with the requirements of stylistic continuity.

Hoppy recognized that Randy was extending a polemical invitation for a rejoinder with his vivid portrayal of his youthful emphasis on learning new songs back in the old days: "I used to LEARN a NEW song once't'week, fifty-two weeks a god-damn YEAR . . ."[17] So Hoppy countered his friend with a move into a nostalgic counterpoint, as a means of deepening the feeling of this conversation. Hoppy thus established a sentimental narrative space that contained Randy's innovative stance within the sociability of the "good old days." The remainder of this example was devoted to curating that sentimental space of "feeling."

Randy saw no conflict at all between Hoppy's argument for the "old stuff" and his own desire for novelty and variety. Indeed, Randy performed the most powerful kind of "feelingful" intensification available in Texas discourse when he marked his agreement with Hoppy by moving briefly into a fragment of song. Of course the song was, again, Haggard's "The Way I Am," the song we had played earlier, which dramatically and intertextually amplified Randy's movement into song. "The Way I Am," he announced, was the kind of a song "I can reLATE to!"

Hoppy's brief interrogation of this point's apparent internal contradiction was then brilliantly topped by Randy's next turn, which cemented the reverent assent of everyone in the room, as he insisted, in a loud staccato, that the newer music is "not . . . down . . . old . . . country . . . style . . . PICKIN'!" Randy continued to personalize his position by arguing from experience, performatively asserting his authority to make such judgments. Significantly, Randy also observed the centrality of embodied movement in the curation of musical "feeling" as he argued against the apathy of younger audiences to "old country" by demanding "Who's interested in them fuckers anyway? You want the guys DANCIN' on that DANCE floor!" By this time the stream of assent from the others in the room had grown nearly continuous: we were closing in on an apotheosis of sociable "feeling."

But Hoppy wanted to continue talking. So he stressed the other side of the dialectic of "feeling," just as he had stressed nostalgia in response to Randy's argument for innovation. Hoppy insisted: "even if they're DANCIN', they're still not hearin' what you say." He argued here for the equal importance of the *verbal* side of "feeling," and his correction was instantly acknowledged by Randy and the others as essential to the "feeling" being co-constructed in this moment.

As the rest of us continued to lend our assent and amplification, Randy refined Hoppy's point by concretizing it further. He referred, specifically, to the way seasoned beer-joint singers often change the lyrics to canonical songs, especially with the use of "dirty" and "nasty" variants and parodies, to express boredom, anger at inattention, or just playfulness and novelty. Randy had a huge number of these rewrites at his command, ranging from altered titles like "Snot Love" (for Merle Haggard's "It's Not Love [But It's Not Bad]") to coarse literalizations of sentimental love songs (e.g., "Take the titty from my mouth" for "Take the ribbons from your hair" in the Kris Kristofferson classic "Help Me Make It Through the Night").

Randy socializes this polemic too, referring to a comic sexual song Justin Treviño had recently written and performed: "How Can I Get Over You (When You're Always Under Him)?"[18] This song is a perfect parody of a conventional punning lyric structure, deftly matched to the 4/4 swing "feel" of which Justin is the acknowledged, albeit youthful, local master.[19] The story constructed in dialogue here dramatizes the affront experienced by a singer when the crowd fails to attend to the words of a song, thus stripping a performance of "feeling" by denying the essential quality of the performer/audience relationship.

Finally, this episode moved toward its climax around the image of the sociomusical ideal: a performance in which the singer and the audience are deeply engaged in the production of verbal and embodied and nostalgic and innovative "feeling." This sequence repaired the image of Hoppy's opening gambit, which pictured, as an image with which to make sense of Randy's departure, the disturbing vision of the mighty Merle Haggard on a bad night, singing without "feeling." Even Merle Haggard (and even Randy Meyer) "can't always feel great." Now, at the feelingful end of this sequence, Randy, Phil, and Hoppy closed in on their vision of perfection: a live performance in a timeless utopian beer joint. Phil added his voice to the increasingly dense pile of parallel and overlapping and back-channeling voices, as he reminded us of the embodied essence of "feeling." "Above all," he said, "you gotta have a certain amount of HEART." The comment was aimed directly at Randy Meyer, dying of heart disease.

This "feeling" was saturated, however, with a sense of impending loss. Randy and Phil stressed, against all the evidence surrounding us in this once intensely musical region of the nation, that one could still set off around the country and find oneself in a utopian musical world, just like in the good old days. The irony here is that in constructing "feeling" as an object of sociable desire for the past, it was salvaged for the present. And in this intense moment, Randy decided to stay for just a while longer. Indeed, Randy stayed and shared the stories of the good old days out "on the road" for at least another hour, until we were all exhausted and it was time for us to go down those stairs together and go "to the house."

Interlude

Photo Essay

Hoppy's Place

Out back

Hoppy looks for a tape

Hoppy talks with a friend

Miss Audrey and Miss Ann share a secret

Randy gives Hoppy a playful punch

A musician enjoys a compliment

Hoppy, Justin, and Bill relax between sets

Hoppy examines a guitar

Judy and Hoppy

Randy singing at the Hilltop Bar, Spicewood, Texas

Randy in the recording studio (1)

Randy in the recording studio (2)

Randy and Hoppy have a reunion (1)

Randy and Hoppy have a reunion (2)

Randy and Judy have a reunion

Randy holds forth with friends between sets

Randy and Ann catch up

Sociability

Miss Ann and Miss Bettie relax

Hoppy argues a point with a friend

Miguel makes himself clear

Checking out a bottle of homemade wine

Candy Sue, the barmaid, at a benefit

Miss Audrey holding Charo, her Chihuahua

Miss Bettie smiles for the camera

Miss Ann on a busy night

The Y'All Come Back Salon, Lockhart, Texas

Drinking alone

Pablo enjoys Justin Treviño's music and a beer

Good Old Boy

Justin Treviño sings at a benefit

Big Joe singing at a jam session

Bill plays the pedal steel guitar

Les the lead-man

Sign in the Y'All Come Back Saloon

Main Street, Lockhart, Texas, U.S.A.

A trailer-home

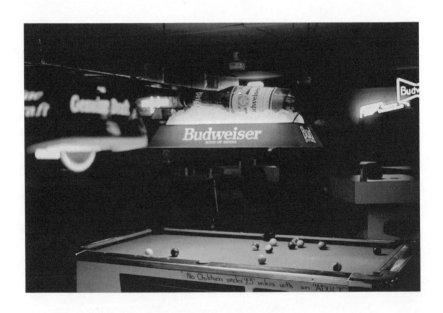

Ann's Other Place, after hours

Down the road a piece

"Bring Me Up in a Beer Joint"

The Poetics of Speech and Song

The "music" of language and the "grammar" of music remain
caught in a metaphysical classification. There is a sense in which,
phenomenologically, spoken language is at least as "musical" as it is
"logical," and if we have separated sound from meaning, then two
distinct directions of inquiry are opened and opposed. But in voiced
word music and logic are incarnate. No "pure" music nor "pure"
meaning may be found. — Don Ihde, *Listening and Voice*

Speech and Song and the Space between Them

Twilight was fading fast outside Ann's Other Place. Inside, we were enveloped in that gauzy, tired quiet that descends over hundreds of beer joints simultaneously in the last hot hour of Texas sunlight, at the end of another workday and the beginning of another night filled with music, talk, and beer. The TV was on with the sound turned all the way down because the jukebox was playing those sad, slow country songs people preferred at this hour. Aching pedal steel guitar lines mingled with humming refrigerators, a clanking old cash register, the whoosh of beer cans being opened, the snap and hiss of lighters being opened and lit, and the muted voices of a few conversations. Cigarette smoke, announced by the exaggerated hiss between pursed lips that accompanies the first few, long-awaited puffs of the evening, seeped into our hair and skin and clothes so completely that you could never wash it out. Trucks sputtered and stopped in the parking lot, grumbling and dieseling with a shower of tinkling gravel thrown up against the tin walls of the bar. Clouds of dust came inside every few minutes when the windowless door opened to admit a shaft of twilight and then slammed shut again and greetings punctuated the quiet.

Someone entering shouted out "Howr' y'doin' Rusty?" Old Rusty barked back, *"TERRIBLE!"* He was shockingly loud in the late-day quiet, and only half kidding, and we all laughed and then turned back to our beers and conversations. Weary, sweaty bodies took their places at the bar. There was Quiet Paul, who drove a delivery truck all day, methodically drinking a can of Miller Lite and talking privately to Pat the barmaid. Old Rusty and his buddy Jerry were leaning into each other, talking playfully about the really BIG dinner you could have if you went to that cook-it-yourself steakhouse up in Austin. Maria, with a fool's broken heart, stared off into space and now and then sang a snatch of a song to herself. When she wasn't talking to Paul, Pat was serving beers, emptying ashtrays, and stocking the beer coolers for the busy night ahead. She seemed a little tired and cranky. She'd been fighting with her boyfriend yet again, and maybe because she was in that mood, the cooler doors slammed a little louder than usual in the air-conditioned quiet, and the icy beers she was serving hit the counter with a louder bang than usual, too.

In this liminal hour between the laboring day and the abandonments of the evening, I was talking to Carl, who drove a propane delivery truck and who was celebrated at Ann's Place as the finest local "comedian." I often used this quiet hour for one-on-one conversations. At twilight, it seemed appropriate to talk seriously and privately. An hour later, after Miss Ann flipped on the Budweiser plastic Tiffany lamps over the bar and turned up the volume on the jukebox, and after the songs got faster and more optimistic, and conversations got a little louder just to compete, and after the fourth or fifth beer began to take effect, there would be little serious, private talk, and no more silence until the last patron departed after midnight, leaving the jukebox to belt out random free selections once an hour through the night in the empty bar.

It was, in fact, nearly time for that seven o'clock swell of noisy sociable talk and loud music and newfound energy. Carl was telling me why he loved beer joints. "I grew up around beer joints," he said. "My father bought one when he got out of the Navy, and I was in there every night." He paused a second and then pronounced, "You can't bring me up in a beer joint, and tell me how to live."

I wrote this last sentence down in my notebook, quickly and nervously, because I knew that writing something down, even something so ordinary as a line from a conversation, was a sure way to derail an interview in this community. To write something down was, like any act of poetic focusing on the submerged meanings of ordinary talk, to open a trap door, and to invite others to join in on the sociable conversation.

As I wrote, Carl practically shouted: "Hey! That'd make a great song. Are you writing that down?" He turned to the others around us at the bar, anticipating the effect of his remark. Promptly, someone else asked, "What's he got there?" in a friendly way, looking for something interesting to talk about. Carl reached for my pad, which I pushed over to him, and he read out my last notation to the bar: " 'You can't bring me up in a beer joint, and tell me how to live!' " Everybody laughed, and the other quiet conversations stopped. "Well, if it makes you rich, remember where you got it. 'You can't bring me up in a beer joint . . .' *Gaaaaaaawd* DAMN!" Our "interview" was, it seemed, over for now, swamped by a wave of talk and laughter and delight.

This scene exemplifies a particular cultural understanding of the relationship between song and the "ordinary" speech registers of everyday working-class life. Blue-collar Texans define "song" precisely as a condensation of conversation into a poetically rich phrase, a movement from epic narration to lyric reflection, a defamiliarizing shifting between the sense and sound of language. Carl's phrase — "You can't bring me up in a beer joint/and tell me how to live" — emerged with only the slightest inflectional marking of its subliminal poetic quality (Jakobson 1985b). Carl had not planned his poetic utterance in advance, though he was regarded by his friends as a gifted speaker. But, as Carl and I both immediately realized, the phrase *is* poetic, and it resonates at many levels with a generically specific kind of country song.[1]

The line possesses regular meter, marked by its alliterative bilabials on the first and third strong beats of the first line ("bring" and "beer"). This effect is heightened by the South Texas English dialectal tendency to implode the /b/ sound slightly in carefully articulated, publicly addressive speech, giving it a percussive, "popping" quality. Those popped bilabials and the more delicate alliteration of the /l/ in "tell me how to live" give the line a symmetrical phonetic shape that compels the playful repetition it inspired among those at the bar. It is pleasurable to speak this phrase. But there is a far more evocative poetry in this line than any invocation of a momentary articulatory delight in paradigmatic projections and symmetric metric patterns can explain.

To people steeped in classic country music, this metrical alliteration echoes a standard formal trope of honky-tonk songwriting. This alliterative pattern is a characteristic of many classic beer-joint songs.[2] Examples include the title line in Loretta Lynn's "Don't Come Home A Drinkin', (With Lovin' on Your Mind)"[3] and the last line of the first verse in Ernest Tubb's "Walkin' the Floor over You": "I don't know why you did dear/but I do know that you're gone."[4] Honky-tonk songs, that is, conventionally use alliteration on strong beats to produce a strong rhythmic "feel" in the vocal line.

Likewise, Carl's phrase features internal syntactic parallelism (an active verb phrase in each clause, with the two clauses together outlining a causal temporal antecedent/consequent sequence). His delivery was marked by metrical regularity (with strong accents on "bring," "beer," "tell," and "live"), and he marked the two-clause structure of his statement with a rising and falling intonational cadence that moves from suspension (at the juncture between clauses) to release (on "live"). This recalls, for these Texans, a conventional syntactic, metrical, and intonational pattern that frequently co-occurs along with metrical alliteration in songs. Numerous canonical country songs organize key lines around such alliterative, metrically bifurcated clause sequences, often at key formal junctures. In song, such lines often follow a series of single-clause or enjambed double-clause lines. These lines delimit the transition from verse to refrain ("chorus") and often end with a dramatic "stop," or silent beat (as in Carl's speech, which was followed by a pregnant pause as we first savored the line and as I decided to commit it to paper). Ray Price's "Heartaches by the Number," for example, fits this pattern in the final lines of its first verse:

END OF FIRST VERSE
"Heartache number two was when you came back again/
+you came back, but never meant to stay.[5] [full band stop]
REFRAIN
Now I've got heartaches by the number . . .

In another variant of this paradigm, the multiple-clause metrically alliterative temporal sequence can be shifted "back" in the song form to occupy the penultimate (rather than final) line in a verse. This sets up a return of the song's title phrase (which may or may not have the same form) as the final line of the verse, prior to its elaboration in the refrain. This "punchline" effect—in which the song's title phrase is framed as a point of rhetorical arrival—tends to occur in song forms in which the verse and refrain are formally indistinguishable in terms of tune, meter, tense, or mood. In such musically (though not textually) strophic song forms, refrains are differentiated from verses only by virtue of their repetition. The refrain must be textually motivated and demarcated by a lyric crystallization in a narrative "punchline" (marked in the examples below with "∧") that rhetorically sets up the refrain's elaboration. We see this in songs like Hank Williams's "Take These Chains from My Heart" and Bobby Helms's "Fraulein."

VERSE

+*If you love somebody new, let me find a new love too*
∧*Take these chains from my heart and set me free.*

REFRAIN

Take these chains from my heart and set me free[6]

VERSE

+*Where I loved her and left her, now I can't forget her*[7]
∧*I miss my pretty Fraulein*

REFRAIN

Fraulein, fraulein, look up to the heavens[8]

This penultimate placement of the alliterative double-clause cause-and-effect sequence in the verse prior to the refrain is also widespread in songs that use the 32-bar AABA form, rather than the more common verse/refrain pattern.[9] Again, the poetic goal is intensification and lyric focusing, and the structural goal is to mark a formal juncture. Typically the double-clause line precedes the title phrase of the song, which in turn completes the "A" section of the poetic form, transitioning to the markedly different tune, mood, harmony, and register of the "B" section (or else ending the song in its final appearance as a "tag"). Some canonical songs I have discussed elsewhere in this work, such as George Jones's "She Thinks I Still Care" and Merle Haggard's "Today, I Started Loving You Again," deploy this structure:

LAST 8 BARS OF "A" SECTION

+*Just because I saw her, and then went all to pieces*
∧*She thinks I still care*[10]

LAST 8 BARS OF "A" SECTION
+*I got over you just long enough to let my heartaches mend*
ʌ*And then today, I started loving you again*[11]

This metrical pattern can also be internally expanded through embedded repetitions and conjunct clauses. For example, in Patsy Cline's "I Fall to Pieces," a line with three sequential clauses (embedded clause marked with [ ]) is contrasted with a background pattern of two-clause lines:

LAST 8 BARS OF "A" SECTION
+*And I try, [and I try,] but I haven't yet*
ʌ*You walk by and I fall to pieces*[12]

Finally, entire songs can be structurally and rhetorically organized as a series of these two-clause temporal sequences. In the next example, Charlie Walker's classic "Pick Me Up on Your Way Down," this is accompanied by a chiasmic alliteration of stressed /p/ and /t/ across the line breaks and by a rigorous maintenance of line-internal phonetic rhyme:

LAST 8 BARS OF FIRST VERSE
Where you tossed it to [alt. 'on'] *the ground* ["it" = the narrator's "heart"],
Pick me up on your way down
REFRAIN
Pick me up on your way down, when you're blue and all alone
When their glamor stars to bore you, come on back where you belong
You may be their pride and joy, but they'll find another toy
Then they'll take way your crown, pick me up on your way down[13]

Bring Me Up in a Beer Joint:
The Sacred Space of Public Domesticity

"I try to write everyday living, everyday life."—Loretta Lynn, quoted in
Dorothy Horstman, *Sing Your Heart Out, Country Boy*

There are, then, complex and pervasive formal similarities between Carl's phrase and the meter, phonology, and syntax of intensification and formal juncture in many important honky-tonk songs. This is one sense in which the phrase would, as Carl observed, "make great song." But the line "You can't

bring me up in a beer joint and then tell me how to live" also drips with semantic and cultural resonance, and this is what ultimately inspires our mutual
recognition of its songlike poesis. The abstract subject of both verbs ("you")
does not refer indexically to Carl's interlocutor (me).[14] Nor does it refer generically to any possible subject, as "one" does in other dialects. Although
both of these uses are common in working-class Texas English, Carl's usage
of "you" is more specific, and rhetorically conventional. It refers to social
forces beyond an "ordinary" person's control, and to a social history that links
the lives of those who were "brought up in beer joints" to those who were
not raised around blue-collar taverns but who are heard to tell working-class
people "how to live."

   This is a poetic usage of "you," one usually handled by the more critical but
still ambiguous pronoun "they" [or "them"/"'em"] which typically refers, at
some level of abstraction, to more powerful classes in society whose asserted
interests are felt to impinge on the local world of working-class existence. One
day, Doc asserted this view to Richard:

DOC: Man it's ridiculous!
They're tryin' to RAPE us!
RICHARD: Yeah I'm tellin' you!
DOC: **They** have . . .
they're havin the EARTH
meeting or whatever it is
down there in BrazIL
or wherever the hell it is
down in
South America
and ALL of the bigwigs are gettin together
and **they've** decided
they're gonna impose all this SHIT on us
an **they're** gonna raise all our electric rates
They're fixin' to raise our electric rates
like YOU ain't never seen 'em!
[loudly, stressing every word]
I GOT NEWS FOR 'EM!
I GOT COAL OIL LAMPS
THEY can cut my electricity OFF!

Such uses of "they" assert local isolation from power, and a sense that one's grievances are not heard by "them." But Carl's "you" asserts a stronger claim to agency. It reflects the addressivity of country music's discourse on class, which is meant to be overheard by those it criticizes (Ann's "what *you . . .* might call country music"). Carl's "you" makes a polemical linkage between oppositional working-class attitudes and the irreversible effects of class experience on his generation of blue-collar workers. This is a generation still clinging to the way of life celebrated in beer joints and country music with a conscious assertion of the oppositionality of their culture and a sense that something valuable is being lost. Carl's articulation of "a beer joint" as the site for the production of his working-class resistance to being "told how to live" represents a key cultural focus and goes right to the heart of why beer joints matter as political institutions to people like the patrons at Ann's.

The perception that "they" are "killing the beer joints" was frequently voiced by Ann's patrons. The laws governing drunk driving and the legal drinking age were increasingly strict and strictly enforced, and the state's promotion of leisure pursuits (like the lottery) was widely felt to be undermining a key institutional basis for working-class cultural and political solidarity. One day, for example, Ann had to decide whether to serve a twenty-two-year-old patron who still had a driver's license issued when he was a teenager, across which was stamped in red letters "UNDER 21." According to the handbook circulated to bars by the Texas Alcoholic Beverages Commission, taverns are not allowed to serve anyone carrying such a license, and twenty-one-year-olds carrying such licenses must pay for a new license whether or not their "Under 21" license has expired. Bo tried to make the rational case for his friend, whom everyone agreed was in fact twenty-two. But Ann was nervous, because infractions in this area could put her out of business quickly and without appeal:[15]

BO: Yeah, he is twenty-two years old
ANN: Yes, it certainly SAYS so
But **they** also . . .
Now where do I come in?
They give me THIS
It's two pages
[opens flyer]
and if a card does NOT match one of these [pictures]
—It's on here and here—

[points to page]
then I'm . . .
It tells you right on there
I'm NOT supposed to take it!
BO: [reading the manual] Hmmmmm
now *that's* something new!
HOPPY: Oh **they're** about to put the BEER joints out of BUSINESS, BO!

With this alliterative summation—itself the potential basis for a "good song"—Hoppy expressed an anxiety about "them" which is widespread in this local world. As a musician, he has a deeply felt anger about the state's hegemonic presence and its crushing effect on his life and livelihood. But country music is far more than a source of livelihood for working-class musicians and their fans. Beer joints are sacred institutions, liturgically centered on country music and verbal art as well as the consumption of alcohol. They are very frequently compared by their patrons to the small fundamentalist churches that also dot these highways. Many people, in fact, move between these institutions throughout their lives, growing up in the church, "falling" into a drinking lifestyle, and dramatically being "saved" in their old age as death approaches. The oral and musical forms that are ritually cultivated in both churches and taverns are, as it were, mutually intelligible, and an air of sentimental fellow-feeling is common to both spheres. Hoppy once put it this way:

AF: I've heard you SAY that beer joints are kinda like churches to you
in some ways?
HOPPY: Weeeeell
There's a lot you can
READ out of people . . .
I made a lot of FRIENDS in beer joints
Course I met a lot of BUMS too
[laughs]
You can do that in CHURCH
y'know?   AF: Right
So what's the difference, then?
And I freak people out a lot of times, y'know
I'm subject to do a religious song in a
BEER joint!   AF: Right

If it happens to be what hits my head
or somebody says somethin, y'know
I'm liable to do it
So I don't care

It is this "sacred" conception of the beer joint that Carl's phrase echoed for all of us as we recognized its poetic resonance with a good country song. The phrase emerged during the hour of transition from the workday to the evening's leisure. It was heightened by our mutual immersion in the oral and aural richness of that hour, which marks the boundary of the nightly ritual of musically mediated beer-joint sociability, an hour saturated with reflection on the politics of working-class experience. It is at precisely this moment that the "sacredness" of beer joints is most palpably salient for patrons, and the fading of noise and daylight outside heightens the smoky darkness, the humming coolness, and the swaddled aural lushness of this cultural space. This "happy hour" is a quiet vigil before the evening's intensifying, quasi-liturgical progression of music, talk, and feeling.

In addition to this sacred resonance, Carl's phrase makes a more explicit and equally canonical equation between beer joints and another marked and cherished social sphere: domesticity. While bars are often considered as "second homes," this parallel is often tinged with a sense of loss, as in Merle Haggard's beloved song "Swingin' Doors," which finds the drinking protagonist "always here at home 'til closing time."[16]

This is, of course, a gendered trope; bars are marked in country music as sites for a male alternative to female-dominated domesticity, while homes (and churches, for that matter) are marked as female spaces. This conflict is delightfully thematized in comedic songs like David Frizzell's "I'm Gonna Hire a Wino (to Decorate Our Home)," sung in the reported voice of a drunkard's wife, who imagines her home as a tavern where her husband's habits can be contained.[17] (Cal Smith's "The Lord Knows I'm Drinking" tells the opposite story, narrating what happens when a female agent of propriety and religion shows up to look down her nose at the folks who drink in a bar; the "self-righteous biddy" is promptly told to go back to church.)

But such songs comically overstate the gulf between the sexes (and their respective spheres of control) in real life. Bars like Ann's Other Place and many other beer joints (especially those that are owned and managed by women and married couples) carefully cultivate an aura of domesticity. They thus become true "second homes" for men, women, and even children. It is therefore possible, as Carl attests, to be "brought up in a beer joint" where adults carefully monitor the environment and attempt to create a homelike atmosphere. The barroom community is often described in the image of family. People express sincere and effusive love for their fellow patrons, even extending to the use of fictive kin terms. Men are "like brothers" to each other; Miss Ann is "like a mother" to musicians, and some older women are affectionately called "Mama [First Name]" by unrelated others. Indeed, bars are not merely adult spaces in rural, working-class communities in Texas. They are full of children.

As Carl implies, a Texan child *can* in fact be born into and brought up in the beer joints. I have seen a newborn baby, hours from the hospital, spend his first social minutes in a beer joint. He was gushed over by his parents' many close friends, who put their cigarettes out and came over to the middle table, away from the smoke and noise, to look and congratulate. At benefits and other community events organized around the bars, adults, including men, take turns supervising children as they play in the interstices of adult sociability, or the supervision is assigned to older children. At these benefits, adults help children set up game booths around the bar or the parking lot and children participate in sign making and decoration. During the charity auctions at such benefits, adults frequently buy gifts for their children and even the children of others, and children can entreat nearly any adult for quarters to play a game of pool or the "crane" games that reward winners with stuffed animals. Adults who win those games frequently give their prizes to the children in the bar.

Bars are an important site for the linguistic socialization of working-class children in Texas. Older, economically stable adults who bring their children and grandchildren into the bars monitor the speech of others, and if profanity is being used they may send the children to play outside or take the children home—or warn the offending speaker that children are present. Indeed, as the following conversation between Sammy and Sally (a relatively well-off retired couple) and Miss Ann suggests, there is not complete agreement on the presence of children in bars:

SAMMY:[18] [confidential, low voiced, falling intonation]
I have a hard time with children in bars . . .
Y'can't (bring a kid in here)
it GETS to me

[high pitched, swooping intonation on each line]
Just DOES . . .
I don' know why
it just DOES . . .
[pounds on bar]
to me this is jus' NOT *a place for children*
's not desIIIIIIGNED for children
they don't SEEERVE things for children . . .
SALLY: Well that's true . . .
SAMMY: and the LANguage is not built for children!
ANN: [firmly]
Now THAT is *very true!*
[pounds bar]
and that BOthers me
MAny times it bothers me!
SAMMY: See that bothers me . . .
but YET by the SAME token
my feelings are
I am not going to tell
all these GROWN adult people . . .
ANN: . . . to clean up your act
Cuz that kid's over there
[points to a baby in the corner of the bar with some teenagers]
just cuz the place is *not designed for children*
SALLY: That's right!
SAMMY: No!
No it's not!
ANN: But yet by the same token I'm still awARE of the fact
that children should not be subjEcted to this
SAMMY: That's riiiiight
there you GO!
ANN: So I'm
I'm always between a rock and a hard place with it . . .
SALLY: When wE brought Shayla[19] here   [their grandchild]
the PEOple that was in here
wasn't talkin' foul-mouthed or anything
cuz if they HAVE

I'd've took her outside
SAMMY: Yeah we'd've LEFT
I guar-an-TEE ya
ANN: So WE gonna HAVE to deal with that
SAMMY: I use plenty . . .
Ann . . .
I use foul language . . .
[the women snicker]
but I don't use it around children!

Despite these sentiments held by some of the older and more conservative members of the community, people do bring children into the beer joints. And children are participants in beer joint life. Small children frequently carry messages between adults and run errands across the bar for adults, like getting sodas and ice from the bar, or cigarettes, tools, or instruments from cars. Adolescent boys may help their fathers set up musical equipment, and even toddlers wander happily across the stage as the adult musicians do their work. Adolescent girls are often expected to watch the younger children for their mothers, and adolescent single mothers occasionally bring their children to the bars seeking impromptu child care.

Adults take delight in the verbal play of children. Such verbal play often shows sensitivity to and awareness of the swirl of adult gossip and narrative that surrounds the children, although like children everywhere, they are still struggling with adult social boundaries. I remember the gales of laughter that ensued when a five-year-old girl, the daughter of a regular patron at Ann's, asked me earnestly and with wide eyes that revealed the bizarreness of my social identity and the kind of talk about me that happened in my absence, "Aaron, are you YANkee?"

The antics of children are often the focus of talk. The story was retold for weeks after a particularly precocious girl toddler seized the training-potty which served as a front-of-the-stage tip-jar (or "kitty") for the musicians, carried it out to the middle of the busy dance floor, and squatted on it, producing what many people regarded as an appropriate bodily comment on the overly loud band that afternoon. Whenever I was filming or taking still photos, I was always asked to document the play of children. Children dance with each other and with their older siblings and parents, and parents will sometimes hold a small child between them as they dance together. In general, children are encouraged to be performative and to weave their way through and around adult social life, although children do not interact much in adult conversations when they are small. Young children *can* freely interrupt adult conversations, however, and meet with only mild disapproval for doing so too often.[20]

Children are disciplined publicly, with little sense of embarrassment. Indeed, to a certain extent any adult can discipline any child verbally with a scold. And parents will sometimes swat their misbehaving children on the rear end, and just as easily pull them close for a spontaneous hug. Adults also discipline their own children with "time out" sessions, in which a child is expected to stay silent and motionless for several minutes to atone for an infraction. When asked, these parents earnestly assert that such "time out" is better than hitting the child. The quickness to justify such punishments reveals that discipline administered in the public sphere of the beer joint is scrutinized by others. Verbally and physically abusive parents are indeed censured by gossip for their excesses, and sometimes reported to social service agencies. Other adults may quietly intervene to comfort a child who has been spanked or yelled at by a parent, plying the child with soda or food or quarters or kind words. And it is common for more stable families to take care of the children of less stable families during times of crisis.

This is not to say that real child abuse does not happen in rural, working-class communities, for it most certainly does, as it does in many other communities in America. But serious abuse tends to happen in the private domestic sphere away from the watchful eyes at the bar. Some locals—especially those raised outside Texas—consider simply bringing children into bars to be abusive, but for some children in abusive families, indeed, the bar is a better place to be than their homes. At the bar there are other children to play with; there are relatively or completely sober adults concerned with their well-being who will feed them, talk to them, and show interest in their development; and there are very real social constraints on their parents' behavior toward them, enforced by consequential gossip.[21]

Teenagers under the legal drinking age sometimes socialize in bars at night, playing pool and drinking sodas. And musical teenagers are welcome as junior participants in jam sessions. Justin Treviño is an example, and he went on to a prominent career as a professional musician in part because he had grown up in the beer joints where he now makes his living. The children of musicians frequently experience such an apprenticeship at their parents' favorite taverns. Some older children and teenagers sit with adults and gradually contribute more fully and competently to conversations. Teenage mothers may enter their own mother's social circle in the beer joints even as they cultivate relationships within their own generational cohort, and mothers and their adult daughters very often remain close friends over the years even as various husbands and boyfriends come and go. Teenage boys and young men, likewise, often remain in their father's social orbit, dropping into their father's regular beer joint for frequent short visits even while they are out cultivating other relationships in other places (which is essential for the assertion of masculine maturity).

Across gender and generational lines, fathers and daughters and mothers and sons also have strong ties. At a beer joint birthday party, Randy Meyer's adult daughter took the stage to sing Holly Dunn's "Daddy's Hands" (a sentimental song about a stern but loving father) for her dad. He was intensely moved. I have since seen several female singers perform this for their fathers. Later that night, Randy performed Merle Haggard's "The Farmer's Daughter" for his daughter, meeting her tear-filled eyes with his own each time he sang the title line of this cherished song about an elderly widowed farmer who gives his daughter away reluctantly but with his blessing to "that city boy from town."[22]

In the beer joints, then, children grow up gradually acquiring knowledge about adult domains of sociability and responsibility. As they themselves begin to figure in local gossip and stories, the emotional ties of obligation and attachment between generations are strongly emphasized. Adults, in turn, lionize their own parents in stories. There is much more to be said about this subject, which goes beyond my project here, but my point is simply that being "brought up in a beer joint" is not an unusual or inaccurate description of a Texas working-class childhood. Crucially, this kind of upbringing, centered on beer joints as community centers, socializes children into markedly working-class forms of speaking, sociality, and sentiment. With this comes a strong sense that beer joints are sacred spaces, vital institutions for the kind of community envisioned by these people as a humane and "ordinary" way to live.

And this was the idea that Carl's line articulated. The vivid local sense that "they're killin' the beer joints" does indeed cause rural, working-class people to feel "told how to live." For people "brought up" around these places, and bringing their children up around them in turn, this has cultural consequences. Carl's poetic line was deeply political and made a fundamental kind of sense in relation to the "ordinary" life he and his friends were carefully cultivating at Ann's bar. Its politicization and poeticization of a shared sense of a good and moral "ordinariness" made the line a fine candidate for conversion into a song—even a hypothetical song. Country song is precisely a medium that discovers the beauty and dignity of an "ordinary" working-class social voice—a voice that might well be "brought up in a beer joint." Carl made explicit the inchoate, implicit significance of every country song worthy of the highest honorific designation this community can bestow: "real country music."

Text and Performance in Country Music and Rural, Working-Class Verbal Art

"Hank [Williams] started telling me about his problems with his ex-wife Audrey. He said that one day her 'Cheatin' Heart' would pay. Then he said, 'Hey, that'd make a good song! Get out my tablet, Baby! Me and you are gonna write us a song!' Just about as fast as I could write, Hank quoted the words to me in a matter of minutes."
—Billie Jean Williams Horton, quoted in Dorothy Horstman,
Sing Your Heart Out, Country Boy

The poetic principles that make country music a recognizable and aesthetically distinct genre for working-class Texans are vividly evident in Carl's recognition of the submerged poetry of his accidental phrase. Canonically, country songwriters claim that they are inspired by overhearing such resonant phrases in ordinary talk, spoken by ordinary working-class people (there are examples of this throughout Horstman 1986). Regular patrons of rural beer joints are, like Carl, quite aware of this mythic connection between their speech and what they hear on the jukebox, and song acquires power and feeling precisely from this resonance.

But this resonance also involves a defamiliarizing movement away from "ordinariness," a movement in which poeticians have discovered the basis of verbal art's social power (Baumann and Briggs 1990; Jakobson 1960; Mukarovsky 1964). Country music, like working-class verbal art more generally, pushes against a sense of the "ordinariness" and "givenness" of language. And yet song and verbal art are sutured tightly together with everyday talk, too.

There are, in other words, two aspects which, in combination, comprise the very definition of what "song" is in relation to "ordinary" speech. The first of these is a "textual" aspect; the second is a "performative" aspect.[23]

I do not want to draw a rigid distinction between these two aspects of country here. Indeed, my examples will show the impossibility of considering either aspect in isolation. But as an analytic model for understanding verbal creativity and the interpretation and experience of that creativity, the text/performance distinction captures a real, locally salient understanding of musical and verbal art. These two facets of verbal and musical art intertwine at the level of discursive practice. But they combine in a cultural attitude that styles poetic creation as an invigorating and sometimes vertiginous "entextualizing" movement *away* from the "naturalness" of "ordinary," unmarked, instrumental discourse. In this model, "performance" is, in turn, the bold assertion of the relevance of such "denaturalizing" poetic movements in the context of "ordinary" discourse and experience.

Such dialectical movements between the de- and re- naturalization of meaning are constitutive of effective and affecting song *and* verbal art in Texas working-class culture. Speech saturates song, and song saturates speech, and in between speech and song lies an enormous and frequently traversed zone of verbal art. Within this zone a subtle range of tropes and vocal inflections establishes a continuum between speech and song. Movements along this continuum are realized by a dense poetic interleaving of speaking and singing practices in song texts, song performances, verbal art, everyday speech about and around music, and even "ordinary" conversational talk.

For these Texans, song is the product of a "denaturalizing" attention to the sound and meaning of everyday speech. As I have argued elsewhere (Fox 1992), this effect is the result of an arsenal of defamiliarizing poetic tropes. These figures and patterns draw a listener's attention to the linguistic construction (the "textuality") of the everyday working-class lifeworld. Country song lyrics are saturated with tropes that call attention to the origin of song's verbal raw material in "ordinary" domains and that simultaneously poeticize that raw material.

These denaturalizing tropes depend, however, on effective performance by musicians and verbal artists. Performance (re-) contextualizes the poet's insight into "real life," situating textuality in the midst of "ordinary" experience. Describing such writerly poetic tropes involves an analytic abstraction, but an abstraction that is not foreign to the spirit of these figures themselves. Carl's previous remark testifies to this spirit of working-class reflexivity. Subtle shadings distinguish metadiscursive reflections on "ordinary" life and language from the most "ordinary" uses to which these reflections are routinely put. At any moment, in other words, "a good song" may emerge out of the texture of everyday talk.

These tropes also differ in their degree of interpretive transparency. Some, like punning and wordplay, mark an orientation to diverse audiences. Such tropes become stereotypical emblems available to celebrators and detractors of country's presumed "simplicity" and "folk wisdom" as well as to people deeply immersed and invested in country music as a historically working-class form of cultural expression (see Fox 2004a). By contrast, other tropes, in particular those that produce the dense intertextuality of country music, require a history of engagement with the genre.

Wordplay and Metaphoric Literalization

Even the most casual listening reveals the centrality of what might be very broadly called "wordplay" in country music. The (forced) pun is a stereotypical emblem of country music, and a frequent basis for parodies of country's poetics. This extensive category takes in a range of specific figures: punning, the literalization and startling juxtaposition of frozen metaphors and the coining of new metaphors, and an orientation toward pithy and aphoristic condensations of "common sense" knowledge about human nature and social life. Embedded and frozen metaphorical tropes with long histories in English poetics are particularly elaborated and typically literalized in country lyrics.[24] These include the "heart" as the independent voiced agent of true thoughts and feelings (e.g., Hank Williams's "Your Cheatin' Heart," which "will tell on you");[25] passion as fire (e.g., Merle Haggard's "Old Flames," which "can't hold a candle to you");[26] or the passage of time as physical movement along a road or railroad track (e.g., Johnny Cash's "Folsom Prison Blues," or Haggard's "White Line Fever," where "the years keep flyin' by like the high-line poles").[27]

The poetic probing of conventional and hackneyed metaphors in song texts canonically involves a "literal" extension of metaphoric entailments that undermine or extend a metaphor's frozen "ordinary" figurative sense. Literalization is engaging and poetic in proportion to the dullness and ubiquity of the metaphor itself, and in proportion to the number of conventional metaphors within a single domain that can be swept up into a single denaturalizing image. Big Judy, for example, often thrilled the crowd at Ann's Place by performing a hit song by the band Highway 101 which combined the classic image of an animated "heart" with a pervasive literalization of the slightly fresher metaphoric linkage between "love" and a "song." *"Our song of love is almost ended,"* the refrain begins, and it ends by asserting *"I won't play second fiddle/to the beat of your honky-tonk heart."*[28] This literalization hinges on the polysemy of the word "beat," conjoining musical and physiological senses. Entire songs can be built out of one extended metaphoric literalization, as in George Jones's "The Race Is On," in which the metaphor "heartbreak is a horse race" is the source for numerous literalized racing metaphors: pride "comes up the backstretch," heartaches "go to the inside," tears "hold back" and "try not to fall," "true love" is "scratched," and "the winner loses all."[29]

Such punning literalization is also a fundamental trope of verbal art in Texas working-class talk, especially in the poetically heightened context of beer-joint conversation. The following humorous example occurred on a quiet late afternoon at Ann's Place, as we sat around "talkin' shit" with no particular intensity. Randy the postman, his wife Val, Miss Ann, and I had been talking about "the old days" as usual, focusing on the observation that people had once married at a younger age, and for life, but didn't do so anymore. Val commented that this was not necessarily a bad social change. Her husband had a quick and witty comeback that literalized Val's unconsidered, conventional metaphor:

VAL: I'd've had a COW if my daughter wanted to get married at fifTEEN!
RANDY: You'd've prob'ly had a SON-in-LAW!

Like the Highway 101 song, Randy's punning literalization was predicated on polysemy, here of the possessive verb "had," which can refer to an embodied emotional state or a kinship relation. Some comedic performances may even raise this trope to a metadiscursive level. For instance, one night at a jam session, an inebriated woman in no condition to sing tried several times to join in on the music making. Carl, who was widely admired for his ability to make just such jokes, intervened on behalf of the musicians, then turned to those of us at the bar and pointed out, with a musical story, that his joke had been predicated on a generalizable species of grammatical ambiguity:[30]

WOMAN: [to the musicians, but loudly] Are you sure I can't SING?
CARL: [interceding] I'm SURE you can't!

HELL no!

[Carl then turns to the others at the bar and in a lower voice adds]

That's like that song me an' the wife was playing

that said

"She don't cry like she used to?"[31]

I said "NO

now she's standin' on her head and cryin!"

Diana said

"No that means she don't CRY anymore . . ."

Lyric and Epic: The Poetry of Mood and Image

This kind of semantic decoupling of words from their "ordinary" sense is the essence of aesthetic quality in both country songwriting and working-class verbal art. Country's entextualization of "ordinary" language is also effected by a generic progression of poetic moods, especially shifts in transitivity and point of view. The contrast between narrative verses and lyrical refrains, and between emergent and repeated aspects of verbal and musical form more generally, is a basic creative and interpretive principle in both song and verbal art.

In both country song verses and working-class conversational style, for example, emergent narratives embody an "epic" modality. Events are introduced, mimetically or diegetically, in temporal sequence, and have a causal, cumulative unfolding. Motivated details of the mise en scène are established through careful description, dialogic elaboration, and layerings of direct and oblique discourse and phonetic icons. Active verbs of movement and speaking predominate; and a parallelistic line structure formally models action as repeated and sequential. Most of these elements are present in the following spoken narrative in which Doc tells of a night when Old Joey had too much to drink: (Parallel narrative and grammatical structures are marked here with diacritics [*, +, ∧].)[32]

DOC: *He come over here one night

He can't DRINK hard liquor . . .

and it . . .

*he set up here

and DAN wasn't mixin' 'em strong enough

and he said

[Doc points across room]
Over there where he's at
*he g . . .
∧*"Mix it stronger"*
y'know
∧*"Put some* BOOZE *in that thing!"*

SUZY: *Put some* BOOZE *in there
I can't taste it!*

DOC: Pretty soon
*he couldn't WALK
y'know? . . .
*So he decided to get along . . .
[confidentially]
You've seen [his] . . .
WIFE
and she WHIPS on him
y'know if he gets outta line!
[laughing]
+Me and Suzy we . . .
ARM in arm y'know
∧CArried him down the stairs
∧WALKED him cross the lawn
∧CROSS the road
∧over there to his house
∧'bout fifty foot from the door
[as an aside]
+we decided
+we didn't any part'a'HER
y'know
She don' particularly care for him
to come over here drinkin'
[end of aside]
and so
+we turned him loose
and boy
*he staggered
#WAAAAAY to the right
y'know

*an' he'd caught his balance
#and WAAAAAY back to the left
*fin'ly got LINED up
*an' headed for the DOOR . . .
*and he got up there t'the door . . .
an' the door was locked!   SUZY: He didn't have a key!
DOC: Suzy an' I
+standin' out there in the DARK
+goin' *"Oh my GAAAAWD"*
y'know
*so he BEATS on the door
And it was so funny
*cuz she YANKED that door open
*an' Ol' Joey jus' FELL in!
[laughter]
Jus' FACE down!
[more laughter]

This story is told, for most of its duration, in a mock-epic mode, elaborating the lyric theme announced parenthetically in Doc's second line ("He can't DRINK hard liquor"). Doc's final line ("Jus' face down!") points to a further requirement for effective narrative: he invokes a visual image that transcends the time frame of the story and crystallizes his own amused subjective point of view. Winding up "face-down" is the ultimate, canonical fate of "drunks" who "can't hold their liquor." Rhetorically powerful songs and narratives should announce their ultimate import in such a lyrical image that bears repetition and earns attention.

Such images are, likewise, the essence of country song refrains. These "choruses," as they are widely called, signal rhetorical closure and universal import, drawing out the ideological conclusions of concrete narratives. Cyclical, repetitive lyric images "freeze" narrative time, as they point out the timeless truths enshrined in detailed and contextually specific narratives. Such "lyric junctures" typically feature verbs of feeling and being and quite often invoke a specifically and literally cyclical trope—wheels turning, life cycles unfolding—and adverbial invocations of the past, such as "anymore" or "still."

This structural opposition between epic and lyric modes is pervasive in country music and can be seen in nearly every example of the genre. It is particularly heightened in songs that specifically invoke cyclicity and time-lessness as overt themes, such as the George Jones and Tammy Wynette duet performance of Bobby Braddock's masterpiece, "Golden Ring."[33]

In "Golden Ring," the female and male voices represent two narrators, tell-ing two sides of a single story. But they also represent, at certain moments in the text, the voices of the story's characters. The song follows a wedding ring from a Chicago pawnshop window, where it is gazed on by a young working-class couple happily planning to wed, to a "little wedding chapel," where the man slips it on the woman's finger, to a "small two-room apartment" where the couple "fight their final round," as the woman "throws down the ring as she walks out the door." Between these narrative verses are refrains sung in harmony by Jones and Wynette (arguably the finest duet singers in country music history). The second line in the refrain is changed with each repetition to refer to the status of the "golden ring" in the most recent verse, thus re-taining some links to the epic narrativity of the verses: in the first refrain, the ring is "waiting there for someone to take it home"; in the second, it has "at last" "found a home"; and in third, it is "cast aside/like a love that's dead and gone." But the refrains shift into the lyric mood to contemplate the "golden ring" as a symbol of cyclicity in the life cycle, ending each time with "By itself, it's just a cold metallic thing/ Only love can make a golden wedding ring."

This complexly voiced song exaggerates the epic/lyric opposition and makes the trope of cyclicity and timelessness its explicit theme. As the male and female voices alternate in the verses, they develop a conventional epic narrative of working-class romance, moving from naive young love through impulsive marriage to a final bitter and disillusioned breakup. The verses rep-resent the voices of the song's protagonists in direct quotation, but not always in parallel with the gender of each singer. In the first verse, Wynette begins the narrative, and Jones directly quotes the male protagonist (handing the ring to the woman, he says "honey that's for you/it's not much but it's the best that I can do"). The second verse follows the same pattern (Jones whispers, "with this ring I thee wed"). In the third verse, however, and after an intesi-fying modulation up a half step, Wynette voices the male protagonist's words ("you won't admit it/but I know you're leaving town"), while Jones voices the female protagonist's angry leave-taking ("one thing's for certain/I don't love you anymore").

The story is timeless and generic, as the refrains emphasize. But this generic narrative is contextually specified with place names ("Chicago," "a little wedding chapel," "a small two-room apartment"); times ("a sunny summer day," "later on that afternoon," "as they fight their final round"); and an abundance of mimetic reported speech meant to recreate the social drama being narrated in dialogue (e.g., "He says 'honey that's for you' "; "She says, 'one thing's for certain: I don't love you anymore' ").

At each stage of development, this miniature epic is interrupted for the harmonized refrain, invoking an omniscient perspective that transcends the gendered polarity of the verses. The refrain obsessively caresses the image of the "golden ring" as this ring moves between the fingers of the young lovers in a chapel, the floor of their small two-room apartment, and the window of a Chicago pawn shop. The ring is itself a symbol of continuity in the wedding ceremony. But it also signifies darkly: entrapment in poverty and a hasty and loveless marriage. (The wedding ring as a symbol of this conflict is generic in country music, in songs such as Randy Travis's "On the Other Hand" and Lefty Frizzell's "Almost Persuaded.") The ring is given extra symbolic weight, in this song, as a lyrical icon of narrative circularity (which is again also a conventional figure in working-class Christian wedding blessings). The variability of the second line in each return of the refrain, referring in each case to the significance of the ring in the previous verse, connects this timeless symbolism to the unfolding miniature epic of the song's verses. The song closes by returning, as a reprise, to the opening lines ("At a pawnshop in Chicago, on a sunny summer's day"). Once again, we are in front of the Chicago pawnshop window, where *another* young couple gazes at the ring, blissfully unaware of the narrative tragedy that predictably awaits them. The final line repeats the phrase "golden ring," with a long fade-out. This delivers one last emphatic abstraction from the song's story, enacting the repetition of the tale asserted as a lyric image in the refrains.

This juxtaposition of lyric and epic moods is equally characteristic of working-class verbal art in Texas. Hoppy's story about how he acquired Sam's furniture (also discussed in chapter 3, above) concludes with a dramatic shift into a lyric image of timeless cyclicity. Like "Golden Ring," it ends by fading away:

HOPPY: [Sam] gave me his table
chairs
bed
EVERYTHING, y'know . . .

'cuz she had all this stuff
he moved her in there and
And I told 'im
I says
"Sam, y'know, I jus'
b'LIEVE I oughta put that stuff up, y'know?"
[Hoppy imitates Sam's rough, drawling voice:]
"Naw, I don't ever need it agin . . . !
Well . . .
GUESS what table he's eatin' on toDAY down there?
[laughter]
The SAME table that he gave away
[trailing off]
and I took back to him cuz he didn't HAVE one . . .

There is a strong preference in oral narrative and sustained conversational dialogues for conclusive aphorisms that move the interpretive perspective "outside" the frame of the immediate situation, summing up a timeless lesson from some mundane story, calling attention to the textuality of the everyday. Such phrases (for example, "[That's] life inside a Texas honky-tonk!" and "SHIT HAppens, I guess!") are ubiquitously used to punctuate and conclude long stretches of casual dialogue. Very often, these miniature lyric refrains draw on actual song refrains for added force. Once, after a long and intense conversation with Ira, an African American truck driver and Vietnam veteran, in which we had exhaustively discussed the violence of war, class difference, racism, drug abuse, lynching, and country music, we settled into a few moments of quiet reflection, drinking our beers and smoking. Vern Gosdin's fatalistic end-of-a-marriage song "That Just about Does It (Don't It?)" played on the jukebox, with its lugubrious "crying" steel-guitar and heavy-hearted lyric hanging in the air with the smoke. Ira was making up his mind to leave, and he announced closure by pushing back from the table with a sigh and declaring, "That just about does it, don't it?" I had to agree. In the flash of a line, Ira had added a lyrical philosophical frame to our conversation that cemented our talk in my memory.

Juxtaposition of Styles

Another constitutive poetic trope of country songwriting involves the jarring juxtaposition of discursive registers, genres, and styles. A classic juxtaposition, for example, is the casting of "romantic" themes in the discourses of business, salesmanship, and advertising. Reba McEntire's "Have I Got a Deal for You" deploys this conventional trope of drawing on the persuasive rhetoric of advertising as she "pitches" her heart to a would-be lover as if it were a used car, offering "a heart that's almost like brand new" that she'll "let go . . . cheap" (this song is discussed in Fox 1992).[34]

This polemical vocal performance of discursive registers like advertising is also common in beer-joint verbal art. At charitable benefit auctions, for example, commonly held to raise money for families facing medical and financial crises, the most skillful local "comedians" like Carl are pressed into service as auctioneers. They have the task of exploiting a subtle knowledge of the socioeconomic order of bar patrons in order to sell a wide assortment of donated items at prices far above their market value (if they even have a market value). The appeal, of course, is indirectly to the charitable spirit of those patrons who have money to spare. Benefit auctions are highly formalized redistributive rituals in which nobody has to offer or accept direct "charity" without something being exchanged symbolically. These "auctioneers" playfully cajole other patrons into purchasing useless items using stylized parodies of advertising and hucksterism:

CARL: Okay, THESE are knickknacks
THIS is a little ceramic DOLL
that ah
y'know you SEE these ceramic deals
in your *PARADE* magazines on Sunday
y'know?
In the Sunday newspaper
And they ask you to
[high-pitched, whining voice, imitating television ads]
"Send in nineteen ninety-five
[pompous, booming voice]
FOR *THREE WEEKS*!
[regular voice]

y'know
Well I tell what I'm gonna do!
THIS is a nail clipper
WITH this ceramic doll
I tell ya what I'm gonna do . . .
If somebody will give me . . .
three dollars   [i.e., for both items]
I'll sell this right NOW!

As with Reba McEntire's "Have I Got a Deal for You," Carl's poetic shift
into the voice of a television salesman denaturalizes the banality of advertising
rhetoric by pairing it with a deeply emotional subtext. How deeply meaningful this subtext was can be discerned in Ann's injunction to the audience at
the beginning of this same auction, as she made the underlying reciprocity
of the ritual explicit. Because she is highly articulate, this was a marked occasion indeed as Ann's voice choked with emotion and she seemed to struggle
to find her words:

ANN: I wanna tell y'all about . . .
I mean about Sunny and . . .
and Jimmy[35]
When ANYtime anybody asks for help
They're the FIRST ones to jump in
an help . . .
When I found a family that didn't have anything to eat . . .
had eight children
the FIRST PEople
to bring me FOOD for them was
Sunny . . .
and Jimmy
And gave me money to go buy MEAT for 'em
So when they jump,
they jump in first to HELP
and I think it's TIME to PAY 'em back!

The specific juxtaposition of the seemingly inappropriate and highly public
register of "advertising" with sentiments so serious that their expression en-

genders inarticulateness is only one version of an essential and more general thematic trope of country song. Country is an articulate, public poetry, but it purports to reveal the inarticulate and pained interiority of subjective experience (Fox 1992 and 1993). Country serves up poetry when "ordinary" speech fails. It is this constitutive irony of "poetic inarticulateness" that makes Marty Robbins's minor 1954 hit "Pretty Words" perhaps the single most emblematic country song for the patrons at Ann's Other Place, the one song I heard more often than any other during the years of my fieldwork. This song was considered Hoppy's theme song. He used it as the title for his only commercial recording, and he almost always began his band's shows with it, singing plaintively: "I want to smile but I cry/ Pretty words make a fool out of me."[36]

People referred (again as a pun) to "Hoppy's pretty words" and said things like "your words are so pretty for us" to him. And yet the song's ostensible claim is that the narrator has been "made a fool" by an untrue lover's "pretty words," left speechless and in tears, iconically represented by Hoppy's powerful vocal "cry breaks" (see chapter 7) in this song. Once again, the juxtaposition of articulate reflection with inarticulate pain is represented here in the powerful image of the "fool."

Intertextuality

As the frequent importation of registers like "advertising" suggests, country music is richly intertextual, comprising an extraordinary world of objectified discourse and specific rhetorical tropes that stands vividly apart from the ordinary life country takes as its principle narrative theme. The verbal texture of country song, like working-class verbal art, is densely layered with both blunt and subtle quotations that import not only words but moods and characters from other songs, as well as from everyday talk.

The device is canonical and stereotypical. Country is famous for its mannerist fixation on certain recurrent thematic tropes, such as "honky-tonk angels," "cheating hearts," "crying in your beer," "drinking," nostalgia for "mothers" and "home." But this pantheon of types is a metadiscursive resource, not a dumbly mechanical template. David Allan Coe's anthemic rendition of Steve Goodman's song "You Never Even Called Me by My Name" is a jukebox and bandstand standard in Texas beer joints, a hilarious reflection on the elements that comprise what Coe calls "the perfect country and western song." The song features a famous metamusical joke. Midway through the performance, Coe breaks the frame of the song's narration and speaks as the performer delivering this song rather than as the song's spluttering protagonist, as he describes (in a spoken verse) telling Steve Goodman that his composition is not "the perfect country and western song" because, in an earlier version, it had failed to mention "drinking, prison, mama, trucks, or trains." Coe, once again as the intratextual narrator, then adds an additional verse (presented as Goodman's response to his challenge) that tells of his getting drunk and driving in his truck to the train station to pick up his mother, who has just been released from prison. Alas, the narrator's mother is run over by a "damned old train" before he can get to the station.[37]

This song has become well known outside the world of working-class country music bars; it is a standard item at college fraternity parties, for example. It excessively stereotypes the more subtle intertextuality of most country music. But it correctly identifies a fundamental quality of good country songwriting, which is a delight in working within severe formal and thematic limits, producing a tightly woven texture of phrases, figures, images, and gestures. It's not particular "trains" or "mamas" that make country songs "perfect." It's the intertextual presence of "mamas" and "trains" as tropes.

Songs like Becky Hobbs's enormously popular "Jones on the Jukebox," for example, rely on a listener's deep familiarity with the tradition they reference. This song hides intertextual references to George Jones classics (e.g., "Golden Ring," "The Race Is On," "He Stopped Loving Her Today," and "Still Doing Time") within the surface meanings of its text. Crucially, these song quotations are motivated by the narrative portrayal of the heartbroken protagonist of the song, who sits listening to George Jones on the jukebox. These song titles are both expressions of her state of mind and elements of the poetic scene (see Fox 1992 for a detailed discussion).

Even more deeply embedded uses of song titles are also conventional. For example, the "foolish" trope of "falling [or going] to pieces" is explicitly foregrounded in Patsy Cline's "I Fall to Pieces." George Strait's "Let's Fall to Pieces (Together)" punningly literalizes this phrase, asking plaintively: "why should we both fall apart?"[38] Such playful variations on "falling to pieces" have appeared in dozens of songs, in as many alternative contextualizations. An example is "I Don't Fall to Pieces (Anymore)," a song I wrote myself using the AABA 32-bar form made popular in country music by Cline. This song embeds the "fall to pieces" trope in a series of Patsy Cline song titles (in boldface type), following a conventional approach to "tribute" songs in country music (e.g., Merle Haggard's "Lefty's Gone"):[39]

*I don't **fall to pieces** anymore*
I don't hurt the way I did before
I don't spend my lonely nights walking the floor
I don't fall to pieces anymore

*I 'm not **crazy** like I was*
It used to haunt me but now it almost never does
I don't stay home and climb the walls because
I'm not crazy like I was

*And I don't go out **walking after midnight***
Wishin' there was someone else
These crazy arms could hold on to
Lately I guess I'm doin' alright
*Because I don't have those **sweet dreams** about you*

Sweet memories, yes I've got one or two
I've even got some pictures I look through
But what good are pictures, when [s]he's got you,
And I've only got a memory or two?

The reception this song earned demonstrates the aesthetic salience of quotation; it was one of my most successful efforts to apply my understanding of local poetic principles. Shortly after I had written it, I was asked to play it repeatedly. Hoppy made his judgment of the song explicit as he cajoled another performance of the composition out of me one evening:

HOPPY: *E*verybody loves that SONG!
[to AF]
Hey Aaron, play that new one!
[to others]
Everybody's gettin' him to do this new one
He just wrote it a week ago but GOD-DOG-it!
It's 'bout all those ol Patsy CLINE songs . . .
and the TItles are all in the song!

Place Names and Metonymic Intertextuality

Like song titles, place names are used in song and verbal art as evocative metonyms for complicated, socially located affective dispositions. In the process, place names acquire the intertextual resonance of song titles, and like titles, they become transportable between songs and across performances. An example of this trope — one that is particularly canonical in Texas — is the opposition between "Dallas" and "Fort Worth." These two North Texas cities, geographically adjacent to one another, are "at least a million miles" apart, as the Austin-based singer/songwriter Chris Wall once put it. They stand for a classic social opposition between Fort Worth's gritty, working-class authenticity and Dallas's polished "high-class" falseness.[40]

Alan Jackson's punning 1991 hit song "Dallas," for example, uses "Dallas" both as the name of the narrator's wife and for the name of the city to which this wife has run off to seek greener pastures, leaving the narrator alone in Tennessee.[41] Jackson's song plays punningly with this gendered map of the class divide as the jilted man bitterly complains: "How I wish Dallas was in Tennessee."

Among the patrons at Ann's Place, and elsewhere in Texas, the most canonical instance of this toponymic trope is "Does Fort Worth Ever Cross Your Mind?," best known from George Strait's 1985 hit recording. In this song, the male narrator imploringly asks the title question of his former lover who has left him drinking "cold Fort Worth beer" while she is in "someone else's arms in Dallas." The working-class character of the song's "Fort Worth" grounds the narrator's misery in the "real world" of a known place, in which life is hard and misery is expected, a place from which "Dallas" glitters in the surreal poetic distance, across the bridges his betrayer is "busy burning."[42]

The emotional power of these metonymic place names is extraordinary when they are effectively performed in ways that marry their poetic power to local landscapes of experience. I remember playing "Does Fort Worth Ever Cross Your Mind?" for a woman who had just been through a devastating breakup with her boyfriend in Fort Worth and had ended up among friends at a bar in the South Texas town of Victoria, where my band was playing, hundreds of miles away. Her friends had passed the story of her misery on to the band, and asked us to play a song for her. As we played the opening notes of the song, the dance floor in the club suddenly cleared and the afflicted woman walked unsteadily and drunkenly to the dance floor, where she danced by herself in a tightly constrained space, with her head down and her eyes closed and her arms wrapped tightly around her own chest for the duration of the song, as her friends watched sympathetically. I have since seen that solo dance repeated numerous times by both women and men; this dancing figure is the paradigmatic "fool," publicly displaying heartbreak and isolation from sociability as embodied performance. But I have never seen this "foolish" dance performed more evocatively and with more poetic power than in this instance, when the song's powerful place name and general affect dovetailed so completely with a personal story.

Localization and Performative Contextualization

"Fort Worth" and "Dallas" are permanently inscribed as an opposition between loss and desire on the textual landscape of country music (Fox 1992), The converse of this geography of metonymic places standing for intense social meanings is the widespread use of novel local place names, injected situationally into song texts by performers. Country song performance is dense with locality, in the same way that working-class talk is dense with figured places and archaeological readings of those places (see chapter 2). Performances in working-class taverns incorporate local references into the very fabric of song, bending and shaping songs to fit specific places. For example, it is a widespread practice for singers to change references to generic place names to the names of local landmarks. When live bands played Charley Pride's classic "Is Anybody Goin' to San Antone" (written by Central Texan Dave Kirby) at Ann's Other Place, for example, the line "Here I am walkin' down sixty-six" would routinely be modified to refer to the state highway ouside the bar's front door ("Here I am walkin' down one-eighty-three").[43]

In live country performance, band members are often introduced by reference to their hometowns. A singer's promotional biography will likely fetishize his or her small-town origins, using the strangely resonant names of otherwise unknown towns to signify both the specificity of a particular locality and the indelible, mythic generality of small towns in general—the trope of the "hometown." Singers' accented voices, too, bespeak local origins in both mythic and precise senses. The covert prestige of a rural, Southern accent is heightened in the styles of singers like Reba McEntire and Becky Hobbs. These singers' nasal, twangy voices and dipthongized vowels reveal their Oklahoma origins. Similarly, accents are implicated in vocal lineages, like the one that connects George Jones to Mark Chesnutt to Tracy Byrd, all sons of the vibrant and rough-edged local scene in the Southeast Texas oil patch around Beaumont. Even locally, such lineages are announced in the phonetic contours of stigmatized regional accents. At Ann's Place, patrons remarked frequently on the wondrous similarity between Randy Meyer's stylized voice, which was raw, lacking in vibrato, nasal, and edgy, and the voice of his young son, just beginning his singing career.

Singers reveal their origins even more unequivocally in performative speech than in song. Both local and touring performers endeavor to refer to local landmarks and concerns in their stage patter; they heighten their accents and performatively evoke "ordinary" conversational tropes in a simulation of face-to-face dialogue, eliciting affirmation and opinion and involvement from the audience.

For example, consider the following recorded stage patter from a performance by Reba McEntire, a major national star, spoken to a live audience on a national television broadcast, in her deep Oklahoma twang, after she had just finished the tear-jerker "Somebody Should Leave":

REBA: [acknowledging applause] Thank you!
Now, y'all
That's whatcha call a SAD country song, isn't it?
[crowd shouts in agreement]
That pretty much takes the cake right there!
[laughter]
[Reba appears to become overcome with emotion]
WHOA!
Y'know?
If it's okay with y'all
I'd like to kinda change the format . . .
This is whatcha call our "sad song segment"
but I'm in a little bit better mood than THAT!
I don' know 'bout y'all . . .

Stage patter on beer-joint stages is not very different. In the following example, Hoppy, like Reba, gives the impression of speaking off the top of his head (as he says, "letting his mind roll along") as he elicits laughter and commentary from the crowd and threads in references to his own biography and a local landmark. Both Hoppy and Reba give the impression of being surprised to find themselves on stage, exaggerating their "ordinariness" and similarity to their audiences. But both are master performers, and like Reba's patter, Hoppy's is in fact carefully crafted and his stories and observations are familiar to his audience:

HOPPY: Man that wrote that [the last song]
knew my sister-in-law . . .
which puts me in the mind of another song . . .
Kinda like it up here [on stage]
I'm just lettin' my mind roll along and do all these weird things . . .
I done this [next] song up at the Catholic church one year
and I told 'em
Mr. Haggard must've had my ex-wife in mind
when he wrote the chorus of this song . . .
[as an aside]
A lot of people out there laugh because they know me!
[directly]
And I told 'em
"just go ahead and laugh"
Cuz they didn't know which one   [i.e., which wife]
I was talkin' about!
[laughter]
And THAT's the damn truth isn't it?
And Lord knows how many MORE there's gonna be!
[sings Merle Haggard's "Don't Just Lay There"]

Both Hoppy and Reba frame their song performances with these explanatory glosses, threading contextualizing speech between songs, justifying the songs they choose to sing with appeals to local and immediate concerns. To take a final example that ties together tropes of literalization, song-title intertextuality, and localization in stage patter, here is a fragment of patter from Hoppy's musical mentor Randy Meyer. Meyer's highly stylized stage patter is considered an especially polished example of the art by his fans. Randy had been singing "Is Anybody Goin' to San Antone?" to a packed dance floor, predictably changing the song's reference to "sixty-six" to the more locally salient "one-eighty-three." As the last chord faded, Meyer announced in his clipped, seamless manner:

RANDY: *WHOA!*
Is anybody goin' to San Antone?
Just *pick me up on your way down!*
We're gonna have a GOOD time tonight!
I guarantee you!

In this minimalist gesture (economy is a hallmark of Randy's style, just as excessiveness is a hallmark of Hoppy's), Randy blended a dialogic appeal to the crowd with a literalization of the song title, and a further literalization of another intertextual song title (Charlie Walker's recording of Harlan Howard's "Pick Me Up on Your Way Down," a beer-joint standard).[44] Following his short poetic outburst, Randy briskly took a drag on his cigarette and a sip of his Pearl beer and turned to the band to call the next tune.

From Poetic Tropes to Socioaesthetic Ideology

Working-class Texans practice a distinctive and elaborate blend of poetic creativity and expressive performance. They locate the roots of song in the textures, grammars, and concerns of everyday talk, and conceive of effective song as deeply attentive to the qualities of working-class social experience. Song is, in this sense, an apotheosis of working-class verbal art. Like other less marked forms of local verbal art, such as narrative and joke telling, song distances itself from the "ordinary" via a series of writerly tropes—grammatical parallelism, wordplay, metaphoric literalization, stylistic juxtaposition, intra- and extramusical intertextuality, and symbolic emplacements. Such tropes are then returned to the domain of everyday discourse via effective musical performance, with its strategies of localization and social contextualization, and via the probing deployment of song's tropes in the flow of stage patter and sociable talk.

But these textual tropes and performative gestures are embedded within even more fundamental ideological commitments and cultural attitudes. Specifically, these include ideologies of gender and gendered discourse; a cultural emphasis on the voice as the medium of both poesis and expressive identity; and a highly personalized view of the working-class artist—especially the country singer—as an organic intellectual. In the following chapters, I turn to these essential aspects of working-class country music and social life.

"The Women Take Care of That"

Engendering Working-Class Culture

Driving south toward Lockhart on Highway 183, you pass an Assembly of God church, with a stern message for thirsty sinners flashing proudly on its sign: *Happy Hour, Sunday Morning*. If you are the sort to be moved but not persuaded by such sentiments, you might turn in at the next driveway and park in the shadow of another sign reading "Y'All Come Back Saloon." The Y'All Come Back, sitting a mere shotgun blast away from the church, is the kind of place where nickel bags and blow jobs are as routinely traded in the parking lot as stories are traded within. The beer joint and the church face off across a patch of grass, in their perpetual struggle for the social soul of small-town working-class Americans, though they are dwarfed by the third contender in this struggle, the giant Wal-Mart superstore that has recently opened in San Marcos.

The people for whom such churches and taverns are central cultural institutions hold several core beliefs about social experience that are foundational for the expressive culture that these institutions ritually reproduce. These ideologies—of gender, the voice, and the "ownership" of working-class popular culture—are critically framed and represented in working-class country musical practice, in local genres of verbal art, and in reflexive discourse about working-class cultural identity. In this and the following chapters, I explore each of these ideological foci, before turning, in an afterword, to the implications of my arguments here for an understanding of the culture described in this book as ultimately expressive of class experience.

"A Blue-Blooded Woman and a Redneck Man"

Under the ideological hegemony of the American "postwar class compromise," as many scholars of class culture have noted, gender ideology is a key symbolic domain in which class experience is expressively reflected (Ortner 1991). The history of country music is intertwined with the fraught development of this allegorical projection over the course of the twentieth century. Within modern industrial working-class culture, and in popular culture more broadly, women appear frequently as symbolic agents of higher classes, and elite culture is widely gendered as effeminate. Authentic working-class solidarity is (or was) prototypically gendered as male.

From the 1950s to the late 1970s, this allegory became an increasingly explicit trope across diverse domains of American popular culture. But this formal trope also codified and sustained more inchoate cultural practices, including "ordinary" expressive practices. Quantitative sociolinguistic work on gender done during the 1970s, for example, showed that working-class women tended to strive to emulate more elite dialects than their male counterparts, sometimes "hypercorrecting" their speech and coming across as affected in the process, and that blue-collar men and women alike tended to evaluate men's command of correspondingly "low status" dialects as "covertly prestigious" within working-class communities, exactly to the extent that such dialects were stigmatized in the broader society.

Popular culture was also saturated with the image, typically from a middle-class perspective, in which the supposed class aspirations of working-class wives for themselves and their families were only slightly less amusing than the destructive, inarticulate male solidarity of their husbands (e.g., in television shows like *The Honeymooners* and *All in the Family*). In popular discourses more directly in dialogue with or emergent from working-class communities, and especially in country music, the same image appeared frequently, but with a more politically charged tone. A gendered critique of wealth, materialism, and status has been a principal rhetorical theme in country music since the 1940s. Country, especially of the "hard" variety (Ching 2001; Peterson 1997) has repeatedly and critically attacked the inauthenticity and emptiness of elite culture through allegories of gender difference and conflict. Canonically, in thousands of songs, women wait at home with "hungry eyes," taking care of the children and the budget and dreaming of upward mobility, while their men carouse and drink in joyous anti-elitist solidarity. The reverse side of this narrative trope appears in songs with a Christian subtext, in which the domestic, feminine sphere is associated with transcendence of earthly pain, while the drunken public solidarity of men appears, both tragically and heroically, to be the sphere of bedevilment, loss, and alienation.

This trope pervades lived working-class experience in a place like Lockhart, Texas, too. I remember, for example, talking to old Jimmy and his wife at a barbecue on a sunny Saturday before Easter. For some reason the talk turned to religion and I asked Jimmy, who was one of the most "respectable" retired men in the local redneck community, whether he planned on going to church on Sunday. "Naaaaw," he said, "but my WIFE will . . . and MOST of my daughters, but us BOYS are a bunch of ASSholes." His wife Shirley interjected, leaning right into my tape recorder, "That's RIGHT, he's telling you the TRUTH."

In this allegorical vision, women consume, nag, and pray. Men—proud "assholes"—work, resist, and carouse. Women represent middle-class ideology, a fatalistic acceptance of capitalist work discipline, and religious piety. They embrace respectability against the heroically disreputable male values of the labor process, shop-floor culture, military experience, and the utopian working-class space of the tavern. In such spaces, society's class hegemony is turned upside down, at women's expense. Prestige accrues to self-proclaimed "assholes," and blue-collar men marked by middle-class ideology as inarticulate, emotionally blocked, and full of *ressentiment* become masterfully articulate, self-assertive performers of highly cultivated verbal arts, such as country music singing.

In American working-class culture, men like Merle Haggard who have mastered those arts are cultural heroes, lionized for symbolizing the identity of a particular kind of class experience. Even on the most local level, certain singers evoke, through performative mastery, nostalgic feelings of beer-drenched musical solidarity remembered by women and men alike as a golden age of working-class culture and community, a time of greater dignity.

One popular local singer in the Lockhart area was widely admired for his masculine charisma, for his ability to conjure the emotionally expressive toughness of singers like Merle Haggard and George Jones. But like Haggard and Jones, for him, musical mastery was only the tip of an iceberg of masculinity. This singer, then, was known in other ways too as a fine specimen of his gender. He was a hard drinker but not "a drunk," a ferocious worker, and, in his earlier years, an abusive husband, contemptuous of his domestic obligations. Once, a long-time musical friend of this man told me a story meant to evoke this aspect of the man:

FREDDY: Oh, he be gettin' married, man
to a little girl who lived down the street
He's a carpenter, and they was madly in love
I think they were married two days, or three days . . .
And he's a down-HOME type guy
I mean he wants what he wants to eat
And it ain't very much y'know
He used to eat like a pig, and now he eats . . .
like a bird
When he came home it was like the old time days
He'd be working from 6 o'clock in the morning til 6 o'clock at night
Framing and all this stuff so   [i.e., building houses]
his supper better be ready to eat
Well, she didn't COOK nothin'
the second or third day they was married
She decided they'd go for hamburgers
Well, he done TOLD her what he wanted to eat, okay?
Which was he wanted red BEANS, fried potatoes, a big old ONION
And, y'know
You don't need no meat back then
That meat, you can live without it
Everything's fine
He got home and
she decided she wasn't gonna COOK
So she didn' COOK . . .
[pause]
Wrong thing to DO!
So he asserted himself very well . . .
He went out and got his hammer and a sixteen   [a large nail]
Put her in the closet, and nailed the door shut
"She ain't gonna cook for me, she ain't gonna eat"
Put TWO SIXTEENS in the top of this closet door
Said *"See you tomorrow!"*
So he left her in there all that night

and all the NEXT day
And he didn't drive 'em all the way up
He drove up about to where he could pull 'em out
And when he got in the next afternoon and asked her if she'd like to cook
some beans
And guess what?
[pause]
She's a BEAN-cookin' THING!

This story (which ends with the canonical summarizing lyric image) reminds us that behind these narrative allegories, the class struggle really was being waged internally as a very real, lived conflict that spilled over frequently into violence and alcoholism and pain. But there is something else, too, in Freddy's tone: a certain reverence for a time now past—"the old time days"—that makes stories like this one ambivalent in meaning, even for working-class women who have experienced such treatment from men. Indeed, I have heard this same story, about this same man, told by women in amused, and even partially respectful, terms. Why is this ambivalent nostalgia for patriarchy so powerful? What does it signify, especially where it is most often expressed—in country music and in working-class verbal art?

From the end of World War II until the early 1970s, the ideological hegemony of American industrial modernity entailed the existence of a solid and socially permeable meritocracy of "middle-class" citizens and consumers. Social mobility, both real and imagined, was abetted by postwar affluence and economic growth, an imperialist foreign policy and Cold War military buildup, the civil rights movement (but also the privileging of whiteness in new ways), and the rise of relatively powerful labor unions in key industries. The United States appeared to be an officially "classless" society with a majority of its (white) working-class citizens invested in the social power of industry and in the apparent encroaching embourgeoisement of the American blue-collar worker.

That hegemony—the "postwar class compromise"—began to shift in the late 1970s and continues its transformation in the present. Wage growth became stagnant, benefits were reduced, jobs were lost, prices were increased, unions were busted, taxes were raised, import tariffs were eliminated, plants, mines, and bases were closed, major industries moved abroad or declined, economic and technical barriers to foreign competition were dropped, banks and corporations and markets boomed and crashed, and the U.S. govern-ment bailed them out. Real income growth and earning power deteriorated for most working-class families (or improved only due to the increasing re-liance of such families on second and third income streams from the work of women and teenagers). The richest segments of American society enjoyed record prosperity, especially in the 1990s. Market-oriented considerations reached increasingly into what had been ideologically quarantined spaces of social reproduction such as schools and family life. And the cultural status and nationalist symbolism of manual labor declined as America entered an "information age."

During this period working families also became increasingly dependent on the waged employment of women. As Harvey writes in his account of this economic transition from modern to postmodern capitalism: "The transi-tion to flexible accumulation has in fact been marked by a revolution (by no means progressive) in the role of women in labor markets and labor pro-cesses" (1989:155).

In places like Lockhart, Texas, this transformation has been profoundly in-fluential, even as it has been vigorously resisted. Through de-skilling and low wages, traditionally "male" jobs have increasingly been targeted to attract women workers, supplementing the low-wage jobs more traditionally open to blue-collar women. Increasingly, families in the lower strata of the white working-class community *depend* on a women's earnings, in addition to in-come earned by men's less regular though often higher-paid work. (On the other hand, gender-based affirmative action programs have created openings for women workers in some better-paid, previously "male" careers, especially jobs in the public sector.) Women's knowledge also contributes much, as it did under the old relations to be sure, to economic survival in the manage-ment of household consumption. Women have long been the everyday money managers in many working-class families; increasingly it is their own earn-ings they are managing, and this has undoubtedly influenced the psychosocial dynamics of gender in those families.

But curiously, what would seem to be a highly residual regime of gen-der relations hangs on in memory and practice and becomes especially fo-cused, as an object and an instrument of aesthetic and political scrutiny, in the performative genres cultivated in small-town bars and churches. Both in-stitutions can seem, in the present, like patriarchal time machines, spaces in which emotionally explosive male performance is celebrated as a nostalgic emblem of working-class identity, especially in song and verbal art. These are places, as well, where most women are commonly expected to conform to norms of femininity that are simultaneously pure and sexualized, and almost always submissive to male interests. These norms are powerfully symbolized in dance and highly thematized in country music. But in country music and in working-class discourse, these norms are also the object of critical reflection, especially in genres of expression that give voice to working-class women's increasingly feminist sensibilities.

In contemporary country music, the hennish wives and hard-drinking husbands of the 1950s and 1960s are largely gone, or banished to the margins of ironically excessive stereotype, especially as the genre has increasingly been marketed to a constituency of working- and middle-class women.[1] But at least one trope rooted in the traditional gender allegory achieved repeated commercial and critical success with country fans in the 1990s: the fantasy narrative genre in which a powerful, authentically masculine blue-collar man seduces a feminine, spoiled, and sheltered "upper-class" woman. This narrative archetype appeals as strongly to working-class women as it does to men, and there are surely interesting parallels to other genres of literature marketed to working-class women, such as romance novels.

The story is usually meant to sound sexy and playful on its surface, and it is almost *always* sung from a male perspective (although singer Shania Twain has advanced a female-voiced version of this tale several times in the last few years). In Alan Jackson's 1990 hit "Blue-Blooded Woman," the class tension, expressed as a conflict of tastes, is the basis of a true if curious love between "a blue-blooded woman" and "a redneck man." The woman in this chromatic fantasy "likes the violin," while the man "loves the fiddle" and prefers his "sushi" to be of the "southern-fried" variety.[2] In an even more erotic version of the trope, Mark Chesnutt's "Old Country" finds a rich woman from Ohio and a sweaty farmer from Alabama meeting for clandestine champagne and sex in a fancy hotel room late at night.[3] But Lady Chatterley's redneck has a darker side too, more willing to force the issue, as Travis Tritt's (1992) hit "Country Club" finds our working-class hero out talking a "country club" woman into hopping into his truck for a picture of life's other side. Against her expressed better judgment, punningly and sexually expressed as "only members are allowed in here," she decides to accept the man's illicit presence at her "country club" and join his club for a brief fling.[4]

Then, finally, there is the inevitable result of such an encounter, which is the redemptive rediscovery of all that is false and shallow about the eroticized, feminized "other." This is powerfully expressed in songs like Randy Travis's huge 1994 hit "A Better Class of Losers," in which a working-class man finally has enough of his upper-class consort and her friends who "pay their bills on home computers" and grind their own coffee.[5] The story told in these songs goes back at least as far as Charley Pride's 1967 hit "Crystal Chandeliers,"[6] in which the singer warns his socially climbing wife that she'll discover wealth won't replace him, and Charlie Walker's 1958 classic "Pick Me Up on Your Way Down," in which the narrator awaits his beloved's disenchantment with her new wealthy friends. Jeanne Pruett's massive 1973 hit "Satin Sheets" (recorded since by many other women singers and a female standard in working-class beer joints) expresses the perspective of the upwardly mobile woman, trapped and miserable in her mansion. (The George Jones/Tammy Wynette 1977 duet "Southern California" is, however, the only case of a hit country song I can think of from the classic era where the *male* character is alienated by his wealth while the female character has remained working–class.)

The logic of this allegory is clear. The gender conflicts of everyday working-class life are projected in these stories *back* onto the terrain of class, taken out of the context of a working-class domestic world into a fantastic space where masculine working-class values and and dispositions are culturally authoritative. For once, in these songs, the (male) workers screw the (female) elites. But only the men get away with it with their class pride intact.

This fantasy of class inversion, however, is not only radical. It preserves the patriarchal form of the traditional working-class gender regime, and in the bars and churches and homes and workplaces where both men and women have "red necks" and where "blue blood" is hard to find, such inversions are subject to further, more local forms of deconstruction. The singer who locked his wife in a closet is on his third wife, and she has him showing up at church and forswearing his macho past. Big Judy, a six-foot-tall truck-driving bass-playing blond, punched out the windows on her boyfriend's van the time she caught him messing around on her. Women are more likely than ever to front their own bar bands, to start their own churches, and to own small businesses. And in the only instance I witnessed of egregious domestic violence during my field research, the abused woman escaped her tormentor and appeared, seeking help, at the Liar's Inn, a tough little beer joint a few miles from Ann's. When her abusive partner showed up to reclaim his girlfriend, a dozen large and angry bikers and cowboys rose as one to throw him out of the place, while his victim was consoled by the other women. The abuser never again showed his face in the area, and soon afterward it was said he had moved to Austin. Patriarchy has its uses, too.

Quotation and Gendered Dialogue

The field of working-class gender relations in Texas is a field of conflict over specific grievances and over the content of a shared identity. This conflict is expressively addressed in local country music practice and in everyday talk and verbal art. I have already described the pervasive use of mimetically vivid direct and quasi-direct discourse to represent another's point of view in verbal art and everyday talk. This fundamental trope is also crucial to country music performance, and to the way gender conflict is represented in country music and working-class discourse. Like the words of social others, songs themselves are framed explicitly as utterances, and song texts are shaped by singers through the frequent use of performative verbs of speaking to announce the transition from speech to song. Masterful singers characteristically begin songs with quickly sung verbs of speaking that are not part of the recorded or written song text. Hoppy, for example, frequently uses "[I] said" to begin a song, transitioning from stage patter into the song narrator's perspective. He nearly always begins his traditional "closing" song, Sonny Burns's obscure "My Blue House Painted White," with a grace note on the word "said," attaching his personal verbal authority to the double meaning of the first line ("The party's all over"). This is at once a description of the narrative mise en scène and an announcement to the crowd that this is the last song of the night. Invariably, as the first notes of this song ring out, somebody lets out a performative moan of disappointment and people quickly get up for one last dance. Hoppy's "said" both elicits and manages the charged poesis of this final moment of a musical evening, claiming both the authority to pronounce the evening's end and the right to focused attention for one more song:

HOPPY: [singing] *Said*
"The party's all over   [the crowd groans]
they're turnin' out the lights . . ."[7]

Verbs of saying are incorporated within the textual structure of songs too, turning songs into complexly voiced miniature dramas. George Jones's classic recording of "He Stopped Loving Her Today" (which many consider to be perhaps the saddest country song ever written, and is discussed in detail in the following chapter) begins with a represented dialogue: *"**He said** 'I'll love you'll 'til I die.'/**She told him** 'you'll forget in time.'"* But instantly Jones asserts the narrator's distinctive point of view ("as the years rolled slowly by . . .").[8] Likewise, in David Frizzell's "I'm Gonna Hire a Wino (to Decorate Our Home)," the refrain is cast in the directly reported voice of the male narrator's long-suffering wife by a quick "she said" placed before each refrain.

In most country songs, lines, verses, and refrains are constantly attributed to particular speakers through verbs of saying and changes in diction and indexical footing. While this is a widespread formal trope, it is particularly essential in songs which, like "He Stopped Loving Her Today" and "I'm Gonna Hire a Wino," enact gender conflict in mimetic dialogue. In "Golden Ring," for example, the male singer quotes the song's male protagonist in the first verse and again in the second verse; in the third verse the female singer quotes the male protagonist and the male singer quotes the female protagonist. Each singer, in other words, vocally "inhabits" each of the song's two protagonists, creating and then undermining gendered identifications between the singers themselves and the narrative's characters. The complicated layering of male and female singing voices with male and female speaking voices (the quoted discourse), and with male and female narrative archetypes, creates a dialogic texture woven from both identification and distance.

This trope of gendered dialogue can be expanded beyond the boundaries of any particular song or conversation, too. The most famous example of this in country music is the "dialogue" between Hank Thompson's song "The Wild Side of Life" and Kitty Wells's polemical "answer" to that song in "It Wasn't God Who Made Honky-Tonk Angels" (Malone 1985: 223–27). In Thompson's song, a number-one hit for nearly four months in 1952, a heartbroken man sings accusingly to his ex-wife who has left him to go "back to the wild side of life," drinking in bars and becoming involved with other men. The song uses a well-known country gospel melody, as Thompson despairingly complains "I didn't know God made honky-tonk angels." In the spring of 1952, Kitty Wells released a female-gendered "answer" song (written by a man) that used the same gospel melody and poetic structure to refute Thompson's sexist accusation (and which spent several weeks in the number-one chart position as well). Thompson's song vividly enters the frame on the first line of Wells's song: *"As I sit here tonight the jukebox playing/that song about the wild side of life."* Wells became instantly famous (she is often called the first woman honky-tonk singer, and is widely known as "the queen of country music") for this song, which explicitly turned the pious complaint of Thompson's song around: "It wasn't God who made honky-tonk angels/like you said in the words of your song."[9]

The two songs comprised a single historical event and a coherent dialogue, and they have been closely linked ever since and recorded several times as a duet, a manner in which they are also frequently performed in working-class bars. In combination, the two songs outline both traditional gender ideology and a feminist critique of that ideology, and working-class fans find their juxtaposition compelling. Hoppy and Big Judy have for years performed a duet version of the song that is structured by a complicated pattern: Hoppy sings Thompson's first verse and refrain (with Judy singing harmony), after which Judy sings Wells's *second* verse and refrain. Hoppy then sings Thompson's second verse and refrain, while Judy ends with the Wells's *first* verse and refrain. Because she sings the last refrain, Judy is entitled to the formally obligatory final tag line, in this case giving the last word to the woman's perspective as she announces that the immorality and sanctimonious hypocrisy of men "has caused many a good girl to go wrong" (to which Judy adds, as a spoken aside to the women in the audience: "Right, girls?")

Judy's inversion of Wells's song's form dovetails with Hoppy's performance (in its original sequence) in a dialogic structure. Her opening performance of the second verse gives the impression of a co-constructed single song (joining the first part of Thompson's version with the second half of Wells's), while her subsequent return to the first verse, with its metamusical opening line ("As I sit here tonight the jukebox playing/that song about the wild side of life") re-creates the quality, within this actual duet form, of a detached "answer" to Thompson's (Hoppy's) song. Not surprisingly, Big Judy gets "the last word" with her tag. Discovering the deep rootedness of this musical dialogue in "ordinary" life and barroom verbal art requires a rudimentary consideration of the politics of language, gender, class solidarity, and discursive authority in working-class culture.

Language and Gender in Rural, Working-Class Life

Working-class barroom discourse in Texas does not conform fully to the conventional sociolinguistic account of the influence of gender on Euro-American conversational style (Coates 1992, see Fox 1995). In Texas, both women and

men are highly competent in numerous shared topical genres, in topic introduction, and in strategies of interruption, overlap, quotation, and affirmation.
Both male and female speech can be characterized by high levels of intonational, amplitudinal, and paralinguistic dynamism, the use of locally prestigious nonstandard forms (including profanity), and by an emphasis on emotional self-revelation. Women and men frequently talk together as equal and
mutually supportive partners in conversation. A densely polyphonic "high-
involvement" speech style is a canonical form of sociability for both men and
women in barroom conversation in particular.[10]

There are, of course, gender-marked topics and forms of communicative
competence. Women are characterized in local linguistic ideology as less inclined (or licensed) to use profanity, and this appears to be statistically true
in practice.[11] In particular, the music making I observed and participated in
during my Texas fieldwork was a male-dominated activity, in which women's
direct participation was to some extent supportive and marginal. Commanding figures like Big Judy were rather more rare than their male equivalents.
And verbal performativity in Texas bars is also somewhat male-dominated
(less so than music making, however).

There are, however, parallel spheres of women's discursive authority. It is
common for women to answer the phone much more frequently than men,
for example, because in general women carry more of the burden of dealing with business contacts "outside" the immediate local sphere.[12] Musicians'
wives and girlfriends are often indispensable as their business agents, han-
dling the booking of jobs, the hiring of players, and often the interpersonal
management of events while the men perform and drink. In relation to certain social spheres (for example, religion, child raising, judgments of character, and knowledge of the ways of other social classes), women's knowledge
is considered especially authoritative, and men defer to it.

Women also have, like men, a distinctive realm of gendered sociability, although obviously my own access to that realm was limited. From a male perspective (as both an ethnographer and a musician), it appears that an enormous amount of women's talk happens at the margins of male-dominated
musical events like jam sessions. But for the women at these events the chance
to talk with other women while the men play music is one reason for attending.[13] For them, the music making is arguably more marginal.

Of course, a good deal of women's talk is overtly *about* men; but women's
talk also involves the cultivation of women's own styles of creativity and emo-

tional engagement. And it can sound very much like men's "talking shit," even in the artful use of profanity (ideologically disfavored for women). On the other hand, its mutual supportiveness and topical focus on "female" subjects such as physical appearance conform in some ways to the stereotypical gendered styles so widely noted by sociolinguists in American speech. The following episode unfolded as Donna, Nora, and Jane came into the bar one evening and struck up a conversation with Alice:[14]

JANE: [entering the bar, shouting] Back AGAIN!
And I got my BOOTS!
ALICE: [to Donna] Did they turn you LOOSE Donna?
How'd you get LOOSE?
DONNA: Real EASY!
I was in here EARlier
ALICE: Huh!
I know you were
I (didn't) get a chance to get back there and talk to you
DONNA: I'm ALways loose
ALICE: Ha! . . . HA!
ALICE: [to Nora] Good to SEE you, lady!
NORA: Good to see YOU!
ALICE: I haven't seen you for a while
NORA: Naw . . .
I BEEN workin' my BUTT off again
ALICE: You look REAL good!
Yeah, I know you are . . .   [i.e., working hard]
Y'look REAL good!
NORA: Thank you!
DONNA: [to Alice]: How've you been doin'?
ALICE: I've been doin' great . . .
I gotta go git . . .
Boy I look great
right now, without MAKEup on!
NORA: You still look great
no matter what you say!
ALICE: bullSHIT!
But thank you anyway

I'll go put my paint on
and it'll BE alright!
NORA: [laughing] ooooohkay!

Moral and discursive authority in both mixed-sex and same-sex contexts is achieved through skilled verbal performance. Powerful speech emphasizes self-revelatory emotional intensity, expressive dynamism, emphatic paralinguistic style, movements into others' social spaces, polemical uses of invective and insults, sustained narrativity, and a command of an arsenal of poetic tropes (especially movements between speech and song). And while, like some men, some women are quite competent in assembling these elements, full performance in mixed-sex sociable discourse is more closely associated with powerful males. Dominant men typically display a wider range of emotion more publicly and more excessively than most women.

Effective verbal performance involves the (highly controlled) modeling of intensity as a loss of emotional control. Such performativity is an intermediate link between gender and discursive dominance. Highly performative, emotionally expressive males (such as singers and "comedians") tend to dominate in mixed-sex groups, taking longer turns, eliciting affirmation from marginal participants, patronizing women and lower-status males with affectionately veiled aggression, pronouncing moral evaluations of others, interrogating silent figures, getting loud and "worked up," orchestrating and suppressing interruptions, and occupying large fields of conversational space through hand gestures, physical intimacy, and eye contact. Such conversational dominance is, however, also locally celebrated as a form of pleasurable, masterful competence in the art of sociability, and therefore as an emblem of working-class cultural style.

Of course, there *are* powerful women who can routinely achieve this level of authoritative performativity (Miss Ann, for example), as well as many men who never do. But this dominance is performatively resisted and playfully reappropriated in turn by women's ways of talking back to male authority (K. Stewart 1990), and men's ways of dramatically conceding their own shortcomings and imperfections. Women remain poised to assert their command over certain socially valued domains in ordinary mixed-sex conversation. For example, in the conversation reported above in which I engaged Jimmy in a conversation about churchgoing, his wife Sandy emphasized the correctness of Jimmy's self-deprecating admission that he rarely went to church: "The women take care of that!"

The Women Take Care of That: Staging the "Reverse"

A more formal means of "talking back" and asserting female competence is through a genre of verbal art which Texas working-class women some-times call a "reverse." A "reverse" is a verbal or musical performance in which women critically parody men's ways of speaking and acting, often for a mixed-sex audience. Reverses may be planned in advance but loosely improvised. A reverse might happen by chance whenever a woman derisively imitated a blustering man, or more formally when Big Judy sang Leroy Van Dyke's manic patter song "The Auctioneer," showing off enunciatory vocal ability that few male singers possess. More elaborate reverses were common too. On a barmaid's birthday at Ann's Other Place, for example, the barmaid and her women friends were entitled to sit at the bar while the men who normally occupied these stools took turns functioning as "barmaids" for an hour at a time, enduring the taunts and teases of the women pretending to be drunken men. I took my turn, of course, emptying ashtrays and serving up cold cans of Milwaukee's Best Light, until I finally sat down to rest. Candy Sue, the bar-maid, asked me, "Are you comfortable?" When I said yes, she said "Good! Now get me another beer!" Later that night Sam Shadow popped out of the hollow center of a table and did a striptease in Candy's honor.

Reverses may also emerge casually in the course of everyday discourse, as a woman takes dramatic control of a conversation with "backtalk." In the fol-lowing example, Robbie — a particularly blustery and aggressively assertive auto mechanic — was holding forth with Carl and Old Blackie on the Texas gu-bernatorial election when Crazy Jane intervened with a polemical challenge to his masculinity, evidently chagrined by Robbie's antiwoman remarks:

ROBBIE: I'm gonna vote for him again!
CARL: Well I ain't gonna swear to that
ROBBIE: Oh who's your choice now?
Old what's-her-name?   [refers to Ann Richards, a candidate for governor]
CARL: HELL NO!
ROBBIE: I wouldn't vote for her jus' cuz she's a damn woman!

Ann Richards?

That's just what Texas needs!

a damn woman!

CARL: Well I damn sure wasn't votin' for the other guy

He was my boss for years

ROBBIE: I know it!

I wanted to vote for that preacher man!

Did you hear that preacher man?

Carl?

Did you hear that preacher

on that debate?

When he come out on TV?

And he said

"There ain't gonna be no more men kissin' men in Texas!"

he said

"There DAMN *sure ain't gonna be no more women livin' with women!"*

And he said

"All you women workin'

you're goin home!"

I like him, he was good

Yeah Jim Mattox and Ann Richards

[makes a sound of disgust]

Jim Mattox is gonna put a lottery in Texas

Ann Richards is gonna put a sewin' bee in Texas!

CARL: Well, I don't care who they are

They gonna do like everybody else anyway

They're gonna turn on you

BLACKIE: Well

They'd 've all got more votes if they'd all run for the county line!

Everybody'd be behind him!

CRAZY JANE: [coming over and interrupting, yelling] ROBBIE!

I LOVE you you son of a bitch!

But you sure do talk a lot of SHIT

when your old lady ain't here standin' beside you!

I've *seeeeeeen* you don't talk so hot

when she's standin' there beside you!

ROBBIE: You see, I'm a firm believer

Every member of the family
ought to have served their term in the military
My wife did
I didn't have to!
Y'know she's bigger 'n I am!

Jane's use of shouted profanity here (a habit for which she is often censured) announces her usurpation of masculine authority. Expressive swearing
in Texas taverns is marked as a masculine privilege, and women are normatively expected to use profanity very sparingly, and never as loudly as men. But
Robbie's self-deprecating response to Jane indicates that the conversation has
entered into the frame of a reverse performance, in which Robbie's wife is seen
as more powerful than her husband, in part because she had served in the military and he had not. Temporarily, at least, Jane's remark overturned the ordi-
narily patriarchal order of tavern discourse. But the ephemerality of the inversion is part of its meaning.

Finally, as in the example discussed next, reverses may be carefully scripted
and framed dramatic performances, and may sometimes rise above the
ephemerality of everyday talk to become touchstones for serious reflection
on gender. In every case, however, the defining feature of a reverse is that
male performativity is critically denaturalized. But this form of gendered critique is itself contained in a joyful and sociability-enhancing performance that
demonstrates women's performative competence. While a reverse polemically
demonstrates female competence in highly valued male performative idiom,
it also ambiguates the critical force of this inversion, by persuasively linking
the exercise of performative power with the pleasure of social play. But this
same linkage is also a feature of the object of the reverse's critique, as the following example demonstrates.

A number of women in Hoppy's social circle had planned for days to stage
an improvised reverse during the course of a party given in honor of the senior singer's fiftieth birthday. Hoppy's wife Mandy played the role of Hoppy;
Denise played the role of her husband, Steve, the guitarist in Hoppy's band.[15]
Steve, an excellent musician, was Hoppy's right-hand man in the operation
of Hoppy's band, responsible for the sound system and a sort of musical di-
rector. Hoppy and Steve had a competitive, agonistic relationship expressed
in constant verbal jousting. But Hoppy, as the singer and bandleader, ultimately dominated in their relationship. Mandy and Denise, playing their hus-

bands, expertly portrayed the constant low-level bickering between the men. Naomi played the role of her boyfriend, Sam the comedian, Hoppy's constant sidekick and the barroom's exuberant clown, with a characteristic maniacal laugh, which Naomi imitates to great effect here. Sam was a foil for Hoppy's jokes, subjected by Hoppy to a steady stream of physical intrusions intended to elicit clownish behavior, and verbal interrogations layered with affectionate diminutives.

The most active participant in the reverse, Big Judy, played herself—unlike the other women who played male roles. Her role in this performance was pivotal. Big Judy's powerful social presence demonstrates that it is possible in this community for a woman to occupy a position of performative authority without losing her feminine identity. She thoroughly ambiguates local gender stereotypes, and most sociolinguistic ones as well. As a bass player and truck driver and as a full participant in male-dominated music making and sociability, Judy lives up to the physically imposing stature that is encoded in her name. But as a singer, her achingly beautiful high voice (saturated with crying articulations), her good looks, and her gentle, dreamy affect are considered exceptionally feminine, an impression she cultivates with her repertoire and her skill as a harmony singer.[16] As a speaker and singer who is equally comfortable with male and female forms of sociability, Big Judy is a key figure in this reverse, at once scheming with her women friends to orchestrate the performance and performing her dramatic role with the most practice and intensity.

In their performance, the four women enacted a typical conversation among three of the four members of Hoppy's band (Hoppy, Steve, and Big Judy) accompanied by Sam, the band's "mascot." Although this tableau was explicitly framed as a peek behind the scenes into the lives of musicians, this conceit also tacitly acknowledged that such "band talk" is a highly stylized masculine display that is meant to be "overheard" and admired for its performative quality. By making explicit this normally tacit overheard quality, the performers achieved the purpose of this framed event. The audience's intense pleasure in this performance, marked by clapping, laughing, shouting out appreciative remarks addressed to subtle details of the imitation, and interpretations of these details for each other, resulted from their recognition of the incredible accuracy of the women's improvised portrayal.

The women sat at a table that had been moved to the middle of the bar's dance floor. In an acknowledgment of the ritual markedness of this fully performative event, the entire crowd (some fifty people) drew their chairs up around the dance floor and attended closely and with enthusiasm. The women spoke through microphones connected to the band's P.A. system and wore signs around their necks indicating their assumed identities. The performance was coordinated and occasionally coached from the sidelines by Miss Ann, a member of these women's intimate circle. Here I transcribe only a few minutes from the middle of the performance, which lasted nearly fifteen minutes in total:[17]

JUDY: [to Denise] By the way, Steve!
I told you many times
how I want that SONG done
And every time we do it
you try to change
how we wanna do it
And I told you a hundred times =
DENISE: = Well you just don't
know how to PLAY it right =
JUDY: = Yeah I DO!
But see
I been tryin' to get this . . .
DENISE: [annoyed, interrupting] Well I had to tell you to
play it THIS way, not THAT way =
JUDY: = Right
I TOLD you the beat I want =
DENISE: = Well I will show you one more time
[repeats more angrily]
I will show you ONE MORE TIME
You just do it the WRONG KEY
FIRST we play the WRONG key
[laughs, breaking frame]
JUDY: We're not in NEW YORK
we in TEXAS
so gimme a BREAK, okay?[18]
[laughter from crowd]
NAOMI: HA HA HA HA HA HA HA!
[Sam's characteristic laugh]

JUDY: No!

I *TOLD* you . . .

MANDY: [interrupting Judy, speaking to both Judy and Denise]

I'm gonna tell you both sompin!

Neither ONE of you do it

the way *I* want it done

and I'M the one . . .

DENISE: [interrupting] I do it right!

MANDY: [ignoring Denise] I'M the one

that runs the band

I'M the one that says what you do   CROWD MEMBER: *TELL 'EM*
                                           HOPPY!

JUDY: Well

you're the one that can SING it, too!

[sustained laughter from crowd]

NAOMI: HA HA HA HA HA HA HA

MANDY: And *I* do [i.e., "sing it"]

DENISE: [interrupting] . . . and *I* play it

MANDY: [changing the subject] And I will tell YOU something Steve[19]

The Lord put you here just to drive me *SLEW NUTS!*[20]

[crowd explodes with raucous laughter, hoots, and applause, continuing into next
few turns]

MANDY: You NEVER shut up!

[Mandy turns to crowd and other actors, with high-pitched, intonationally
dynamic voice]

He never shuts up!

You can't get a word in EDGEwise!   CROWD MEMBER: *TELL 'EM*
                                             HOPPY!

MANDY: *He just won't shut up*

[Denise tries to speak, but Mandy preempts Denise]

SEE?

You're doin' it again!

DENISE: [looking around, beginning to get up]

Where's my BEER?

Where's my beer?

I gotta get another beer!

The agonistic, dialogic sociability of male musicians' talk is brilliantly poeticized in this performance. But the women's remarkable improvisational competence with this genre reveals that this is by no means an exclusively male skill. Precisely coordinated overlaps, cues, repetitions, and seamless transitions indicate a nongendered emphasis on the continuity of talk, on the drawing out of interlocutors, and on shaping the form of talk to emphasize humorous climaxes that elicit laughter and comment. The essence of this performance is the women's achievement of canonical agonistic dialogism, in which all participants attend closely to each other and to audience reactions, reacting rapidly and dramatically to each other. Women possess discursive competence in modes of speaking stylized as male. This is conscious metalinguistic knowledge, as well as relatively unreflexive practical knowledge.

On the other hand, the women also model the emergence of male dominance and hierarchy in this reverse performance. In the opening sequence, Judy (as herself) and Denise (as Steve) accuse each other of musical incompetence, a topical index of male "band talk." As in "real" male conversations, such talk quickly turns confrontational. Judy and Denise sequentially interrupt each other and grow more and more aggressive, stressing first-person pronouns and self-aggrandizing verbs of telling and showing. When Denise asserts her claim to dominance through repetition, emphatic gestures, and staccato delivery, Judy counters with a devastatingly artful comeback that she uses often to gain the upper hand in her frequent arguments with the "real" Steve: "We're not in New York, we in Texas, so gimme a break, okay?"[21] This polemical remark elicits wild approval and delighted recognition from the crowd, and from Naomi (as Sam), who mimics her boyfriend's characteristic cackling laughter.

Mandy (as Hoppy) steps into this battle to address both subordinates and to assert a claim to ultimate authority here, "telling them both something," with a hectoring intonation and stressed repetitions of the first-person pronoun at the head of each clause. Denise interrupts Mandy with a low mutter, referring back to the earlier sequence, but this has no effect. Mandy's performance of Hoppy's persona is so accurate that it elicits, here and elsewhere during the performance, shouts of "Tell 'em Hoppy!" from the audience. Sociable performativity draws power from other speakers' engaged affirmations.

As she would do to Hoppy in real life, Judy takes up Mandy's challenge and tops her: "Well, you're the one that can SING it, too!" This also elicits approval from the audience, and again from Naomi's Sam, in the form of a maniacal cackle. Mandy, aware of having been topped, then seizes on Denise's barely audible interruption ("and *I* play it") to demonstrate another male technique of discursive power: she changes the focus of her verbal aggression to engage a weaker opponent. Mandy then delivers the most effective lines of the performance, using a phrase that Hoppy characteristically speaks to express exasperated resignation: "I will tell you something, Steve. The Lord put you here to drive me SLEW nuts." As her husband Hoppy often does, Mandy mixes affection with a finalizing gesture of discursive authority.

Mandy then moves to solidify her advantage, using an increasingly dynamic intonation and the first direct appeal to the crowd for affirmation to crush Denise's attempts to resist Mandy's dominance. Denise's defeated response enacts a typical male tactic when a verbal contest has been lost: she withdraws briefly to "get another beer." Mandy next employs a classic male technique of discursive hegemony, suddenly turning sympathetic (and gracefully patronizing) in victory, but opening the door to further conversation: "Alright, you get another beer and we'll discuss it."

In these reverses, then, women performatively inhabit a polemically figured "male" voice and simultaneously offer both a feminist critique of male authority and a working-class critique of class hegemony itself. They mimic male discourse and simultaneously exhibit female competence, not only in the subtle details of male interactional dominance but in the symbolic idiom of expressively "out of control" performance associated with male sociability and with a nostalgia for "traditional" working-class culture and social relations. In so doing, these women empower themselves to assert their own interests and perspectives; but they empower men too, as they craft a critical reflection on the continued salience of gender and gendered narrative in the formation of working-class identity in an era of rapid change and perceived loss of power and promise.

Driving On . . .

Refreshed by your pause for an hour or two at the Y'All Come Back Saloon, you continue driving down the highway and into the town of Lockhart, past the increasingly busy intersection of Main and San Antonio streets, the feed warehouse, the new supermarket, the grungy laundromat, the Mr. Taco stand, and the pawn shop. Turning right onto County Road 142, toward Martindale, you might go about a mile past the high school football field and pass an un-assuming strip of retail stores on your left, in what used to be the headquarters of an oil-drilling outfit. Look carefully and you'll see one of the new women-owned businesses in town, a hair and nail place known as The Y'All Come Back Salon.

The Art of Singing

Speech and Song in Performance

Speech and Song: Phenomenological Intertwining

The most fundamental poetic characteristic of country music, and of rural working-class verbal art, is the pervasive intertwining of speech and song as vocal modalities, with divergent yet linked valences of meaning. Underlying all the parallels between song, verbal art, and "ordinary" talk is the possibility that, at any moment, a singer will speak or a speaker will sing, and that either might do something in between singing and speaking.

The act of singing consciously structures the pitch, timbre, volume, signal-to-noise ratio, and rhythm of vocalization, in order to express the meaning of an independently structured poetic text, and to convey the interpretation of that text and the moment of performance by a singer. Singing heightens the aural and visceral presence of the vocalizing body in language, calling attention to the physical medium of the voice, the normally taken-for-granted channel of "ordinary" speech. Singing is by its very nature *phatic* communication. In focusing on the "channel" or medium of expression, it emphasizes the significance of that medium's distinctive contribution to the communicative act. Singing may even eclipse the referential content of expression in highly embodied and sense-interrupting forms like vocables, yodeling, melisma and polyphony, and iconic vocal articulations (cry breaks, pharyngealization, nasalization).

Vocality exceeds textuality, but the voice is also bound to the word in the oral culture of working-class Texans. Texted song compels singers, listeners, and analysts to attend to the interplay of embodied sound and the abstraction of affect and reference in linguistic forms. Song is also, in other words, by its very nature *poetic* communication, heightening attention to the formal organization of language and social discourse. The musical organization of song imposes highly redundant formal organizations of melody, meter, amplitude, and interactional dynamics on the less redundant and predictable material of "words themselves." Singing and vocal movements in the direction of song mark the embodied and emplaced sociality of language, which may even achieve temporary dominance over referential sense. Song marks and reveals, as I argued in chapter 6, the taken-for-granted structuring of "ordinary" speech (Feld and Fox 1994). In song, the fundamental tension in all language use between the context-bound materiality of the utterance and the abstracting (but never fully abstract or decontextualized) textuality of grammatical, semantic, sonic, and interactional structure establishes a zone of explicit experiment and contemplation. In the following pages, I explore this fundamental tension in relation to the sounding materiality of real voices in Texas working-class culture and country music performance practice. For these Texans, I argue, the sounding voice, pivoting between speaking and singing, is a summarizing symbol of identity and a fundamental medium of class-conscious social practice.

The Art of Singing: Some Aspects of Country Vocal Style

In Texas working-class culture, the art of singing "country" music is highly valued and carefully cultivated, as is critical discourse *about* singing. Local "lead" singers, like Randy Meyer, Justin Treviño, or Larry Hopkins, are musical specialists, both privileged and obligated to be responsible to their audiences and local communities for a wide range of performance skills and social tasks. They are especially evaluated in terms of their mastery (and creative extension) of a canonical set of distinctive vocal techniques. These same techniques are equally normative for recording artists, at least for those whose music is regarded as "real country" by blue-collar Texans. Here I consider several of those vocal techniques, in order to present the larger significance of singing as a working-class cultural practice.

Many articulatory possibilities are available to country singers as elements of canonical stylistic practice. Fully pitched, metrically regular, and dynamically shaped singing (with an expansive and exploitable range of voice qualities, vibratos, registers, and dialects of "ordinary" speech) is, of course, a basic mode of vocalization. Professional country singers tend to develop excellent vocal technique, pitch control, sustain, and vibrato. While both head and chest registers are used in country singing, neither predominates across the board, and different singers are known for different vocal characteristics. Larry "Hoppy" Hopkins, for example, produces a smooth, even, primarily diaphragmatic tone. His preferred repertoire emphasizes the beauty of his chest voice, although he uses effects such as nasalization and yodeling—where the chest voice is "broken" by head resonances—extensively and with fine control. He consistently applies a fast and wide vibrato to midrange and high tones. Hoppy's voice is considered "sweet" by his fans. It is a delicate instrument as well. Hoppy often refuses to sing if his voice is not in decent condition.

Randy Meyer, on the other hand, was called a "hard" singer by his many fans. He produced a piercing, vibratoless head register as his default style, though with enough breath control and power that he was reputed not to need amplification to be heard in front of a band (this was an exaggeration, and he generally used a microphone quite effectively). Justin Treviño, who has acquired a national reputation as a vocal virtuoso in recent years, can perform in either sweet or hard styles but normally produces a highly trained chest register vocal tone that approaches operatic bel canto in its consistent vibrato, portamento, and diaphragmatic breath control (reflecting his long apprenticeship with Johnny Bush, the "country Caruso"). Similar distinctions are applied to female singers as well.

In addition to these sorts of basic "fully sung" sonorities, country singers also routinely produce intonationally heightened "speech" that is metrically closer to the rhythm of "ordinary" talk, within the boundaries of song performance. When this technique predominates in a particular song, country fans and musicians refer to such sung-spoken vocalization as "recitation." "Recitation songs" have a significant place in the historical canon of country music, though they became less common in commercial country recording after the early 1970s.

Nonetheless, recitations remain fixtures in the working-class tavern repertory, and reciting is a skill that serious singers are expected to master. Typically, recitation is used for the narrative verses of a song, while refrains are fully sung, as in Hank Williams's 1951 "Pictures from Life's Other Side," in which Williams "recites" tales—cast in the same poetic meter as the refrains—

of desperation and loss, interrupting these stories to draw the lyric conclusion, in his sung refrains, that these horrors are essential dimensions of human experience.[1] More often, recitation is reserved for a particular climactic verse, typically prior to the last refrain, as in George Jones's "He Stopped Loving Her Today" (discussed in detail below). More rarely, recitations are (or begin as) improvised commentary on a song or a performance event, or emerge spontaneously when a singer recites a normally sung text.

Country performance practice also involves the frequent use of metrically nonregular and nonpitched speech in the course of managing musical structure, timing, and contextualization, as singers "speak" (sometimes performatively and sometimes as an aside) to their supporting musicians and to their audiences, both within and in between songs. This happens, for example, when a singer announces the name of a soloist (Ernest Tubb's "Pick it out, Billy Byrd!" or Randy Meyer's "Heeere's Mister Aaron!"), or offers metacommentary on the meaning of a song (as when Big Judy turns to the women in the crowd during her performance of "It Wasn't God Who Made Honky-Tonk Angels" and demands "Ain't that right girls?"). Such dramatic speech tends to be intonationally heightened, though less so than in recitation, and it tends to be metrically assimilated into the rhythm of the song even if it breaks the frame of sung narrative.

Even more fully "spoken" discourse also shapes the boundaries around song performances. Stage patter, bandstand talk, and interactions with audience members (using intonationally and dynamically heightened speech) can also be used to move between the spoken frame of song performance and full singing. Examples include bandstand "count-offs," which verbally establish the meter of the song (and which singers develop into stylized aspects of their performance), introductory words summoning full attention from audiences or announcing forthcoming song titles, and stylized formulae for marking song as reported speech, such as Hoppy's frequent use of "I said" to launch a new song.

Competent singers are consciously aware of this range of articulations and may refer to a corresponding set of theoretical concepts to describe specific formulae, articulations, and voice qualities. More often, both among singers and among listeners, metamusical discourse proceeds by analogy, usually comparing one singer's stylistic gestalt to another well-known singer's example (e.g., "he does it Marty Robbins style"). Fans and musicians also deploy a metaphorical vocabulary that emphasizes gestalt vocal qualities of "hardness," "sweetness," "sadness," "volume," "power," and "precision."

These dimensions of vocal style in country singing can be approached analytically through a fine-grained description of particular techniques employed by esteemed singers. Many properties of vocal sound (e.g., vibrato, amplitude, articulatory noise, nasalization, melodic shape, etc.) can be correlated with the communicative and expressive features of song texts. Particular inflections and textures are evocatively paired with affective verbs, references to feeling states, and canonical moods. Similar correlations, considered quite important by most Texas singers with whom I have worked, can be made between vocal techniques and the language-structural properties of song texts. For example, many vocal inflections, such as the cry breaks discussed below, appear to be conditioned equally by phonological environments and by affective connotations of the referential text.

A continuum of intonational markedness, ranging from unpitched, metrically irregular but intonationally heightened speech to fully pitched, metrically regular singing, is routinely employed to mark structural divisions in song texts, changes of point of view and narrative voice, contrasting affects, and degrees of expressive engagement by the singer. Timbral quality deserves special attention in this respect. Country singers evoke key affective gestalts through distinctive changes in the site and manner of voice production. A pharyngealized tone, for example, can be iconic of the ravaged voice of a character textually narrated as "crying." "Crying" itself can be iconically represented with specific inflections known categorically as "cry breaks"— sharp deformations of the melodic line effected through intermittent falsetto or nasalization, glottal or diaphragmatic pulsing of the airstream and thus the melodic line, or the addition of articulatory "noise" to an otherwise timbrally "smooth" vocal tone.

Much of the repertoire performed by local singers in Texas is comprised of covers of the classic country canon. Most singers tend to apply (or imitate) the style of the original recording artist associated with any particular song to the performance of that song. This is especially true for less accomplished singers, and for those still learning their craft. As Texas singers become more competent and develop individual styles, and as they acquire a repertoire of original songs or covers of songs by obscure artists whose styles are not familiar, they increasingly apply their own distinctive stylistic signature to everything they perform. Eventually they may be said to have "made a song their own" by restyling a canonical song, sometimes with dramatic modifications to the canonical recording.

Typically, however, even highly accomplished singers retain an affinity for one or two major stars' styles (and repertoire), and these styles can be instantly recognized as "influences" on their personal styles. Singers are known for the accuracy and authenticity with which they embody these archetypal models: Randy Meyer for his Merle Haggard; Larry Hopkins for his Marty Robbins; Justin Treviño for his Johnny Bush; Jack Hill for his Johnny Cash. This does not imply that a singer is simply competent in a derivative, imitative sense. An entire cultural conception of voice and orality underlies such tropes of classification. This stylistic emphasis on the embodiment of another's voice obviously extends from the pervasive elaboration in working-class speech of direct and quasi-direct discourse and extensive voice imitation in reported speech constructions.

George Jones's "He Stopped Loving Her Today"

The field of vocal possibilities and styles deployed within country music performance is therefore complex and subtle, as well as foundational to the genre. Movements within this range of possible articulations are ubiquitous expressive resources. An astute listening to George Jones's classic "He Stopped Loving Her Today," for example, reveals why Jones is widely regarded as the greatest vocalist in the history of country music, especially by his fellow Texans, and why this song is considered his greatest recorded performance by many fans.[2]

Jones begins the narration, which is introduced as reported speech (*"He said 'I'll love you 'til I die . . .'"*) by singing lightly, at times coming close to a spoken articulation, glancing off each word with a breathy tone and very delicate vibrato. Over the course of the song's unusually long sequence of four verses prior to the first refrain, Jones uses modulations in voice quality to intensify the poetic scene. These timbral modulations become ever more ornamented and intense as the narrator gradually reveals the depth of the male protagonist's obsession with a lost love. The narrator describes a character living out a "half crazy" life surrounded by objects that serve as shrines to the memory of his beloved ("her picture on the wall," the letters by the bed with every "I love you" underlined in red). The vocal line gradually acquires more intensity, as Jones increasingly sustains and amplitudinally shapes his notes and produces an ever-richer tone. His voice acquires a broader vibrato, as the song modulates up a half-step. Jones reaches for a high note (the first appearance of the third above the tonic that begins each verse) on the desperate line "hoping she'd come back again." Gradually, Jones adds and extends his trademark vocal melismas and increases his overall dynamic amplitude. Finally, in the fourth verse we find out that the narrator has gone to see the abject protagonist of this tale as he is "all dressed up to go away" and finally smiling for the first time in years. The song text carefully distinguishes and distances the narrator from this protagonist, who is apparently the narrator's friend, but Jones's vocal intensity suggests an emotional investment out of proportion to this scenario. When the first refrain finally arrives, Jones has arrived at a full-throated, elaborately melismatic, sustained and vibrato-rich sonority as he reveals why the protagonist has finally "stopped loving her today": the protagonist has died. He is dressed up and smiling because he is at his own funeral. The protagonist's emotional release from obsessive love — "today" — is suddenly and vertiginously revealed as a trope of compulsion rather than choice.

After the first refrain, the narrator withdraws to observe the arrival of the protagonist's beloved at the man's funeral. Here, Jones suddenly reverts, with an eerie effect, to recitation — a loosely metric spoken articulation (breathy, with elongated vowels and heightened intonational movement). This recitation preserves the poetic structure of the composition (rhyme, line breaks, and scansion): "she came to see him one last time/and we all wondered if she would. . . ." Behind this, a wordless female voice laments in an operatic descant, layering the most extreme form of singing (fully pitched, wordless, rich vibrato). The total effect is to juxtapose nonreferential "pure song" and song straining toward referential speech in the form of a recitation.

This recitation moves from a description of the funeral scene to the first reported inner speech of the narrator himself (who has hitherto been merely the reporter of events). This thought is couched as wordplay, and it delivers the final refrain on the heels of a mordant joke that plays on a trite romantic cliché: *"And it kept runnin' through my mind/ this time, he's over her for good."* The refrain returns, one last time, more fully and powerfully sung than previously, in Jones's all-out quasi-operatic apotheosis, and ends as Jones fades out on the word "today," around which the poetic effect of the song has been built.

The Vocal Art of Larry "Hoppy" Hopkins

I have heard Hoppy compared, as a singer and a "character," to George Jones many times by his fans. This extraordinary compliment is proffered in part because Hopkins is a master of this same subtle range of expressive vocal articulations. His singing style is built on carefully shaped and controlled gestures. His notes have clearly delineated onsets and offsets, and if his pitch wavers it is with expressive purpose. His dynamic control is extraordinary. He controls form-articulating crescendos and decrescendos, accents and *sforzandos*, and ornamental inflections, using these techniques to call attention to individual notes, key phrases, whole lines, structural divisions of song forms, and even relationships between different songs.

The dynamic shaping of whole lines is evident in Hoppy's performance of "My Blue House Painted White," where he gradually and very smoothly crescendos through the lines that lead up to the refrain's climax with a mysterious setting of the mise en scène, beginning near a whisper at the bottom of his register and building to a full-throated expressive peak (in the next octave). The narrator of the song comes home to discover that his wife has left him because of his "partying" lifestyle, finally arriving on the powerful lexical trope "anymore," which contains within it the whole sad history preceding this moment, suddenly made vividly present: *"Well the teardrops they started as I walked through the door/ The silence it tells me she's not here anymore."*[3] The amplitude (i.e., volume level) of this line, in Hoppy's performance, rises with perfect regularity, punctuated by strongly accented peaks on the meter-defining alliterative sibilants in "silence" and "started." With this crescendo, Hoppy builds smoothly to the expressive catharsis of the song's title line, sung in a full-voiced style with frequent cry breaks, in which the narrator "calls her name out every night," receiving no response in his "blue house painted white."

Hopkins's attention to the structuring of vocal intensification is also evident in smaller gestures. For example, in Marty Robbins's song "Pretty Words," on the poetically intensifying line "I'm not sorry we met," Hopkins sets each syllable to a clearly distinguished note; he drops his volume rapidly after the onset of "sorry," and he imbues this note with a wide, even vibrato. He incrementally raises his volume and pitch until the end of the line, "bending" the pitch of the "we" expressively upward as he completes his crescendo, to the amplitudinal and intonational peak of the line.[4]

These carefully delineated fully sung articulations, however, hardly exhaust

Hoppy's techniques for shaping his "pretty words." When he performs Randy Meyer's song "When I'm with Me," for example, he varies his articulation within the first two lines of the refrain. He moves from "sung" rhetorical declamation to "recited" micro-epic explanation, shifting from a highly emotional tone (rich vibrato, high amplitude, definite pitch, and careful shaping of notes in a melismatic line) to an almost offhandedly spoken, though still metrical and slightly pitched, articulation:

1. [sung at full volume, with full vibrato, and with a melisma on "world"]
What makes a man live in two different wo——rlds?
2a. [quasi-spoken, metrically regular, exaggerated intonational movement]
I'm here at home tonight
2b. [fully pitched, full vibrato, syllabic articulation, lower amplitude]
the next night I'm with a girl.[5]

In addition to these kinds of sung and quasi-spoken articulations, singers superimpose on the sung/spoken vocal stream a variety of icons of embodied affect (notably, "crying" effects) and virtuosic departures from texted singing (e.g., yodels, which break rapidly between falsetto and normal registers; melismatic vocal ornaments like turns and shakes; and vocables). These articulations are coordinated with song forms and specific affective goals. "Crying" effects, in particular, are both generalized aspects of a subgeneric style ("hillbilly" style, for example, permits as many cry breaks as possible subject to phonological constraints) and specifically coordinated with "sad" songs, verbs of crying, and affectively potent moments.

Certain singers are known as specialists in "sad songs," and such singers frequently adopt a consistently pharyngealized timbre. Vern Gosdin is a revered example. His morose song of marital conclusion, "That Just about Does It (Don't It?)," plays in the background of many of my field tapes, as his pharyngealized voice, practically dripping with mucus, intones hollowly: *"That just about does it, don't it?/ That'll just about kill it, won't it?"*

Gosdin's pervasive "crying" tone loads his lines with embodied meaning. Big Judy's voice has something of this pharyngealized timbre (in a much higher pitch range), and people tend to describe it as a profoundly "sad" voice. Other singers may, like Larry Hopkins, sing with a clearer, more fronted timbre and more even vibrato. But such singers can also convey tragic affects, by controlling a range of "crying" effects that fall under the general local heading of "breaks." These are sudden constrictions of the vocal articulatory mechanism that "pinch" a note in midstream, producing either momentary silence or grace-note movements into falsetto registers (the same effect as yodeling, but done once, briefly, rather than over a sustained period of time). If a cry break is followed by a sustained pitch, that pitch may be imbued with a wide vibrato or tremolo to mimic a chest pulse or "sob," or it may be sharply bent upward, or both.

Like pharyngealization, these "crying" breaks, bends, and pulses vividly express the upwelling of bodily processes in the sound-stream of texted song, fracturing, bending, interrupting, and overwhelming ordinary phonetic patterns, intonational contours, and metric regularities. Breaks, bends, and pulses may be used at any point in singing where they are phonologically possible, generally on the boundaries between liquid, fricative, and nasal consonants and vowels, as in Hank Williams's 1949 classic "I'm So Lonesome I Could Cry." When he sings the song's title phrase at the end of each strophe, Williams often "breaks" both the "o" in "lonesome" (following the liquid sound /l/) and the second "I" (which follows the nasal sound /m/).[6] Such "breaks" express "feelingful" poetic intensification, especially at moments when the singer wishes to appear overwhelmed with emotion to the point of encroaching inarticulateness. Most conventionally, these articulations are virtually obligatory when a song text mentions "crying." But the phonological constraints of the song text must also be observed, making decisions about cry break placement complicated and significant.

Hoppy, whose "sweet" voice is not inherently "sad," has mastered a subtle range of cry breaks, bends, and pulses as an expressive resource. He has been extremely consistent in his stylization of particular songs, lines, and melodic contours over the twelve years during which I have been recording his singing. Consider his performance of Gene Watson's "Farewell Party," a magnificently miserable song in which the narrator imagines a party at which he will be sent off from his lover's life (the implication is that it's a funeral, as in "He Stopped Loving Her Today").[7] On the refrain's first line (*"There'll be flowers from those/who'll cry when I'm gone"*) Hopkins builds to an intense climax on the word "cry." He quietly and evenly intones the first half of the line but suddenly rears back for a high and quick pitch-bend up to the top of his range on "who'll." Coming off the sharply aspirated /wh/ segment, he "breaks" the vocalic portion of the note ("who'll), before settling back on the high note as an appoggiatura on the verb "cry," which he shapes carefully as a long (more than one second) and fully sung note with a decrescendo and strong fast vibrato.

Another form of crying articulation is a pulsing or "stuttering" effect, in which the singer "splits a note" (the vocalic nucleus of a syllable) in half, often with a corresponding up-step in pitch. This is somewhat similar to a cry break, but it involves little or no emphasis of the singer's falsetto or nasal "head" register in the offset or onset phases of the note. It entails a full interruption of the vocal stream rather than a break across vocal registers. In "Pretty Words," for example, Hoppy performs this pulsed/stuttered articulation on the word "sorry" in the couplet "I'm not sorry we met/I'm not so^^^orry I let/pretty words make a fool out of me." This adds variety to the reiteration of the word "sorry," and it contributes to the stylized irony of this kind of song, in which a narrator protests his indifference despite vocal evidence to the contrary (as in George Jones's "She Thinks I Still Care").

Yet another possibility that Hoppy frequently exploits is the conjoining of a "cry break" with a sharp, expressive upward "pitch bend." For example, when he performs Merle Haggard's "Shelly's Winter Love," an obscure recording but one of the staples of Hoppy's repertoire, he uses this technique to articulate the word "hers" in the line *"When those friends of h$_\wedge$ers start calling her from town."* This is a vividly sad song about a pathetic rural man who is grateful for the occasional affections of a woman who leaves him every spring when "those friends of hers" call her "from town." (This is another, rather unusual example of the "blue-blooded woman and redneck man" trope.) Here, Hoppy inflects the word "hers" with a slight cry break after the aspirated consonant. He then returns to a fully pitched articulation on the vowel as he bends the note upward into the highest part of his vocal range. The effect is very poignant, as the line demands, expressing the abjection of the song's abandoned narrator.

To take one final example, Hoppy will also string together several nuanced cry breaks and pitch bends in the course of a single line, usually over a repeated note in his highest register (the fifth above middle C). In his version of Marty Robbins's "The Hands You're Holding Now" (a lover's plea to his woman not to leave him before she considers the many things his hands have given her), Hopkins hits an expressive climax on the line *"In the ashes of our love that's lost its glow."*[8] Because the line is set to a repeated high note leading to a falling melodic cadence in the second clause, Hoppy strains to delineate the note boundaries and to make the line intelligible. (The close proximity of the sounds /l/ and /r/ and /sh/ and /s/ in this line present special difficulties for a singer.) To impart the intensification that the line demands, Hoppy uses a series of subtly different cry breaks and bends, breaking upward on the first vowel in "ashes" to the melodic climax of the line on the E above middle C, pulsing the stressed initial vocalic nucleus of the word.[9] He then produces a series of small falsetto breaks at the onset of each word in "of our love," beginning on the high E, and as he bends the note downward to the D, before (in the next line) stepping down to the tonic A (220 Hz) for the resigned conclusion ("that's lost its glow").

Hoppy's expressive vocal precision weds personal style and received tradition through technical mastery, the crucial elements of any art. Many of his inflections were learned from Randy Meyer, although the two singers have very different voices and styles. Hoppy's technical command reflects a knowledge of the natural limitations and strengths of his own voice, and a sure sense of the expressive possibilities and requirements of particular songs (emphasized because of his conscious preference for commercially obscure repertoire), particular lines, particular syllables, and particular performance situations. Even at this microanalytic level, the vocal nuances that comprise virtuosity in country music performance explore a complicated terrain between embodiment and textual meaning, between more "sung" and more "spoken" articulations, between concrete sound and abstract grammar, and between emotion and its manifold and disciplined vocal stylizations.

Singing, Speaking, and Playing in Country Performance Practice

Because of its emphasis on vocal subtleties like the ones Larry Hopkins and George Jones command, country music performance and recording practices entail supporting and framing the lead singer's voice and voice-mediated aesthetic presence. Country music is canonically recorded and performed with the lead singer's voice "out in front" of the mix, significantly louder than any other component of the ensemble. The intelligibility of the song text and the audibility of subtle modulations of voice quality are aesthetic prerequisites for effective performance, especially for working-class audiences. These same standards apply in achieving a proper live "mix" in beer joint performance.

Bar owners are fanatical about policing the volume level of bands, and the most common criticism of a band one hears in working-class beer joints is that the instruments are drowning out both the singer's voice and the audience's conversations. Bar owners make no bones about enforcing their standards and may even fire a band in midperformance for repeated failures to heed calls to turn the instruments down. I have even seen a bar owner simply walk behind the stage and unplug the band's power supply.[10]

Ensemble texture in country must support the singer's voice. Over a solid and relatively spare rhythm section (bass, rhythm guitar, drums, and sometimes keyboards), playing tightly in one of only a few standard rhythmic "feels," various lead instruments (fiddle, steel guitar, and lead guitar, and, more rarely, mandolin, banjo, harmonica, keyboard, or saxophone) take turns playing "fills." This is the melodic filigree that counterpoints the voice, decorates vacant melodic spaces in the phrase structure, and articulates structural divisions in song form.

Good singers are rigorous in their expectations of sidemen or "pickers," whether they perform with professional bands, the shifting pool of "pick-up" or freelance players who work in the beer joints, or even randomly assembled players who convene at jam sessions and picking parties. Accomplished singers show little patience for sidemen who overwhelm the vocalist with volume, or for instrumentalists whose "fill work" is too busy, too loud, or too close to the vocal melody, overlapping it too completely or cluttering up its registral space. For "lead pickers," the most basic skill one can bring to the bandstand is the ability to negotiate the sequencing of fill responsibilities in performance so that multiple players' fills do not overwhelm the texture. This can be done through eye contact, hand signals, or the establishment of routine sequences for all songs (e.g., steel on the first verse, guitar on the second, etc.). If sidemen compete too obviously to dominate the fill role, they are considered incompetent no matter how technically proficient they might be on their instruments.

Though lead players do move to the front of the mix briefly for their "rides," these solo turns are generally kept to a single verse, or to half a verse when a ride is shared among soloists (the ride sequence is another basic stage-managed task). A ride must remain close enough to the song melody so that the singer is carefully "brought back in." The best lead players tend to conclude their rides with close approximations of the song's introductory "turn-around" or "kick" melody. And in any case, a lead player is evaluated first on his or her fills, turnarounds, and kicks, and only secondarily on the ingenuity or technical skill of his or her rides, a lesson that musicians schooled in rock performance often struggle to learn when they work in country bands.

Everything in ensemble practice is focused, in other words, on supporting the vocalist. Good pickers, especially pickers who work steadily, are fanatically attentive to the nuances of the lead vocalist's expression. Long-term relationships develop between singers and respected lead men, who are nominally subordinate but often function as "music directors" for a band. Lead men often take responsibility for the rehearsal of new material, the selection of appropriate songs for "sit in" players and singers, the setup and running of the P.A., and the fielding and management of requests delivered while the band is playing.[11] They may also take charge of remembering which birthdays and anniversaries the singer is supposed to announce, and the general coaching of the other players in the course of performance. Good "lead men" (and they are usually men, regardless of the lead singer's gender) in other words, allow the singer to focus on the projection of their own performance.

Harmony or "backup" vocalists (usually instrumentalists who also handle some of the lead vocal duty, making them "front men") also heighten the centrality of the lead vocal in country performance. Good harmony singers are highly valued, but a bad harmony singer is considered worse than no harmony singer at all. Again, the best harmony singers are those who submerge themselves in the lead vocalist's every nuance of rhythmic articulation, note shaping, and pitch bending, and they are fanatical about matching the details of the harmony and lead vocal parts (which are usually a third or sixth apart, though fourths and fifths are also used in two-part harmony; multipart harmony singing is also highly valued). Big Judy, Hoppy's long-time bass player (and a stunningly good lead singer herself), exemplifies this impeccable sense of nuance.[12] Judy has spent many years developing her sense of the subtle details of Hoppy's vocal style. Her distinctively "ragged" (i.e., pharyngealized) vocal tone adds timbral depth and complexity to Hoppy's "sweet" and smooth tone. She matches his phrasing so completely that Hoppy's fans assert that they hear the two singers' best performances as a single biphonic and bitimbral voice. This is an aesthetic ideal to working-class fans, and harmony singing is the subject of extensive comment.

But harmony singing, like fill work, also counterpoints the lead vocal. Judy, for example, uses a fully *spoken* delivery to step away from this unified texture. She has developed a range of "back-talking" responses to certain lines in Hoppy's standard songs. When Hoppy performs Waylon Jennings's waltz "Amanda," in which an aging country singer apologizes to his long-suffering wife for his failures as a husband, he focuses a great deal of intensity on the line "*I got my first guitar/when I was fifteen.*"[13] Hoppy sings the line using a rich vibrato and a dramatic dynamic shaping of the line's high, arching melody. But as the last word fades, Judy slyly undercuts this melodramatic effect (in the form of a small reverse) as she performatively mutters "*I* was fourteen." The line, delivered in a hurried spoken rhythm, usually gets a laugh, even after years of repetition. Of such nuances are great harmony singers made.

Boundaries, Borders, and Frames: Speech around Song

Songs frame periods of intense aesthetic and embodied concentration on the range of vocal articulations, the sound of a voice, the presence of a performer, and the meaning of a text. Consequently, the temporal borders around song performances (e.g., movements into and out of song, introductions, and "walk-on" and "walk-off" formulae) are saturated with multiple and complex movements between singing and speaking.

A framing convention that has its probable origins in Anglo-American folk singing is still widely practiced in modern country music: songs often begin and/or end on a spoken word or line (Fox 1992). Such boundary-marking gestures, which are still encompassed by the textual poetic form of the song, serve to move vocalization gradually along a continuum from stage patter to full-throated singing and back again.

In live country performance, there are additional levels of framing song with speech, and additional movements between speech and song. Even if a song is sung throughout, it may be introduced in stage patter by a metrically and intonationally heightened invocation of its name or the name of the artist it is associated with. Such framing movements are decisively intensified from the background "conversational" tone of stage patter discussed above. There is often a moment, before the band has actually started playing but during which the song has already begun for the listeners, when the air is charged with anticipation. In such moments, speech/song movement marks the cathartic emergence of full performance. Randy Meyer, who is considered a master of stage patter, provides an example:

RANDY: [on microphone] Drink up folks!
The more you drink the better we sound . . .
Alright!
Now here's a Hank Williams number
Aw, honey . . .

[slightly more intoned, in the meter of the song]
"Take these chains from my heart and set me FREE!"
[the band begins the song immediately]

To work effectively, this focusing device must be immediately followed by a "count-off" or, among skillful players, an immediate instrumental kickoff ("kick" or "turnaround") from the guitar, fiddle, or steel guitar player. The picker playing the kick may vocally count the band in ("one . . . two, one TWO . . ."), ideally *while* the singer is speaking, or s/he may simply begin the kick on his own at the appropriate moment, trusting the band to pick up the song's meter and key promptly, usually on the first downbeat of the kick following a two- or three-beat "pickup" figure. A kick should be both elegantly melodic (usually based on the song's vocal melody) and rhythmically forceful and unambiguously directed toward arrival at the first full-band downbeat. Experienced players often require only that the singer announce (either privately to the band or publicly to the audience) the song title and (if it is not known already) the key; in an instant they have begun the appropriate kick.

If a singer is unsure whether his or her musicians know the song s/he wants to play but trusts them to figure it out with a minimal clue, then s/he may turn to the band (before announcing the next song) and quietly *sing* the song's tag line or "punchline" (the last line of either the refrain or a verse). This line supplies the melodic and harmonic skeleton for the stylized kick (or "turnaround") to a song. The singer (or a delegated musician in the band) may instead turn to the band and announce the chord sequence (using a numeric shorthand for scale degrees) and metrical structure of the song and then begin the count (e.g., "slow shuffle . . . *four-five-one* [harmonic cadential pattern] . . . one . . . two, one TWO"), trusting that the sideman responsible for the kick will come in as required (repeated failure can get a picker fired). Alternatively, a solid lead player may inform the rest of the band about the harmonic pattern and rhythmic shape of the kick by rehearsing it once quietly while the singer talks to the audience (although this is considered somewhat amateurish). If the singer or another musician knows the kick but the lead instrumentalist does not, they may play or sing it to the lead player (although, again, this is not desirable because it breaks the flow of the performance).

Master singers like Randy Meyer sometimes compensate for an informal or hastily assembled band or low-skilled musicians by forgoing an instrumental kick and instead formally *singing* an introductory tag line (e.g., *"Take these chains from my heart and set me free!*"). These sung kicks use the text and melody of the song's turnaround line (the same source the instrumentalist uses) and often exaggerate the rhythmic feel of the line. If the pickers are unable to kick songs reliably, singers resort to announcing the song title and key and then "kicking it cold." This entails beginning with the first line of the first verse and playing a simplified "straight rhythm" pattern forcefully on the rhythm guitar (and praying for the drummer and bass player to lock in quickly, as their failure to do so results in a "train wreck").[14]

Likewise, at the end of a song, as the last chord is struck, a singer may reiterate the song title, the name of the artist with whom the song is associated, or a stylized phrase using a heightened speech articulation (again, intonationally dynamic and metrically regularized) as the crowd applauds. Such phrases include "Oh yeah!" or "There's a [Merle Haggard] song!" or more extended patter, as when Randy Meyer ends "Is Anybody Goin' to San Antone" with "WHOA! 'Is anybody goin' to San Antone?' Just pick me up on your way down!" as the song's final chord is sounded.

Many bands frame entire sets (conventionally about an hour long in Texas bars) by playing "walk-on" and "walk-off" music, usually instrumental standards (Leon McAuliffe's version of "Steel Guitar Rag," for example). The same music is repeated at the beginning and end of each set, thus creating a musical border between the layering of conversation and jukebox music and the more focused layering of conversation and dance with the louder and more closely attended music of the band. Whether the music comes from the stage or the jukebox, however, this layering is carefully preserved. As the bandleader finishes his last song, or as the band plays "Steel Guitar Rag," the singer or one of the pickers gets on the microphone and shouts "Jukebox, please! We're gonna take a short pause for a very good cause and be RIGHT back!" (or some other stylized closing formula). As the musicians step off of the stage, skillful bar employees and owners have their hands on the volume control and instantly turn up the jukebox to preserve the music/speech balance. In larger dance halls where the Top-40 bands hold forth, these transitions are carefully coordinated with the band's soundman (running a tape or CD machine) or the club's DJ, who attempts to keep dancers on the floor by supplying musical continuity. Likewise, as the pickers assemble onstage at the beginning of a set and begin to tune and warm up, the singer or one of the pickers will call out "Jukebox, please!" to signal the bar manager to turn down the jukebox just as the band prepares to start. The aesthetic goal, in other words, is to achieve a soundscape in which talk and music are consistently layered, although one or the other may be in focus at any given moment.

Speech and Song at Jam Sessions and Musical Parties

These same conventions of performance practice are applied, in a more relaxed manner, at informal musical events like jam sessions and picking sessions around the tables in a bar. The close proximity of conversations and music making in such situations, and the fact that the musicians are also parties to ongoing conversations, leads to dense integrations of speaking and singing, and partial and fragmentary movements into and out of song that would be inappropriate in staged performance.

For example, at one picking party at Ann's Place, several patrons prevailed upon Big Judy to perform a certain song, but she demurred, claiming to have forgotten the words. Justin Treviño "fed" her the opening line by singing it softly, and the rest of the musicians launched into the song instantly, with Judy confidently picking up the text exactly where Justin left off. At these sessions, anybody could begin a song by experimenting vocally with its opening line, and selections were usually chosen this way. To sing an opening line, even quietly to yourself, was an invitation for the others to join in, though often with some intervening conversation and frequent false starts.

Such invitations to sing could have a critical thrust, too. Late at night during another jam session at Hoppy's place, the whiskey and beer and smoke had put us in a tired mood, and we fell silent for several minutes, making desultory attempts at conversation and contemplating going home. Richard judged the situation critically, and sang, *"It was all that I could do to keep from yawning."* This was a sarcastic parody of the opening line of David Allan Coe's "You Never Even Called Me by My Name" (see chapter 6), which begins *"It was all that I could do to keep from cryin'."* When the laughter died down, we launched into a proper rendition of the song that energized us for another hour of music making.

Jam sessions are occasions for many other kinds of verbal art, of course. Songs and stories and jokes overlap and interpenetrate in quick succession, amplifying one another with intertextual references across the speech/song boundary. For example, one evening I was telling Hoppy about my new digital electronic effects processor, purchased so I could achieve the wide range of guitar tones necessary for playing contemporary country music hits in a Top-40 dance hall band (and utterly unnecessary in beer-joint performance). This was an invitation for critique, of course, though Hoppy delivered it gently with a story. But the story in turn suggested a song, which, in the manner I have discussed, served as the kind of lyrical denouement that tropes of cylicity provide in other stories:

HOPPY: I don' know
Those things SCARE me sometimes
That's like . . .
We was playin' one night at a
th'American Legion and ol . . .
EVan[15]
Johnny Mac's BRother
was playin' bass
They like to pull . . .
PRANKS!
Now Evan was the type of guy
He played bass
But he had EVERYthing you could imagine!
All kinds a little buttons and hookups
And I was not suspicious at all
of this stuff he was hookin' up, see?
And . . .
What he DID
He hooked an ECHO chamber up!
Now, boy I went out there and . . .
[sings]
"Smoke smoke smoke that cigarette"[16]
[strums a chord]
Anyway
Pretty soon I hear this
[slightly sung, repeating and fading away]
"Smoke smoke smoke smoke smoke smoke . . ."[17]
[Hoppy makes a quizzical expression and imitates his own words
in the narrated event]

What in the . . . ?
[laughter]
[Hoppy breaks into song: "Smoke, Smoke, Smoke (That Cigarette)"]

Finally, these informal musical events also invite extensive participation by nonmusicians, whose discursive contributions further enrich the dense texture of speech and song overlaps. Attendees call out song titles, sing along with performers, and launch into conversations stimulated by songs, including stories about performers, and discussions of music-related topics. One night, several hours into a session of playing around a table in Ann's bar, Hoppy finished "Shelly's Winter Love" and announced:

HOPPY: Another old MERLE song!
RICHARD: What's that other song he did?
"Carolyn?"
Something like that?
I think it's on the same album . . .
HOPPY: Yeah, yeah he did one
"CArolyn"
"Carolyn"
I'm trying to think . . .
what was that . . . ?[18]
RICHARD: Wasn't that [on]
"The Roots of My Raisin' " album?
"The Roots of My RAIsin' "?
HOPPY: What was that one about . . .
He tells you
Love for mom . . .
What the HELL was the name of that?
RICHARD: That's the "Roots of My Raisin' " album . . .
BEAUtiful album . . .
And it's hard to find too
"The Roots of my Raisin' "?
He does it!
HOPPY: [sings]
I sell the morning papers sir, my name is Jimmie Brown
Never mind sir how I lived . . .

[Hoppy stops singing suddenly]

HOPPY: Ah, I wisht I KNEW all that!

I think we GOT that somewhere on tape don' we? . . .

"Jimmie Brown the Newsboy"

Think ol' MAC Wiseman done that . . .[19]

ANN: Jimmie BROWN?

HOPPY: Yeah . . .

RICHARD: [sings]

The roots of my raisin' run deep!

[speaks]

I feel better tonight . . .

HOPPY: [to Joanna] Why don't you TRY some different ones Joanna

that you haven't TRIED before?

JOANNA:[20] Such AS?

HOPPY: Such AS . . .

you know what songs you know

better'n I DO!

ANN: [sings] *"Sweet violets . . ."*

JOANNA: I don' KNOW that one Ann! [laughs]

ANN: HOPPY does!

HOPPY: [sings "Sweet Violets," a slightly bawdy folksong]

RICHARD: Hoppy?

Ever done any . . .

Y'ever done any WRITIN'?

HOPPY: Very LITTLE

I get too SERIOUS about writin' songs . . .

AF: There's a couple of them I've heard

HOPPY: Yeah that, "Guilty" I wrote

mmmmm

I've got several back in the back . . .

Don' bring 'em OUT much

Cuz USUALLY when I write about sumpin

I write about a personal experience

A lot of times that . . .

brings up bad MEM'ries

So I don't wind up never doin' 'em, y'know?

[long silence]

AF: How 'bout "When I'm with Me"?
HOPPY: [sings "When I'm with Me"]
[applause]
HOPPY: [seriously] That's a Randy MEYer tune there!

This graceful sequencing of talk about songs and artists, talk about other subjects, fragments of songs, jokes, and full performances of songs can go on for hours at a jam session. At other times, these events can be the occasion for a riotously dense piling up of speech and song. Late one night, we were near the end of a long evening of music making in Hoppy's "house of mem'ries." Hoppy was playing a tape he had made on an old boombox of that evening's jam session. Sam was telling us about a band he had recently seen perform, and how much he appreciated their faithfulness to the classic concluding gesture in country performance: ending with a gospel song. To illustrate his point, Sam began to sing a gospel classic, the one the band had ended with: Hank Williams's "I Saw the Light."[21] As Sam sang, the tape in the boombox suddenly began to replay an earlier conversation about the song "There's a Tear in My Beer," a "recently discovered" Hank Williams Sr. song that Hank Williams Jr. had released in 1989 as an electronically faked "duet" with his dead father (discussed in Fox 1992). The song was one of the major hits of 1989, but it was controversial among working-class fans for its ghoulish conceit.

As Sam finished singing a few lines of "I Saw the Light," his recorded voice could be heard on the tape playing in the background, this time singing "There's a Tear in My Beer." On the tape, Hoppy began to sing "When I'm with Me," Randy Meyer's song, which literalizes the metaphor of the "split subject," a figure strongly evoked by the splitting of present and past in that moment, as the tape had resurrected a past moment when Sam had evoked a song that resurrects a dead country music star. Completing the bizarrely symmetrical layering of the moment, as Hoppy sang "When I'm with Me" on the tape, Sam joined him in the present, singing the second line of Meyer's song ("I go out to all the barrooms") with comedic delight.

We fell into sustained laughter, overwhelmed by the density of the interplay of taped and live discourse and music, speech and song, past and present, serious and humorous images, and the way that movements into song could condense so much meaning that they overflowed their moment and bubbled up again and again in voices on the speakers.

Speech and Song in "Ordinary" Conversation

These movements, layerings, and juxtapositions of speech and song are ubiquitous, then, in the context of performance practice, musical events, and musically mediated sociability. But they also comprise a key rhetorical resource for "ordinary" conversation, even where music is backgrounded. The functions of these movements include exemplification, punctuation and emphasis, opening momentary spaces for reflection, emotional intensification, and the management of difficult topics.

In discussions about music, especially among musicians, movements into song are, of course, frequent and virtually unmarked as a means of exemplification. Country musicians, in conversation, routinely break into song when words fail them or when they want to make a point about musical style economically and unambiguously. In an early conversation with Justin Treviño, for example, we began talking about his mentor, the great Texas singer Johnny Bush. At the time, I knew very little about Bush, and to make his point about Bush's importance Justin cited Bush's best-known composition, the song "Whiskey River," which had been a huge hit record for Willie Nelson:[22]

JUSTIN: He wrote "Whiskey River"
I don't know if you've heard him do that
He's got a completely different version than Willie
AF: I don't think I have
JUSTIN: It's a shuffle thing
Kind of a two-step
[Justin makes drum sounds with his mouth]
Like medium speed
[sings while tapping the swing rhythm]
"I'm drownin' in a whiskey river"
He just kinda creates the atmosphere for it
It's unique
He was real famous in HIS time
the late 60s . . .
Then he was into some voice problems

The continuous presence of music, on the jukebox or live or on people's minds, means that song is frequently available as a conversational resource. Movements into song can signal a desire for sociability, filling a sudden silence with an interesting observation about music on the jukebox or some particular feature of a song. And conversationalists can bond socially around such movements. For example, during a lull in a conversation one afternoon, Donna Fargo's goofy, chirpy "Happiest Girl in the Whole USA" came on the jukebox. The song is fairly absurd, especially when Fargo breaks into a nursery-rhyme chant on the phrase "Skippedy doo da" to mimic the carefree heart of the "happiest girl." Like so many truly banal songs, however, this one could be humorously infectious, and in the quiet, Terri and Linda both began to sing along with the jukebox:

TERRI AND LINDA:[23] [singing along]
"Skippedy doo da, thank you . . ."
PAT: Why do you PLAY that?
Someone has to jump up and reject it!   [i.e., hit the "reject" button to stop the song]

I also hate THAT song!
LINDA: [laughs] I'd have 'em take that damn thing OFF!   [i.e., remove it from the jukebox]

PAT: Ann LOVES it
TERRI: [laughs] I always play one that Ann likes
Most of 'em she takes off
cuz I play them so much!
[laughter]

Movements into song can also serve to restore balance in more charged moments, when there has been a breach or failure of sociability. For example, a group of middle-aged couples were conversing one evening when their talk turned, for no apparent reason, to the subjects of aging, sickness, and death. As the conversation stalled, they looked uncomfortably around at each other, searching for a humorous intervention in this glum topic. One of the men walked over to the jukebox, which was uncharacteristically silent, and played Hank Thompson's "The Older the Violin, the Sweeter the Music." The joke was instantly understood by everyone, and laughter and talk flowed once more. In this case, the movement into song involved the third party of the speaking object, and the jukebox is often this kind of "participant" in talk.

Movements into singing can also signal an opposite meaning. Feeling "tore up" or withdrawn from sociability is very often signified by a show of musical immersion (see chapter 4). Such displays may signal a desire for sociable attention, but often they serve to erect a wall of music around a genuinely reflective or solitary mood. Obsessive fixation on a particular song is a much remarked-upon sign of being "tore-up." On numerous occasions, I have seen people in the throes of depression or loss play a single song over and over again, as Maria did with "Here in the Real World" (discussed in chapter 4). On a smaller scale, feelings of sadness can be signaled by singing quietly to yourself, avoiding eye contact and other conversations.

Pat, the barmaid at Ann's, had a reflective streak to her personality, and when she was feeling distant she would play long sequences of her favorite songs on the jukebox and sing quietly along with them as she worked, conspicuously avoiding getting drawn in to the conversations all around her.[24] It was on one such occasion that the next example occurred. Pat was feeling "tore up" indeed, as her boyfriend had left her the night before, after yet another argument (they had a decidedly rocky relationship). She'd been singing to herself a lot that afternoon, and had been close to tears a few times. Pat put on a feisty show of barroom feminist bravado, however, when Rusty, who was a good friend of hers, inquired into her state of mind.

She told Rusty she didn't care if her boyfriend never did come back, as she could do without him anyway. But there was no doubt about the subtext as Rusty and then Robbie began to tease her to see how sincere this bravado was, as Jerry looked on in amusement. The two men were intent on bringing Pat back into the conversational fold, drawing her out and socializing her depression. As Becky Hobbs's "Jones on the Jukebox," a classic instantiation of the trope of the divided subject and the speaking jukebox, played on the jukebox (thanks to Pat's quarters), Rusty quietly observed:[25]

RUSTY: Ah, you never gonna drop him . . .
He's pretty quiet anyway
He's hard to READ . . .
PAT: Well he wasn't last night on the telephone!
RUSTY: He's hard to read . . .
JERRY: That's his hangup![26]
RUSTY: He's hard to read
PAT: Well, you see how heartbroke *I* am!
RUSTY: Oh yeah I noticed y' all broke up   [Jerry laughs]
PAT: Shit happens, I guess

RUSTY: Nyaaah!

Thirty minutes, he be back

PAT: Think so?

RUSTY: Whadaya bet?

Whadaya bet?

PAT: [in a high, "feline" voice] *Kitty, kitty, kitty, kitty!"*

[Pat gestures toward her crotch]

RUSTY: Right! Right! [laughs] . . .

HE be back!

PAT: Well, if he ain't it's his LOSS

That's all I can say

RUSTY: Oh OH!

NOW you're braggin'!

ROBBIE: [laughing] She's all shook up!

RUSTY: Hah!

I love ME!

Oh yeah . . .

HIS LOSS!

Gaaaaawd DAMN!

PAT: Would you rather see me like this?

Or would you rather see me sittin' over here cryin'?

ROBBIE: [suggestively] I'd console you! [laughs]

RUSTY: Boy, I'd like to have your ego!

PAT: What'd you say?

RUSTY: I'd like to have your ego!

HIS loss . . . !

PAT: I could be standin' over here cryin' . . .

RUSTY: HIS loss!

PAT: I could be standin' over here cryin' cuz I'm brokenhearted!

ROBBIE: [sings] *"I've got this cryin . . ."*

[ca. 3 seconds of silence]

You got the right attitude

Always go through life thinkin' what someone else is missin' out on

Someone tears me down

I go, *Pppt!*

"Get lost!"

[long pause]
Then I go home and cry!
[everybody laughs]

Minutes before this conversation, Pat had gone out behind the bar to be by herself and cry, adding much ironic resonance to her insistence that her bravado is better than "sittin' up here cryin'." Rusty's repeated insistence that her boyfriend is "hard to read" applies as much to Pat herself. The men nervously interrogate her seeming lack of affect. They refuse to allow her to dismiss the topic, and then duplicitously attempt to shame her for her for her immodest show of unconcern. "HIS loss, *GaawdDAMN!*" Rusty snarls at her in humorous disbelief.

Pat is equal to the challenge, however, as she poeticizes the gendered tension in this dialogue with a bawdy gesture and a half-sung expression invoking female control over male sexual desire. Three times, then, she asks if the men would prefer to see her "sittin' over here cryin'" rather than shrugging off her abjection, questioning their apparent sympathy. By repeating this phrase, Pat revels in the intertextuality between her "split" affect: her articulate condition of being "tore-up," and the country music trope of "cryin' songs." This "cryin'" trope is vividly present in the air around this conversation as Becky Hobbs's voice comes out of the jukebox saturated with cry breaks as she sings: *"There's a fool in the mirror lookin' back across the bar/ reflections of a woman whose world just fell apart."*[27]

It is this poetic resonance that Robbie seizes in his fleeting musical intensification of this moment. Sensing that Pam is close to losing her vigorously asserted control over her feelings, and realizing that the song on the jukebox has just ended, leaving behind a vertiginous moment of silence, he inserts a quietly sung fragment that blends Becky Hobbs's song and Pam's "cryin'." His brief, almost offhand line borrows its melody and verb from Hobbs's song, in which the refrains begin "I've got (Jones on the jukebox)." But like a good country songwriter, Robbie borrows a small fragment of the speech around him to construct a new, if miniature, text, echoing Pat's repeated use of the verb "cryin'" as he sings: *"I've got this cryin'..."*

He breaks the line off, and another silence follows in which the entire moment is now dramatically placed at risk. How will Pat respond to this latest intensification? The mood is charged with danger. But like a good country singer working the crowd with stage patter, Robbie quickly recovers his poetic intensification, switching back to sympathetic speech, and self-reflexively in-habiting the figure of the "split subject" himself in a perfectly placed joke that devolves this dangerous moment into a wave of sociable laughter.

In this working-class community, speech and song abut and adjoin each other at numerous points and overlap and interpenetrate and blend in count-less ways. Verbal art and song performance demand the control of innumer-able articulatory nuances that blend text and embodied sound, emotion and the stylization of emotion. Speech frames song in the discourses of stage pat-ter, in musicians' technical talk, and in constant discussions about music and musicians. Song, conversely, is always in the air as people speak, coming from the jukebox, the stage, the TV, the stereo, or a few "old boys" picking around a table. One of the most generic features of my field tapes, made under very different circumstances over the years, is the constant background of music, the aural soundscape that my interlocutors take for granted as the canvas on which everyday life is painted in conversational brush strokes. Social life is vividly colored by the myriad shades of the sounding, speaking, and singing human voice, in everyday acts of verbal and musical creativity.

An extremely dense network of vocal practices and ideologies constitutes the discursive and experiential world of working-class Texas culture. This net-work is focused and attended to explicitly in singing practice, but it extends well beyond the boundaries of song per se. An analysis of the vocal practices of country singers, verbal artists, and ordinary working-class speakers reveals dense relationships between song and speech in this culture. Vivid acoustic refractions of sociality are materialized in every act of vocalization. But some voices are especially valued for the symbolic work they do. This will be the subject of my final chapter.

"I Hang My Head and Cry"

The Character of the Voice

In songs, words are the sign of the voice . . . song words are

always spoken out, heard in someone's accent. Songs are more like plays

than poems . . . [they bear] meaning not just semantically, but also as

structures of sound that are direct signs of emotion and marks of

character. — Simon Frith, "Why Do Songs Have Words?"

Characterizing the Voice

The first time Miss Ann ever mentioned Randy Meyer to me, on my second visit to her bar, this is what she said:

ANN: He [Randy Meyer] is THE legend of country music
in South Austin
for the last twenty-five or thirty YEARS
He played for me every Friday night at the Little Bottle
and he PACKED my house
He played HERE
I 'd moved out here
Within a WEEK or two or three weeks
And he had already start packin' this house
He has the most fantastic chaRIsma

And everbody knows him
EVerybody loves him
He can sing MERLE Haggard
all NIGHT long
He says
"I know FIVE hundred songs
and I ain't learned a new one in the last ten YEARS"
But . . .
[Ann's voice starts to choke with emotion]
He's livin' up at the lake right now
He had a STROKE
RIGHT here in this place!
But he, he's come back
and within a month or so
he was back PICKin' for me
He has the most fanTAstic amount
of charisma and volume
and VOICE

In this chapter, I consider one final constitutive trope of verbal art, social life, and "real country music" in working-class Texas culture: the intimate linkage between voice, character, and identity. Although this is a complicated idea, it has a simple refraction in Texas beer joints: the vivid presence of country music stars, and, by extension, the starlike charisma of local heroes like the singer Randy Meyer. Among these Texans, certain figures walk like omnipresent ghosts. Their voices and the things those voices stand for are never far from consciousness, and the mere mention of their names or the mere intimation of the sound of their voices can powerfully focus "feeling" and "mem'ry" in moments of condensed social poetry. There are only a few such voices whose power is undisputed, certainly including George Jones, Merle Haggard, Hank Williams, Patsy Cline, Marty Robbins, Jim Reeves, Willie Nelson, Loretta Lynn, Johnny Cash, and a few others. But vividly standing in these same ranks are a select few local voices, the voices of singers like Larry Hopkins, Randy Meyer, Big Judy, and Justin Treviño. A few towns away, the list might be different.

The big stars and the local heroes alike are figures in everyday narrative, and the role of stars in these stories is to appear "ordinary." The subtle and highly disciplined vocal art of these stars and local heroes is at every level imagined in tandem with the origins of such voices in a local, "ordinary," working-class milieu. And because country music is an everyday topic of conversation, these stars can enter at any "ordinary" local moment:

SONNY: To me, to me, to me
Roger Miller is a storyteller . . .
ANN: He is!
SONNY: And there's a lot more to it than just . . .
ANN: But you could dance to his music . . .
SONNY: Ya, but he was still a storyteller . . .
[pounds on bar to make point]
every . . . song . . . he . . . ever . . . sang . . . told . . . a story!
ANN: Well so did Jim Reeves!
SHIRLEY: Oh, I LOVE Jim Reeves!
God I still love him . . .
SONNY: But he's a storyteller!
He woulda been a . . .
If he couldn't 'a sang
he'd a been a storyteller   ANN: Yeah!
SONNY: He'd'a sat down and told you
the SAME story in verse rather than in song, y'know?
ANN: Right before Jim Reeves died
I was workin' at the Western Inn steakhouse?
SHIRLEY: uhhuh?
ANN: And he'd come in
come in there and . . .
I didn't know Jim Reeves from a big-eyed BUG!
But he walked up to the counter
and he handed me a card
And on the card it said "I'm Jim Reeves . . ."
"Hello"
or somethin' like that
"I'm Jim Reeves,
and I would like to . . .
have dinner and would like not like
to be disturbed"   SONNY: mmm, yeah

Real *NICE* man!

Real *PLEASant!*

And just wanted to eat and be on his way!

SHIRLEY: Quietly!

ANN: And so I put him over in a corner

and turned his back to everybody

And he had his dinner,

And he was a *very very* sweet . . .

gentle, loving, caring man!

SONNY: [reverently] That was my MOther's favorite artist of all time . . .

ANN: And he was a perfect gentleman . . .

SHIRLEY: He was real good   SONNY: Oh yeah

ANN: And he just had his dinner

and he went his merry way

But I guess . . .

It wasn't too long before he was dead

Although Jim Reeves was one of the biggest stars of his day, he was, or so the story goes, the kind of gentleman (and his nickname was "Gentleman Jim Reeves") who spoke silently to working-class waitresses, never even using his awesomely rich and smooth baritone in the entire encounter. How do stars and their voices come to carry so much significance, power, and sacred grace in everyday life, even years after their death? For the remainder of this chapter, I consider one such sacred voice: that of Johnny Cash.

"I Hang My Head and Cry"

The "jammers' reunion" had been going on for three days and three nights when the fleeting, locally unmemorable incident I wish to consider at some length here occurred. This "reunion" was Ann's annual summer music marathon. Nearly every musician who had ever worked for Ann or jammed at one of her bars would appear over the three-day event to participate in a nonstop jam session that overflowed the stage and took over the bar and even extended into people's homes and other beer joints.

A good percentage of the serious working-class country musicians living between South Austin and San Antonio, and some from further off than that, would show up to join in this musical marathon. These included established local singers like James Casey, Jack Hill, Jan Tyson, Bud Robbins, Ted Lacy, Fran Allen, and of course Larry Hopkins (who stage-managed the event), Randy Meyer, and Justin Treviño. And then there were all the "kids" (as the older pickers called the younger ones, when they weren't known as "little fuckers"), some pushing hard to move into the higher ranks of reputation after years of apprenticeship marked by an increasingly regular schedule of $150-per-night weekend beer-joint jobs, and others just trying to find their voice. The "drunks" and the many working men and women who just liked to pick a few songs every now and then also put in some time on the stage. There were even some *real* kids urged up on stage by their parents. Some pickers played for a single set and then left, while some hung around for days, like Les, who reliably covered the lead guitar role when others weren't willing to do so, and Bo, who could be counted on to supply an all-important bass part under any conditions. Those who stayed wound up sleeping on the pool tables or the old sagging couches along the walls (where little babies and toddlers napped during the day). The most esteemed visitors—guests of honor—crashed in one of the trailers behind the bar, where more serious forms of partying also took place, away from the barroom throng. The event was ritually framed and anticipated all year long through lovingly assembled "mem'ries" from previous reunions, such as videotapes, photographs, a sign-in sheet on which all visiting musicians left greetings, and, of course, many, many stories.

The dance hall's stage was occupied by both established and makeshift bands ("jammers") each day of the reunion, from midafternoon until one in the morning, as different crowds came through, and different assemblages of "jammers" formed. But things quieted down at around 2 A.M., at which point a small group of musicians—those staying at the bar, and Hoppy and his guests, since he lived nearby—would gather around a few tables in the back of the dance hall with acoustic guitars. Ann couldn't sell beer after midnight, or 1 A.M. on Saturdays. During the reunions, that made little difference, however. There were plenty of bottles and joints circulating out in the parking lot, in the band trailers behind the bar, and in the cabs of trucks. For the sober, Ann and her sister Bettie kept the coffee brewing, and warm plates of food would miraculously appear on the musicians' amplifiers as long as they kept going into the night. There was an emphasis on "keeping going." Everything possible was done to maintain a deeply altered ritual state of focus and sociable intensity and heightened consciousness of music's orchestration of "feeling." Sleep could wait.

During busier hours, most of the musicians and the many working-class fans who would show up over the course of the event came and went, a few hours here and a few more there, bouncing back and forth between the bars along the highway, or going off to work or to their homes and coming back for more the next day or evening, children in tow. But a core group made it a point of honor to stick out the entire event, holding on for all three days and three nights of nonstop sociability, almost without sleeping. There was Ann, of course, and Bettie, and Ann's adult daughter, Nita. Bettie, along with Nita and another musician's girlfriend, had worked at the bar for the entire event, selling beer and clearing tables despite her advancing arthritis. She had also cooked the continual supply of food arrayed on a table along the dance-hall wall. Randy Meyer's son Anthony was there the whole time too, just starting to sing onstage at the age of twenty-one. "Sounds just like his dad," people said, although they meant only his voice quality. Nobody could hope to phrase like Randy Meyer, at least not without many years of experience.

Quiet Paul and his friend José would stay until late at night too, hanging out together under the overhanging roof out behind the bar, sitting on old trash barrels and broken barstools, drinking beer, smoking, and talking in Spanish as they tended to the barbecue on which some huge piece of meat was always cooking, giving off a smokey, greasy smell that wafted through the open door and across the dance floor. A sociable tour through the bar always included fifteen minutes outside talkin' shit with Paul and José, standing with them inhaling barbecue smoke, watching the sun go down behind the bar over the simmering cotton fields and pastures.

And, always, among the die-hards who never seemed to sleep, there was Robert, a hard-drinking music-obsessed, self-identified "redneck" songwriter, and something of a ne'er-do-well, and Big Joe, Robert's drinking buddy, a huge bear of a man who had installed highway signs for the state for forty years. This is a late-night story about Robert and Big Joe and a singer named Johnny Cash, and about how much the tone of a voice can mean in a culture where it always means something.[1]

Big Joe was a slow-moving, slow-talking, sweet-tempered "country boy" who liked his beer and loved country music with an unmatched intensity. Many said that, at one time, Joe had been "a hell of a drummer." Now he played his acoustic guitar and sang, and although he played with great reserves of "feeling," he lacked musical precision. He tended to drop and add beats, and he knew only partial versions of most of the songs he sang. But no one begrudged him a few songs on the stage during jam sessions, which is all he ever wanted to do, before he would fall back and bang out rhythm chords on his big old yellow acoustic guitar. Only the musicians noticed that he never plugged the guitar in, so that you wouldn't hear him unless you were right next to him onstage, where he grinned widely as he played for the crowds. He'd play as long as anybody else did, though. After the stage grew quiet, he'd be right there in the circle around the tables over near the bar, singing one or two songs, dropping a beat here and there, making sweeping gestures with his hands to try to bring us back in with him, and stomping his huge foot. And after he'd sung a few local favorites (hard country tunes like Haggard's "Swingin' Doors" and sentimental songs like Bill Monroe's "Footprints in the Snow"), he'd go back to his rhythm guitar, and to urging songs out of the other singers, both good and bad, with infectious enthusiasm. "PICK one HOPPY!" he'd shout, using the standard local exhortation to make some music.

Joe was a limited guitar player. He'd lost most of the little finger of his left hand on the job years ago, like so many local men. But he had a grubby prosthetic finger that he would pull out of his pocket and attach to his hand when he played. That odd plastic finger was "a beautiful thing," people said, poeticizing an all-too-common injury among working-class men, a metonymic reminder of the costs of hard physical labor. The prosthesis was "beautiful" because it allowed Joe to play music, which was the one thing he most loved to do. The extra effort this required made it more significant. It gave Joe's music an extra dose of "feeling" and imbued it with a sense of a mighty struggle for a little bit of humble joy.

As long as we were making music, any music, Joe had a grin on his wide, furrowed, sun-leathered face, and his deep-set eyes would shine. I finally understood the clichéd phrase "pickin' and grinnin' " in its full symbolic depth when I met Joe. And Joe's enthusiasm was infectious, able to imbue even tired songs with new, sometimes compelling deconstructive possibilities (like his 5/4 version of "Blueberry Hill," which took some getting used to).

When he was strongly moved by music, Joe would grab any woman who would let him and dance her around the floor in a heavy swirl, smelling of hard labor in the Texas sun and cold beer under a neon moon and smiling at everyone who caught his eye. But when he wasn't playing or listening to good music, Joe often had a sad look on his face. He'd sit quietly at the bar, lost in thought, speaking only once in while, and often cryptically, unless it was to say "when are we gonna PLAY some MUSIC again, pardner?" He'd light up like a beer sign, though, when another picker would walk through the door, and he'd get impatient if you talked too long and didn't set down to some pickin'. When you said goodbye to Joe, he always demanded a commitment: "When 're you gonna come on back out and PICK sometime? We'll be playin' Sunday up at J and J's!"

Robert was a different kind of man. Like Joe, he lived for music, and Texas music was his consuming passion. But whereas Joe was content to play and listen to music, Robert sought every possible chance to talk, argue, and read about music. Joe was a big, slow-moving, slow-talking man who was deeply respected for his modest talents and simple manner. Robert was a smaller man physically, but he lacked a less obvious kind of stature too. He had a quick temper and an urgent manner. He was easily engaged but also restless and quickly bored. He was highly intelligent, but highly polemical about his tastes. He was an adequate musician, but inappropriately critical of other players' skills. Big Joe spoke slowly when he spoke at all, and he knew only a few words to a few songs. Robert was extremely verbal. He was a gifted songwriter, and he would write a new song nearly every week. He knew the complete lyrics to a large number of songs. He had read numerous books on country music, and in fact he read my academic papers and made valuable criticisms of them. He loved to argue and joke, and he sought emotional intensity in conversation and in musical sociability.

Joe loved to make music with others but shunned the spotlight. Robert loved to play too but sought the center stage too insistently. He was a solid, forceful rhythm guitar player and could "carry" other players of lesser skill. He knew the chords to most standard songs, and if he didn't he could pick them up quickly, after a few bars. If the stage was empty for a minute between sets at a benefit or a jam session, Robert would gather the younger and more rowdy musicians and seize it, often to the chagrin of the more senior musicians. Once onstage, Robert would sing song after song, especially his own songs, which were often raunchy and aggressive. One of his songs, for example, ran down a long list of excremental bodily functions to analogize the narrator's romantic misery. The younger men laughed at this if they were drunk, but the women and the older men called it "that disGUSTin' song," and they dreaded the moment in any jam session when some "drunk" would call out for it. Robert also loved to play loud "southern rock" music (e.g., songs by Lynyrd Skynyrd and the Marshall Tucker Band) which, again, infuriated Ann and the senior musicians, who resented "that loud rock and roll shit."

Big Joe had labored in the weather for forty years, and often wore his sweat-drenched work clothes to the bar on weeknights. Robert avoided labor, and he dressed sharp if he was going to play, in a vest and a cowboy hat, felt for winter, straw for summer. To him, I was always a "Yankee," even after we shared many adventures, even if I was an exception that proved the rule: "You're the only damn Yankee I'll TALK to," he once told me. He took the idea of "Texas music" very seriously, and he frequently tested me on my knowledge of it, chiding me when I fell short of his knowledge of its history. He knew this history in detail, and he had strong opinions about what counted as "REAL" Texas country music. He drank only a locally produced beer (Shiner Bock), which Ann carried almost exclusively for him. And he knew and was known in just about every bar in Central Texas. He had the time to circulate widely through these taverns because he was often unemployed. People said of him: "He's like so MANY musicians, he'll live off a DAMN woman 'til she kicks him out on his BUTT." His relations with his girlfriend and her child were stormy and tense, and his behavior toward his family was a source of constant opprobrium from more respectable members of the tavern community.

In a classic pairing of opposites, Joe and Robert were devoted friends and rarely appeared separately. They enacted a mythic mode of male friendship centered on music and "raisin hell" together.[2] Both men were talked about as eccentric, imperfect, and sometimes infuriating, but of course, they were always welcome. Their imperfections made them "characters" in the social drama, and thus full persons. The deep sociability that music organized in the community was unthinkable without these two men. They made life interesting and musical. Like every other full person in this world, they were the objects of incessant gossip aimed at socializing their imperfections, layering their eccentricities onto local sociability, thinking through and with their suggestive pairing as friends, the way that categorical oppositions are always suggestive of interpretive openings into the primal figures of social life.

Late on a Saturday night during the reunion, we were sitting around the tables in the back of the dance hall, over by the bar itself. Nita had her feet, out of their shoes at last, resting in her mother's lap, tired from a long day of tending to the needs of several hundred drinkers. Bettie and another woman sat talking off to the side, in that quiet but serious way that seemed more congenial to women. There were a few others sitting quietly at the table or the bar. It was perhaps three in the morning, and the rest of the crowd had long since dissipated. The stage was piled high with guitars and amplifiers and overflowing ashtrays and empty beer cans and congealing plates of cold, half-eaten food.

That stage, for the past day the site of continuous action, stood empty now, bathed in the half-light coming from the single row of fluorescent lights Ann had left on in the otherwise darkened dance hall. Buddy, Big Joe, Robert, and I were sitting in a circle "trading songs." A mood of quiet exhausted peace lay upon us all, and even Big Joe, who never flagged, was looking like he might be ready for some rest.

We went several minutes without playing a song, just chatting and drinking coffee, enjoying the mood, thinking about sleep and the next day's music. But suddenly Joe got a second wind. "Come on! PICK one!" he suddenly barked, causing a few nodding heads to snap to attention, and looking at me expectantly.

Into the tired late-night silence, I listlessly played the opening lick from Johnny Cash's "Folsom Prison Blues."[3] This lick is one of the most recognizable and symbolic musical figures in country music. Originally played by Luther Perkins on Cash's 1956 Sun Records recording, it has come to stand for a whole rural, working-class structure of feeling, if it is played with the right "feel" and at the right moment.[4]

Folsom Prison Blues:
On the Meaning of Johnny Cash's Voice

I expected the "Folsom" riff to pass, as it so often did, for a joke about running out of material. I stopped after I had played the twanging intro, damping the strings for a percussive timbre and playing down near the bridge to simulate the sound of Perkins's out-of-phase electric guitar pickups, repeating the low B like a machine gun, pouncing upward onto the D-sharp which always seemed dissonant because it didn't resolve immediately to the E above it, instead slinking back down through the low B to a slurred, bent blue-note G moving almost to a G-sharp, marking the ambiguous tonality of the song, halfway between E major and E minor, symbolizing the "blues" of the title and of the song's narrator, then winding down through a bent F-sharp moving almost to the G, and finally sliding off that bend onto a sharply attacked open-string tonic low E on the downbeat. It's that downbeat where the band is supposed to come in—and come in hard and fast and tight—with what country musicians call a "train" beat, modeling the incessant mechanical groove of a train with slightly uneven sixteenth notes accented on the second and fourth beats of the bar.

This standard country "feel" iconically signifies the huffing sound of a train straining down the tracks. But the theme precedes the groove. "Folsom Prison Blues" is only the most canonical example of a trope that has been ubiquitous in country since Jimmie Rodgers, "the Singing Brakeman," first sang of "waiting for a train" with the unemployed and the hobos around the station water tower in 1929.[5] "Folsom" is about this mythic train that runs through twentieth-century American experience, a train the narrator hears off in the distance while he sits locked up for shooting a man in Reno, "just to watch him die." This unseen train "tortures" the narrator as he imagines it full of "rich folks drinkin' coffee" and "smokin' big cigars," on their way "down to San Antone" (a mere fifty miles from where we sat that night). "Folsom" exaggerates and symbolizes all the fantastic American movement and luxury and historical "progress" that has always happened just beyond the horizon of rural working-class existence, but always within earshot: "But those people keep a-moving," Cash sings, "and that's what tortures me."

"The Man in Black"—Johnny Cash—had a voice that continues to stand for all this brooding darkness and historical marginality in every sung phoneme,[6] a mysteriously "ordinary" voice that found its metaphoric "vehicle" in this train coursing through a prisoner's tortured imagination. Low and gravelly and accented and weary and dour, Johnny Cash's voice will always signify pain and entrapment and struggle, the sonic equivalent of the black garments he always wore in solidarity with the poor and the oppressed of the world. "Folsom Prison Blues," in particular, will be forever associated with its canonical performance on an album recorded live at California's Folsom Prison in 1968, where the prisoners unleashed a mighty cheer as Perkins's opening riff sounded out. They were identifying instantly with the tortured narrator, and with Cash as his cipher, a man who kills for pleasure (that line earned another loud cheer from the inmates), a dark working-class antihero, connected by marriage (to the late June Carter Cash, daughter of Mother Maybelle Carter of the Carter Family) to the mythical origins of country music, by his ironic name to a parodic joke about poverty and deprivation, and by his voice and manner to a childhood of cotton-farming poverty in Dyess, Arkansas.[7]

Cash's singing voice, with its drawled, broad Ozark vowels, its hollow depth, its pungent back-of-the-throat midrange and gravelly texture, its complete lack of ornament or vibrato, and its deep, almost impossibly resonant low register, is so completely unique and identifiable and "extra-ordinary" that it surely qualifies as one of the most inherently compelling voices in the history of recorded American song. Within country music Cash's voice belongs in the very select company of Jones and Haggard and Williams and Cline. In Cash's commercial heyday, from the early 1960s through the mid-1970s, there were singers who worked the steakhouse and county fair circuit who made a living off of doing a "Johnny Cash show," imitating the singer's voice, dress, and repertoire.

And Cash imitations are a standard part of rural working-class musical humor too. One trashy example that delighted my friends was a comedy record, titled "Dear John," which somebody found at a garage sale. The song begins, of course, with a distorted, off-key version of the opening lick in "Folsom Prison Blues," in which a screechy-voiced Cash-crazed fan struggles valiantly through a ridiculous series of obstacles in order to get tickets for a Johnny Cash show. At the end of the song, Johnny Cash himself intervenes to give the fan tickets, in the guise of a good imitation of Cash's voice. At the moment this iconic voice comes over the speakers, my friends always laughed uproariously. The old scratchy record on which this routine resides was played again and again, always producing the same delight.

Cash imitations are also ubiquitous in working-class verbal art and musical performance. Justin Treviño, for example, has spent his life immersed in the study of canonical singers, and in performance he often playfully imitates Johnny Bush, Willie Nelson, Marty Robbins, and Ernest Tubb. (Tubb has another frequently mimed voice, even more startling in its "ordinariness," with its distinctive Texan accent, its utter lack of vibrato or ornament, and its quavery pitch control.) But the voice Treviño reaches for most often when he is seeking a humorous effect is the voice of Johnny Cash. One night during a jam session, the subject of Johnny Cash came up, as it so often did, as we were discussing a popular deep-voiced local country singer, Jack Hill:

JUSTIN: Jack could prob'ly be
one of the BEST Johnny Cash impersonators in the WORLD
if there was a market for that kinda thing, y'know
JOANNA: Yeah, yeah!
but there is NOT and never will be!

HOPPY: I don't think there's too much market for that kinda thing y'know

JUSTIN: I know it . . .

he's got the VOICE for it though

HOPPY: [sings in imitation of Cash's voice] *I fell in to a ring of FIRE!*[8]

SAM: [loud and slightly sung] *I FELL IN TO A BURNING RING OF FIRE!*

JUSTIN: They're gonna use that for a . . .

"Preparation H" commercial here!   [a hemorrhoid ointment]

[uproarious laughter]

[Justin sings in an imitation of Cash's voice]

"And it burns burns burns

Ring of fire

Ring of fire . . ."

Such jokes are ubiquitous and usually ephemeral, but occasionally they take on a long, storied life of their own. Another story illuminates how Cash was a symbol of resistance to the increasingly corporate control and commodified character of country music, a source of major irritation for working-class country fans. Many of the working-class bars in the small towns of South Texas pay no licensing fees to the performing rights organizations (ASCAP and BMI), although as live-music venues they are legally obliged to do so, since semi-professional and amateur musicians play ASCAP- and BMI-licensed songs in these bars, and presumably contribute thereby to the generation of revenue by these beer joints. ASCAP in particular undertook a vigorous enforcement campaign during the years of my fieldwork, and bar owners routinely received intimidating letters, calls, and visits from ASCAP lawyers and field representatives.

Like many local bars, Ann's Other Place received regular letters, visits, and phone calls, offering various terms and threatening lawsuits for continued noncompliance. This infuriated Ann and her patrons. The concept of intellectual property rights did not extend, for these fans, into the live performance of cover songs by well-known country artists, although they were more than accepting of the rights of an artist to receive revenues from the sale of recordings and for live appearances. Quite reasonably, in fact, they understood that cover performances of popular songs contributed to the general popularity of particular artists as well as country music more generally and hence had an incalculable positive effect on the revenue artists did earn from public appearances and recordings.

But more than this, these fans and musicians understood the nature of musical "property" and its "ownership" very differently than did music industry institutions like ASCAP. They were shocked to hear that I (or my academic publisher) had to pay money in royalties to publish short quotations from some songs in an academic article (Fox 1992). They were even more furious when an ASCAP representative told them which songs they were technically not allowed to play without payment of license fees. A defining moment came when Ann asked a visiting ASCAP agent just *who* would get the money she was being asked to pay as a yearly fee. The agent showed Ann and some other patrons at the bar a brochure with pictures of ASCAP artists, including one of Johnny Cash. The agent left the brochure at the bar, where it was circulated with disbelieving remarks for days after the visit.

The sentiment this event inspired was crystallized in phrases I heard several times as this story was retold in subsequent weeks. People said things like "Johnny Cash wouldn't stand for this," or "If Johnny knew *who* was playin' his songs, he'd let us have them for free." Ann talked of writing to Johnny Cash to explain the whole situation. The incident seemed to energize anti-ASCAP sentiment. Ann had heard that record stores were exempt from live-performance licensing fees, since music played in such stores could be legitimately described as advertising and promotion for particular artists' recordings. Within days, a large bin of old LP records appeared at the back of the dance hall, under a hand-painted yellow plastic insert stuck onto an electric beer-sign: ANN'S LITTLE RECORD SHOP.

It wasn't long, too, before a huge white banner was draped across the graffiti-covered wall behind the stage, reading: NO ASCAP MUSIC PLAYED HERE. This sign was not meant to be taken literally; I offered to do some research and make a list of songs licensed by ASCAP, so that we could, indeed, avoid these songs when we were jamming in the bar, but the suggestion was laughed off. The sign meant, of course, that music played "here" was by definition not "ASCAP music" but the intellectual property of the people who bought Johnny Cash records and went to Johnny Cash shows and knew the words to every Johnny Cash song. It was simply unimaginable to the patrons and musicians of this humble working-class establishment that Johnny Cash, whose voice stood for so much to these people, would have expected money from them before he would have allowed them to play "Folsom Prison Blues" as they sat around unsteady tables on old plastic chairs drinking cheap beer and talkin' shit. Everybody knew, deep in their hearts, that Johnny would probably have joined us around the table if he were coming through town, and that even if he never came through this particular town, he would have been pleased to hear that his voice still mattered in a place like this.

Where Was I?

Johnny would have been pleased, indeed, then, by the turn of events on that quiet evening during the "jammers' reunion." I had expected my musical joke to pass only a few listless seconds in the late-night haze. But as the "Folsom" lick left my guitar's soundhole, Big Joe seamlessly grabbed the "train beat" groove from out of the air, chunking an open E chord on his big yellow guitar with mighty strokes, and he began to sing, *"I hear that train a' coming, it's rollin' round the bend. . . ."* As he often did, Joe forgot the words beyond the memorable opening lines. He kept singing though, slurring together a phonetic approximation of the lyrics in his deep voice. As he got to the last line of the second verse, however, sound and meaning realigned in the most important line in the song. Joe lowered his large head iconically and bellowed the line, word for word, with the most incredible amount of gravity, sinking down to the resonant low E on the last word, sung with enough *profundo* power that it vibrated our bones, the way only a few singers besides Johnny Cash can do. Suddenly, Johnny Cash *was* in the room with us:

JOE: [singing] *When I hear that whistle blowin'*
I hang my head . . . and . . . CRY!

Joe stopped playing after this line. He looked up suddenly to discover that we had fallen silent, all eyes and ears on him. This momentary breakthrough into the most evocative and profound sort of performative "feeling" had been so effective that Cash's song, by now usually a hackneyed joke, suddenly acquired substantial new power. Joe's long life of grueling labor and his veiled pain seemed laid out before us in the flash of a single line, converging on the image of loss and passing time mashed inside the word "cry."

Not used to commanding this level of musical "feeling" by himself, Joe acted sheepish at having drawn our fixated attention. He looked soulfully around at the other pickers and implored us to continue for him, saying: "I don' know the words."

Robert knew the words—all the words. He knew the words to nearly every canonical country song, and he had little patience for those who didn't, with the exception of Joe. Stepping into this sudden pregnant breach to rescue his friend, he picked up the "train beat" on his own guitar and began to sing the third verse, word for word, all the way through to the end of the song. Although he was singing in the same octave, and with a marked command of the song's lyrics and mood, the spell was broken. His voice lacked the weight and power and ineffable fit with the song that Big Joe's inarticulate, half-remembered rendition had so compellingly exposed. Following the convention among pickers, Joe and I continued playing our guitars to support Robert's performance, but the others turned back to their conversations and coffee cups and cigarettes before Robert reached the final verse. Johnny Cash had come and gone in a second, wafting in on Joe's voice and out again on Robert's.

This brief moment was an epiphany to me, all its dense layers of meaning demanding pages of interpretation that have barely scratched the surface of its local complexity and embeddedness. Big Joe's transcendent performance stands out as a milestone in my understanding of just how salient the sound of the biographically embodied voice might be for my friends. The incident made new sense, for me, of the enormous importance of singers in general, and of particular, individual singers, in the rural, working-class social world. Indeed, it made new sense out of the importance of *all* individual voices in this world, an importance given textual presence in nearly every conversation in every rural, working-class beer joint in which careful attention is paid to the evocation of others' voices through a poetics of direct mimetic quotation. Timbral, inflectional, articulatory and grammatical details come together to make the sound of another's voice as instantly recognizable to the ears as another's face is to the eyes.[9] And yet words and voice, though they were intimately intertwined, were not reducible to one another. Knowing all the words did not mean knowing a song. The right words had to be saturated with the sweat and specificity of a particular body, a particular life, and a particular voice.

Coda

Indigenous to Modernity

"Singing is in a line of descent from the psalms, a way of puncturing

reality, the ordered structure of things as they are. As soon as we start

to sing, dance, remember, things are not as they are. . . . it's a weird

thing to do—a non-animal-like thing to do. The angel in us."

—Dennis Potter, quoted in Fuller, *Potter on Potter*

The sound of the voice is the sound of social life—of Marx's "social being" and "social consciousness" alike—in working-class Texas culture. Subtle shifts in vocal articulation encode knowledge about and intervention in every dimension of "ordinary" life. "Ordinary" categories of self, person, identity, place, space, time, memory, knowledge, gender, and feeling are emergent from the close attention these Texans pay to the speaking/singing voice, and critical elaborations of these categories can be discerned in the smallest details of speaking and singing. The interpenetrated rhetorical tropes of country songs and beer-joint talk open onto a world of social and individual experience.

"REAL country music" is a rather striking and distinctive poetry of the voice not only because it is the music of the highly oral and musical culture I have been describing here, and not only because it is stitched so tightly into the fabric of life in this culture. It is also and undeniably a mass-mediated and highly commodified art form, imbued at the moment of its production—and of its consumption—with ephemerality, novelty, and potential alienation. Country music is saturated with desire, but "out the country" this desire is modulated by a poetic obsession with loss and the looming presence of the past.

This is a fundamental irony, the complexity of which belies both paeans to country music as the simple poetry of simple people, and still-common dismissals of country music as commodified trash with no aesthetic value (see Fox 2004a). Country music, in the context of rural, working-class life, is the complicated poetry of complicated people, albeit people who think proudly of themselves as simple and profoundly "ordinary." It is situated at the very crux of a struggle for local meaning and the value of class-specific experience that of necessity endeavors to reappropriate the commodity form to the local lifeworld, constituted in discourses of aesthetic cultivation and moments of sociable and musical "feeling." It is hardly surprising, then, that the phenomenological interface between song and speech, and the personal and voiced qualities of country music stars, are central cultural axes in working-class social life. Nor should it be a surprise that some working-class people still struggle to claim this music—"REAL country music"—for their own cultural heritage, against the inexorable logic of its—and their—commodification, and all that commodification implies about the worth of music, art, and human beings and their local, "ordinary" concerns in our capitalist society.

The culture I have described here appears almost folkloric in its residuality, its orientation toward a collectively imagined past, and the pervasive orality that symbolizes that orientation. This culture is mythologized in commercial country music, though its image becomes more burnished with the patina of antiquity with each passing year. It is oversimplified, sometimes polemically, in its popular cultural representation, reduced to "redneck" stereotypes and subject to a disparaging cosmopolitan gaze when it is noticed at all in some segments of American society, or else sweetened with saccharine nostalgia or cloying nationalist sentimentality. No wonder that in recent years country music scholarship has obsessively deconstructed the rhetorics of cultural "authenticity" in the discourses of commercial country music. Country, as mass culture, begs to be seen as an ironic fantasy.

Yet to the Texans who appear in these pages, country music, verbal art, and the authentic representation of their social experience are inseparable ideas. The "fantasy" of country music is their discourse on "the real." "Authenticity" is indeed the issue that organizes an understanding of country music in a Texas bar. But the local claim on country music, which is as rooted in a suspicion of the commodity form as the perspective of any academic critic or cosmo-politan fan, asserts an alternative notion of the "authentic" — "real" — essence of the art form, rather than an ironic or despairing abandonment of the idea of musical truth or beauty.

Blue-collar, small-town country music performance is a waning art, to be sure. Even in the early 1990s, when I conducted the primary field research re-ported here, the scene at Ann's Other Place struck me (and many knowledge-able others) as exceptionally vibrant and coherent. I looked far and wide for a field site where live country music performance mattered deeply, across the American South and Midwest, and I performed as a touring musician in hun-dreds of bars and dance halls around Texas. I repeatedly returned to Lockhart, only an hour from my Austin home, increasingly convinced that the scene at Ann's Place was the one I *had* to write about, a rare place in modern America where live musical performance was the object of a vigorous intellectual and practical communal passion, imagined in intergenerational terms as a *tradi-tion*. In the years since I left Texas, that scene has itself declined in coherence and quality, with many of its principle actors scattered on the winds of time and rapid social change. Like the most thoughtful of my interlocutors in Lock-hart, Texas, I worry about the fate of a rich and important American musical tradition, and I worry about the loss of ritualized live music as a community-building institution for working-class people whose communities are often in a fragile condition.

In the face of impending residuality, the working-class country music prac-tices described here assert a strong claim on the present in the key of nostal-gia. Country music, as working-class culture, is a music of protest, accom-modation, self-realization, and mythological fantasy. It articulates a structure of feeling I have come to view as comparable to "indigeneity," though not to a particular, aboriginally inhabited *place* (though emplacement is one of its principle cultural idioms) but to a particular historical social formation, to a moment in *time*. That time, for most of the Texans who appear in this book, is the era of the postwar class compromise, the era of an advanced industrial political economy in which manual workers enjoyed both dignity and economic power unprecedented in the history of capitalist society. That these were also years of war, anxiety, and violent racial and class conflicts is understood, as is the extent to which working-class empowerment entailed real compromises — the acceptance of highly routinized work discipline, and the continued existence of many barriers to class mobility. Such hegemonic contradictions (high wages for stigmatized, mind-dulling work; publicly subsidized safety nets for the victims of unfettered markets) are also forgotten, however, through a fantastic blurring of a recent modern-industrial social history with elements of a more conjured and mediated rustic past and with elements of nationalist, racial, and gender hegemonies. This blurred image is precisely summoned when working-class Texans speak the word "country."

Globalization changed all that. The shift was well underway by the early 1990s, and most of the Texans I represent here were fully aware of the storm breaking on their community's shore. NAFTA and the high-tech boom in Austin were then nascent forces, but the national economy had absorbed so much deindustrialization and industrial deterritorialization already that working-class common sense was imbued with pessimistic, defensive anxiety in the years of research I report here.

Live music, verbal art, and a rich tradition of "ordinary" talk have served American workers as weapons, as solace, and as expressions of social identity throughout the twentieth century even as they have been commodified, folklorized, stigmatized, and mummified in American national popular culture. Songs and stories, materialized in the voice and memorized in communal rituals of working-class cultural solidarity, continue to serve as barriers thrown up to halt the alienating progress of an uncertain global postmodernity that appears to disparage manual work, dismiss the obligations of capital to labor, disdain the distinctiveness of place, and disrespect working-class experience. In the face of confusing times, a new identity emerges, one that attaches to communities and their lineages as well as to the biography of a particular generation or two of American workers. In claiming to be indigenous to a vanishing modern mode of production and its signal social relations, blue-collar Texans find common cause with other victims of progress, and it is only initially surprising to consider that country music — and especially the kind of "country music" practice described here — has become a globally popular genre among aboriginal and indigenous peoples, including Native North and South Americans, Aboriginal Australians, and many black Africans. But this is a subject for another book (Fox and Yano, forthcoming).

Dennis Potter's words, quoted above, remind us that the sounding, singing voice is a vital human resource for the critical construction of local worlds of meaning. Texans sing to reappropriate the vocal materiality of language as the stuff of (their) culture, and to reunite alienated, commodified sound with local canons of sense. Moments of high musical "feeling" summon Potter's "angels," who make uncanny voiced entrances into the very ordinary, and sometimes grim, times and places of working-class social experience. Vocalization performs, in working-class Texas, an intertwining of self and other, and an aesthetic and ethical projection of the self into the experience of the other that is the basis for sociality in this community. Singing is at the heart of a working-class way of living, the most privileged commentary on this way of life as well as a cherished source of its meaningfulness.

I close with the story of another rainy March night, a night when the weather was bad enough that almost no one came out to the bar for the usual Wednesday jam session. Hoppy and I were listlessly trading songs on acoustic guitars, but doing more talking than singing. Joanna, Miss Ann, and a few other loyal patrons sat with us at the round table. We had been discussing the current popularity of a parodic country song called "Help I'm White and I Can't Get Down" by the Geezinslaw Brothers, an Austin musical comedy act. The song's overt if harmless racial polemic had pushed conversation in an unusually frank direction, and jokes and serious thoughts about race relations were flying thickly when a group of five tough-looking Chicano teenagers entered the bar and, after ordering sodas in the suddenly silent tavern, told us they were a band and had come for the jam session advertised on the roll-away sign outside. They asked if they could use the instruments and drums and microphones currently set up against the back wall of the bar's front room.

It was late, and most of Ann's patrons were in no mood for any amplified music, and certainly not amplified *Messican* music, as the local slur had it. But Miss Ann had a long-established and virtually sacred policy that she strictly enforced: *any* musician was always welcome to play, at any time. I had seen Ann keep the coffee flowing long after closing time to accommodate pickers who were in a groove, and these Chicano kids were challenging the place to live up to its ideology.

They set up quickly, bringing in armloads of electric guitars, drums, and cymbals from their gaudy pickup truck, parked just outside the door (where armed robbers would be likely to place their getaway vehicle, as someone pointed out sotto voce). But these kids had apparently come here on this rainy night for the purpose of showing off their musical skills, as had so many young Anglo country bands just trying to break into the semiprofessional beer-joint circuit. Miss Ann prided herself on providing opportunities for young musicians, a subject about which she spoke frequently and passionately. Nervously, she turned down the old country song on the jukebox she had switched on when the kids had first come in to discourage them from staying.

The kids were, it became apparent, nervously excited and eager to please the seven or eight Anglos staring at them across the bar. But they began their set with a terrifyingly loud version of a Credence Clearwater Revival song with a pounding rock groove. Annoyed glances passed among the patrons seated at tables and along the bar, and at least two patrons left during the song.

Sensing that her minimal business for the evening was at serious risk, Ann forcefully asked — no, demanded — that the band play *country* music, not "that rock and roll shit." She did not specify the consequences of failure, but the tension was thick enough that several of the Anglo men present tensed their muscles and stabbed out their cigarettes in anticipation of a physical confrontation. The kids conversed quickly and nervously among themselves, and then with a quick count-off they launched into a familiar riff, and a familiar song. Alas, the bass player began in the wrong key, causing more glances to fly. But a second attempt took off seamlessly and suddenly bodies relaxed, smiles broke out, and cheers erupted as the kids began to play a Norteño-style version of "Folsom Prison Blues," with the lightly accented backbeats of Cash's country version now hammered into a proper and infectious polka groove. Fear and mistrust dissolved instantly under a wave of "feeling." The kids played for another half hour to respectful applause and eventually joined the rest of us around the tables, talking shit and playing songs late into that rainy night.

Notes

Prelude

1 "Johnny Mac" is a pseudonym.
2 "That's the Way Love Goes" by Lefty Frizzell and Sanger D. Shafer. © Copyright 1972. APRS and SONY/ATV Acuff Rose Music Inc. Meyer's recording, like most recordings by local musicians mentioned in this volume, will be available on my website (see preface).

1 Voicing Working-Class Culture

1 To demonstrate this last argument, I will also discuss examples drawn from my ethnographic experiences in other rural working-class communities in the United States, in Texas, Illinois, and Nevada.
2 There is, of course, an extensive ethnographic literature on American working-class taverns. Important examples include Bell 1983; Jensen 1998; LeMasters 1975; Limon 1994; and most recently, Lindquist 2002, an excellent study of working-class barroom rhetoric that reviews the relevant literature on this topic.
3 There are, however, significant regional differences that affect barroom culture in Texas.
4 Interestingly, I heard far more racist jokes in my early fieldwork than I did as the project progressed, which suggests to me both that my white interlocutors were concerned not to offend my well-known liberal sensibilities and that the original abundance of racially charged remarks was intended to test the limits of my own willingness to engage with a "redneck" point-of-view. The most telling evidence for this was a joke I was told during my first month of fieldwork: a mechanic sitting next to me at the bar asked me if I knew the "first line" of every racist joke. When I demurred, he looked rapidly and nervously over each shoulder, suggesting that "every" racist joke begins with the teller checking to see if it is safe to proceed.

5 One of my striking memories is of watching the 1992 LA riots that followed the verdict acquitting the policemen charged with beating Rodney King on the television at Ann's Other Place. Expecting to hear racially charged condemnations of the African American mob, I was taken aback to hear a series of comments sympathizing with the mob's frustration and rage over the police abuses. Race was not mentioned once.

6 Among some of my interlocutors, "Christian" was also an important and central identity. This was relatively less important for the people who appear in this book, most of whom would consider themselves "Christians" but for whom religion is not a central ideological or practical focus. This is an artifact of my focus on country music and tavern culture. Although I did spend a good deal of time in working-class churches and revival meetings and in dialogue with serious, practicing Christians over the course of my field research, to take this "Christian" cultural formation seriously as an object of analysis is beyond the scope of this book.

7 The community I report on here has expressly intended to occupy this peri-urban margin, to the extent that virtually the entire community, including Ann's Other Place, transplanted itself, moving to Lockhart from the formerly more peri-urban southern margin of the city of Austin during the late 1970s and early 1980s.

8 I think this approach will illuminate several important questions about country music as a commercial genre of popular music. Perhaps most importantly, I hope to call attention to how little serious attention has been paid to issues of poetics, narrativity, and even musical and performative style in historical, sociological, and literary work on country music as a commercial genre (with work by Barbara Ching [2001] and Pamela Fox [1998] as exciting recent exceptions). In addition, I hope to challenge a tradition of assuming the univocality and ideological obviousness of country's cultural politics, a challenge Barbara Ching has already issued forcefully (2001; cf. Fiske 1989: 166–67).

9 It is interesting to note that most of the few examples of attested full indirect discourse I have recorded are "self-quoting" routines, where the speaker represents something s/he had said in another setting, e.g.:

RANDY: *I told Dwight*
that if she won a million dollars
on that entry she got in
that I'd buy him a BEER!

Obviously in such a case, there is an identity established between the voice of the speaker in the present and in the past, anchored by the dual character of the pronoun "I" (see Urban 1989), mitigating the need for maintaining the boundary between indexical contexts. This also conditions an exception to the rule I am describing, a fairly common rhetorical figure Texans use to begin a statement of contrary opinion: *I still say that . . .*

10 An intermediate formal possibility—"quasi-direct" or "free indirect discourse"— was uncommon, though not as rare as full indirect discourse. Grammatically, free indirect or quasi-direct discourse has no subordinating conjunction, and deictic modulations ambiguate the context of the reported utterance so that it is not clear where the boundary is between narrator and character, or between the reporter and the reported speaker.

11 Given the prevalence of direct discourse in this speech community, any verb of saying should in fact suffice to specify that what follows is a directly reported utterance. In Texas English, verbs of saying do significant evaluative and rhetorical work that will be discussed in subsequent chapters.

12 This approach is an extension already well underway in a range of musicolinguistic ethnographies (E. Basso 1985; Feld 1990a; Roseman 1991; Seeger 1987; Titon 1988) and in some recent work in linguistics, anthropology, and ethnomusicology on funerary lament and sound symbolism (Feld and Fox 1994).

13 Ironically, these representations of rural "redneck" existence are exactly paralleled (on the same television shows) with representations of inner-city black culture, complicating the meaning of the rural/urban distinction with the politics of race and class.

14 There are antecedents for my view, of course. Marx's original theorization of "ideology" in *The German Ideology* (1978b) proceeded from precisely the dialectical account of the voice I want to develop here, as the epigraph which opens this chapter indicates. Far from seeing talk as superstructural, Marx stressed the constitutive materiality of language as sound. The implications of this point for a theory of language as the terrain of social conflict have too rarely been taken seriously, except by Voloshinov (1973). In addition to this, "the voice" has emerged as a key metaphor in poststructuralist social thought (drawing on a long history of this metaphor in Western culture) as anthropologists and others have struggled to forge a "dialogic" practice and theory, to understand the dynamics of hegemony and resistance, and to reform the troubled historical relationship between anthropology and colonialist ideology. In this sense, anthropologists have sought to define a writing and fieldwork practice that will "give voice" to silenced "others," and to represent voices that are silenced even within "other" social formations (e.g., Abu-Lughod 1993).

The voice has been considered as a site for the eruption of bodily drives and non-sense intertwined with or articulated against the "ordinary" dominance of sense as segmental, arbitrary linguistic meaning, in song, and in such phenomena as "icons of crying" in funerary lament, glossolalia in Protestant worship, and vocables in Native American song (Csordas 1994; Feld 1990a, 1990b; Frisbie 1980; Hinton 1980; Urban 1985, 1988). Simon Frith and Roland Barthes have asserted that the embodied voice, marked by its social origins and its bodily drives, is in a deep and foundational tension with the textual meaning of popular song lyrics

(Barthes 1977; Frith 1988). For Frith and Barthes, the aesthetic and sensual force of popular song is entirely contingent on the "grain" of the voice, to the point that song lyrics are mere vehicles for vocality.

Julia Kristeva (1986) has taken a similar view of the voice in her critique of Saussurian semiology through her psychoanalytic theorization of the deep and foundational tension in language between the embodied realm of desire which wells up in the speech act (which she calls "the semiotic chora") and the structured, lawlike meaningfulness she identifies as "the symbolic." Her work suggests a gendering of language in which voicing embodies a natural/feminine impulse. At a similar level of abstraction, phenomenological philosopher Don Ihde (1976) has proposed a focus on the speaking/singing voice in its dual material and symbolic dimensions as a critique of the limited account of experience and knowledge characteristic of the Western philosophical tradition's dependence on textual evidence and argument.

Linguist Dwight Bolinger (1980, 1986) has urged linguists to reconsider the iconic and nonsegmentable meaningful primitives (he glosses these as "emotions") that are conveyed by the "musical" dimensions of language structure (primarily sentence intonation) considered least significant by cognitivist and structuralist theories of grammar. His work has inspired and connected with a renewed attention in linguistics to the pragmatics of oral prosody more generally. Linguists such as Woodbury (1985) and McLemore (1990) have taken these insights still further and reconnected the domains of grammar, prosody, and discourse function, a linkage Woodbury refers to as "rhetorical structure."

Bruce Mannheim (1986, 1987) has made explicit the claim about the dual musicality and linguisticality of the voice which underlies many ethnographic considerations of the power of song texts (e.g., Abu-Lughod 1986; Fernandez 1986; Firth 1990; Hinton 1980, 1984), when he asserts, following Jakobson's theory of parallelism (1960), the metalingual and metacultural thrust of song's poetic objectification of grammatical and cultural categories. Finally, Dennis Tedlock (1983a) has criticized Derrida (1978) by emphasizing the irreducible poesis of the sounding voice, and its rootedness in material reality. For Tedlock (as for me), there is a sense in which the materialized voice of speech and song really *is* an experiential and social primitive, although I argue in this work that it is also ideologically figured as such in country music and working-class culture, as Derrida asserts it is in Western metaphysics more generally (1978).

15 This argument draws on several critical responses to the limits of Derridean views of textuality and presence. Giddens, for example, argues that "we cannot best explicate what language or signification are through writing. In this, Derrida is wrong. We should assert the priority not of *speech*, but of *talk*, over writing. But this should not lead us to suppose that writing is simply a 'representation' of talk" (1987: 217). Tedlock, too, has taken the Derridean account to task, finding in it

a surprising correlation with the structuralist tradition in linguistics (one of the main objects of Derrida's critique), again for its elision of the real, sounding voice in oral verbal art, in favor of an idealist opposition between a purely abstract structure (phonology) and a purely atomistic instantiation of structure (the phoneme). He suggests that the elision of the *phonetic* level of linguistic reality in Derrida's thought parallels the reduction of descriptive phonetics and phonography to a technology rather than an epistemology in linguistics (1983a: 196–97).

2 Knowing Lockhart

1 My use of "redneck" here is intended to call attention to the complex political and cultural resonance of this term, which is both derogatory and celebratory at the same time. The term has received only scattered scholarly attention. The best example, by a working-class scholar, is Huber 1994.

2 My video work was often expertly assisted by my friend and colleague at the University of Texas, Randal Tillery. We have coproduced one commercially released video segment from one of these shoots (Fox and Tillery 1994).

3 Described at length in chapter 9. A subsequent jammer's reunion, which I attended, was in fact organized in the summer of 1998.

4 Emblematically, the new proprietors renamed the cleaned-up bar after a nationally popular Top-40 country line-dancing song by the duo Brooks and Dunn, which most locals hated. The resentment felt over the song amplified the resentment felt over the changes in the bar.

5 The description in this section is largely based on an analysis of census data for Caldwell County, collected in the U.S. Census Bureau's "County and City Data Books" for 1984, 1994 (http://fisher.lib.virginia.edu/ccdb/), and in some cases, the same agency's USA Counties Database (http://tier2.census.gov/usac/index.html), which carries the same statistics forward to 1998, as well as several other data sources. The descriptions are also supplemented by my own anecdotal familiarity with the conditions of existence the statistical data evoke.

6 See Foley 1990 for an ethnography of a South Texas high school in a very similar community. Foley shows how the school he studied very efficiently reproduced the town's historically racialized class distinctions.

7 This number is harder to determine from available statistics, but in 1990, 735 persons between the ages of 16 and 19 were neither high school graduates nor currently enrolled in high school. By a reasonable and generous extrapolation from known figures (approximately 6 percent, or 1,660 persons, were between the ages of 18 and 20), there were probably fewer than 4,000 persons between 16 and 19 in the county (a significant number leave the area for work or military service at the age of 18). This suggests a dropout rate in the low double digits. The Lockhart Independent School District claims a current dropout rate of 1.6 percent,

based on a rating of Texas school performance by the Texas Education Association (http://www.tea.state.tx.us/perfreport/account/2002/listall.html). Jay P. Greene, a researcher at the Manhattan Institute for Policy Studies, has published a study of the radical divergence between actual school attrition rates and "official" dropout rates, entitled "High School Graduation Rates in the United States" (2002), in which he calls a similar disparity in figures for the Dallas Independent School District "simply unbelievable." For the state of Texas as a whole, he calculates a "graduation rate" (for 1998) of 68 percent (amounting to an "attrition" rate of 32 percent, in contrast to the state's claim of 1.6 percent per year). The Intercultural Development Research Association (IRDA) has also calculated attrition rates (broken down by race) for Texas schools and proposes an "attrition index" of 43, comparable to the statewide average (http://www.idra.org/Research/dout2001.htm) and supportive of Greene's scathing dismissal of official "dropout rate" statistics.

The calculation of actual rates of school completion is a complex problem, well beyond the scope of this study. However, my intuitive sense is that critics of official dropout statistics are correct. The dropout rate in Caldwell County is probably higher than the Lockhart Independent School District claims, and it is beyond question that school dropout rates are worse among low-income students and among ethnic minorities. The IRDA cites studies by the National Center for Education Statistics to argue (for the United States as a whole) that family income is a fundamental factor in school completion (http://www.idra.org/Research/edstats. htm#dropout).

8 See O. Davidson 1990 for a thorough discussion of race and class in Texas political culture, with an argument for the submerged but salient alignments along class lines which are often obscured by discourses of "race." For histories of Chicano/Anglo relations, see Limon 1994 and Montejano 1987. For a description of Anglo/Chicano relations in a contemporary South Texas small town, see Foley 1990.

9 African American consultants uniformly told me that overt racial violence was rare in Caldwell County in this generation, and had been relatively uncommon even during the civil rights era and before. Many reported moving to the area to escape the more overtly racist environments of other Southern communities. However, Caldwell County probably had a far higher level of racial violence and intimidation prior to World War II.

10 More than 17 percent of occupied housing units in Caldwell County were without a telephone in 1990. This number significantly overlaps the percentage of families living below the poverty line (22 percent).

3 "Out the Country"

1 A pseudonym.

2 "Y'All Come" by Arleigh Duff. © Copyright 1953. Fort Knox Music Co.

3 "Place of business" is a working-class euphemism for a tavern.

4 "Dave" and "Doc" are pseudonyms.

5 The EPA had shut down this landfill because it was full of toxic chemicals. The mine nearby had been shut down recently too, because its soft coal was too sulfurous to be burned under the Clean Air Act. Neither closing made much sense to the locals, who were already suffering from high unemployment levels because of these closings and major cutbacks at the railroad switching-yards, historically the town's major employer.

6 This is quoted from memory (hence the absence of line breaks), and I have intentionally changed some details.

7 Both are pseudonyms. Some place and road names have been changed here.

8 "Nothing's News" by Clint Black. © Copyright 1988. Howlin' Hits Music.

9 Some of my most intensely feelingful sociable moments during the past few years have been spent just outside the doors of various beer joints, staring out across the fields, reading the horizon with friends, trying to spot nascent tornadoes and hailstorms and thunderheads, or rain during long, hot summers. In such moments, a quiet repose, and a sense of the smallness of humans on the land, often takes hold intersubjectively. The experience is qualitatively different from watching the skies in the city. At these moments "slow talk" gives way to *no* talk, and yet these moments feel exceedingly sociable.

10 A pseudonym.

11 Observe this richly tropic phrase: it will be echoed in later examples.

12 "Diggin' Up Bones" by Paul Overstreet, Al Gore, and Nat Stuckey. © Copyright 1985. Sawgrass Music Publishing (Songs of Polygram International, Inc.) and Scarlet Moon Music; Writers Group Music; Tree Publishing Co, Inc.

13 "Two Story House" by David H. Lindsey, Douglas Glen Tubb, and Tammy Wynette. © Copyright 1980. Sony/ATV Music LLC.

14 "The Grand Tour" by Norro Wilson, Carmel Taylor, and George Ritchey. © Copyright 1974. Al Gallico Music/Algee.

15 "Mike" is a pseudonym.

16 "Joanna" is a pseudonym.

17 The following example must be taken as a canonical example of "talkin' shit," even if I did elicit it with a simple question. The transcript of this conversation was metadiscursively identified several times by locals as the apotheosis of "talkin' shit," because of its dialogism, its humor, its redundancy, and its dense overlaps. "Talkin' shit" is also a metadiscursive genre of urban African American barroom

speech, according to Michael Bell (1983), although I think it is less framed as a genre in rural, working-class metadiscourse. The compelling links between the tropes and genres I describe here and African American musical and speech genres is an important topic in need of further research.

18   "Pat" is a pseudonym.

19   The use of this cliché ("doesn't last too long") is a potent example of the local aesthetic preference for concluding a conversational episode with a lyric, summational image or maxim, preferably dialogically affirmed. Note that this is the same trope with which Rusty and Jake dialogically ended their exchange about the weather above.

20   "White Lightning" by Jape Richardson. © Copyright 1959. Glad Music Co.

21   This is in a class of icons that includes another famous example, Jim Ed Brown's imitation of a bottle-top being pulled off in "Pop-A-Top." The performative exaggeration of the burn of whiskey, using some variant of this sonic icon, is frequently a part of ritualized male social drinking when a bottle is passed around out behind a club or in the cab of a truck. Of course, this is an icon that is physiologically wedded to a real bodily source: cheap whiskey does burn!

22   This laugh continued the "hillbilly" parody, using a combination of breathiness and forcefulness which is frequently deployed to mimic the voice of an elderly, rural person who has smoked all his life. I have known several country musicians to deploy this icon as a shorthand critique of a particularly troublesome "blue hair" (as they say).

23   I have excised some names and ranks from this story.

24   "Owen" is a pseudonym.

25   "Now, That's Country" by Marty Stuart. © Copyright 1992. Songs of Polygram.

26   This is quoted from memory.

4 "The Fool in the Mirror"

1   Randy Meyer claims to have written this song in the 1970s. As far as I can determine from discussions with Meyer, it has not been published.

2   A very partial listing (those works that have influenced my own thought the most) includes Ewing 1990; Geertz 1973; Kondo 1990; Levy 1973; Mauss 1979; Rosaldo 1980, 1984; Spiro 1993.

3   This section is written with a middle-class American reader in mind, of course. But the issues involved in "native ethnography" across the social dividing line of class are salient for all anthropologists.

4   As some scholars might say, it is also a "Southern" ethos, a "white" ethos, a "Christian" ethos, and a "small-town," or even "rural" ethos, factors that shape its apparent if ironic obviousness as a typical "American" ethos. To argue that it is a "class" ethos is more disruptive of that obviousness. But that is my point. Rural,

working-class culture and the country music which is its soundtrack have often confounded efforts to think about the sharedness of "American" culture.

5 "I'm Only Human" was recorded in the late 1960s or early 1970s by a minor rocka-billy and country artist named Barney Tall. I have researched the song with BMI and ASCAP and made extensive inquiries, but have been unable to ascertain the author or publisher of the song. It was a ubiquitous item in Larry Hopkins's reper-toire, and a much-loved song at Ann's Other Place.

6 Like many of the tropes of person, place, and time that I will discuss here, the idea of human imperfection as a sacred quality has obvious historical and experiential roots in the explicitly sacred realm of Christian theology. Most of the people I dis-cuss in this work consider themselves to be Christians, and many grew up in fun-damentalist Christian communities and homes. Some are currently churchgoers. However, I am describing a world that is in many respects constructed in opposi-tion to the institutional realm of the church, as a culture centered on alcohol and other sensual pleasures. Nonetheless, a Christian ethos pervades my interlocu-tors' discourse, music, and culture, and my materials contain pervasive references to Christian ideologies. A consideration of the relationship between bar-centered social life and church-centered social life reveals deep parallels in the way the two spheres invoke important shared ideological narratives and are significantly an expression of gender and generational conflicts and differences. For example, country-style gospel music is an important local genre of musical practice in Lock-hart, even in beer joints, where the most affecting gospel songs are those sung by a powerful older male singer joined by his loyal wife, closely modeling the role of the preacher and his wife in a fundamentalist Protestant church (Titon 1988). But there is another side to the re-creation of churchlike reverence. The bars, of course, are carnivalesque, sinful spaces. Drinkers (and their discourse) are con-structed as oppositional by religious discourse. (I'll never forget having a preacher angrily level a shotgun at me as I made the mistake of crossing his parking lot in an attempt to offload some equipment at the back of a bar for a show.) Drink-ers return the favor in a loud and sharp-tongued critique of religious hypocrisy. (Cal Smith's "Hello Mrs. Johnson" provides country music's finest example of this critique.) Matching the "conversion narratives" of the saved, many drinkers will tell narratives which mythicize the moment in which they lost faith in the church, through a traumatic discovery of the "ordinary" imperfections of preachers and religious people.

7 Jimmy's artistry here is remarkable in details that depart from my point but which are interesting for their resonance with other arguments in this work. Observe that he gradually elides markers of formal dialogue, modeling an increasing intimacy through a move from relatively formal dialogue to relatively more sociable and intimate talk. He moves from full to contracted verb forms, gradually removes verbs of speaking which convert this from a narrative with voiced characters and

an objectively specified illocutionary force to a purely voiced dramatic scene, and eventually addresses his interlocutor with "God-damn" in an ironic characterization of "God" *Himself* as an "ordinary" imperfect polemical conversationalist who is not bothered by the use of blasphemous profanity by his egalitarian interlocutor.

8 This refers to Marty Robbins's song "Pretty Words," which is also Hoppy's emblematic theme song and the title of his one commercial recording.

9 Note that in this situation, where characterization is very explicitly in the air, Richard refers to Joe as "Old Joe Briggs," using all three slots in the naming paradigm to express a high level of objectification of Joe Briggs's social person as a "character."

10 A pseudonym.

11 Examples such as this show the importance of alcohol and inebriation in the shaping of some aspects of performative speech in this community. Alcohol is, indeed, a ritually central part of the kinds of social events and situations I am discussing here. Alcohol clearly affects rate and intensity of speech and phonological precision, as well as more general dispositions, memory, and inhibition. But most of the grammatical features I am attending to here are only *exaggerated* in drunken speech and can also be seen to be operative in the speech of community members who do not drink at all.

12 Note the extensive use of direct voicing in the remainder of this example.

13 This is similar to what Friedrich (1991:24) calls a "terminal commutation of values" trope, a sudden indexically decentering revelation about the context of an otherwise mundane or inexplicable narrative which has unfolded under a different, ostensibly less intense, mood. This trope is crucial in George Jones's "He Stopped Loving Her Today," for example, when the narrator reveals that the title phrase is true only because the protagonist has died, and in Lefty Frizzell's "The Long Black Veil," where only in the final verse do we find out that the narrator sings "from his grave" because he had preferred to be hanged for a murder he did not commit rather than reveal that he had been, at the time of the killing, "in the arms of [his] best friend's wife." The most ubiquitous form of this trope in country music and in working-class oral narrative, however, is the revelation that a heartbroken first-person narrator has been talking about a lost love which ended in the distant past as if it had ended yesterday. This trope of obsessive return to the intensely present but impossibly distant past is closely linked to the trope of speaking mnemonic objects (Fox 1992). The protagonist of these narratives is also, very often, the "fool in the mirror" character whom I discuss in this chapter and in Fox 1993.

14 "Fifteen Years Ago" by Raymond A. Smith. © Copyright 1992. Peach Music and Hello Darling Music.

15 "Jane" is a pseudonym.

16 "Kenny," "Joanna," "Nora," and "Dave" are pseudonyms.

17 Hoppy slyly thematized his own prominent personality in the course of narrating

about Sam, thereby accruing even more status as a person to himself. Near the end of his story, he further heightened the performativity and the poesis of his narrative by representing his own voice in pictorial direct discourse in dialogue with his imitation of his old friend Sam's voice.

18 In a subtle and iconic expansion of this trope of cyclicity, Hoppy's amplitudinal "trailing off" at the end of this performance (in the middle of a powerful lyric image) may actually be poetically coordinated with the idea of temporal cyclicality in country music songs. In Gordon Lightfoot's "Cotton Jenny," for example, this image of cyclic return is explicitly figured through the repetition of the phrase "the wheel goes round, the wheel goes round," as the singer mimics a record "fade out" and evokes a gradual trailing off of the image "into the future." Likewise, in the classic George Jones/Tammy Wynette duet "Golden Ring," the story follows a wedding ring from a pawnshop window to a wedding and finally to a breakup, tracking this everyday cyclicality of love, marriage, and divorce with a repetition of the chorus (see chapter 6). This song also ends, like "Cotton Jenny," in medias res with a fade-out on the title phrase. My intuition is that Hoppy's trailing-off effect is an extempore version of this trope, which is supported by the fact that Hoppy's performance of the sung fade-out on "Cotton Jenny" is regarded as especially masterful by both listeners and fellow singers, as, indeed, is his performance of "Golden Ring."

19 This is the ethical core of diverse Western social philosophies, such as the human rights movement, humanism, Christian evangelism, radical free-market capitalism, and libertarianism.

20 The extent to which this really is an exclusively Western account of the self is a subject of debate. It is undoubtedly at least Western (Spiro 1993).

21 A pseudonym.

22 A pseudonym.

23 "Sam S.'s" name, with its alliteration-driven but honorific use of the most respectful local name-form, [first-name]+[last name], suggests the undercurrent of respect which attends his more public "foolish" persona or "character."

24 "The Prisoner's Song" by Guy Massey. © Copyright 1924. Shapiro and Bernstein Co. Inc.

25 "Statue of a Fool" by Jan Crutchfield. © Copyright by Sure-fire Music (BMI).

26 "Paul" is a pseudonym.

27 A phrase that echoes across all my tapes and aural memories is "Ain't that right, Paul?"

28 "Doc" is a pseudonym.

29 "I Never Go Around Mirrors" by Sanger D. Shafer and William "Lefty" Frizzell. © Copyright 1976 Acuff-Rose Publications (BMI). Although this song's copyright is registered as 1976, Lefty Frizzell recorded it in the early 1970s, and he died in 1974.

30 "Jones on the Jukebox" by Mack Vickery, Becky Hobbs, and Don Goodman. © Copyright 1983. Tree Publishing Company, Inc., Beckaroo Music, Guyasuta Music, and Write Road Music. Hobbs cowrote this song with Mack Vickery and Don Goodman in a motel bar while on the road (Hobbs, personal communication), and it has achieved the evasive distinction (especially for a female artist of the modern era) of being considered a "classic," or canonical, work by my interlocutors. I am not the only academic writer to have discovered its delightfully complex and artful poetic structure (Ching 1993; Fox 1992).

31 "Bartender's Blues" by James Taylor. © Copyright 1977. CBS Songs.

32 This is an important cultural function of the best bartenders in rural, working-class communities.

33 Such control is, rather obviously, gendered in a complicated way. Briefly, in the local ideological constructions, males traverse a wider zone between self and person, and go to greater extremes of both positive and negative expressions of feeling between themselves and other men (public embraces and fistfights or threats to kill, for examples of extremes), and in a more narrow way between themselves and women (examples of extremes are warm platonic public embraces as well as public expressions of sexual desire for women, sly "dirty" jokes, angry words, cruel parodic imitative revoicings in narrative, private domestic violence, and suicides by one or the other party to a broken love relationship). Women display more restrained and balanced affects, showing an articulate clipped anger or a dialogically engaged delight, but avoiding some of the wider extremes of affect shown by men in favor of an endlessly subtle system of implicit cues for irony, disbelief, and anger. Each gendered regime of affective ambitus is equally complicated, and the two are enmeshed in innumerable ways. But I think that the way male expression seems to occupy a "bigger canvas" in real experience (and in space and time) is a naturalized ideology which underlies the pronounced male dominance of public-sphere discourse in rural, working-class communities. I take up some of these issues at length in chapter 8.

34 Some of these functions are semantic. Other functions are prosodic, like the short "I saids" and other verbs of saying which tend to be placed consistently between long bursts of reported speech, marking a regular breath-rhythm and holding a turn while the speaker prepares to continue with direct discourse segments. There are also poetic intersubjective functions for first-person verbs of saying which make the narrator's turn pleasurable for the listener and sustain interest. These constructions set off or frame direct discourse and create a heightened effect of parallelism between direct-discourse segments.

    Verbs of saying have, important metadiscursive functions too. They establish narrative details about the illocutionary and perlocutionary forces of the quoted and voiced utterances they introduce, and they fill in situational contextual features such as the intensity of a situation (e.g., "I'm tellin' you . . ." and "I'm gonna tell you . . ."). I suspect that there are also interactional functions still to be assessed for such formulaic devices.

35 It is interesting to compare "myyySELF" with the idiom which means the same thing in some of the Northeastern dialects I know, "You SAID it!" Both expressions signify complete agreement and a sufficiency of words on the subject. But "you said it" focuses dialogically on the original speaker's performative rhetorical success, rather than on the alignment of mutually revealed selves implied in "myyySELF."

36 "Maria" is a pseudonym.

37 "Here in The Real World" by Alan Jackson and Mark Irwin. © Copyright 1989 by Mattie Ruth Musick, Seventh Son Music, Inc., and Ten Ten Tunes.

38 "I Fall To Pieces" by Harlan Howard and Hank Cochran. Copyright 1960. Sony-Tree Music. Howard's and Cochran's title has inspired numerous playful experiments with the trope of "falling to pieces," including George Strait's "Let's Fall to Pieces Together" and my own "I Don't Fall to Pieces (Anymore)" (discussed in chapter 8).

39 "She Thinks I Still Care" by Dickey Lee. © Copyright 1962. Glad Music Co. and Jack Music.

40 "Today I Started Loving You Again" by Merle Haggard and Bonnie Owens. © Copyright 1968. Sony-Tree Music.

41 Harmony singers are likewise judged on the basis of such details, which they must command in order to mirror the lead singer's phrasing (see chapter 8).

5 "Feeling" and "Relating"

1 Cognitive and symbolic anthropology have combined in efforts to confront the problems such categories present for models of culture as an autonomous, isolated map of meanings, characterized by pervasive discreteness and economy of form (Wierzbicka 1992). The key problem for understanding sedimented emotional tropes as semantic structures is the need to view their complex referential meanings in the context of their social, pragmatic, and affective meanings.

2 Rollings's focus on the recent popularity of country music's feeling in this industrial part of rural, central Illinois is important for the way it links feeling to the social tensions brought on by the deep regional depression and consequent high unemployment which had gripped the area for several years prior to this conversation. These troubles were much on people's minds during my time in Illinois, and the air was heavy with a sense of loss and frustration and fear and social breakdown. In her linkage, then, we gain some sense of the connections between feeling and the particularity of working-class experience, and some understanding of the

importance of sociability, constructed through musical feeling, as a class resource for rural workers in dangerous times. "Feeling" as I define it here is specifically a working-class sociomusical aesthetic concept.

3 "I Love a Rainy Night" by David Malloy, Eddie Rabbitt, and Even Stevens. © Copyright 1980. Screen Gems-EMI Music, Inc.

4 Hoppy has an unusual fondness, among Texas country singers of his generation, for songs from the folk revival era.

5 And, although it departs from my main point here, this song is carefully chosen for its evocative intertextuality with Hoppy's story of losing his friend to the Vietnam War. "Talking Vietnam Blues" is a humorous portrayal of the irrationality of the Vietnam War from a soldier's perspective. Its amused portrayal of drug use contrasts with more serious songs of the same name by Johnny Cash and Phil Ochs.

6 His mastery is suggested by his awareness of the tape recorder at all times in this talk, as he makes clear by asking me to shut it off when the performative turn has come to an end and a more confidential subject has been broached. I have, albeit gratefully, lost control of an "interview" once again!

7 Both songs were released as 45 rpm singles by MCR, a small-scale independent label. I played them hundreds of times as the guitarist in Becky's band.

8 "Feel" is also an aspect of musical individuality. Singers prefer some sidemen over other, equally skilled, players on the basis of their particular "feel" and the sympathies that a particular player's "feel" generates with a particular singer's repertoire and "feel" for that repertoire.

9 "Jukebox in My Mind" by Dave Gibson and Ronnie Rogers. © Copyright 1991. Maypop Music (a Division of Wildcountry, Inc.).

10 The point suggests, also, Hoppy's song-linked remembrance of his friend Bill, again indicating the way repetitive singularity, relationship, and narrativity are not schematic components but rather woven strands of the cloth of feeling.

11 This draws on the hidden additional meaning of "to relate," although this is not explicitly used in ordinary talk, of "relating" as "telling (or 'goin' into') a story." Though this sense of the verb is not widely used in conversation, it sometimes appears in country song texts.

12 Ann is claiming that country star Reba McEntire declined to perform in front of the standard "Austin skyline" backdrop when she performed on the popular PBS country music live-performance program, *Austin City Limits*, in 1987. I have been unable to determine if this account is accurate. Because McEntire is from Oklahoma, this would tend to inflame opinions in Texas.

13 The highly personalized quality of country performer/audience relationships is widely remarked on in the critical and pop literatures on country and is in wide circulation as a metadiscourse among country musicians and people in the music business at all levels. Even local musicians spoke to me often of having to cultivate the appearance of being "everybody's friend" and maintain relationships which

they secretly resented. I discuss this further in my treatment of stage patter in the following chapter. See also Ellison 1995.

14 I recorded this excerpt from the Larry King radio program sometime during 1990.

15 "The Way I Am" by Sonny Throckmorton. © Copyright 1980. Cross Keys Music.

16 Note that this iconic phrasing ("over and over and over") is an intertextual trope; it echoes, for example, Randy's critique of the repetitive lyrics of Eddie Rabbitt's "I Love a Rainy Night." Randy repeats it in a reduced form several seconds later, advancing a critique of repetition through both the internal repetitiveness of the phrase and through the repetition of the phrase itself. Such everyday verbal iconicity is an almost unremarkable substrate of rural working-class discourse, as it is in many other highly aural/oral cultures. It is obviously related to the pervasive iconic animation of others' voices in direct and quasi-direct discourse.

17 This was no exaggeration and may even have been an understatement based on what Randy's long time fans have told me. His repertoire was very large. Other singers have said things like "Randy has forgotten more songs than I ever learned." In 1994, Randy estimated his current song list at over five hundred songs. The significant point is that each one of those songs was known entirely from memory (unlike most local singers, he used no notebook full of lyrics), and, more importantly, that each one of those songs was carefully stylized at the most detailed levels of phrasing, expression, and articulation.

18 This song is pervasively sexual, and Justin would not normally play it in a paid public performance. Randy, Hoppy, Judy, Justin, and Phil refer to a recent performance at Kelly's Bar, south of Lockhart, where the night was so awful (the bar's air conditioner had failed, there were very few patrons in attendance, and the drummer was so inebriated that he could not keep a steady beat) that Justin performed "How Can I Get Over You" out of anger and frustration, brought on by the recognition that the few people who *were* sitting in the steamy barroom had been neither dancing nor listening to his vocals.

19 Justin Treviño is an accomplished singer and musician in his early twenties, an age when many working-class men first take up singing. He began singing in beer joints at age twelve. He has long been a protégé of Hoppy and, to a lesser extent, of Meyer. Hoppy is Meyer's protégé. This generational continuity is highly storied, and an important local narrative concerns the time that Justin (then fourteen) first met Hoppy and Randy as the two older men were pickin' together out at the "old Hideaway bar" (referred to obliquely in this excerpt, in fact, since "Kelly's" is in the same building as the Hideaway once was, which focuses and intensifies the generational dialogue here). According to legend, Justin refused to sing any more songs that night after he heard Randy and Hoppy sing. This fanatical devotion to local masters and to "traditional" or "hard" country (especially Texas swing—Justin has gone on to apprentice himself to the great Johnny Bush) has made Justin something of a hero among local musicians and fans, although he wears this mantle

with discomfort. Interested readers may purchase Treviño's most recent recordings on the Texas Music Group label ("Scene of the Cryin'" [2002] and "Traveling Singing Man" [2001]) from major Internet music retailers. A short film of Treviño performing at a Lockart-area honkeytonk is also available on *The New Smithsonian/JVC Folkways Video Anthology of Music and Dance of the Americas* (Fox and Tillery 1995).

Interlude (Photo Essay)

The photos in this essay were taken at various points over the course of my fieldwork, for the most part with a Nikon E series 35mm camera, using both color and black and white film. Many of the indoor photos were taken using high-speed color film in order to avoid using a flash, which would have been disruptive of the very sociability I was trying to document. Such film yields images with a significantly grainy texture and is very sensitive to movement, leading to certain blurring effects, both of which are somewhat magnified in the black and white conversions of these photos as reproduced here. Where color photos have been converted to black and white here, they will be available in color on the book's website (see preface). My conscious goal as a photographer, overriding concerns of image clarity and density, was always to try to capture the intimacy and spontaneity of everyday working-class sociability, and I was deeply influenced by the "snapshot aesthetic" of my subjects' own approach to photography, and in particular by the work of documentary photographer Dick Blau.

In most cases, the photos are reproduced here with the full consent of the subjects in the photos. In other cases, consent was obtained at the time the photo was taken. Most of the people who appear in these photos also appear in the text of the book, but where they appear under pseudonyms in the text, I have chosen not to match the photos to the pseudonyms, which would render the pseudonyms potentially decipherable. Where real names or pseudonyms keyed to the text are used in the captions in this essay, the subject(s) of the photos have consented to this practice, or are deceased. In most cases, where subjects are deceased, I have the consent of their survivors to use the images herein.

6 "Bring Me Up in a Beer Joint"

1 As a songwriter for many years, I was subliminally prepared for phrases like this in a sense that transcended my role as an ethnographer. But my friends did not yet know me as a songwriter when this incident occurred, adding to the odd rightness of the moment. As several examples in this chapter will show, songwriting is a powerful field methodology (cf. Feld 1990a).

2 Every song quoted in this section is a "standard" or a "classic" (to make a local

distinction) in Texas beer joints. A band would not work steadily without being able to perform these songs competently.

3 "Don't Come Home A Drinkin' (With Loving on Your Mind)" by Loretta Lynn and Peggy Sue Wells. © Copyright 1966. Surefire Music Company, Inc.

4 "Walking the Floor over You" by Ernest Tubb. Copyright © 1941. American Music, Inc. Copyright renewed, assigned to Unichappell Music, Inc. (Rightsong Music, Publisher).

5 "Heartaches by the Number" by Harlan Howard. © Copyright 1959. Tree Publishing Co., Inc.

6 "Take These Chains from My Heart" by Fred Rose and Hy Heath. © Copyright 1952, renewed 1980. Milene-Opryland Music, Inc.

7 In addition to alliteration, this example contains internal vowel assonance.

8 "Fraulein" by Lawton Williams. © Copyright 1956. Unart Music Corp. Rights assigned to CBS Catalogue Partnership.

9 This song form was imported into country music from more urbane popular song genres during the 1950s, becoming briefly ascendant over the pattern of alternating verses and refrain.

10 "She Thinks I Still Care" by Dickey Lee. © Copyright 1962. Glad Music Co. and Jack Music. While this example lacks the canonical alliteration, the metric and syntactic structure is clearly parallel to the other examples. In addition, note the pervasive alliteration of sibilant segments throughout the lyric.

11 "Today, I Started Loving You Again" by Merle Haggard and Bonnie Owens. © Copyright 1968. Sony-Tree Music.

12 "I Fall to Pieces" by Hank Cochran and Harlan Howard. © Copyright 1961. Pamper Music Inc. and Sony-Tree Music.

13 "Pick Me Up on Your Way Down" by Harlan Howard. © Copyright 1958. Tree Publishing Co., Inc. In this case, although each two-clause phrase might be transcribed as two separate lines according to metrical and musical criteria, this is contravened by the song's syntactic poetic structure because these paired lines are parallel with *single-clause* lines which are also built around a line-internal rhyme, but follow the form VP+PP+PP rather than VP+VP (e.g., "And you've never once looked back at your home across the track"). I have also observed that this is consistent with the form in which songs like "Pick Me Up" are transcribed by country singers who use notebooks full of song lyrics as mnemonic aids.

There is another interesting poetic detail in this example which supports my claim that the two-clause phrases are conceived as single lines. Although I have transcribed the correct published and recorded version of this song's lyric, the first line of my example is *usually* sung, in live performances, as "*When* they take away your crown, pick me up on your way down" (vs. "*Then* they'll . . ."). An apparently trivial variation, this alternative for the penultimate line in the chorus in fact is poetically motivated for singers because of its parallelism with a line which occurs later in the song, in the second verse (*"When* you learn these things are true, I'll be waiting here for you"). The performative variation is also motivated by the clause-relativizing force of "when," which requires the second clause in the line as its complement, thus enforcing the impression that the two clauses do in fact comprise a single grammatical line, since they comprise a single sentence. Out of such subtle and apparently trivial subliminal decisions, made spontaneously in performance and crystallized as style, the grammar of poetry emerges from and reflects the poetry of grammar (Jakobson 1985a).

14 I am metonymically associated, as someone from outside this local world, with the diffuse extralocal agency Carl implies. In the early days of my fieldwork, my social identity and loyalty were frequently tested through jokes about "country" vs. "city" ways, and sometimes through direct interrogations about my cultural loyalties.

15 Again, observe the generic "they" used to characterize the state in this exchange.

16 "Swingin' Doors" by Merle Haggard. © Copyright 1967 Sony/ATV Tree Music.

17 "I'm Gonna Hire a Wino" by DeWayne Blackwell. © Copyright 1982. Careers Music/BMG Music Publishing.

18 A pseudonym.

19 A pseudonym.

20 My description in this section has been strongly influenced by Shirley Brice Heath's extraordinary ethnography, *Ways with Words* (1983). Interestingly, however, my limited observations of child language socialization would place the children of this predominantly white, rural working-class community somewhere between the white and African American rural working-class communities Heath surveyed in the early 1970s in the Carolina Piedmont ("Roadville" and "Trackton") in terms of many aspects of their sociolinguistic upbringing. For example, very young children in Lockhart are actively encouraged to interact verbally with multiple nonkin adults, especially in teasing situations.

21 Late hours, omnipresent cigarette smoke, and dealing with drunken adults must be weighed against this, of course. Employment is the crucial variable. Fully employed parents making an adequate income are more careful about bringing their children into the bars and tend to limit the time their children (and they themselves) are in the beer joints. The connections between un(der)employment, divorce, alcoholism, and despair were deeply palpable and obvious in rural working-class communities in the 1990s.

22 "The Farmer's Daughter" by Merle Haggard. © Copyright 1971. Sony/ATV Tree Music.

23 Country music has historically emphasized these aspects as distinctive phases of its constitutive creative and economic processes. In part this has been reflected in a standard division of labor which has stressed singing as interpretation and

songwriting as creation or discovery (a distinction which influenced most American popular music until the rock era, but which has persisted in country). The singer/writer split has defined the dominant mode of production for the Nashville music industry up to the present day. This mode of production both reflects and constructs an aesthetic distinction which structures the creation, performance, marketing, and interpretation of country music, and which is rooted in the cultural contradictions of aesthetic production and experience in capitalist society (Fox 1992). Some of the most important singers in country music have written few of their own hit songs (Ray Price, George Jones, Reba McEntire), while several songwriters have dominated the country charts but do not record their own songs (Harlan Howard, Bobby Braddock). On the other hand, the historical magnitude of country's singer/songwriters (Jimmie Rodgers, Merle Haggard, Hank Williams, Loretta Lynn, Dolly Parton, Johnny Cash, Willie Nelson, and most recently Dwight Yoakam) calls into question any facile reduction of the poetic distinction between text and performance.

24 These tropes also resonate strongly with what have been considered the foundational cognitive metatropes of English discourse (cf. Lakoff and Johnson 1980; Lakoff and Kövesces 1987).

25 "Your Cheatin' Heart" by Hank Williams. © Copyright 1952 Renewed 1980. Acuff-Rose Music and Hiriam Music.

26 "Old Flames (Can't Hold a Candle to You)" by Hugh Moffatt and Pebe Seibert. © Copyright 1980. Rightsong Music.

27 "White Line Fever" by Merle Haggard. © Copyright 1969. Sony/ATV Tree Publishing.

28 "Honky-Tonk Heart" by James Photoglo and Howard Russell Smith. © Copyright 1989. Berger Bits Music and Universal MCA Music Publishing.

29 "The Race is On" by Don Rollins. © Copyright 1964. Tree Publishing Co., Inc. and Glad Music Co.

30 This demonstrates my point that working-class Texans are quite capable of theorizing abstract poetic principles. Carl's metalinguistic observation was hardly unusual.

31 I believe this refers to the Billy Ray Cyrus song "She's Not Crying Anymore." But it is interesting to note that Carl's joking paraphrase imputes wordplay to this otherwise banal and noncanonical song, which lacked wordplay in its original form. More country songwriters should perhaps spend time talking to Carl.

32 "Doc," "Dan," "Suzy," and "Old Joey" are pseudonyms.

33 "Golden Ring" by Bobby Braddock and Rafe Van Hoy. © Copyright 1971. Sony-Tree Music.

34 "Have I Got a Deal for You" by Jackson Leap and Michael P. Heeney. © Copyright 1985. Careers Music, Inc.

35 "Sunny" and "Jimmy" are pseudonyms.

36 "Pretty Words" by Marty Robbins. © Copyright 1952 (Renewed 1980). Acuff-Rose Music, Inc.

37 "You Never Even Called Me by My Name" by Steve Goodman. © Copyright 1972. Jurisdad Music.

38 "Let's Fall to Pieces Together" by Tommy Rocco, Dickey Lee, and Johnny Russell. © Copyright 1983. Sunflower County Songs and Universal/Songs of Polygram Inc.

39 The copyright to this song is owned by the author of this book, making it possible for me to reproduce the song in its entirety here. Among other song quotations in this example, I refer to Patsy Cline's "I Fall to Pieces," "Crazy," "Walkin' after Midnight," "Crazy Arms," "Sweet Dreams (of You)," and "She's Got You." Note the double-clause penultimate lines in the verses. The song also uses musical quotations (the introduction to "I Fall to Pieces"), the A A B A verse form, and a harmonic vocabulary familiar from many Patsy Cline songs.

40 A commanding knowledge of these metonymic effects is taken for granted in beer joints. I remember writing a song in which I used the name "Dallas" in an inappropriately positive context (I needed the /d/ sound to alliterate with "Detroit" and "Denver"). Miss Bettie, who lived in Fort Worth and brought many Fort Worth friends to Ann's over the years, listened to me sing the newborn song one night, and at the end she looked disapprovingly at me and said "Everybody hates Dallas!" The song died on the vine at that moment, and I have never sung it since. Among Austin musicians, Jimmie Dale Gilmore's "Dallas," which asks "did you ever see Dallas from a DC-9 at night?," is often jokingly parodied as "did you ever see Dallas from a B-52 at night?" There are dozens of country songs in which Dallas represents glittering, heartless, and impossibly distant wealth.

41 "Dallas" by Alan Eugene Jackson and Keith Stegall. © Copyright 1991. Warner-Tamerlane Publishing Co.

42 "Does Fort Worth Ever Cross Your Mind?" by Darlene K. Shafer and Sanger D. Shafer. © Copyright 1985. Sony/ATV Music and Acuff-Rose Music.

43 "Is Anybody Goin' to San Antone?" by Dave Kirby and Glen Martin. © Copyright 1970. Sony/ATV Tree Publishing.

44 Harlan Howard claims that he wrote this song in 1957 after hearing the title expression uttered by a man on the phone in a tavern (Horstman 1986: 180). This again demonstrates that songs are canonically inspired by everyday talk, and their verbal insights are returned to everyday talk via a medium such as Randy Meyer's stage patter.

7 "The Women Take Care of That"

1 According to the 2000 *Country Music Industry Overview*, published in Nashville by the industry-based Country Music Association, in that year 54 percent of country

music record buyers were women, which is probably a significant increase from even the early 1990s. The same report notes that slightly over half have an income exceeding $50,000 per year (CMA 2000:3)

2 "Blue-Blooded Woman" by Alan Jackson, Keith Stegall, and Roger Murrah. © Copyright 1989 by Mattie Ruth Musick, Seventh Son Music, Inc., Tom Collins Music Corp., and Murrah Music.

3 "Old Country" by Bobby Harden. © Copyright 1992. EMI/April Music, Inc.

4 "Country Club" by Catesby Jones and Dennis Lord. © Copyright 1988. Triumvirate Music, Inc., C/O New Clarion Music Group.

5 "A Better Class of Losers" by Alan Eugene Jackson and Randy Traywick (Travis). © Copyright 1994. Sometimes You Win Music and Chrysalis Music.

6 "Crystal Chandeliers" by Cliff Harris. © Copyright 1967. Plainspoken Music Publishing / Talbot Music Group.

7 "Blue House Painted White" by Walter M. Breeland, Sonny Burns, and Buddy Word. © Copyright ca. 1960. Glad Music Co.

8 "He Stopped Loving Her Today" by Bobby Braddock and Curly Putnam. © Copyright 1978, 1980 by American Music. Copyright renewed, assigned to Unichappell Music, Inc. (Rightsong Music, Publisher).

9 "The Wild Side of Life" by W. Warren and A. A. Carter. © Copyright 1952 by Travis Music Co. "It Wasn't God Who Made Honky Tonk Angels" by J. D. Miller. © Copyright 1952 by Peer International Corp.

10 All of these features conflict with the stereotypical account of the interaction of language and gender which has emerged in sociolinguistics in recent years (see Coates 1993 for an overview).

11 Certainly, extensive use of profanity by a woman is styled as transgressive. But there are situational constraints on profanity that influence both men and women.

12 And this *does* conform to the sociolinguistic stereotypes for working-class communities; it is apparently rooted in the nature of working-class women's typical jobs, which may involve more extensive contact with members of higher social classes and the cultivation of discursive and technical skills for dealing with bureaucracy and financial matters. This is often advanced as an explanation for the gendering of phenomena like "covert prestige" and "hypercorrection."

13 Such talk is styled (by both men and women) as "gossip" in contrast with the way the "boys" are said to "talk shit." But neither style of sociability is overtly less valued within the linguistic ideology of the community.

14 All of the names in this transcript are pseudonyms.

15 "Mandy," "Denise," and "Naomi" are pseudonyms.

16 For the most part, Judy sings very feminine songs, and she is perhaps the finest harmony singer I have ever heard (a formally subordinated talent), with an extraordinary and widely noted ability to coordinate her timing and pitch bending to Hoppy's lead vocals. But Judy is capable of showing up most male singers with

virtuoso solo turns on songs like Leroy Van Dyke's 1965 hit "The Auctioneer," which accelerates to breakneck speed in imitation of the rapid vocal articulation of professional auctioneering. She also performs gender-neutral songs or songs which are canonically sung by men, such as Buck Owens's "Together Again" and Hank Williams's "I Can't Help It If I'm Still in Love with You." Another woman once told me, "I admire Big Judy. She's not afraid to get up there and play with the boys and run with the boys, and still throw her head back and let you know she's a big beautiful woman."

17 This excerpt was originally transcribed for analysis in Fox 1995, where it is presented in greater detail and at greater length. The "=" notation indicates rapid transition with no intervening silence.

18 This was an insult Hoppy frequently used against Steve, who had moved to Texas from upstate New York.

19 Mandy uses both the standard and vernacular variants of "something" in this excerpt (i.e., "sompin'" and "something," including the final velar nasal). In both cases, she is performing a marked imitation of Hoppy, who also uses both variants depending on the formality with which he is speaking. Phenomena like this escape the analytic capacity of concepts like gendered hypercorrection and covert prestige.

20 Mandy, who is a quiet and very dignified and respected woman, insists with embarrassment that she used a more vulgar expression here (which would have been highly characteristic of the man she is imitating). Upon reading this transcript, she thanked me for changing her word to this "meaningless" epithet ("slew"), which I have never heard before or since. I'm not sure whether the Whorfian grooves here are hers or mine, but I am certain that I hear this epithet as "slew" on my tape. In other words, I am not sure if she self-censored here, or if my inability to hear a more conventionally profane epithet is an error in my transcription or the fault of my recording. In any case, this confusion speaks volumes about the complexity of gendered discursive norms regarding profanity and emotiveness.

21 Again, note Judy's use of both standard and local vernacular syntax ("we're not in New York" vs. "we in Texas"). This is obviously a poetically meaningful choice: the opposition between New York and Texas is made to stand for an opposition between elite and "ordinary" culture; the verbs Judy uses reflect this allegorical characterization.

8 The Art of Singing

1 "Pictures from Life's Other Side" by Hank Williams. © Copyright 1951, renewed 1979, Acuff-Rose Music, Inc., and Hiriam Music, administered by Rightsong Music, Inc.

2   Spectrograms and audio clips for the examples discussed in this section are available on the author's website. See the preface for details.

3   "Blue House Painted White" by Walter M. Breeland, Sonny Burns, and Buddy Word. © Copyright ca. 1960. Glad Music Co.

4   "Pretty Words" by Marty Robbins. © Copyright 1952, renewed 1980. Acuff-Rose Music, Inc.

5   "When I'm with Me" by Randy Meyer. This song has not, to my knowledge, been previously published.

6   "I'm So Lonesome I Could Cry" by Hank Williams. © Copyright 1949. Acuff-Rose Music/Hiriam Music, Inc. Administered by Rightsong Music, Inc.

7   "Farewell Party" by Lawton Williams and Gene Watson. © Copyright 1979. Western Hills Music Corp.

8   "The Hands You're Holding Now" by Marty Robbins. © Copyright 1960. Mariposa Music Inc. and Unichappell Music Inc.

9   Hopkins's preferred keys are A major (which allow the use of this distinctive high E as a structural climax tone, the dominant) and D major (which allows the use of the high D above middle C as a climactic tonic, with the high E as an available appoggiatura for bends and cry breaks). He is praised by fellow singers for the power and beauty of his upper register, though he has a resonant low register too, with a powerful low A at 110 Hz. This is the tonic in his preferred A tonalities, and the important low dominant root when he sings in D.

10 This problem is exacerbated because many of the sidemen willing to work for low pay in beer joints are not schooled in country music performance and consider their work in country bars to be "dues paying," unrelated musically to their desire to play rock or blues. Many sidemen are young, urban musicians (often with long hair and a preference for marijuana over beer, which makes matters somewhat worse). Bandleaders must work hard to discipline such players, and many sidemen (myself included) have been summarily fired for playing too loud.

11 I have frequently had to field requests, requiring me to engage in dialogue with an audience member standing at the edge of the stage, while I have been playing a lead ride.

12 Once, while absent-mindedly singing along with the jukebox, which was playing George Jones's obscure version of Haggard's classic "Today, I Started Loving You Again," Big Judy inattentively sang the last line of the refrain using Haggard's articulation rather than Jones's (as discussed in chapter 4). Haggard artfully separates the word "today" from the word "I" in the last line, while Jones does not make this distinction, and repeats the "Today-I" phrasing used in the first line of the refrain. Instantly, Big Judy became conscious of this minute error, and she looked annoyed and then taken aback. When I asked her about this, she told me Jones "sang it wrong."

13 "Amanda" by Bob McDill. © Copyright 1972, 1978. Vogue Music.

14 Some singers, like Hoppy, often prefer to "kick it cold" even with experienced musicians. Pickers then demonstrate skill by the tightness and tastefulness of their entry on a staggered "walk-up" or "walk-down" in the beats following the singer's first notes.

15 "Evan" is a pseudonym, as is "Johnny Mac."

16 "Smoke, Smoke, Smoke (That Cigarette)" by Merle Travis and Tex Williams. © Copyright 1947 by American Music, Inc. Copyright renewed, assigned to Unichappell Music, Inc. (Rightsong Music, publisher) and Elvis Presley Music, Inc.

17 This acoustic icon of the sound of a word fading away on an "Echoplex" (a tape-loop echo machine popular in the 1960s and 1970s) is itself a version of the trope of narrative conclusion, a timeless summational device designed to bring a narrative to poetic closure. "Fading away" is an essential predicate of this trope. Hoppy's choice of the Echoplex sound for this function is inspired.

18 Hoppy and Richard refer to Haggard's 1971 recording of "Carolyn," written by Tommy Collins. "The Roots of My Raising," also a Tommy Collins song, was released in 1976.

19 "Jimmie [also spelled "Jimmy"] Brown the Newsboy" by A. P. Carter. © Copyright 1952. APRS, Inc. The song was in fact a hit for Mac Wiseman around 1960.

20 "Joanna" is a pseudonym.

21 "I Saw the Light" by Hank Williams © Copyright 1948. Acuff-Rose Music/Hiriam Music, Inc. Administered by Rightsong Music, Inc.

22 "Whiskey River" by John Bush Shinn. © Copyright 1973. EMI Full Nelson Music.

23 "Terri," "Linda," and "Pat" are pseudonyms.

24 Once, over a late night drink, we were discussing the merits of being drunk when one is depressed. I remarked that time seemed to "blur" for me when I was inebriated. Pat got a faraway look in her eyes and said, slowly and deliberately, "I LIKE the blur."

25 "Robbie" is a pseudonym.

26 This pun from Jerry, otherwise a marginal participant in this exchange, is another example of the productivity of metaphoric literalization in beer-joint humor.

27 "Jones on the Jukebox" by Mack Vickery, Becky Hobbs, and Don Goodman. © Copyright 1983. Tree Publishing Company, Inc., Beckaroo Music, Guyasuta Music, and Write Road Music.

9 "I Hang My Head and Cry"

1 "Robert" is a pseudonym.

2 Ann once told me: "The thing I've always felt about MEN is that there's nothing in the world like the FRIENDship among men. . . . They have the most BEAUtiful friendships. I WISH women could have that, but they don't. They don't have the

same mentality! (. . .) Men form relationships and friendships that are lifeLONG and they think a lot of each other (but they don't get as close as women do!) (. . .) And men can have more damn fun by themSELVES. (. . .) You can take four, five MEN [and they'll be] (. . .) settin' out there pickin' guitar, talkin', raisin' hell."

3 "Folsom Prison Blues" by John R. Cash. © Copyright 1956 by Hi Lo Music. Administered by Hill and Range Songs, Inc.

4 Countless times I have been in bands where "Folsom Prison Blues" was used as a fallback or punctuating song, played for a few seconds after the singer told a bad joke or when the band couldn't decide what to play next. People would invariably whoop and scream as the opening lick was played, and laugh when the song was cut short.

5 "Waiting for a Train" by Jimmie Rodgers. © Copyright 1929. APRS, Inc.

6 Which is why Cash has been rediscovered as an icon for the dark side of American rural working-class music by punk/alternative rockers in search of "roots" authenticity, like Glen Danzig, the rock star who produced Cash's 1994 all-acoustic "comeback" recording, *American Recordings*. See Fox 2004b for further details.

7 Hence there are songs with titles like Jack Clements's "If I Had Johnny's Cash and Charley's Pride." Not coincidentally, Merle Haggard's last name is a hidden iconic poem too, as is Waylon Jennings's first name. Also intriguing in this context are assumed names like "Johnny Paycheck" (who made his name, so to speak, by singing "Take This Job and Shove It").

8 Hoppy, Sam, and Justin quote from "Ring of Fire" by June Carter Cash and Merle Kilgore. © Copyright 1963. Painted Desert Music Corp.

9 A great deal of importance is attached to the recognition of voices in greetings in working-class Texas. "(Do) you know who this is?" is a frequent opening gambit in phone conversations. More often, phone conversations begin without *any* formal greeting, on the assumption that voice recognition is automatic, and that the phone is an extension of the local face-to-face interactional context (this is, of course, common among intimates in American culture more generally). Among my consultants and friends, however, the phone is regarded as an inadequate medium for serious social discourse between friends, and answering machines in particular are regarded derisively. I have also been greeted several times by friends coming up behind me and covering my eyes with their hands and saying "Guess who?" (An example can be seen in the transcript in Fox 1994). Such voice recognition, with the associated physical intimacy of the in-person greeting, tests mastery of a key cultural skill and symbolizes achieved levels of friendship.

References

Abu-Lughod, Lila. 1986. *Veiled Sentiments: Honor and Poetry in a Bedouin Society.* Berkeley: University of California Press.

———. 1993. *Writing Women's Worlds: Bedouin Stories.* Berkeley: University of California Press.

Bakhtin, Mikhail. 1981a. "Discourse in the Novel." In M. Holquist, ed., *The Dialogic Imagination: Four Essays by M. M. Bakhtin,* 259–422. Austin: University of Texas Press.

———. 1981b. "Forms of Time and Chronotope in the Novel." In M. Holquist, ed., *The Dialogic Imagination: Four Essays by M. M. Bakhtin,* 84–258. Austin: University of Texas Press.

———. 1984. *Problems of Dostoevsky's Poetics.* Minneapolis: University of Minnesota Press.

———. 1986 *Speech Genres and Other Late Essays.* Austin: University of Texas Press.

Barthes, Roland. 1977. "The Grain of the Voice." In *Image—Music—Text,* 179–89. London: Fontana.

Basso, Ellen. 1985. *A Musical View of the Universe.* Philadelphia: University of Pennsylvania Press.

Basso, Keith. 1990a. " 'Stalking with Stories': Names, Places, and Moral Narratives among the Western Apache." In *Western Apache Language and Culture,* 99–137. Tucson: University of Arizona Press.

———. 1990b. " 'Speaking with Names': Language and Landscape among the Western Apache." In *Western Apache Language and Culture,* 138–74. Tucson: University of Arizona Press.

Bauman, Richard. 1986. *Story, Performance, and Event: Contextual Studies of Oral Narrative.* Cambridge: Cambridge University Press.

Bauman, Richard, and Charles L. Briggs. 1990. "Poetics and Performance as Critical Perspectives on Language and Social Life." *Annual Review of Anthropology* 19: 59–88.

Bell, Michael. 1983. *The World from Brown's Lounge: An Ethnography of Black Middle-Class Play*. Urbana: University of Illinois Press.

Boas, Franz. 1927. *Primitive Art*. Cambridge: Harvard University Press.

Bolinger, Dwight. 1980. "Intonation and 'Nature'." In M. Foster and S. Brandes, eds., *Symbol as Sense*, 9–23. New York: Academic Press.

———. 1986. *Intonation and Its Parts: Melody in Spoken English*. Palo Alto: Stanford University Press.

Brenneis, Don. 1987. "Talk and Transformation." *Man* 22: 495–510.

Ching, Barbara. 1993, "Acting Naturally: Cultural Distinction and Critiques of Pure Country." *Arizona Quarterly* 49(3): 107–36.

———. 2001. *Wrong's What I Do Best: Hard Country Music and Contemporary Culture*. New York: Oxford University Press.

Coates, Jennifer. 1993. *Women, Men and Language*, 2d ed. London: Longman.

Country Music Association. 2000. *2000 Country Music Industry Overview*. Nashville: Country Music Association.

Csordas, Thomas. 1994. *Embodiment and Experience: The Existential Ground of Culture and Self*. Cambridge: Cambridge University Press.

Davidson, Chandler. 1990. *Race and Class in Texas Politics*. Princeton: Princeton University Press.

Davidson, Osha Gray. 1990. *Broken Heartland: The Rise of America's Rural Ghetto*. New York: Free Press.

DeMott, Benjamin. 1990. *The Imperial Middle: Why Americans Can't Think Straight about Class*. New York: Morrow.

Derrida, Jacques. 1978. "Sign, Structure, and Play in the Discourse of the Human Sciences." In *Writing and Difference*, 278–94. Chicago: University of Chicago Press.

Dirks, Nicholas, ed. 1998. *In Near Ruins: Cultural Theory at the End of the Century*. Minneapolis: University of Minnesota Press.

Dudley, Kathryn. 1994. *The End of the Line: Lost Jobs, New Lives in Postindustrial America*. Chicago: University of Chicago Press.

Ellison, Curtis W. 1995. *Country Music Culture: From Hard Times to Heaven*. Jackson: University Press of Mississippi.

Ewing, Katherine P. 1990. "The Dream of Spiritual Initiation and the Organization of Self-Representations among Pakistani Sufis." *American Ethnologist* 17(1): 56–75.

Feld, Steven. 1988. "Aesthetics as Iconicity of Style, or, 'Lift-Up-Over-Sounding': Getting into the Kaluli Groove." *Yearbook for Traditional Music* 20: 74–113.

———. 1990a. *Sound and Sentiment: Birds, Weeping, Poetics, and Song in Kaluli Expression*, 2nd ed. Philadelphia: University of Pennsylvania Press.

———. 1990b. "Wept Thoughts: The Voicing of Kaluli Memories." *Oral Tradition* 5(2–3): 1–24.

Feld, Steven, and Aaron Fox. 1994. "Music and Language." *Annual Review of Anthropology* 23: 25–53.

Fernandez, James. 1986. *Persuasions and Performances: The Play of Tropes in Culture.* Bloomington: Indiana University Press.

Firth, Raymond, with M. McLean. 1990. *Tikopia Songs: Poetic and Musical Art of a Polynesian People of the Solomon Islands.* Cambridge: Cambridge University Press.

Fiske, John. 1989. *Understanding Popular Culture.* New York: Routledge.

Foley, Douglas E. 1990. *Learning Capitalist Culture: Deep in the Heart of Tejas.* Philadelphia: University of Pennsylvania Press.

Fox, Aaron A. 1992. "The Jukebox of History: Narratives of Loss and Desire in the Discourse of Country Music." *Popular Music* 11(1): 53–72.

———. 1993. "Split Subjectivity in Country Music and Honky-Tonk Discourse." In G. Lewis, ed. *All That Glitters: Country Music in America*, 131–39. Bowling Green: Bowling Green State University Press.

———. 1994. "The Poetics of Irony and the Ethnography of Class Culture." *Anthropology and Humanism* 19(1):61–66.

———. 1995. "The 'Redneck' Reverse: Language and Gender in American Working-Class Women's Verbal Art." *SALSA II Conference Proceedings*, 189–99.

———. 1997. " 'Funny How Time Slips Away': Talk, Trash, and Technology in a 'Redneck' Bar." In G. Creed and B. Ching, eds. *Knowing Your Place: Rusticity and Identity*, 105–30. New York: Routledge.

———. 2004a. "White Trash Alchemies of the Abject Sublime: Country as Bad Music." Forthcoming in C. Washburn and M. Derno, eds. *Bad Music.* New York: Routledge.

———. 2004b. " 'Alternative' to What?: 'O Brother,' September 11th, and the Politics of Country Music." Forthcoming in C. Wolfe and J. Akenson, eds., *There's a Star-Spangled Banner Waving Somewhere: Country Music Goes to War.* Lexington: University Press of Kentucky.

Fox, Aaron, and Randal Tillery. 1995. "Soft Rain" (Video documentary segment featuring Justin Treviño). In *The New Smithsonian/JVC Video Anthology of World Music and Dance*, Vol. 26.

Fox, Aaron, and Christine Yano, eds. Forthcoming. *Songs Out of Place: Country Musics of the World.* Durham: Duke University Press.

Fox, Pamela. 1998. "Recycled 'Trash': Gender and Authenticity in Country Music Autobiography." *American Quarterly* 50(2): 234–66.

Friedrich, Paul. 1991. "Polytropy." In J. Fernandez, ed., *Beyond Metaphor: The Theory of Tropes in Anthropology*, 17–55. Stanford: Stanford University Press.

Frisbie, Charlotte. 1980. "Vocables in Navajo Ceremonial Music." *Ethnomusicology* 24(3): 347–92.

Frith, Simon. 1988. "Why Do Songs Have Words?" *Music for Pleasure*, 105–28. London: Routledge.

Fuller, Graham. 1993. *Potter on Potter.* London: Faber and Faber.

Geertz, Clifford. 1973. "Person, Time and Conduct in Bali." *The Interpretation of Cultures*, 360–411. New York: Basic Books.

———. 1983. *Local Knowledge: Further Essays in Interpretive Anthropology.* New York: Basic Books.

Giddens, Anthony. 1987. "Structuralism, Poststructuralism, and the Production of Culture." *In* A. Giddens and J. Turner, eds., *Social Theory Today*, 195–223. Stanford: Stanford University Press.

Gramsci, Antonio. 1971. *Selections from the Prison Notebooks.* New York: International Publishers.

Greene, Jay P. 2002. "High School Graduation Rates in the United States." New York: The Manhattan Institute. (online at: http://www.manhattan-institute.org/html/cr_baeo.htm#08)

Halle, David. 1984. *America's Working Man: Work, Home, and Politics among Blue-Collar Property Owners.* Chicago: University of Chicago Press.

Halperin, Rhoda. 1990. *The Livelihood of Kin: Making Ends Meet "The Kentucky Way."* Austin: University of Texas Press.

Harrison, Bennett, and Barry Bluestone. 1988. *The Great U-Turn: Corporate Restructuring and the Polarizing of America.* New York: Basic Books.

Hartigan, John. 1999. *Racial Situations: Class Predicaments of Whiteness in Detroit.* Princeton: Princeton University Press.

Harvey, David. 1989. *The Condition of Postmodernity: An Enquiry into the Origins of Cultural Change.* London: Basil Blackwell.

Heath, Shirley Brice. 1983.*Ways with Words: Language, Life, and Work in Communities and Classrooms.* New York: Cambridge University Press.

Hinton, Leanne. 1980. "Vocables in Havasupai song." In C. Frisbie, ed., *Southwestern Indian Ritual Drama*, 275–305. Albuquerque: University of New Mexico Press.

———. 1984. *Havasupai Songs: A Linguistic Perspective.* Tübingen: Gunter Narr Verlag.

Horstman, Dorothy. 1986. *Sing Your Heart Out, Country Boy.* Nashville: Country Music Foundation Press.

Huber, Patrick J. 1994. " 'Redneck': A Short Note from American Labor History." *American Speech* 69(1): 106–12.

Ihde, Don. 1976. *Listening and Voice: A Phenomenology of Sound.* Athens: Ohio University Press.

Jakobson, Roman. 1960. "Concluding Statement: Linguistics and Poetics." In T. Sebeok, ed., *Style in Language*, 350–77. Cambridge: MIT Press.

———. 1985a. "Poetry of Grammar and Grammar of Poetry." In K. Pomorska and S. Ruby, eds. *Roman Jakobson: Verbal Sign, Verbal Time*, 37–46. Oxford: Basil Blackwell.

———. 1985b. "Subliminal Verbal Patterning in Poetry." In K. Pomorska and

S. Ruby, eds. *Roman Jakobson: Verbal Sign, Verbal Time*, 59–68. Oxford: Basil Blackwell.

Jensen, Joli. 1998. *The Nashville Sound: Authenticity, Commercialization, and Country Music*. Nashville: Country Music Foundation Press and Vanderbilt University Press.

Keil, Charles. 1966. "Motion and Feeling through Music." *Journal of Aesthetics and Art Criticism* 24: 337–49.

———. 1985. "People's Music Comparatively: Style and Stereotype, Class and Hegemony." *Dialectical Anthropology* 10: 119–30.

King, Joyce. 2002. *Hate Crime: The Story of a Dragging in Jasper, Texas*. New York: Pantheon Books.

Kondo, Dorinne. 1990. *Crafting Selves. Power, Gender, and Discourses of Identity in a Japanese Workplace*. Chicago: University of Chicago Press.

Kristeva, Julia. 1986. "The System and the Speaking Subject." In T. Moi, ed., *The Kristeva Reader*, 24–33. New York: Columbia University Press.

Lakoff, George, and Mark Johnson. 1980. *Metaphors We Live By*. Chicago: University of Chicago Press.

Lakoff, George, and Zoltan Kövesces. 1987. "A Cognitive Model of Anger Inherent in American English." In D. Holland and N. Quinn, eds., *Cultural Models in Language and Thought*, 195–221. Cambridge: Cambridge University Press.

LeMasters, E. E. 1975. *Blue-Collar Aristocrats: Life-Styles at a Working-Class Tavern*. Madison: University of Wisconsin Press.

Levy, Robert. 1973. *Tahitians: Mind and Experience in the Society Islands*. Chicago: University of Chicago Press.

Limon, José. 1994. *Dancing with the Devil: Society and Cultural Poetics in Mexican-American South Texas*. Madison: University of Wisconsin Press.

Lindquist, Julie. 2002. *A Place to Stand: Politics and Persuasion in a Working-Class Bar*. Oxford: Oxford University Press.

Lutz, Catherine. 1988. *Unnatural Emotions: Everyday Sentiments on a Micronesian Atoll and Their Challenge to Western Theory*. Chicago: University of Chicago Press.

Malone, Bill C. 1985. *Country Music, USA*, 2d ed. Austin: University of Texas Press.

Mannheim, Bruce. 1986. "Popular Song and Popular Grammar, Poetry and Metalanguage." *Word* 37(1–2): 45–75.

———. 1987. "Couplets and Oblique Contexts: The Social Organization of a Folksong." *Text* 7(3): 265–88.

Marx, Karl. 1978a. *Capital, Vol. 1*. In R. C. Tucker, ed., *The Marx-Engels Reader*, 294–438. New York: Norton.

———. 1978b. *The German Ideology*. In R. C. Tucker, ed., *The Marx-Engels Reader*, 147–202. New York: Norton.

Mauss, Marcel. 1979. *Sociology and Psychology: Essays*. London: Routledge and Kegan Paul.

McLemore, Cynthia. 1990. *"The Pragmatic Interpretation of English Intonation: Sorority Speech."* Ph.D. diss., University of Texas at Austin.

Montejano, David. 1987. *Anglos and Mexicans in the Making of Texas, 1836–1986.* Austin: University of Texas Press.

Morningside Research and Consulting. 2000. "Report to the Technical Advisory Committee." Austin: Morningside Research and Consulting, Inc.

Mukarovsky, Jan. 1964. "Standard Language and Poetic Language." In P. L. Garvin, ed., *A Prague School Reader.* Washington, D.C.: Georgetown University Press.

Negus, Keith. 1999. *Music Genres and Corporate Cultures.* New York: Routledge.

Ortner, Sherry. 1991. "Reading America: Preliminary Notes on Class and Culture." In R. Fox, ed., *Recapturing Anthropology: Working in the Present,* 164–210. Santa Fe: School of American Research Press.

Paredes, Americo. 1958. *"With His Pistol in His Hand": A Border Ballad and Its Hero.* Austin: University of Texas Press.

Peterson, Richard. 1997. *Creating Country Music: Fabricating Authenticity.* Chicago: University of Chicago Press.

Ricoeur, Paul. 1971. "The Model of the Text: Meaningful Action Considered as a Text." *Social Research* 38(3):529–62.

Roediger, David R. 1991. *The Wages of Whiteness: Race and the Making of the American Working Class.* London: Verso.

Rosaldo, Michelle. 1980. *Knowledge and Passion: Ilongot Notions of Self and Social Life.* Cambridge: Cambridge University Press.

———. 1984. "Toward an Anthropology of Self and Feeling." In R. Shweder and R. Levine, eds. *Culture Theory: Essays on Mind Self, and Emotion,* 137–57. Cambridge: Cambridge University Press.

Roseman, Marina. 1991. *Healing Sounds from the Malaysian Rainforest: Temiar Music and Medicine.* Berkeley: University of California Press.

Rosenzweig, Roy. 1991. "The Rise of the Saloon." In C. Mukerji and M. Schudson, eds., *Rethinking Popular Culture,* 121–56. Berkeley: University of California Press.

Sapir, Edward. 1925. "Sound Patterns in Language." *Language* 1:37–51.

Schieffelin, Bambi, and Elinor Ochs. 1986. "Language Socialization."*Annual Review of Anthropology* 15: 163–91.

Seeger, Anthony. 1987. *Why Suyá Sing: A Musical Anthropology of an Amazonian People.* New York: Cambridge University Press.

Slobin, Mark. 1993. *Subcultural Sounds: Micromusics of the West.* Hanover: Wesleyan University Press/University Press of New England.

Spiro, Melford. 1993. "Is the Western Conception of the Self 'Peculiar' within the Context of the World Cultures?" *Ethos* 21(2): 107–53.

Sterne, Jonathan. 1997. "Sounds like the Mall of America: Programmed Music." *Ethnomusicology* 41(1):22–50.

Stewart, Kathleen. 1988. "Nostalgia: A Polemic." *Cultural Anthropology* 3: 227–41.

———. 1989. "On the Politics of Cultural Theory: A Case for 'Contaminated' Critique." *Social Research* 58(2): 395–412.

———. 1990. "Backtalking the Wilderness: 'Appalachian' Engenderings." In F. Ginsburg and A. L. Tsing, eds., *Uncertain Terms: Negotiating Gender in American Culture*, 43–56. Boston: Beacon Press.

———. 1993. "Engendering Narratives of Lament in Country Music." In G. Lewis, ed., *All That Glitters: Country Music in America*, 221–25. Bowling Green: Bowling Green State University Popular Press.

Stewart, Susan. 1984. *On Longing: Narratives of the Miniature, the Gigantic, the Souvenir, the Collection*. Baltimore: Johns Hopkins University Press.

Tedlock, Dennis. 1983a. "Phonography and the Problem of Time in Oral Narrative Events." *The Spoken Word and the Work of Interpretation*, 194–215. Philadelphia: University of Pennsylvania Press.

———. 1983b "The Analogical Tradition and the Emergence of a Dialogical Anthropology." *The Spoken Word and the Work of Interpretation*, 321–38. Philadelphia: University of Pennsylvania Press.

Théberge, Paul. 1997. *Any Sound You Can Imagine: Making Music/Consuming Technology*. Hanover: University Press of New England/Wesleyan University Press.

Thompson, E. P. 1991. *Customs in Common: Studies in Traditional Popular Culture*. New York: New Press.

Tichi, Cecilia. 1994. *High Lonesome: The American Culture of Country Music*. Chapel Hill: University of North Carolina Press.

Titon, Jeff. 1988. *Powerhouse for God: Speech, Chant and Song in an Appalachian Baptist Church*. Austin: University Texas Press.

Urban, Greg. 1985. "The Semiotics of Two Speech Styles in Shokleng." In E. Mertz and R. Parmentier, eds., *Semiotic Mediation*, 311–29. New York: Academic Press.

———. 1988. "Ritual Wailing in Amerindian Brazil." *American Anthropologist* 90(2): 385–400.

———. 1989. "The 'I' of Discourse." In B. Lee and G. Urban, eds., *Semiotics, Self, and Society*, 27–51. Berlin: Mouton de Gruyter.

Vanneman, Reeve, and Lynn Cannon. 1987. *The American Perception of Class*. Philadelphia: Temple University Press.

Voloshinov, Valentin. 1973. *Marxism and the Philosophy of Language*. New York: Seminar Press.

Wierzbicka, Anna. 1992. *Semantics, Culture, and Cognition*. New York: Oxford University Press.

Williams, Raymond. 1973. *The Country and the City*. Oxford: Oxford University Press.

Willis, Paul. 1981. *Learning to Labor: How Working-Class Kids Get Working-Class Jobs*. New York: Columbia Teachers' College Press.

Wilson, William J. 1978. *The Declining Significance of Race: Blacks and Changing American Institutions*. Chicago: University of Chicago Press.

Woodbury, Anthony C. 1985. "The Function of Rhetorical Structure: A Study of Central Alaskan Yupik Eskimo Discourse." *Language in Society* 14:153–90.

Zuckerkandl, Victor. 1956. *Sound and Symbol: Music and the External World*. Princeton: Princeton University Press.

Appendix

Index of Songs

Index

AARON A. FOX

is Associate Professor of Music

at Columbia University.

Supplemental audio, video, and photographic

materials and interactive content for this book are

available online at www.aaronfox.com.

Library of Congress Cataloging-in-Publication Data

Fox, Aaron A.
Real country : music and language in working-class
culture / Aaron A. Fox.
p. cm.
Includes bibliographical references (p.   ) and index.
ISBN 0-8223-3336-8 (cloth : alk. paper)
ISBN 0-8223-3348-1 (pbk. : alk. paper)
1. Country music—Texas—Lockhart—History and criticism.
2. Working class—Texas—Lockhart—Songs and music—
History and criticism.   3. Music and language.   I. Title.
ML3524.F69 2004
781.642'09764'33—dc22   2004006964